THE POLITICAL ECONOMY OF TERF

The Political Economy of Terrorism, Second E
ble political economy approach to the study o.   ...omic
methodology – theoretical and empirical – comb   ..al analysis and
realities to the study of domestic and transnation.   ..irorism. In so doing, the
book provides both a qualitative and quantitative investigation of terrorism in a
balanced, up-to-date presentation that informs students, policymakers, researchers, and the general reader of the current state of knowledge. Included are historical aspects, a discussion of watershed events, the rise of modern-day terrorism,
examination of current trends, the dilemma of liberal democracies, evaluation of
counterterrorism, analysis of hostage incidents, and much more. The new edition
expands the coverage of each chapter, adds a new chapter on terrorist network
structures and organization, accounts for changes in the Department of Homeland
Security and the USA PATRIOT Act, and discusses insurance against terrorism.

Rational-actor models of terrorist and government behavior and game-
theoretic analysis are presented for readers with no prior theoretical training. Where relevant, the authors display graphs using data from International
Terrorism: Attributes of Terrorist Events (ITERATE), the Global Terrorism
Database (GTD), and other public-access data sets.

Walter Enders holds the Bidgood Chair of Economics and Finance at the
University of Alabama. He has published numerous research articles in
such journals as the *Review of Economics and Statistics, Quarterly Journal of
Economics, American Economic Review, Journal of Economics Literature, Journal
of Business and Economic Statistics*, and the *American Political Science Review*.
He is on the editorial board of the *Journal of Conflict Resolution*. Dr. Enders's
Applied Econometric Time-Series is a leading book in the field. In 2003, he was
the corecipient with Todd Sandler of the National Academy of Sciences Award
for Behavioral Research Relevant to the Prevention of Nuclear War.

Todd Sandler is the Vibhooti Shukla Professor of Economics and Political
Economy at the University of Texas at Dallas. He has written or edited twenty-
one books, including *Global Collective Action; Economic Concepts for the Social
Sciences; The Political Economy of NATO* (with Keith Hartley); and *Global
Challenges: An Approach to Economic, Political, and Environmental Problems*,
as well as more than two hundred journal articles in economics and political
science. His work on terrorism dates back to 1983.

Professors Enders and Sandler coauthored the first edition of this title.

The Political Economy of Terrorism

Second Edition

WALTER ENDERS

University of Alabama

TODD SANDLER

University of Texas at Dallas

CAMBRIDGE UNIVERSITY PRESS

Cambridge, New York, Melbourne, Madrid, Cape Town,
Singapore, São Paulo, Delhi, Tokyo, Mexico City

Cambridge University Press
32 Avenue of the Americas, New York, NY 10013-2473, USA

www.cambridge.org
Information on this title: www.cambridge.org/9780521181006

First published 2006
Second edition published 2012

Printed in the United States of America

A catalog record for this publication is available from the British Library.

Library of Congress Cataloging in Publication data
Enders, Walter, 1948–
The political economy of terrorism / Walter Enders, Todd Sandler. – 2nd ed.
p.   cm.
Includes bibliographical references and index.
ISBN 978-1-107-00456-6 (hardback) – ISBN 978-0-521-18100-6 (paperback)
1. Terrorism.   2. Terrorism – Economic aspects.   I. Sandler, Todd.   II. Title.
HV6431.E54   2011
363.325–dc22 3   2011015035

ISBN 978-1-107-00456-6 Hardback
ISBN 978-0-521-18100-6 Paperback

To Linda Enders
and to the memory of Henry Sandler (1939–2005)

Contents

Tables and Figures

TABLES

FIGURES

Preface

The first edition of this book was published in 2006. Since its publication, there has been a tremendous amount of research in economics, political science, operations research, and related fields on terrorism. This is due to the continued security threat to society posed by terrorism and to the large quantity of resources allocated to defensive and offensive counterterrorism measures. Another driver of this interest has been the funding made available by the US Department of Homeland Security (DHS), the US Department of Defense, the European Union, and other institutions for the study of terrorism and the practice of counterterrorism. The Science and Technology agency in the DHS has funded twelve Homeland Security Centers of Excellence to study various terrorism-related issues – for example, protecting critical infrastructure against terrorist attacks and preparing for biological terrorism. Some of these centers have degree programs to teach students about the analysis of terrorism, so the need for an up-to-date version of our book has grown.

This second edition is a substantial revision of the first edition; nevertheless, the new edition maintains the structure, analytical orientation, and accessibility of the first edition. The new edition incorporates a number of key changes. First, it brings topics up to date in terms of current thinking and the recent literature. In particular, there is now a lot more insight and knowledge about the economic impact of terrorism, the prospects for international cooperation to thwart terrorism, and the efficacy of alternative counterterrorism tools. Recent research articles have incorporated more agents – for example, terrorist operatives, the general population, and targeted governments – into the strategic analysis of terrorism. There are more models that address suicide terrorism. Second, the new edition updates the statistical displays to include terrorist-event data through 2008. Unlike the first edition, which focused on transnational terrorism, the second

edition also investigates domestic terrorism. Statistics on domestic terrorist incidents come from the Global Terrorism Database, maintained at the
University of Maryland. Third, the new edition accounts for changes with
respect to DHS, the USA PATRIOT Act, insurance against terrorist incidents, and other institutional concerns. Fourth, the new edition uses recent
terrorist incidents – for example, the attempted downing of a Northwest
Airlines flight on 25 December 2009, the failed terrorist plot to blow up
transatlantic flights with liquid explosives in August 2006, and the Mumbai
armed attacks on 26 November 2008 – as relevant illustrative examples.

The new edition expands the coverage of each chapter so that topics
from the first edition are discussed in greater detail. Moreover, new topics
are added to each chapter – for example, the study of target substitution is
addressed in Chapter 5; an analysis of hostage-taking dynamics is included
in Chapter 7; and the psychic costs of terrorism and the Life Satisfaction
Approach are considered in Chapter 10. In addition, key factors affecting hostage-taking dynamics are indicated in Chapter 7. More graphs and
tables have been added throughout the second edition. There is also a new
chapter on terrorist groups and their organization. Among other things,
this chapter considers how terrorist groups trade off their functionality
and connectivity for security when determining their institutional form.
This new chapter also investigates characteristics of terrorist groups based
on their orientation – that is, religious, nationalist/separatist, left-wing, or
right-wing. The longevity of terrorist groups is also discussed, along with
their tendency to splinter into more groups. In addition, dynamic issues,
including recruitment, are investigated.

Since its publication we have used the book in many classes that we have
taught on terrorism. These in-class experiences have provided us insights
into where concepts and analyses in the first edition needed clarification
and/or expansion. We drew from these experiences and student feedback
in order to improve the book.

This edition presents a widely accessible political economy approach
that combines economic methods with political analysis and realities. In so
doing, the book provides both a qualitative and quantitative investigation
of terrorism in a balanced, up-to-date presentation that informs students,
practitioners, policymakers, researchers, and the general reader of the current state of knowledge. We also indicate fruitful areas for future research.
Most books on terrorism focus on historical, cultural, factual, and conceptual details and shy away from rational-choice-based analyses backed by
statistical inference. Our book presents not only the historical and conceptual issues, but also scientific-based analyses of the behavior of terrorists and
government policymakers. Moreover, we are concerned with knowing how

these adversaries make rational decisions in a strategic interactive framework. That is, how do the choices of the terrorists influence governments' counterterrorism policies, and how do these policies affect the choices of the terrorists? Strategic interactions among targeted governments are also investigated. Since the publication of the first edition, these strategic analyses have become more complex, with the actions of more agents being incorporated into the studies. To establish the relevancy of the theories presented, we display data and review statistical findings from a variety of studies.

Although we are particularly interested in rational-choice models and their empirical verification, we are no less interested in the history of terrorism, the causes of terrorism, and the dilemma faced by liberal democracies. Unlike most other books, this book identifies rational explanations for observed behavior – for example, why terrorist groups often cooperate and form networks, while targeted governments are slow to cooperate. We address many questions, including the following: When confronted with a common terrorist threat, why do targeted governments rely on defensive measures that merely deflect attacks to soft targets, and often eschew proactive responses that would reduce the threat for all governments? Why do countries fail, at times, to adhere to a stated policy of not conceding to hostage takers' demands when it is in their long-run interests never to concede? Which counterterrorism policies work best? How successful have terrorists been in creating economic consequences for targeted countries? Could the 9/11 attacks have been predicted with advanced forecasting tools, and how has transnational terrorism changed since 9/11?

By applying simple economic models and statistical analyses, our book provides a unique and important perspective on the study of terrorism. This perspective is increasingly being applied by researchers at the Centers of Excellence funded by the DHS. It is also used by researchers funded by other grant-giving organizations. To better understand terrorism and to counter its threat, society must utilize varied techniques and knowledge from many disciplines – for example, history, sociology, law, psychology, operations research, statistics, and economics. Our book draws upon insights from all of these disciplines. If one looks through a typical book on terrorism, especially those used in college courses, one will find few, if any, statistical displays of the incidence of terrorist events over time. More important, these books do not present any analysis or explanation of these patterns of events. Most books rely, instead, on some "watershed" events or case studies to draw some general principles. By contrast, we present data on terrorist events over time to bolster our investigation of numerous watershed incidents. Thus, our book is rich in detail about past terrorist events and the changing pattern of terrorism.

Our book is intended for use in college-level economics, political science, and public policy courses on terrorism. The book is also appropriate for classes at military colleges. Our approach will particularly appeal to teachers who want to emphasize a rational-choice basis for understanding terrorism and policies to ameliorate its threat. The book assumes no pre-knowledge of the techniques used. Thus, the game-theoretic methods are explained in detail for readers who have never seen a game matrix or game tree. The book is also useful for researchers who are new to the field and who may be driven to study terrorism because of their interest in the topic or the availability of funding from numerous sources since 9/11. Our book allows a researcher to gain the requisite background in the field, because we have incorporated a rich and diverse set of references and techniques. The interested reader can consult our plentiful references for further details about a particular approach or analysis. In addition, the book should interest people in DHS, the intelligence community, the defense sector, law enforcement, and the insurance industry, all of whom have to address myriad issues concerning modern-day terrorism. Our book provides a different way of thinking about terrorism.

We have profited from perceptive comments on various drafts from anonymous reviewers. We have received helpful support and counsel from Scott Parris, the economics editor at Cambridge University Press. We also appreciate the efforts of the production staff at Cambridge, who transformed the typescript into a book. We acknowledge our debt to our coauthors of articles, where some of the concepts applied here were originally developed. Prominent on this list are Dan Arce, Subhayu Bandyopadhyay, Patrick Brandt, Jon Cauley, Khusrav Gaibulloev, Kate Ivanova, Paan Jindapon, Harvey Lapan, Kevin Siqueira, and John Tschirhart. Others include Scott Atkinson, Peter Flemming, Beom S. Lee, Dwight Lee, Edward Mickolus, B. Peter Rosendorff, Adolfo Sachsida, John Scott, Xuejuan Su, Donggyu Sul, and Javed Younas. This project has succeeded because of the support of our wives – Linda Enders and Jeannie Murdock – and our children. Todd Sandler acknowledges that his research was funded, in part, by the DHS through the Center for Risk and Economic Analysis of Terrorism Events (CREATE) at the University of Southern California, grant numbers 2007-ST-061–000001 and 2010-ST-061-RE0001. However, any opinions, findings, and conclusions or recommendations are solely those of the authors and do not necessarily reflect the views of DHS or CREATE.

Tuscaloosa and Dallas
March 2011

ONE

Terrorism

An Introduction

The events on 11 September 2001 (henceforth, 9/11) served as a wake-up
call to the world that transnational terrorism poses grave risks. The four
simultaneous hijackings on 9/11 represent watershed terrorist incidents
for a number of reasons. First, the deaths associated with 9/11 were
unprecedented: the human toll was equal to the number of deaths from
transnational terrorism from the start of 1988 through the end of 2000
(Sandler, 2003). Second, the losses associated with 9/11 topped $80 billion
and caused insurance companies to end automatic coverage of terrorist-
induced losses.[1] Following 9/11, many companies were unable to afford terrorism insurance. To address the insurance concern, the US government
enacted the Terrorism Risk Insurance Act (TRIA) on 26 November 2002.[2]
Third, 9/11 showed that ordinary objects can be turned into deadly weapons with catastrophic consequences. Despite the huge carnage of 9/11, the
death toll could have been much higher had the planes struck the towers
at a lower floor. Fourth, 9/11 underscored the objectives of today's fundamentalist terrorists to seek maximum casualties and to cause widespread
fear, unlike the predominantly left-wing terrorist campaigns of the 1970s
and 1980s that sought to win over a constituency.[3] Fifth, 9/11 mobilized a

---

[1] On the implications of 9/11 for the insurance industry, see Kunreuther and Michel-Kerjan
    (2004a) and Kunreuther, Michel-Kerjan, and Porter (2003). Approximately half of the
    losses from 9/11 were covered by the insurance companies, including $11 billion in lost
    business, $2 billion of workers' compensation, $3.5 billion in property losses at the World
    Trade Center, and $3.5 billion of aviation liability.
[2] TRIA is now extended to 31 December 2014 and provides for the US government to cover
    85% of the insured losses on large-scale terrorist incidents. Government-supported pay-
    outs are capped at $100 billion annually.
[3] On the changing nature of terrorists, see Brandt and Sandler (2010), Enders and Sandler
    (2000, 2005a, 2006), Hoffman (1998, 2006), Rapoport (2004), White (2003), and Wilkinson
    (2001).

huge reallocation of resources to homeland security – since 2002, the US Department of Homeland Security (DHS) budget has grown by over 60% to $36.2 billion for the fiscal year 2004 (DHS, 2003). In fiscal year 2005, the DHS budget grew another 10% to $40.2 billion (DHS, 2004). The proposed DHS budget for 2010 is $55.1 billion, with approximately 65% of the budget, or $35.7 billion, going to homeland security proper (DHS, 2009, p. 155). In past DHS budgets, between 60 and 65% went to defending against terrorism on US soil. This expenditure is small compared to proactive or military measures taken in fighting the "war on terror," including the invasion against the Taliban and al-Qaida in Afghanistan on 7 October 2001 and the ongoing operations against these groups in Afghanistan in 2009, 2010, and 2011. Still other proactive spending involves improving intelligence, tracking terrorist assets, and fostering cooperative linkages with other countries. Sixth, protective actions taken by rich developed countries have transferred some attacks against these countries' interests to poorer countries – for example, the post-9/11 attacks in Indonesia, Morocco, Kenya, Saudi Arabia, Turkey, and elsewhere.

The events of 9/11 heightened anxiety worldwide and resulted in trade-offs in terms of accepting reduced freedom in return for greater security; society had not been willing to surrender as much freedom prior to 9/11. Society lost innocence on that fateful day that it will never regain. The threat of catastrophic terrorist events – though remote – is etched indelibly in everyone's mind. The Madrid train bombings on 11 March 2004 and the 7 July 2005 London transport bombings have made Europe more aware that large-scale terrorist events can occur on European soil. Other noteworthy European attacks include bomb-laden sedans discovered in London's Haymarket district on 29 June 2007 and the crash of a flaming SUV into the doors of the main terminal at Glasgow Airport on 30 June 2007. The anxiety that terrorists seek to create is amplified by people's proclivity to overreact to low-probability but ghastly events.

Although terrorist attacks are generally fewer in number since the late 1990s, terrorism continues to pose grave security risks to society. As will be shown in Chapter 3, each terrorist attack results, on average, in more casualties than those of earlier decades. Some modern-day terrorists are bent on causing attacks with large numbers of casualties – for example, al-Qaida, Lashkar-e-Taiba, and Jemaah Islamiyah. Select terrorist groups have displayed a desire to acquire weapons of mass destruction (Intriligator, 2010). The attempted bombing of a Northwest Airlines flight on 25 December 2009 highlights the fact that terrorists will innovate to circumvent static security measures, so that weak points must be constantly plugged in order to forestall catastrophe. The reliance on reactive measures (for example, inspecting shoes after the shoe bomber incident) is not the best way to avert disaster. Terrorists will always have a tactical advantage because they can seek weak spots after governments allocate defensive measures to alternative targets. Many terrorist groups harbor great animosity to Western interests and will patiently wait for their opportunity.

The study of terrorism has been an active field of research in international relations since the early 1970s and the start of the modern era of transnational terrorism (that is, terrorism with international implications or genesis). Of course, the interest in the study of terrorism grew greatly after 9/11, with many new courses being taught at the undergraduate level worldwide. Subscriptions to the two field journals – *Terrorism and Political Violence* and *Studies in Conflict & Terrorism* (formerly, *Terrorism*) – that publish scholarly articles increased following 9/11. Ever since 9/11, there has been a greater appreciation for the application of scientific methods to the study of terrorism. This is reflected in the growing number of articles on terrorism in economics, political science, operations research, criminology, and sociology journals. General journals in the social sciences are now more willing to publish articles on terrorism. In recent years, special issues of journals have been devoted to the study of terrorism – for example, the *Journal of Monetary Economics* (2004), *European Journal of Political Economy* (2004), *Risk Analysis* (2007), *Economics and Politics* (2009), and *Journal of Conflict Resolution* (2010). Scientific methods have been emphasized by the twelve DHS Centers of Excellence that have funded a vast network of researchers studying terrorism. Grant opportunities are also available from government agencies (for example, the National Science Foundation and the Department of Defense) and private foundations. These funding opportunities are also available abroad. Scholarly conferences on terrorism have also grown in number during the last few years.

The purpose of this book is to present a widely accessible political economy approach that combines economic methods and political analysis. Where possible, we apply theoretical and statistical tools so that the reader can understand why governments and terrorists take certain actions even when, on occasion, these actions may be against their interests. Often, we are able to explain behavior that appears counterintuitive once the underlying *strategic* interactions among agents (for example, among targeted governments) are taken into account. Throughout the book, we provide insights that go against conventional wisdom but that are supported by the data. Our reliance on statistical analysis means that we do *not* simply eyeball the data in order to draw conclusions that may not hold up to statistical scrutiny. Our approach gives the reader statistical inference that is less apt to change tomorrow as new terrorist groups with new objectives and modes of action come on the scene. Our intention is to offer a fresh approach that can inform not only students but also researchers, practitioners (for example, insurers), policymakers, and others interested in an up-to-date treatment of the political economy of terrorism.

We acknowledge that our scientific-based, political economy approach is not the only fruitful way of studying terrorism. Like other social scientific topics, terrorism is best understood by using complementary methods that draw on history, mathematical modeling, statistical inference, psychology, and culture. We are, however, constantly amazed at how mathematics and statistical inference can identify important stable relationships heretofore missed by other approaches – for example, some kinds of hostage-taking incidents are not deterred by governments' raids to free the hostages.[4] Unlike other methods, statistical analysis can also quantify a relationship, such as how long stock markets were impacted by 9/11 (Chen and Siems, 2004).

DEFINITIONS OF TERRORISM

Terrorism is the premeditated use or threat to use violence by individuals or subnational groups to obtain a political or social objective through the intimidation of a large audience beyond that of the immediate victims. Two essential ingredients characterize any modern definition of terrorism: the presence or threat of violence and a political/social motive. Without violence or its threat, terrorists cannot get a political decision maker to respond to their demands. Moreover, in the absence of a political/social motive, a violent act is a crime rather than an act of terrorism. Terrorists broaden their audience beyond their immediate victim by making their actions appear to be random, so that everyone feels anxiety. In contrast to a drive-by shooting on a city street, terrorist acts are not random but well-planned and often well-executed attacks where terrorists account for risks and associated costs, as well as possible gains.

In addition to violence and a political motive, a minimalist definition hinges on three additional factors: the victim, the perpetrator, and the audience. Of these three, the most controversial is the identity of the *victim*. Is

---

[4] Brandt and Sandler (2009) found that government-orchestrated violent ends to kidnappings did not deter future kidnappings. Kidnappers apparently reasoned that better efforts on their part to keep their location secret would prevent such a disastrous outcome.

an attack against a passive military target or a peacekeeper a terrorist act? The Israelis include an assault against a passive military target as a terrorist attack, whereas other countries may not if the military person is part of an occupying force. Virtually all definitions consider terrorist attacks against civilians as terrorism. The data set International Terrorism: Attributes of Terrorist Events (ITERATE) includes terrorist actions against peacekeepers but not against an occupying army as acts of terrorism.[5] While not as contentious as the victim, the *perpetrator* also presents controversy. If a state or government applies terror tactics to its citizens (for example, Stalin's reign of terror), is this terrorism? We apply the convention to call such actions *state terror* but not terrorism. In our definition here, the perpetrators are individuals or subnational groups but not the state itself. States can, however, support these subnational terrorist groups by providing safe havens, funding, weapons, intelligence, training, or by other means. When a state assists a terrorist group, the resulting terrorist act is known as *state-sponsored terrorism*. Libya is accused of state sponsoring the downing of Pan Am flight 103 over Lockerbie, Scotland, on 21 December 1988, and agreed in 2003 to compensate the victims' families. The US Department of State brands a number of nations – Cuba, Iran, North Korea, and Syria – as state sponsors of terrorism.[6] Finally, the *audience* refers to the collective that the terrorist act is intended to intimidate. For example, a terrorist bomb aboard a commuter train is meant to cause anxiety among the public at large, because such bombs can be placed in any train or public place. The audience thus extends beyond the immediate victims of the attack. On 9/11, al-Qaida's audience was everyone on the planet, not just the unfortunate victims associated with the four hijackings and their aftermath.

Why do terrorists seek such a wide audience? Terrorists want to circumvent the normal political channels/procedures and create political change through threats and violence. By intimidating a target population, terrorists intend that this population will apply pressure on political decision makers to concede to their demands. From a rational calculus viewpoint, political decision makers must weigh the expected costs of conceding, including possible countergrievances from other groups,[7] against the anticipated costs of future attacks. If the latter costs exceed those of concessions, then

[5] On ITERATE, see Mickolus (1980, 1982) and Mickolus, Sandler, and Murdock (1989).
[6] In the April 2003 issue of *Patterns of Global Terrorism 2002*, the US Department of State (2003) also included Iraq on this list. In recent years, Libya and Sudan have been removed from the list of state sponsors.
[7] Such other groups may view a government's concessions as an invitation to engage in their own terror campaigns.

a besieged government should rationally give in to the demands of the terrorists. Suicide attacks have gained prominence since 1983, because they raise the target audience's anxiety and, in so doing, greatly increase the government's anticipated costs from future attacks. This follows because a suicide attack kills on average twelve to thirteen people, while a typical terrorist incident kills on average a single person (Pape, 2003, 2005). Thus, governments have more readily given in to *modest* demands following suicide campaigns – for example, Hezbollah's car bombing of the US Marine barracks in Lebanon on 23 October 1983 resulted in the US withdrawal from Lebanon, whereas the October 1994–August 1995 Hamas suicide campaign against Israel led to the partial Israeli withdrawal from the West Bank (Pape, 2003, Table 1). Concessions also encourage more terrorism as the government loses its reputation for toughness – these reputational costs must also be weighed against the gains from giving in (for example, released hostages or an end to attacks). Terrorist tactics are more effective in liberal democracies where governments are expected to protect lives and property. Understandably, suicide campaigns have been almost exclusively associated with liberal democracies.

Some Alternative Definitions

To show how definitions may vary, we investigate a few official ones starting with that of the US Department of State, for which "terrorism means premeditated, politically motivated violence perpetrated against noncombatant targets by subnational groups or clandestine agents, usually intended to influence an audience" (US Department of State, 2003, p. xiii). An interesting feature of this definition is the characterization of the victims as "noncombatants," meaning civilians and unarmed or off-duty military personnel. Accordingly, a bomb planted under a US soldier's private vehicle in Germany by a Red Army Faction terrorist is an act of terrorism. This nicely illustrates how the designation of a victim can be quite controversial. The State Department's definition is silent about whether a threat is a terrorist act.

The US Department of Defense (DoD) defines terrorism as "the unlawful use or threatened use of force or violence against individuals or property to coerce or intimidate governments or societies, often to achieve political, religious, or ideological objectives" (White, 2003, p. 12). Three contrasts between the DoD's and the State Department's definition are worth highlighting. First, the *threat* of violence is now included. Second, the noncombatant distinction is dropped, so that the roadside bombing of a US convoy in Iraq would be terrorism. Third, religious and ideological motives are explicitly identified. Even two departments of the same government cannot fully agree on the definition! Nevertheless, these definitions identify the same five minimalist ingredients – that is, violence, political motivation, perpetrator, victim, and audience. The definitional problem lies in precisely identifying these ingredients. Slightly different definitions for terrorism also characterize those of the Federal Bureau of Investigation (FBI), the Defense Intelligence Agency, and the Vice President's Task Force on Terrorism in 1986 (White, 2003, p. 12).

The political nature of defining terrorism comes into focus when the official UN definition is examined: "terrorism is the act of destroying or injuring civilian lives or the act of destroying or damaging civilian or government property *without the expressly chartered permission of a specific government*, this by individuals or groups acting independently … in the attempt to effect some political goal" (emphasis added) (White, 2003, p. 12). A difficulty with this definition is that it may not brand a state-sponsored skyjacking or bombing as an act of terrorism if it is sanctioned by a specific government – for example, Iran's action to maintain the takeover of the US embassy in Tehran on 4 November 1979 for 444 days. Loopholes such as this arise when so many nations have to agree on a definition and governments do not want to tie their own hands. Since 9/11, the United Nations has ignored its official definition and taken a more pragmatic approach, branding violent acts perpetrated by subnational groups for political change as terrorism (United Nations, 2002a, p. 6). This new pragmatic definition closely matches our own definition.

Another definitional issue concerns distinguishing terrorism from warfare. In its classic sense, war targets combatants with weapons that are highly discriminating in order to limit collateral damage to civilians. Unlike war, terrorism targets noncombatants in a relatively indiscriminate manner, as 9/11 or the downing of Pan Am flight 103 illustrates. Unfortunately, the firebombings of Dresden and Tokyo during World War II blur the wartime distinction about noncombatants and discriminating attack. For our purposes, we distinguish warfare from terrorism in this standard way despite some issues. The Dresden and Tokyo bombings were not terrorist attacks, because they were perpetrated by governments, not by subnational groups, during a declared war.

Another essential distinction concerns insurrection, guerrilla warfare, and terrorism. An insurrection is a politically based uprising that is typically intended to overthrow the established system of governance. Insurgencies may also be leveled at occupying armies. Terrorism and guerrilla warfare are *tactics* used by an armed movement to achieve political change. Guerrilla warfare often involves large bands of rebel forces attacking superior government armies. Guerrillas rely on surprise and cover to harass and defeat government troops. Generally, guerrillas control territory within a country – for example, the Revolutionary Armed Forces of Colombia (FARC) controls jungle tracts in southeastern Colombia. This control can be short- or long-term. In contrast to terrorism, guerrilla warfare may be a more pervasive tactic that puts many more people at risk. Typically, terrorists do not try to control territory, nor do they operate as military units that engage government troops (Hoffman, 2006, p. 35). At times, some of these distinctions can become blurred – for example, Sendero Luminoso or Shining Path in Peru controlled territory. As we will discuss, many terrorist groups rely on urban guerrilla tactics to ambush police and military forces. These terrorists do not control the urban areas; rather, they use a city as cover to conduct their surprise attacks.

Definitions are essential when putting together data to examine propositions, trends, and other aspects of terrorism. A well-defined notion is needed so that events can be classified as terrorism for empirical purposes. To this end, we rely on our definition, which takes a middle ground with respect to other definitions and comes close to the US Department of State's definition and the pragmatic UN definition after 9/11.

Domestic versus Transnational Terrorism

Another essential distinction is between domestic and transnational terrorism. *Domestic terrorism* is homegrown and has consequences for just the host country, its institutions, citizens, property, and policies. In a domestic incident, the perpetrators, victims, and audience are all from the host country. The Weather Underground in the United States engaged in domestic terrorist attacks; this group operated from 1969 until about 1981. Other US domestic terrorist groups include the Animal Liberation Front, the Army of God, and the Earth Liberation Front ("The Elves"). On 19 April 1995, Timothy McVeigh's bombing of the Alfred P. Murrah Federal Building in Oklahoma City was a domestic terrorist event, as was the 27 July 1996 Centennial Olympic Park bombing in Atlanta. The latter attack was claimed by the Army of God, which protests abortions. The Unabomber – Theodore Kaczynski – mailed sixteen bombs to universities, airlines, and other targets from 1978 to 1995.[8] In addressing domestic terrorism, a country can

---

[8] The facts in this paragraph come from various Wikipedia entries.

be self-reliant if it possesses sufficient resources. Antiterrorist policies need not involve other countries insofar as neither the terrorist acts nor the government's responses need impose costs or confer benefits on foreign interests. Domestic terrorist campaigns result in a country taking measures to limit the threat. A targeted country is motivated to curb the threat; elected governments may lose the next election if domestic terrorist attacks are not curtailed.

Over the last two decades, most terrorist events directed against the United States have not occurred on its soil. The kidnapping in January 2002 and subsequent murder of the reporter Daniel Pearl in Pakistan; the destruction of the Al Khubar Towers housing US airmen in June 1996 near Dhahran, Saudi Arabia; and the bombing of the US embassies in Kenya and Tanzania in August 1998 are but three gruesome examples of *transnational terrorism*. Another example is the August 2006 plot in the United Kingdom to blow up ten or more transatlantic flights from the United Kingdom to the United States and Canada with liquid explosives. British authorities arrested the plotters, thereby averting disasters. Terrorism is transnational when an incident in one country involves perpetrators, victims, institutions, governments, or citizens of another country. If an incident begins in one country but terminates in another, then it is a transnational terrorist event, as in the case of a hijacking of a plane in country *A* that is made to fly to country *B*. An attack against a multilateral organization is a transnational incident owing to its multicountry impact, as in the case of the suicide car bombing of the UN headquarters in Baghdad on 19 August 2003. The toppling of the World Trade Center towers was a transnational incident because the victims were from ninety different countries, the mission had been planned abroad, the terrorists were foreigners, and the implications of the event (for example, financial repercussions) were global.

With transnational terrorism, countries' policies are interdependent. Efforts by the European countries to secure their borders and ports of entry may merely shift attacks aimed at their people and property abroad, where borders are more porous (Enders and Sandler, 1993, 1995; also see Chapter 5). US actions that deny al-Qaida safe havens or that destroy its training camps limit the network's effectiveness against all potential targets, thereby conferring a benefit on other countries. Intelligence on a common transnational terrorist threat that is gathered by one nation can benefit other potential target countries. As a result, transnational terrorism raises the need for countries to coordinate antiterrorist policies, a need that countries had resisted until 9/11. Even now, this coordination could be much improved (see Chapters 6 and 7).

OTHER ASPECTS OF TERRORISM

The motives of terrorists may vary among groups. Traditionally, many terrorists are motivated by ethno-nationalistic goals to establish a homeland for an oppressed ethnic group. The now-defeated Tamil Tigers in Sri Lanka fell into this category, as did the Sudanese People Liberation Army's (SPLA's) struggle against the Muslim majority in the north of Sudan.[9] The Palestinians are also applying terrorism in order to gain a state. Terrorism may also be motivated by nihilism, left-wing ideology, religious suppression, intolerance, social injustice, or issue-specific goals. In recent years, some groups have resorted to terrorism to establish a fundamentalist-based regime (Hoffman, 1998, 2006). For example, Harakat ul-Jihad-I-Islami/Bangladesh wants to establish Islamic rule in Bangladesh; Al-Jihad (also known as the Egyptian Islamic Jihad) wishes to set up an Islamic state in Egypt; and Jemaah Islamiyah intends to create a pan-Islamic state out of Indonesia, Malaysia, Singapore, the southern Philippines, and southern Thailand (US Department of State, 2003). Many other rationales – for example, publicizing an alleged genocide, a millennium movement, and animal protection – have motivated terrorists' wrath on innocent victims.

Terrorists employ varied modes of attack to create an atmosphere of fear and vulnerability. Some common tactics are displayed in Table 1.1. Hostage missions are logistically complex and risky, and include kidnappings, barricade and hostage taking (that is, the takeover of a building and the securing of hostages), skyjackings, and the takeover of nonaerial means of transportation. Ransoms from kidnappings have been used by some terrorist groups as a revenue source to support operations. This is especially true of some Latin American terrorist groups (for example, FARC), which have kidnapped business executives for ransoms. Bombings can take many forms, including explosive, letter, and incendiary bombs. Bombings are by far the favorite tactic of terrorists, accounting for about half of all transnational terrorist incidents (Sandler and Enders, 2004). Assassinations are politically motivated murders. Threats are promises of future action, while hoaxes are false claims of past actions (for example, a falsely claimed bomb

---

[9] The Liberation Tigers of Tamil Eelam (LTTE) was defeated by the Sri Lankan military on 16 May 2009. The SPLA and the Sudanese government signed an accord in January 2005 that ended hostilities. This long-term struggle between the SPLA and the Muslim majority must not be confused with the state terror of the Sudanese government directed against the inhabitants of Darfur in 2004 and 2005.

Table 1.1. *Some Terrorist Tactics*

Terrorist Operations

- Hostage missions (e.g., skyjacking, kidnapping, and barricade and hostage taking)
- Bombings
- Assassinations
- Threats and hoaxes
- Suicide attacks
- Armed attacks
- Sabotage
- Nuclear-related weapon attack
- Chemical or biological attack

Other Actions

- Bank robberies
- Propaganda
- Legitimate efforts to gain political recognition

---

aboard a plane). Suicide attacks can involve a car, a lone terrorist carrying explosives, or some other delivery device (for example, a donkey cart). Other terrorist modes of attack include armed attacks (including sniping and shootouts with authorities) and sabotage.

Since the 20 March 1995 sarin attack on the Tokyo subway by Aum Shinrikyo, the growing worry has been that terrorists will resort to weapons of mass destruction (WMD) in the form of a nuclear weapon, a radiological ("dirty") bomb, a chemical weapon, or a biological weapon (see Chapter 12). The dirty bomb consists of a conventional bomb that disperses radioactive material, which contaminates an area for years afterward and causes delayed deaths. Other terrorist actions involve bank robberies or criminal acts to finance operations. In some cases, terrorists also spread propaganda and use legitimate political actions to induce change. For example, Hamas, Hezbollah, the Irish Republican Army, and Euskadi ta Askatasuna (ETA) have political wings that promote the group's viewpoint.

Terrorists must allocate resources between terrorist attacks and legitimate means for achieving political goals. Ironically, actions by the authorities to limit protest may close off legitimate avenues of dissent and push terrorists into engaging in more attacks. Even among attack modes, terrorists must weigh expected costs and expected benefits from various actions in order to pick the best combination for their campaigns.

POLITICAL APPROACH TO THE STUDY OF TERRORISM

The primary contributors to the study of terrorism during the last forty years have been the political scientists, who have enlightened us on terrorist campaigns, groups, tactics, motives, finances, state support, and trends. Much of their analysis has been comparative – for example, when researchers distinguish among terrorist groups or countries harboring terrorists. The comparative approach has taught us much about what is common and what is different among terrorist groups. For instance, political scientists have characterized many of the European terrorist organizations coming out of the antiwar protests of the late 1960s as "fighting communist organizations" with a Marxist-Leninist ideology, an anticapitalist orientation, a desire to limit casualties, and a need for an external constituency (Alexander and Pluchinsky, 1992). Over the last few decades, political scientists have identified the changing nature of terrorism – for example, the rise of state sponsorship in the early 1980s and the more recent increase in fundamentalist-based terrorism. Political scientists have also analyzed the effectiveness of antiterrorist policies, but typically without applying statistical inference – the work of Brophy-Baermann and Conybeare (1994) is an important early exception. Since 9/11, political scientists have been more interested in empirical analyses of terrorism (see Li, 2005; Li and Schaub, 2004; Piazza, 2008). Moreover, political scientists now rely on rational-actor models of terrorist behavior – for example, Asal and Rethemeyer (2008), Bapat (2006), Bueno de Mesquita (2005a, 2005b), Powell (2007), and many other recent papers.

An advantage of the political science approach has been its eclectic, multidisciplinary viewpoint encompassing historical, sociological, and psychological studies. Historical studies identify common features among terrorist campaigns and indicate how the nature of terrorist tactics and campaigns has evolved over time. Sociological analyses examine norms and social structure within terrorist organizations. In recent psychological studies, researchers identify internal and external variables associated with the escalation of violence in terrorist events.[10] Factors that induce an individual to become a suicide bomber include both sociological – the approval of a group – and psychological considerations. Other psychological studies indicate the personality traits of different types of terrorists, including those who use the internet to coordinate attacks.

---

[10] Major contributors to psychological studies in terrorism include Jerrold M. Post and Eric D. Shaw – see Post, Ruby, and Shaw (2000, 2002). See also the excellent survey by Victoroff (2005) on the mind of the terrorist. John Horgan's (2005) book, *The Psychology of Terrorism*, is an outstanding source on myriad aspects of terrorists' psychology.

ECONOMIC APPROACH TO THE STUDY OF TERRORISM

Economic methodology has much to offer to the study of terrorism because it adds theoretical models and empirical analyses that have not been prominent. The application of economic methods to study terrorism started with Landes (1978), who applied the economics of crime and punishment to the study of hijackings in the United States. His study derived an "offense function," which relates the number of hijackings to policy variables – for example, the probability of apprehension, the presence of sky marshals, the probability of conviction, and the average length of sentence – that can be controlled by the authorities. Landes then estimated this offense function using data from past US hijackings from 1961 to 1976 to ascertain the marginal impact that each variable had on the number of hijackings. For example, Landes quantified the immediate and large influence that the installation of metal detectors at US airports in January 1973 had on the number of hijackings. In a scientific tradition, Landes first built a theoretical behavioral model of terrorists that he later tested using the data. In the next thirty-two years, other economists and political scientists have followed his methodology.[11] After 9/11, many economists have turned their attention to examining terrorism insurance, antiterrorism policy evaluation (see Chapter 4), terrorist-imposed risks, the causes of terrorism, and the economic impacts of terrorism (see Chapter 10).[12]

Economists have applied rational-actor models in which terrorists are portrayed as calculating individuals who optimize some goal subject to constraints. If the parameters of these constraints change, then a rational actor is anticipated to respond in a predictable fashion. Thus, actions taken by a government to harden a target should induce the terrorists to shift their attacks to relatively less-guarded venues (so-called softer targets). While this insight is now commonplace, we encountered a good deal of initial resistance to this notion when we utilized it in a series of articles over twenty-seven years ago.[13] People resisted characterizing terrorists as rational, because their goals and methods are not only repugnant but also differ from those of most people. In economics, however, rationality is not judged

---

[11] See, for example, Brophy-Baermann and Conybeare (1994), Enders, Sandler, and Cauley (1990a, 1990b), Li (2005), and Piazza (2008).

[12] Recent examples include Abadie (2006), Abadie and Gardeazabal (2003, 2008), Barros and Gil-Alana (2006), Drakos and Kutan (2003), Heal and Kunreuther (2003), Kunreuther and Heal (2003), and Viscusi and Zeckhauser (2003).

[13] Articles in this series include Enders and Sandler (1993), Im, Cauley, and Sandler (1987), Sandler, Tschirhart, and Cauley (1983), and Sandler and Lapan (1988).

by objectives or norms of acceptable behavior but by the manner in which an agent responds to environmental and other constraints. *By responding in a sensible and predictable fashion to changing risks, terrorists are judged to be rational.* Although weak compared to the governments that they confront, terrorists have waged some long-lived campaigns with small amounts of resources against formidable odds. They have also conducted numerous successful operations in the process. Terrorist groups order the operations in their campaigns according to risks: the least risky operations are used the most often and the most risky operations the least (Sandler, Tschirhart, and Cauley, 1983). Terrorist logistical success rates are very high. These stylized facts bode well for the rational-actor characterization of terrorists; this characterization is also applied to governments that oppose the terrorists.

In keeping with a rational-actor depiction, economists and later political scientists have applied game theory to study terrorism.[14] Game theory is an appropriate methodology for examining terrorism for a number of reasons. First, game theory captures the strategic interactions between terrorists and targeted governments, where actions are interdependent and, thus, cannot be analyzed as though one side were passive. Second, strategic interactions among rational beings, who are trying to act according to how they think their counterparts will act and react, characterize the interfaces among terrorists (for example, between hard-liners and moderates) or among alternative targets (for example, governments that are taking defensive measures). Third, game theory permits adversaries to issue threats and promises to gain strategic advantage – for example, a no-negotiation declaration intended to keep terrorists from taking hostages, or a terrorist group's pledge to engage in suicide bombings in order to gain concessions. Fourth, game-theoretic notions of bargaining are applicable to hostage negotiations and terrorist campaign-induced negotiations over demands (see Chapter 7).[15] Fifth, uncertainty and learning in a strategic environment are relevant to all aspects of terrorism in which the terrorists or government or both are *not* completely informed. Game theory concerns the knowledge possessed by the players and allows earlier actions to inform players over time.

The economic approach also provides for the testing of theories with advanced statistical methods. For example, consider the potential impact of terrorism on tourism. When deciding the appropriate vacation spot,

---

[14] Early game-theoretic papers include Lapan and Sandler (1988, 1993), Overgaard (1994), and Selten (1988).

[15] Bargaining papers include Atkinson, Sandler, and Tschirhart (1987), Gaibulloev and Sandler (2009a), Lapan and Sandler (1988), and Sandler, Tschirhart, and Cauley (1983).

tourists consider not only the exchange rate, costs, scenery, temperature, and other amenities, but also the risk of terrorism. After Greece experienced a spate of terrorist attacks in the mid-1980s, the Greek tourism industry suffered significant economic losses as tourists vacationed elsewhere. Enders, Sandler, and Parise (1992) formulated a consumer choice model to indicate the nature of the tourist trade-off and then tested this trade-off using data from Greece and other countries. Their methods put a price tag on Greek losses. A follow-up study applied their method to Greece, Israel, and Turkey for 1991–2000 (Drakos and Kutan, 2003).[16] The subsequent testing of theories provides many policy insights in the study of terrorism. For example, once the price tag for tourist losses is identified, a country can make a more informed decision on the potential gains from securing airports and other tourist venues. Knowing the losses more precisely allows a government to better allocate resources to curbing terrorism.

Economic methods have been applied to evaluate the popular consensus that poverty is the root of modern-day transnational terrorism. If this were true, then foreign assistance to limit global poverty might serve as an effective counterterrorism device. To investigate this consensus, economists have applied a variety of empirical tools. Using a terrorism risk index, Abadie (2006) showed that, ceteris paribus, poverty is *not* a significant determinant of terrorism risks. In his study, political freedoms are an important nonlinear determinant of terrorism risks. "Countries with intermediate levels of political freedom are shown to be more prone to terrorism than countries with high levels of political freedom or countries with highly authoritarian regimes" (Abadie, 2006, p. 51). He also found that certain geophysical characteristics – larger area, higher elevation, and greater jungle cover – are associated with a higher risk of terrorism, presumably because terrorists have havens to hide from government forces. In a complementary study, Krueger and Laitin (2008) separated the terrorists' country of origin and their venue country, and discovered that political repression, not economics, explained the transnational terrorists' country of origin. Thus, the lack of political freedom is a prime motivator of terrorism. Target countries tended to be rich, a conclusion that agrees with the findings of Blomberg, Hess, and Weerapana (2004). Other researchers – for example, Drakos and Gofas (2006) – have found similar results, so poverty does not appear to be a main driver of terrorism.[17]

---

[16] Another relevant paper is Enders and Sandler (1991), which examines the impact of terrorism on the Spanish tourist industry. See Chapter 10 for a fuller discussion.

[17] This paragraph draws from Sandler (2009).

POLITICAL ECONOMY APPROACH

We combine economic methods and political analysis to provide a political economy orientation. At times, each approach stands by itself; at other times, they must be joined to help us understand terrorism issues. Economists often lose track of the roots of their discipline as a highly policy-relevant political economy put forward by Adam Smith, David Ricardo, and Thomas Robert Malthus. To accomplish our study of terrorism, we return to these roots and include the implications of political factors. Why, for example, are liberal democracies more prone to terrorist campaigns than autocracies? The answer to this question requires a political economy orientation (see Chapter 2). In addition, both political and economic factors are important when ascertaining whether governments will cooperate sufficiently when addressing common terrorist threats. We must account not only for the potential gains derived from such cooperation, but also for the proclivity of nations to maintain autonomy over security concerns. Another essential factor in evaluating collective action against terrorism is the tendency of governments to rely on the efforts of other governments when the terrorist threat is truly common. The possibility of international organizations (for example, INTERPOL) and agreements circumventing this tendency is a political issue that can be better understood using economic methods – for example, the analysis of public goods. Our focus on policy questions also gives our study a political economy orientation.

Political factors are particularly relevant when distinguishing between domestic and transnational terrorism. In the case of domestic terrorism, a central government is empowered to act and direct resources using income, value-added, and other taxes to finance security and other measures against terrorism. After 9/11, the US government moved swiftly to create the DHS, thereby bringing twenty-two agencies together in the same department to improve coordination. To address the weaknesses in airport security, the federal government trained and deployed professional screeners country-wide in order to shore up any weak links. At the international level, there is no supranational government that can direct efforts to eliminate weakest links in a globalized world where a vulnerable airport poses potential risks to all the passengers passing through. Even baggage originating at such an airport can jeopardize passengers 10,000 miles away when transferred unscreened to the cargo hold of their plane.[18] Solving such interdependent

---

[18] See the careful analysis of such airline security risks and what can be done about them in Heal and Kunreuther (2005).

security concerns internationally presents a much different political dilemma than fixing the problem domestically (see Chapters 4 and 6).

For completeness, we must acknowledge that there are other approaches to the study of terrorism. For example, Zhuang and Bier (2007) have investigated the allocation of defensive measures to balance the risks of terrorism and natural disasters. Such an operations research orientation represents an engineering viewpoint that is less interested in the political context than our own orientation. Nevertheless, an operations research approach is elegant and can inform policymakers. Other methods stress legal, mathematical, or sociological concerns.

HISTORY OF TERRORISM

Terrorism is an activity that has probably characterized modern civilization from its inception. One of the earliest recorded examples is the *sicarii*, a highly organized religious sect consisting of "men of lower orders" in the Zealot struggle in Palestine during 66–73 A.D. (Laqueur, 1978, p. 7). Our brief historical survey of terrorism starts at the Age of Enlightenment in the eighteenth century, a time when commoners were no longer the property of the state but persons whose lives and property were to be protected by the state. Thus, the notion of liberal democracy was born out of the American (1775–1783) and French Revolutions (1789–1795). Ironically, the term *terrorism* was first used with the advent of state terror as the post-revolutionary government of France massacred the French nobility and associates (White, 2003).

The Russian Anarchists and Revolutionaries

The more common use of the term "terrorism" arose a half-century later with the appearance of the socialist radicals in Europe during the 1840s. These radicals resorted to bombings and assassinations – modern-day terrorist tactics – to terrorize the established order in a failed attempt to bring about a revolution.[19] Following the philosophy and teachings of Pierre Joseph Proudhon, anarchists later adopted the same terrorist tactics in the 1850s and thereafter, with the aim to create a government-less state. Basing their ideas on the writings of Mikhail Bakunin and Sergey Nechaev, the Russian anarchists formed Narodnaya Volya (henceforth, the People's

---

[19] The material in this section draws from Combs (2003), Hoffman (1998), White (2003), and other sources.

Will) and engaged in a terrorist campaign involving the assassination of government officials. The People's Will operated between 1878 and 1881; its most noteworthy assassination victim was Czar Alexander II, whose murder resulted in Alexander III ending reforms and repressing those who sought political change in Russia. Though its campaign was unsuccessful, the People's Will was a major factor in shaping modern-day terrorism. First, the People's Will exerted clear transnational influence by exporting its tactics, adherents, and philosophy abroad, most notably to the labor movement in the United States. Second, the terrorist tactics of the People's Will were copied by anarchist and nationalist movements throughout Europe in the late 1800s and early 1900s. Third, the People's Will was the forerunner to the Russian Revolutions in 1905 and 1917. In 1917, the world saw that a well-planned terrorist campaign with a large constituency could overthrow a ruling government – this was a shocking revelation that influenced nationalist/separatist struggles thereafter. Fourth, the Irish Republican Army (IRA) under the leadership of Michael Collins applied and honed the terrorist tactics of the People's Will during Ireland's 1919–1921 fight for independence from Britain. Once again, terrorist tactics were applied successfully in a nationalist movement.

After the Japanese defeat of the Russians, the 1905 Russian Revolution began with two events: a demonstration by unemployed workers in St. Petersburg and a mutiny by the Russian navy. The revolution was repressed by the Russian government, whose brutality forced the movement underground and sowed the seeds for a future revolution. This second revolution began in February 1917 with a general strike in St. Petersburg that resulted in a countrywide revolt, with the Russian army joining the workers. A new Russian government headed by the Menseviks gained power but became unpopular because of Russian participation in World War I. Aided by the Germans, Lenin returned to Russia and took over the leadership of the Bolsheviks with the intention of engineering a revolt to topple the Mensevik government. During this second revolution of October 1917, Lenin and Trotsky used terrorist tactics – bombings and assassinations – against the government and its middle-class constituency. Once in power, Lenin and Trotsky applied state terror to silence opponents. While in exile in Mexico, Trotsky was later assassinated in order to silence him. To ensure that there was no going back to czarist Russia, the Bolsheviks executed Czar Nicholas II and his family in 1918. An important innovation was Lenin's threat to export terrorism (White, 2003) – not unlike the Islamic revolutionaries' threat over sixty years later, following the establishment of an Islamic government in Iran under Khomeini – as a means to keep other governments out of the new communist government's affairs.

Terrorism and the State of Israel

Next, we turn to the Middle East and the Zionists' struggle for a homeland during 1947–1948. Two terrorist groups – Irgun Zvai Leumi and the Stern Gang – applied and refined the methods of Michael Collins in order to make British rule in Palestine costly. These groups relied on bombings and assassinations directed at British targets to raise the cost of not conceding to Jewish demands for statehood. To raise British stakes further, the Jewish terrorists escalated their campaigns into urban guerrilla warfare in order to keep British troops occupied. The terrorists hoped that the British public would tire of the casualties from hit-and-run attacks and grant Israel independence – the strategy eventually worked. In so doing, they demonstrated the effectiveness of urban terrorism worldwide. Ironically, the Jewish terrorists initially applied the Irish methods of Collins, which they perfected and then "exported" back to the Irish to be used in their confrontation with British troops after 1969.

Algeria and Cyprus

We next turn to the anticolonial revolutions as represented by those in Algeria (1954–1962) and Cyprus (1956–1969). The Algerian revolt against French rule was led by the Front de Libération Nationale (FLN), which took its tactics from those of the Jewish terrorists, as laid out in Begin's book, *The Revolt*. The movie *The Battle of Algiers* illustrated the urban guerrilla warfare waged by the FLN, whose primary targets were the police, the French military, and symbols of authority. Because attacks on these targets were having little influence on French or Algerian public opinion, the FLN raised the stakes and bombed the milk bars. Women were used to plant the bombs in these bars, where victims included ordinary French citizens. These brutal attacks resulted in the French military being brought in. From the movie, one learns that the subsequent repressive and brutal measures – the tortures and executions – by the French military backfired, hardening the terrorists' resolve and giving the FLN the high moral ground and more recruits. The Muslim majority in Algeria started to turn against French rule because of its repressive response.

By staging its attacks in Algiers, where there were many foreign journalists and residents, the FLN succeeded in capturing world attention. The FLN *internationalized* its struggle further by having terrorist campaigns coincide with propitious events – for example, the opening session of the UN General Assembly (Hoffman, 1998, p. 57). Although the FLN knew that it could never defeat the French forces, it reasoned correctly that a terrorist-based war of attrition would eventually raise the cost to the French suffi-ciently that independence would be granted. A similar tactic was used by the Cypriot insurgents, who also borrowed their tactics from the Jewish terrorists of the 1940s and also tried to internationalize their campaign.

Irish Troubles after Independence

Irish independence in 1921 did not end the trouble in Ireland, because Northern Ireland remained under British rule. As the civil rights and eco-nomic prospects of the Catholic minority waned in Northern Ireland, Catholic discontent grew. From 1930 until the end of the century, the fight for Irish unification was orchestrated by the IRA and the more militant Provisional IRA. The bloodshed increased greatly when the British army was deployed to Northern Ireland in 1969 to maintain order. With the arrival of British troops, the Provisional IRA evolved urban guerrilla warfare tactics; their attacks against police and soldiers in Belfast, Londonderry, and other urban centers in Northern Ireland appeared random and relentless. The Provisional IRA borrowed methods used in the late 1940s by Jewish terror-ists in Palestine and in the 1950s by Algerian terrorists. The cities provided cover for the terrorists, who could tie down the British troops and make British rule difficult and costly. To place additional cost on the British pub-lic, the Provisional IRA exported its bombing campaigns to British cities in the hopes that a besieged and fearful British public would pressure its gov-ernment to support Irish unification. Once again, we see the importance of the audience in a terrorist campaign.

The Tupamaros

In Uruguay (1968–1972) and elsewhere in Latin America, similar tactics were applied in other nationalist and separatist struggles. The Tupamaros in Uruguay added kidnappings and bank robberies to their urban guer-rilla war tactics as a means to finance their activities. Like the Jewish and Algerian terrorists, the Tupamaros practiced urban terrorism. Clearly, these terrorists were influenced by both the Irgun Zvai Leumi and the FLN when they designed their 1968 urban terror campaign for Montevideo. Like their predecessors, the Tupamaros refined the technique of urban terrorism and managed to tie up the authorities. Unlike their predecessors, they failed to win over a constituency; people viewed the Tupamaros as needlessly brutal. Moreover, the working class never identified with these privileged students, who claimed to be leading a Marxist-Leninist revolution of redistribution.

The group is important because its urban terrorist method influenced the fighting communist organizations in Europe during the modern era of terrorism (see Chapter 2).

Terrorism and a Palestinian State

A final noteworthy historical terrorist campaign is the ongoing Palestinian struggle against Israel for a Palestinian state, a struggle that began after the 1967 Arab-Israeli War. The Palestinian Liberation Organization (PLO) and its splinter groups studied IRA, Jewish, and Algerian terrorist tactics in designing their own campaign against Israel. The PLO saw the importance of internationalizing their fight, which was made even more important because Israel refused to recognize them. If the world came to recognize the PLO and its grievances, then the PLO believed that Israel too would have to address its concerns. The PLO's new tactics signaled the rise of modern transnational terrorism; terrorists began to stage their acts abroad in order to attract the world's attention. The advent of satellite broadcasts meant that terrorist acts half a globe away could be viewed live as dramatic events unfolded. We return to the PLO in Chapter 2.

Summing Up

We summarize our brief history in Table 1.2, where the first column indicates the cause of the terrorist campaign, the second lists the terrorists, and the third denotes their tactics. A number of important lessons can be drawn from this select historical record. Throughout history, terrorists have borrowed from their predecessors and, in so doing, have improved their methods. Terrorists pay attention to other terrorists' operations even when they are on opposing sides – for example, the Palestinian terrorists copied the Zionist terrorist methods. To attract media exposure, the terrorists tend to stage their campaigns in urban centers where the media can report their attacks.[20] Over time, terrorist campaigns have been increasingly internationalized in order to capture world attention. Some nationalist/ separatist campaigns have succeeded, becoming too costly for the authorities owing to a war of attrition waged by the terrorists. If the terrorists manage to maintain a constituency, they have a greater likelihood of success. Brutal countermeasures by the authorities increase this constituency

---

[20] Shining Path in Peru is something of an exception to this general rule, since most of their attacks occurred in rural settings.

Table 1.2. *Historical Terrorist Campaigns*

Cause of Terrorist Campaign	Terrorists	Tactics
French Revolution	The new government's treatment of those once in power	Applied state terror.
Socialist revolution in Europe, 1840s and beyond	Subversive radical democrats; anarchists (e.g., Pierre Joseph Proudhon)	Bombings and assassinations.
Russian anarchists, 1878–1881	Narodnaya Volya (People's Will); leaders included Mikhail Bakunin and Sergey Nechaev	Assassinations of government officials.
Russian Revolutions, 1905, 1917	Anarchists and Bolsheviks	Assassinations, bombings, and other tactics. A threat to export terrorism abroad to governments meddling in communist affairs.
Irish independence and unification, 1919–1921	Irish Republican Army led by Michael Collins	Studied tactics of Narodnaya Volya and applied their methods.
Irish unification, 1930 on	Irish Republican Army	Changing methods over time, including adopting urban guerrilla tactics.
Israel's struggle for a homeland, 1947–1948	Irgun Zvai Leumi, Stern Gang	Studied methods of Collins from the IRA. Bombings and assassinations, urban guerrilla warfare.
Anticolonial revolutions – e.g., Algeria (1954–1962), Cyprus (1956–1959)	Various groups – for example, Front de Libération Nationale	Bombings and assassinations. Urban guerrilla warfare.
Latin American revolutions – for example, Uruguay (1968–1972), Cuba (1950s)	Tupamaros in Uruguay, Ernesto (Che) Guevara in Cuba, and Carlos Marighella	Urban guerrilla warfare. Kidnappings, bombings, assassinations, propaganda, and bank robberies.
Palestinian struggle against Israel for a Palestinian state, 1967 on	Palestine Liberation Organization (PLO) and splinter groups (e.g., Black September)	Studied IRA's and Israel's methods. Used transnational attacks.

Sources: Hoffman (1998), White (2003).

and *do not* work in the authorities' favor. Similarly, terrorists' brutality may lose them support.

Our brief history can be related to David Rapoport's (2004) "four waves" of modern terrorism. The first wave – the Anarchists – began in the late 1870s with the People's Will and lasted until about 1920. Thereafter, the Anti-Colonialist wave ensued as terrorist groups in aspiring countries – for example, Algeria, Cyprus, Ireland, Israel, and Yemen – relied on terrorist tactics to gain their independence. The third wave started with the Vietnam War in the late 1960s with the PLO and the fighting communist organizations in Europe, South America, the Middle East, and elsewhere. This third wave waned in the late 1980s, just prior to the fall of the Berlin Wall. Our brief history has focused on the first two waves; Chapter 2 will address the third and fourth waves. The latter includes the Fundamentalist wave, which started in 1979 and is the dominant influence of terrorism today. Elements of each wave persist outside of its demarcated time interval – for example, there are leftist terrorist groups still active today, and there are other groups fighting for independence (for example, the ETA). Moreover, some terrorist organizations may fall into more than one wave.

SOME KEY CONCEPTS

To set the stage for our political economy approach, we must define a few terms that appear at various points throughout the book. An *externality* arises when the action of one agent imposes consequences – costs or benefits – on another agent, and when these consequences are not accounted for by the transaction or its associated price. In its simplest terms, an externality means that a market price may not result in resources being directed to their most valued use, because important costs and/or benefits are not reflected in the price. In the case of a negative externality or external cost, an externality results in too much of the activity, as the provider is not made to compensate for harm done to others. In the case of a positive externality or external benefit, an externality results in too little of the activity, as the provider is not compensated for the benefits conferred on others. When an externality-generating activity provides benefits or costs to agents in another country, a *transnational externality* occurs.

If defensive measures taken by one country divert a terrorist attack to another country, a transnational externality results. Ironically, actions by a country to secure its own airports may merely transfer the attack to a less-secure foreign airport, where the diverter's own citizens are murdered (Arce and Sandler, 2005; Sandler and Lapan, 1988; Sandler and Siqueira,

2006). This example constitutes a negative externality, where countries engage in too much security in an arms-race-like attempt to deflect attacks. If countries become aware that their citizens may still be at risk, then this may curb somewhat their overprovision of defensive measures. As a second example, intelligence on a common terrorist threat provided by one country to the authorities in another country represents a positive externality. Here, underprovision is the concern. As terrorists refined their tactics, as in the case of the IRA, the Zionist terrorists, and the Tupamaros, these terrorists generated a positive externality for other terrorists. Actions by the world press to report successful terrorist tactics speed the dissemination of these external benefits.

Another essential concept is that of a *pure public good*. "Publicness" here does not necessarily refer to government provision; rather, it means that the good's benefits possess two properties that distinguish these goods from those that can be readily traded in markets. First, a pure public good's benefits are nonexcludable, with both payers and nonpayers gaining from the good once it is provided. If a targeted country preempts a terrorist group by capturing its members and destroying its infrastructure, then this action protects all potential target countries from attacks. In so doing, preemptive action against a common terrorist threat confers nonexcludable benefits. Since the provider cannot keep others from benefiting from the public good, consumers have a natural incentive to take advantage of the public good without paying for it, which leads to a *free-rider* problem and an anticipated underprovision of the public good.

Second, the benefits of a pure public good are nonrival in the sense that one users' consumption of these benefits does not detract, in the least, from the consumption opportunities still in store for others. Like magic, a pure public good keeps giving benefits as more consumers show up. Again consider the preemption of a common terrorist threat. The safety stemming from the action does not diminish in the slightest if there are six, seven, or fifty potential target nations. Each at-risk target receives the same enhanced safety, but may value it differently. Once taken, the preemption protects all potential target nations. Next, suppose that the provider of a pure public good has the means to exclude someone from benefiting from the good. Is it socially desirable to do so? The nonrivalry property of a pure public good makes it inefficient to deny access to anyone who gains, because extending consumption to another user creates benefits but costs society nothing. That is, there is zero additional cost to society from extending consumption, and the extra benefit to the new consumer makes for a net gain to society, thereby justifying making consumption as inclusive as possible. If, however, there is congestion or other costs from extending consumption, then there is a rationale for excluding someone unless she compensates for the costs that her consumption causes.

An important class of public goods, where exclusion should be practiced, is the *club good*, whose benefits are easily excluded and only partially nonrival owing to congestion considerations. Congestion costs mean that another consumer diminishes the benefits to the existing consumers. If, for example, the same security force that guards ten airports is made to guard an eleventh, then the safety provided to the original ten airports is diluted as the force is thinned. When the new airport must compensate for this thinning or be denied protection, the hiring of new guards can be financed from the compensation in order to maintain the same level of vigilance. Clubs finance club goods by charging members for the crowding that they cause.

PURPOSE OF THE BOOK

The purpose of this book is to present an up-to-date survey of the study of terrorism, while incorporating contributions from political science, related disciplines, and economics. To our knowledge, our book is the first to highlight theoretical and statistical contributions in the study of terrorism. In so doing, we demonstrate the novel insights that follow from applying such methods, including game theory. For example, empirical methods can identify cycles, trends (if any), and abrupt changes in terrorists' behavior. Such methods can also be used to generate forecasts, evaluate policies, or to gauge the economic consequences of events (for example, the effects of a series of hijackings on airline revenues). Theoretical analysis can address such questions as: should governments share information if they do not coordinate defensive operations? When theoretical methods are applied, conclusions may be initially surprising owing to perverse incentives among adversaries or targets. Thus, nations may work at cross purposes as they put more weight on their own benefits and ignore how their actions impact others. There are many collective action problems associated with the way in which governments decide upon counterterrorism measures. As a consequence, many measures are inefficiently supplied.

Our study investigates both domestic and transnational terrorism. The policy implications of addressing terrorism often differ between the two forms of terrorism owing to institutional and other concerns. Nevertheless, some insights with respect to domestic terrorism extend with little alteration to transnational terrorism. Although our empirical investigation focuses on the latter, we will also address issues concerning domestic terrorism when data are available.

PLAN OF THE BOOK

The body of the book contains eleven chapters. The dilemma for liberal democracies posed by terrorism is discussed in Chapter 2. Liberal democracies walk a tightrope: too small a response makes them look unable to protect lives and property, while too large a response makes them look tyrannical. Either an underreponse or an overresponse will lose the government support. Many factors in liberal democracies (for example, freedom of movement and freedom of association) provide a supportive environment for terrorism. In Chapter 3, a statistical overview is presented that examines past patterns of domestic and transnational terrorism. Additionally, we demonstrate how statistical analysis can inform policy evaluation and forecasting.

Chapter 4 investigates counterterrorism policies with the use of elementary game theory and related tools. These policies are divided into two classes: proactive and defensive policies. Strategic implications are shown to differ between these two policy classes. Proactive or offensive policies are more difficult to implement, while defensive policies are easier to implement but may generate negative impacts on other countries. At the transnational level, greater coordination of antiterrorism policies is needed but has been slow to materialize. Chapter 5 further investigates these negative implications by focusing on the *transference* of attacks caused by the policy choices of targeted government. Transference results when actions to secure borders deflect the attack to a country with less-secure borders. In Chapter 6, we contrast terrorist cooperation with government noncooperation. We are especially interested in elucidating the collective action implications associated with government cooperation. Means for fostering greater government coordination are indicated.

Chapter 7 concerns hostage-taking incidents, where a game-theoretic analysis is sketched. The efficacy of a policy of never negotiating and never conceding to hostage-taking terrorists is evaluated. Terrorist groups are studied in Chapter 8. We are interested in what distinguishes long-standing groups (for example, the PLO and ETA) from short-lived groups. We are also interested in fractionalization and in how groups evolve over time. The role of networks on a group's vulnerability is also examined. In Chapter 9, we apply some statistical analysis to investigate how things are different after 9/11. Chapter 10 displays how statistical tools can be applied to study the economic impact of terrorism – for example, its impact on economic growth, tourism, and/or foreign direct investment. An evaluation of US homeland security is presented in Chapter 11, followed by an evaluation of the future of terrorism and concluding remarks in Chapter 12. This last chapter also looks at the possibility of chemical, biological, radiological, and nuclear terrorism.

TWO

The Dilemma of Liberal Democracies

A liberal democracy rules by the mandate and wishes of its citizens. Periodic elections place candidates into legislative and executive offices based on some voting rule, such as a simple majority or plurality of votes cast. The political system may be two-party majoritarian, proportional representation, or some similar system. The "liberal" adjective underscores that the system preserves the civil and political rights of citizens and foreign residents (see Doyle, 1997). In a well-functioning liberal democracy, the political and civil rights of the minority are protected by the ruling government. The press is allowed to report the news, and everyone has the right to express his or her views. As a result, people can criticize the government and its policies without fear of reprisals. Suspected criminals have civil rights – for example, to be charged with a crime, to obtain counsel, and to have a fair trial. Election results are tallied in an open and accurate fashion. When a government loses an election, it relinquishes office and allows for a peaceful and orderly transition of power.

An essential requirement of a liberal democracy is the protection of its people's lives and property. A government that fails to provide this security will lose support and be voted out of office. If, for example, a liberal democracy is unable to control a terrorist campaign that murders innocent individuals on city streets or on public transit, then the government will appear inept and lose popularity. Ironically, a liberal democracy protects not only its citizens and residents but also the terrorists who engage in attacks on its soil. The political and civil freedoms that define a liberal democracy provide a favorable environment in which to wage terrorist campaigns. To date, evidence indicates that liberal democracies are more likely to be plagued by transnational terrorism than their autocratic counterparts, even though grievances may be greater in autocracies (Drakos and Gofas, 2006;

28

Eubank and Weinberg, 1994, 2001; Li, 2005; Li and Schaub, 2004; Savun and Phillips, 2009; Weinberg and Eubank, 1998).

The primary purpose of this chapter is to examine the dilemma posed by terrorism for liberal democracies, first noted by Wilkinson (1986), and to indicate their likely response. This dilemma involves engineering a reaction to the terrorist threat in which the government is viewed as providing security without compromising the principles upon which a liberal democracy rests. A secondary purpose is to depict the changing nature of terrorism since 1968 and its implications for liberal democracies. As terrorists seek to surpass past atrocious attacks in order to capture headlines, the carnage associated with terrorism has escalated. This progression has crucial implications for the way in which liberal democracies respond, because citizens may be willing to sacrifice civil freedoms for greater security as terrorists' innovative attacks demonstrate heightened risks. A tertiary purpose is to examine the role of the media in the fight against terrorism. Often simple solutions – for example, not reporting terrorist attacks in order to starve terrorists of the publicity that they crave – have consequences that may be worse than the alternative of not restricting the press. A nonreporting policy may allow other kinds of censorship that a government deems to be in "our" security interest. An important message of the chapter is our call for further research to quantify the relationship between liberal democracies and terrorism.

WHY ARE LIBERAL DEMOCRACIES PRONE TO TERRORISM?

The simple answer is that many of the protections provided to a country's citizens by a liberal democracy serve to aid and abet terrorists in their campaigns of violence (Schmid, 1992). Factors conducive to terrorism include freedom of association, which allows terrorists to form groups and networks with other groups. There is also freedom of speech, which permits terrorists to spread dissent through political wings. Many terrorist groups – for example, Hamas, the Palestine Liberation Organization (PLO), the Irish Republican Army, Euskadi ta Askatasuna (ETA), and Hezbollah – have political wings that disseminate their message through legitimate means that might be quashed in less liberal societies. These political activities can reinforce recruitment to the military wing. Terrorists rely on free speech to spread their propaganda, but the same is true of targeted governments. In liberal democracies, people have freedom of movement and greater rights to cross international borders than in autocracies. This enhanced mobility is conducive to transnational terrorism. Liberal democracies present terrorists with a target-rich environment. Efforts in recent years to put barriers outside of federal buildings in the United States after the 19 April 1995 Oklahoma City bombing will merely deflect future attacks to high-profile business and public buildings with less robust defenses. The right to privacy makes it more difficult for governments to spy on suspected terrorist groups without showing just cause. Liberal democracies also provide greater opportunities to obtain weapons, paramilitary training, and bomb-making information and materials than autocracies. There are greater funding possibilities through legal and illegal channels.

Perhaps the greatest facilitators of terrorism in liberal democracies are the built-in *restraints* that protect people's civil liberties and inhibit actions against suspected terrorists. Restraints on government – for example, the prohibition of unwarranted search and seizure – allow terrorists the freedom to acquire vast arsenals, provided that their actions do not arouse the suspicions of authorities. At the time of the sarin attack on the Tokyo subway on the morning of 20 March 1995, Aum Shinrikyo had $1.4 billion in financial assets, a stockpile of 4.2 million lethal doses of sarin, a biological weapons program, and AK-47 production facilities (Campbell, 1997). The group had even acquired a Russian MI-17 helicopter with a spray attachment to disperse sarin or other chemical agents into the air over Tokyo. Aum Shinrikyo had 10,000 members in Japan and upwards of 30,000 followers in Russia. Obviously, Japanese liberalism had allowed this organization to become quite formidable before any action was taken. Only luck and incompetency kept the death toll from the subway attack to just twelve people. Liberal democratic restraints not only permit a terrorist group to become a significant threat, but also limit actions against suspected and known terrorists. Differences in punishment practices among countries can inhibit extradition – that is, countries without a death penalty will not extradite captured terrorist suspects to a country with a death penalty. Once captured, suspected terrorists are guaranteed the right to a fair trial and to appeals if convicted. After 9/11, however, the Bush administration limited many of these legal rights; suspected terrorists apprehended in Afghanistan and elsewhere have been held at Guantánamo Bay, Cuba, in indefinite detention as enemy combatants. The Obama administration seeks to close the prison in Guantánamo and bring individuals charged with terrorist offenses to trial. Individuals not charged are being released from prison. As of June 2011, the prison in Guantánamo is still open.

Another factor that supports terrorism in a liberal democracy is the presence of press freedoms. Terrorists seek publicity for their cause and grievances, which they can achieve when the media is allowed to report terrorist attacks. Autocracies limit these freedoms and, in so doing, motivate terrorists to stage attacks in foreign capitals, where media coverage is more extensive. Thus, press freedoms in liberal democracies may result in transnational terrorist attacks. We return to the role of media later in the chapter.

A related issue concerning the relationship between liberal democracy and terrorism has to do with the form of democracy. Which kind of democratic system – proportional representation or majoritarian rule – is more conducive to terrorism? Because proportional representation (PR) gives more viewpoints, even extreme ones, a presence in government, terrorism *may* be less prevalent under PR than under a majoritarian system. In an *ideal* PR system, seats in parliament are allocated in proportion to the percentage of votes that a party wins. An *indirect* test of this hypothesis is provided by Eubank and Weinberg (1994, pp. 429–30), who related the number of parties in a country to the presence of terrorist groups. Contrary to expectations, they found that "the more parties, the more likely that a nation will have terrorist groups" (Eubank and Weinberg, 1994, p. 430). This finding is consistent with a reverse causality – the presence of more parties implies more extreme views, whose proponents may resort to terrorism. A more direct test by Li (2005), discussed in the next section, gives evidence that PR *is* associated with less terrorism than other democratic systems, as conventionally hypothesized.

There is another consideration that encourages an association between liberal democracy and terrorism. Terrorists are after political concessions that stem from a besieged and threatened public pressuring a government to restore security. In some instances, this pressure may induce the government to concede to some of the terrorists' demands, as was the case when Hezbollah executed the suicide attack against the US Marine barracks in Lebanon on 23 October 1983. Just over four months after the attack, which killed 241 Marines, the United States withdrew its peacekeepers from Beirut as demanded by Hezbollah. A suicide campaign waged by Hezbollah against Israel in the early 1980s resulted in the Israelis withdrawing their military from southern Lebanon (Pape, 2003, 2005). An autocracy is less likely to concede to terrorists' demands, because an autocratic government is less responsive to public pressure and can apply draconian measures against the terrorists or their families. Furthermore, some terrorist attacks may not be reported, thereby limiting public awareness.

There are a few factors that inhibit terrorism in liberal democracies. Perhaps the greatest inhibitor is the opportunity for *political participation*,

Table 2.1. *Supporting and Inhibiting Factors for*
Terrorism in a Liberal Democracy

Supporting factors

- Freedom of association
- Freedom of speech
- Freedom of movement within and between countries
- Target-rich environment
- Right to privacy
- Opportunity to obtain weapons, paramilitary training, and bomb-making information
- Executive and government constraints
- Press freedoms
- Political concessions

Inhibiting factors

- Political participation
- Proportional representation systems
- Periodic change in government

where free and fair elections can remove unpopular leaders and change unpopular policies (Crenshaw, 1981; Eyerman, 1998; Li, 2005; Ross, 1993). Unlike autocracies, liberal democracies give citizens peaceful means to create change through voting and political parties. By allowing for more viewpoints to be represented in the government, PR systems reduce the need to resort to violence to air grievances. Elections allow for periodic changes in government and its composition, which also curb the need for violent dissent.

By way of summary, Table 2.1 lists the supporting and inhibiting influences for terrorism in liberal democracies. The preponderance of supporting factors suggests that these democracies are more likely than autocracies to be plagued by domestic and transnational terrorism. However, the presence of opposing factors means that it is an empirical question whether there is more terrorism in liberal democracies. This question is addressed shortly.

BASIC DILEMMA OF LIBERAL DEMOCRACIES

Terrorism poses a real dilemma for a liberal democracy. If it responds too passively and appears unable to protect life and property, then the government loses its legitimacy and may be voted from office. If, however, the government reacts too harshly, then it also sacrifices popular support and may even increase popular support for the terrorists. President Carter's inability to end the Iranian takeover of the US embassy in Tehran probably cost him the 1980 election. The failed rescue mission on 24 April 1980, where a US helicopter crashed into one of the transport planes, killing eight soldiers, in the desert near Tabas, Iran (Mickolus, 1980, p. 884), also made the Carter administration appear inept. The Italian government of Bettino Craxi collapsed on 17 October 1985, just five days after it released Abu Abbas, the mastermind of the hijacking of the *Achille Lauro* cruise ship (Mickolus, Sandler, and Murdock, 1989, vol. 2, p. 285). Following the 11 March 2004 Madrid train bombings, the Spanish government lost the general election after it tried to pin responsibility for the bombings on Euskadi ta Askatasuna (ETA) when the evidence pointed to Islamic fundamentalists. Ineptitude in handling terrorism clearly has consequences for liberal democracies.

Too strong a response can also have severe and harmful consequences. This was the case when French troops tried to crush the Front de Libération Nationale (FLN) terrorists in Algeria in the late 1950s and early 1960s; French brutality turned the native Algerian Muslim community against the French and in favor of the terrorists (Hoffman, 1998). In some instances, world opinion may turn against a government when its antiterrorist measures are too harsh – for example, world reaction to US handling of detainees at Guantánamo Bay, Cuba, or to Israel's assassination of Hamas leaders in 2004 and 2010. Recent theoretical analysis shows how direct action against terrorists – known as proactive measures (see Chapter 4) – can increase terrorist recruitment, which harms all potential targets at home and abroad (Frey, 2004; Frey and Luechinger, 2003; Rosendorff and Sandler, 2004; Siqueira, 2005). Thus, such offensive measures may have a downside, known as *backlash*.[1]

IS THERE MORE TERRORISM IN LIBERAL DEMOCRACIES?

Given the supportive environment that liberal democracies offer to terrorists, we would expect to find more terrorism in liberal democracies compared to their autocratic counterparts. The first analysis of this correlation was done by Eubank and Weinberg (1994); their study ascertained whether terrorist groups tended to be more prevalent in liberal democracies than in

---

[1] Backlash arises when heavy-handed proactive tactics of the government create new grievances and increased support for the terrorists. This support may take the form of increased recruitment. On backlash, see Arce and Sandler (2010), Bloom (2005), Bueno de Mesquita and Dixon (2007), Jacobson and Kaplan (2007), Pedahzur (2005), and Rosendorff and Sandler (2010).

Table 2.2. *Odds Ratio for Presence of Terrorist Group*

	Democracies	Nondemocracies
Terrorist group presence	44	27
Terrorist group absence	27	58
Odds of terrorists' presence	1.6296	0.4655

Odds ratio = 3.50, chi-square = 14.24, N = 156.
p < .001, standard deviation = 1.39.
Source: Eubank and Weinberg (1994).

nondemocracies for the 1954–1987 period based on an odds-ratio test. In Table 2.2, countries are pigeonholed into four categories: democracies with and without terrorist groups, and nondemocracies with and without terrorist groups. In the third row of Table 2.2, the odds that terrorists are present are computed for each type of political system by taking the ratio of groups being present to their being absent – that is, these odds are 44/27 = 1.6296 for democracies and 27/58 = 0.4655 for nondemocracies. A ratio greater than one indicates a positive association between the political system and the presence of terrorist groups, while a ratio less than one denotes a negative association between the political system and the presence of terrorist groups. The statistical significance of the odds in Table 2.2 is computed by finding the *odds ratio*, which equals 3.5 (= 1.6296/0.4655). Thus, terrorist groups are 3.5 times more likely to be found in democracies than in autocracies. This odds ratio has a chi-square (goodness-of-fit) statistic of 14.24, which gives a one-in-a-thousand chance that it occurred randomly. Thus, democracies are associated with terrorist groups operating on their soil. When the authors compare other categories of democracies – for example, interrupted and partial democracies – the results are similar.

Although this analysis is very innovative, it suffers from some problems. There is a tendency in authoritarian regimes to underreport terrorism; this tendency biases the results in favor of the authors' hypothesized association. The tendency for underreporting is greater for the presence of terrorist groups than for the occurrence of terrorist incidents. Although an authoritarian regime would have difficulty hiding the fact that a bomb had exploded in a major city or that a commercial aircraft had been hijacked, it could easily keep quiet the name of a group claiming responsibility unless the claim were made directly to the media. Even then, the government could bring pressure on the domestic media not to disclose the group's identity. The government has an interest in hiding such information so that people do not believe that the government faces significant challenges to its rule.

Terrorism may be present in repressive regimes but carried out at the individual level, owing to the risks involved in forming groups that might attract government attention or be infiltrated. Thus, we should see more acts by individuals as opposed to groups in authoritarian regimes, but this does not mean that the nation is free from terrorism. Timothy McVeigh had an accomplice but was not part of an established group; thus, the group measure may miss the presence of terrorism even in liberal democracies. Nevertheless, this underreporting bias is anticipated to be higher in autocracies.

In the Eubank and Weinberg (1994) analysis, the hosting of one or more terrorist groups characterized the country as confronting terrorism. This measure is particularly poor at capturing spillover terrorism, where groups stage their terrorist activities in one country while being based elsewhere. Throughout the 1970s and 1980s, Middle Eastern terrorism spilled over to Europe; for example, forty-three incidents in Europe were of Middle Eastern origin in 1987 (US Department of State, 1988). A country such as Austria experienced a lot of spillover transnational terrorism – forty-one incidents from 1980 to 1987, including the 27 December 1985 armed attack on Vienna's Schwechat Airport (Mickolus, Sandler, and Murdock, 1989) – but hosted no groups during the sample period considered by Eubank and Weinberg. Thus, the presence or absence of terrorist groups can give a very misleading view of terrorist activities.

State sponsorship also presents a problem for Eubank and Weinberg's group-based analysis. During the Cold War, it is believed that the communist bloc was responsible for sponsoring terrorist events in the West. State-sponsored groups had home bases (for example, Syria, Libya, Algeria, and Tunisia) outside the country where the acts were staged. For example, the North Korean agents responsible for blowing up Korean Air Lines flight 858 on 30 November 1987 are thought to have acquired the bomb from another North Korean operative in Belgrade (US Department of State, 1988). Eubank and Weinberg (1994) listed North Korea, a repressive regime, as having no terrorist groups; the implication is, then, that North Korea is not involved in terrorism.

Similarly, failed or failing states, which lack coercive and administrative capacity, often host terrorist groups that attack abroad. This empirical relationship between failed states and transnational terrorism was established by Piazza (2008). This means that failed states generate terrorism in such a way that the venue country does not necessarily host the attacking terrorist group. However, Piazza showed that failed states also experienced more terrorist attacks. Unlike some other researchers, Piazza did not find a significant negative relationship between political participation and terrorism in venue countries where terrorist attacks took place.

A more accurate way to test for the presence or absence of terrorism in liberal democracies is to use terrorist event data, which indicate the level of terrorism in a host country. In a follow-up study, Weinberg and Eubank (1998) took this recommendation (see Sandler, 1995) and analyzed the correlation between regime type and the presence of terrorist *events* for 1994–1995. They indeed found that terrorism was more prevalent in democracies. Moreover, they discovered that democracies are more prone to terrorism during a regime transition period.

Although their study is an improvement over their earlier work, it raises further issues that must be addressed. First, only two years of data were examined; these years might not be representative of other years. Data are available for the entire 1968–2008 period. Has the relationship between political system and terrorism changed over time? Only a more complete study can answer this question. Second, the authors have not investigated a crucial issue raised, but not really answered, in their first study – that is, to what extent has terrorism been exported from autocratic to democratic regimes?[2] This migration may be motivated, in part, by the greater anticipated media coverage in democracies. The migration question can be addressed if event venues and the perpetrators' home country are related to one another. Third, Weinberg and Eubank (1998) used only transnational terrorism, which includes no domestic terrorist incidents. Surely, domestic incidents must be included in order to determine whether terrorism is related to a country's political regime. Fourth, these authors reported only correlations and did not examine what factors, including regime type, explained the prevalence of terrorism. In this regard, one needs to quantify what *level* of terrorism, in terms of the number of incidents, is related to regime type and other determinants. Researchers have begun to address this concern by reporting some regressions that indicate the factors that influence the level of terrorism in countries (Blomberg, Hess, and Weerapana, 2004; Li and Schaub, 2004). Such quantitative measures can assist governments in allocating resources to counterterrorism activities.

In a recent study, Li (2005) provided a careful analysis on the relationship between democracy and transnational terrorism. His study distinguished essential characteristics of democracies – for example, press freedoms, political constraints on the executive, and political participation among potential voters. Among other results, Li found that press freedoms and

---

[2] A proper answer requires an examination of the nationality of the perpetrator, the home base of the terrorists, and the location of the terrorist incident (Sandler, 1995).

political constraints are positively associated, as hypothesized, with greater transnational terrorism. Proportional representation systems experience significantly less transnational terrorism than other democratic alternatives. Greater regime durability reduces transnational terrorism at home.

To date, all of the evidence points to liberal democracies being associated with transnational terrorism. While this relationship appears robust and unequivocal, there is still much to learn about it. For example, is the relationship sensitive to sample period and sample countries? Is the terrorism homegrown or exported from abroad?

LIBERAL DEMOCRACIES: DOMESTIC VERSUS TRANSNATIONAL TERRORISM

In a provocative study, Savun and Phillips (2009) went beyond the simple relationship between terrorism and democracy in two important ways. First, these authors distinguished between domestic and transnational terrorist attacks in liberal democracies. Second, they investigated possible root causes of domestic and transnational terrorism in liberal democracies. Savun and Phillips (2009, p. 886) showed that characteristics of democracies (that is, press freedom, executive constraint, political participation, and civil liberties) were *not* significant determinants of domestic terrorism during 1998–2004. By contrast, these democratic characteristics were significant determinants of transnational terrorism. Thus, the type of terrorism appears to make a difference. Why is this the case? With the help of empirical tests, these authors showed that liberal democracies attract transnational terrorist attacks when they are involved in foreign policy crises with other states, when they have alliance ties with the United States, and when they intervene in other countries' civil wars. If the democratic states' foreign policy involvement is controlled, then the positive relationship between democratic characteristics and transnational terrorism diminishes greatly. Thus, an apparent cause of transnational terrorism in liberal democracies is foreign policy interventions.

Other causes of terrorism must be identified. Possible causes may be political, economic, religious, or geophysical (for example, the presence of jungles and mountains, or propinquity to failed states). In a recent study, Krueger and Laitin (2008) found that countries with fewer political freedoms are the source countries for transnational terrorism, while richer countries are the target countries for transnational terrorism. Their results indicate that political oppression, rather than economic deprivation, is a root cause for the exportation of transnational terrorism.

CIVIL LIBERTIES VERSUS PROTECTION TRADE-OFF

To explain how civil liberties are traded off against greater security in a liberal democracy, we present a microeconomic-based indifference curve analysis of this trade-off.[3] In Figure 2.1, expected damage from terrorist attacks is measured on the vertical axis, while the level of civil liberties is measured on the horizontal axis. Curve AB represents the constraint that a society faces in a liberal democracy confronted with a terrorist threat. The minimal expected terrorism damage is $0A$ in the absence of any civil liberties. At a given point in time, all choices on or above AB are feasible, but trade-offs below AB are infeasible. The "cost" of increased civil liberties is greater exposure to terrorism and its expected damage for the reasons discussed earlier in the chapter – for example, freer media make the country a more attractive venue for terrorist attacks. With enhanced liberties, terrorists can engage in larger organizations and larger-scale attacks. Along AB, each increase in civil liberties comes at the expense of larger expected terrorism-induced losses, so that the constraint is positively sloped. In moving from a to c and then from c to e along AB, civil liberties increase by ab and cd, respectively, where $ab = cd$, but the change in anticipated terrorism losses escalates from cb to ed, where $ed > cb$. As a consequence, constraint AB rises at an increasing rate. This implies that a very free society can achieve the largest reduction in terrorist risks as some freedoms are first removed – say, in moving from e to c. Each additional sacrifice of freedom gains less additional security from terrorist attacks. In Figure 2.1, curve AB represents the perceived terrorism–civil liberties constraint before 9/11. The events of 9/11 made people aware that for each level of civil liberties, the expected terrorism damage is higher. Thus, the perceived post-9/11 constraint, $A'B'$, is above and steeper than AB.

An upward shift in the perceived constraint can stem from other terrorists' innovations that result in greater terrorist risks being associated with each level of civil liberties. For instance, Richard Reid, the shoe bomber on American Airlines flight 63 on 22 December 2001, increased the terrorism risk with respect to flying and other transportation modes. The underwear bomb employed on 25 December 2009 is a variant of the shoe bomb. Similarly, the plot to use liquid explosives to bring down transatlantic flights in August 2006 also resulted in a more binding (upward-shifted) constraint.

---

[3]   This analysis modifies and expands on the presentation of Viscusi and Zeckhauser (2003). Their presentation is a standard analysis of the trade-off between a risk and a return.

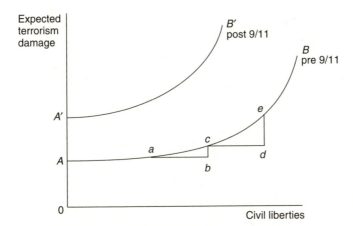

Figure 2.1. Terrorism–civil liberties constraint.

The taste side depends on society's indifference map, which indicates how society is willing to trade off terrorism risks for civil liberties.[4] Consider indifference curve 4 in Figure 2.2, which depicts all combinations of expected terrorism damage and civil liberties – for example, bundles *a*, *c*, and *e* – that provide equal levels of satisfaction to society. Because expected terrorism losses represent a "bad" and civil freedoms denote a "good," the indifference curves are upward-sloping, indicating that society is willing to accept greater anticipated losses only if compensated with more civil liberties.[5] Similarly, society is *willing to sacrifice* some of its liberties in return for greater security – that is, fewer and less severe terrorist attacks. The shape of an indifference curve shows that for each increase in civil liberties, society is less willing to accept further risks in terms of terrorism. In moving from *a* to *c* and then from *c* to *e* on indifference curve 4, each equal increment in civil liberties (*ab* = *cd*) results in smaller tolerated increases in risk as *ed* < *cb*. We have chosen this trade-off because it conforms to the notion that societies are less risk-accepting as freedoms expand; thus, a very free society is more willing to *sacrifice* freedoms for security (in moving from *e* to *a*) than a less free society.

4 Indifference maps are discussed in any intermediate microeconomics textbook. Most introductory textbooks in economics have a discussion of indifference curves in the consumer theory chapter. For more about indifference curves, the reader should consult one of these books. Also, see Chapter 5.

5 On the vertical axis, we could have put *reduced terrorism risk* instead of *expected terrorism losses* so as to show the trade-off of two goods. With *reduced terrorism risk* on the vertical axis, the indifference curves would have the normal shape – that is, convex-to-the-origin, downward-sloping curves. Moreover, the constraint would be a concave-to-the-origin downward-sloping curve.

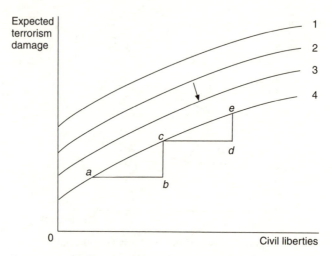

Figure 2.2. Indifference map for terrorism–civil liberties trade-off.

In Figure 2.2., the well-being of society *increases* when moving from indifference curve 1 to lower indifference curves (in the direction of the arrow), so that indifference curve 4 represents the highest satisfaction level of the four curves displayed. This follows because lower indifference curves have *reduced risks for each level of civil liberties* and, thus, are improvements in social welfare. Only four indifference curves are drawn in Figure 2.2, but through any point there is an indifference curve. If a society or group within the society is more accepting of risks or less willing to give up freedoms, then their indifference curves would be steeper, indicating that they would tolerate greater risk for every gain in freedom.

In Figure 2.3, the constraint and tastes are put together to find the social equilibrium, where the greatest feasible level of social welfare is attained on constraint *AB*. Part of the indifference map – four of the multitude of indifference curves – is displayed. Because social welfare increases with lower indifference curves, the social optimum is reached at tangency *E* between *AB* and indifference curve *xx*. Lower indifference curves, while desirable, are unobtainable given the constraint. At equilibrium *E*, society experiences C_e civil liberties and D_e in expected terrorism damage. If society is less accepting of risks, then its entire indifference map will be flatter, with an optimum to the left of *E* along *AB*, where security is increased at the expense of freedom. When, however, society is less willing to accept restraints on its civil liberties, its indifference curves (not shown) will be steeper, and the equilibrium will be to the right of *E* along *AB*, where liberties are expanded at the

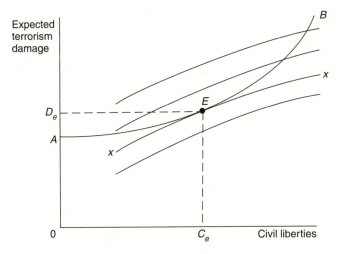

Figure 2.3. Social equilibrium.

expense of greater risks. At point E, society's optimal trade-off of risks and liberties equals the feasible trade-off along AB.

Authoritarian regimes are less accepting of challenges to their rule for fear that tolerance may encourage further challenges. Moreover, such regimes have little or no interest in civil liberties. The ruler's indifference curves are effectively horizontal, and the ruler's optimum is at point A, where measures are taken to limit terrorism to the minimum feasible level of damages. This would then explain why Eubank, Weinberg, and others found so little evidence of terrorism in authoritarian regimes.

The potential effect of 9/11 is displayed in Figure 2.4. Ignore the dashed indifference curve and consider citizen Group 1 both before and after 9/11. Prior to 9/11, Group 1 is in equilibrium at E, with a relatively high level of civil liberties and a low level of expected terrorism damage. After 9/11, AB shifts to $A'B'$ as terrorists' innovations demonstrate greater risks for every level of civil liberties. Also, 9/11 sets in motion a drive for terrorists to find new, more devastating attacks in an escalation process. $A'B'$ is also steeper than AB, so that each increase in civil liberties results in a greater increase in the risk of terrorism. In Figure 2.4, Group 1's indifference curves become flatter as people become less risk-accepting, so that all indifference curves in this group's preference map become flatter. Only one representative indifference curve is displayed in the two scenarios to prevent clutter. The post-9/11 equilibrium for Group 1 is at F, with higher risks and reduced civil liberties compared to E. In the United States, this explains why the

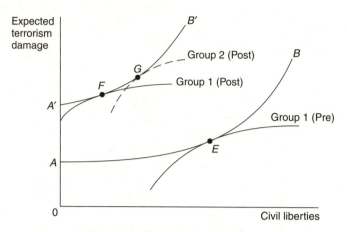

Figure 2.4. Alternative equilibriums.

public was generally accepting of the PATRIOT Act, which curtailed many civil liberties (for example, limitations on habeas corpus, reduced immigration rights, and greater electronic surveillance) in the name of providing security against terrorism. In West Germany, the population basically supported the issuing of identity cards during the height of left-wing terrorism in the 1970s and 1980s. Since August 2006, airline passengers limit their liquid carry-on bottles to three ounces or less. Passengers are more willing to undergo revealing full-body scans after the incident of the underwear bomber in 2009.

Next, consider the presence of a second group in society – Group 2 – with a reduced willingness to trade away civil liberties for lower terrorism risks. This may be due to a worry that they may be singled out owing to past experiences – for example, police profiling of African Americans in traffic stops. In Figure 2.4, Group 2's representative (dashed) indifference curve favors a higher level of civil liberties at the cost of greater terrorism risks compared to Group 1. Its equilibrium is at point G along $A'B'$. Using surveys, Davis and Silver (2004) showed that this was indeed true after 9/11 – "African Americans are much less willing to trade civil liberties for security than whites vs. Latinos" (p. 28). In an experimental situation, Viscusi and Zeckhauser (2003) found analogous results; people whose rights have been infringed upon in the past were less willing to sacrifice civil freedoms after 9/11 than those whose rights had never been compromised.

In Figure 2.5, we examine the change that ensues with enhanced counterterrorism. Suppose that a government severely limits an existing terrorist

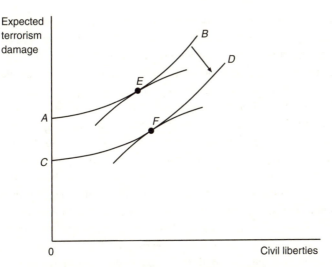

Figure 2.5. Influence of increased counterterrorism.

group's threat by making a series of arrests. This action shifts the trade-off constraint in the southeast direction from *AB* to *CD* as shown. At each level of civil liberty, there is now a smaller terrorism risk. The social equilibrium moves from *E* to *F*, where there will be more civil liberties and reduced terrorism risk. Thus, our analysis is entirely consistent with improved pro-active measures increasing civil freedoms and curbing terrorism. A crucial rationale for such measures is to reduce the civil liberty–security trade-off. A downward shift of constraint *AB* will also occur with the deployment of greater defensive measures. If, however, privacy is infringed by the new defensive measures, then the new constraint becomes steeper (not shown). In this case, the new equilibrium may involve more security and reduced civil liberties. Technological innovations and/or greater international coop-eration may shift the *AB* constraint down, thus lowering potential terrorism losses for each level of civil liberty.

THE ROLE OF THE MEDIA

The media involves all means and channels of information and entertain-ment (Wilkinson, 1997). As such, the media includes television, movies, documentaries, theater, music, newspapers, magazines, books, photogra-phy, and other visual arts. The influence of the media in every facet of our lives has grown with technological innovations that have effectively shrunk the globe.

Periods of globalization have been associated with increased international terrorism. The first wave of globalization beginning in the 1880s coincided with the anarchists, who emigrated from Russia to Europe and then North America (see Chapter 1; Rapoport, 2004). The anarchists assassinated political leaders, planted bombs, and engaged in sabotage in order to foment revolution. Their terrorist acts coincided with advances in global communications (for example, the telegraph and daily newspapers) and transportation (for example, faster and larger ocean liners). The second wave of globalization in the latter third of the twentieth century also coincided with an era of increased terrorism. Innovations in communication and transportation – communication satellites, the internet, high-speed commercial air travel, and the digital revolution – were associated with the new era. Over the last two decades, the internet has been increasingly used by terrorists to disseminate propaganda, spread terror (for example, the beheading of Nicholas Berg posted on the internet on 12 May 2004), coordinate activities, make demands, and send warnings.[6] Terrorists have also relied on the internet to gather intelligence – for example, an al-Qaida computer, found in a cave in Afghanistan, contained a downloaded copy of a US General Accounting Office report on US infrastructure vulnerabilities.

Terrorists and the media represent a symbiotic relationship. To create an atmosphere of fear, terrorists need the media and their ability to reach every corner of the globe almost instantaneously. The events of the Munich Olympics on 5 September 1972 and the toppling of the World Trade Center on 9/11 were transmitted live worldwide. More recently, this was also the case for the 7 July 2005 attacks on the London transport system and the 26 November 2008 armed attacks on various Mumbai venues. The terrorists exploit all forms of the media to gain wider support and recruit new members. During the 1970s and 1980s, left-wing terrorists relied on the media to confirm their claims of responsibility through coded communications, passwords, and other tell-tale signs that allowed groups to get credit for terrorist acts that could be claimed by others (Alexander and Pluchinsky, 1992; Mickolus, Sandler, and Murdock, 1989). In essence, the media made a terrorist act a private good that could not be shared among groups. Coverage of horrible terrorist acts – for example, the massacres at Vienna's Schwechat Airport and Rome's Fiumicino Airport on 27 December 1985, masterminded by Abu Nidal – traumatized a global community. These attacks

---

[6] On information terrorism and the use of the internet, see Post, Ruby, and Shaw (2000). Also, consult Bunker (2000) on weapons of mass disruption that rely on networks for replication purposes. Computer viruses are examples of weapons of mass disruption that may be used by terrorists to create large economic losses in a targeted economy.

changed the flying public's concept of airport risks for many years to come. Such publicity augments the economic consequences of terrorist acts; for example, media coverage of 9/11 added to the huge losses suffered by the airline industry (Chapter 9; Drakos, 2004; Ito and Lee, 2005).

Terrorists may use the media to spread their propaganda. A case in point involves the hijacking of Trans World Airlines (TWA) flight 847 en route from Athens to Rome on 14 June 1985. Prior to the release of the remaining thirty-nine hostages on 30 June 1985, the hooded terrorists held news conferences during which they indicated their views and grievances (Mickolus, Sandler, and Murdock, 1989, vol. 2, p. 224). In many hostage-taking incidents, terrorists issue statements about their cause during negotiations. The publication of a political statement is often a condition for the release of the hostage(s) (Mickolus, 1980; Mickolus, Sandler, and Murdock, 1989). Terrorists will frequently send propaganda statements to the media when claiming responsibility for a terrorist act. The *New York Times* and *Washington Post* published a rambling 35,000-word manifesto by the Unabomber that condemned technology and modern civilization. On 3 April 1996, the arrest of Theodore Kaczynski, the Unabomber, came after David Kaczynski recognized his brother's writings from the published manifesto and alerted the authorities to his brother's whereabouts in Montana.

Terrorists also rely on the media to portray government responses as brutal in the hopes of winning popular support. This tactic was particularly true of the left-wing or "third-wave" terrorists of the 1970s and 1980s. This motive is less applicable to fundamentalist terrorists, who are less interested in winning over a constituency. However, this motive may apply to Hamas, which wants to show Israeli reactions as excessive so that world opinion will turn against Israel.

By reporting logistical innovations, the media inadvertently assist terrorists to adopt new methods that prove effective. On 24 November 1971, D. B. Cooper hijacked Northwest Airlines flight 305, a Boeing 727 en route from Washington, D.C., to Seattle. Cooper demanded $200,000 in twenty-dollar bills and four parachutes, which he was given on the tarmac in Seattle in exchange for the passengers and two of the stewardesses (Mickolus, 1980, pp. 287–88). He then demanded to be flown to Mexico via Reno, Nevada. While en route to Reno, he parachuted from the rear door of the plane and was never seen again.[7] His method was then copied unsuccessfully by

---

[7] He jumped somewhere over Oregon or Washington when the plane was cruising at 200 miles per hour at an altitude of 10,000 feet. When he left the plane in his blue business suit, the wind chill was −69° F. Apparently, the parachutes had been sewn shut, so there is little chance that he survived the jump (Mickolus, 1980, p. 287).

seventeen hijackers, leading the airlines to redesign the Boeing 727, DC-8, and DC-9 so that their rear doors could not be opened in flight (Landes, 1978, p. 4). Unintentionally, the media can encourage a wave of copycat events, which was also true in the 1980s after the media reported that a hijacker had commandeered a plane to Cuba by claiming to have a flammable liquid in a bottle. Many subsequent hijackers used this method (Enders, Sandler, and Cauley, 1990a, 1990b). Such *demonstration effects* can lead to cycles in terrorist attacks as successful methods disseminate rapidly and failures quickly lead to cancellation of some planned attacks.

Like the terrorists, the media are interested in the size of their audience. A larger audience means higher viewer ratings and advertisers' demand for television and larger profits for the print media. Thus, the goals of the media and terrorists are, at times, aligned so that grisly terrorist acts or the tense drama of a hijacking that at any moment might end in bloodshed serve the interests of both. Over time, the terrorists see a need to escalate the shock value and the death toll of their attacks in order to capture and maintain the media's attention. Driven by the need for viewers and readers, the media focus on the more spectacular events, thereby increasing the terrorists' demand for such events.

The media can also serve useful purposes. First, the media can inform the public about heightened terrorism alerts. In so doing, they can pass along vital information about what to watch for. Second, the media can assist in the capture of terrorists, as was the case with the Unabomber. The media published sketches of the parachuting terrorist D. B. Cooper, in the hope that someone might see him and turn him in; but this never happened. Third, the media can provide a forum for discussion so that the public can better assess the risks and learn the measures taken to curtail them. Such forums can teach the public how to respond if they become the target of a terrorist attack. Fourth, the media can expose the hypocrisy of the terrorists, when appropriate, thereby reducing their support. When the brutality of the Tupamaros was reported to the people of Uruguay in the 1960s, it alienated their supporters (White, 2003, pp. 119–29). Once a terrorist group loses its constituency, the authorities can show less restraint, and the terrorists risk being turned in by reward seekers. The media may facilitate this process by exposing terrorists' excesses. Fifth, the media may provide the government with a means to take its case to the public to counter charges made by the terrorists (Scheuer, 2006). Sixth, the media are the sources of event data used by researchers to study terrorism. Important event data include International Terrorism: Attributes of Terrorist Events (ITERATE) and Global Terrorism Database (GTD). ITERATE records observations on transnational terrorist incidents, while GTD records observations on domestic and transnational terrorist incidents.

The net impact of the media can be evaluated only if both the beneficial and not-so-beneficial aspects are compared. To date, there has been very little empirical work to assess the net impact of the media on terrorism. In an innovative paper, Nelson and Scott (1992) applied statistical techniques to determine whether media coverage encouraged additional terrorist events.[8] In particular, these authors tested whether media attention, as measured by the number of column inches devoted to terrorism in the *New York Times*, influenced terrorist events during the ensuing period. For 1968–1984, these authors showed that media coverage of high-profile terrorist incidents did *not* induce additional terrorist acts. In addition, terrorist events in the previous period did not explain media coverage in the next period; only current terrorist incidents determined contemporaneous media coverage. Finally, these authors identified incidents' characteristics that attracted the most media coverage. US and Israeli attacks gained attention in the *New York Times*, especially when Americans were killed. The number of hostages, the sequential release of hostages, and the passing of terrorists' deadlines (for example, a deadline for killing a hostage) had important influences on the amount of media attention afforded to hostage incidents. Their study should be extended to include additional newspapers in order to circumvent the *New York Times* bias for US and Israeli events, which clearly showed up in the results. Such extensions require a lot of effort to record the data in terms of news media coverage of terrorist incidents. Research like the Nelson and Scott study is essential to gauge the impact of media coverage on terrorism.

In a recent paper,[9] Rohner and Frey (2007) applied the Nelson-Scott empirical methodology to investigate the causal relationship between media coverage and terrorism from January 1998 to June 2005. Rohner and Frey drew their domestic and transnational terrorist fatality data from the National Memorial Institute for the Prevention of Terrorism (MIPT) event database. Media coverage was confined to the *New York Times* and the *Neue Zürcher Zeitung*, both highly regarded newspapers. These authors found that past terrorist fatalities increased future media coverage, and that past media coverage increased future terrorist fatalities. This causal relationship held for both newspapers. Apparently, there is a greater symbiotic

[8] These authors used a vector-autoregression (VAR) technique – see Chapter 3 on time series methods and Chapter 5 on their application to other terrorism scenarios.

[9] Rohner and Frey (2007) also built a two-agent game model involving the media and the terrorists in a symbiotic relationship.

relationship between the media and terrorism in today's globalized world as compared to the earlier period (1968–1984) studied by Nelson and Scott (1992). The events on 9/11 may have stimulated this causal relationship.

A standard policy recommendation to curb any negative impact of media coverage of terrorism is to rely on the media to exercise voluntary self-restraint (Wilkinson, 1997). Forced restraint of the media is censorship, which constitutes a loss of civil liberties. There are times where the media must decide whether showing a grisly act is in poor taste, or whether reporting terrorists' innovative methods may encourage further terrorist acts. The media may also need to restrain themselves from reporting a rescue operation while it is in progress, because such coverage could alert the terrorists and jeopardize the mission – for example, the dispatch of Delta Force was reported by the media during the *Achille Lauro* hijacking (Mickolus, Sandler, and Murdock, 1989, vol. 2, p. 283). A similar news tip-off occurred during the hijacking of Pan Am flight 73 at the Karachi airport on 5 September 1986. The *New York Times* reported that a Delta Force commando unit had been dispatched to the scene. Prior to its arrival, the hijackers began killing the passengers – 22 died and 100 were injured (Mickolus, Sandler, and Murdock, 1989, vol. 2, pp. 454–5). There was, however, no evidence that the hijackers knew of the *New York Times* report. The bloodshed ensued when the airplane's lights dimmed as the plane's generators ran out of power. The hijackers mistakenly thought that the Pakistani officials had deliberately lowered the lights to allow for a rescue operation.

TERRORISM IN THE AGE OF GLOBALIZATION

The modern era of terrorism is often characterized as starting in 1968, after the 1967 Arab-Israeli War. In contrast to earlier epochs of terrorism, the modern era is said to be marked by the "internationalization of terrorism" (Hoffman, 1998, pp. 67–75). In a seminal study, Rapoport (1984) indicated that early terrorists – the Thugs in the thirteenth century and the Assassins in the eleventh, twelfth, and thirteenth centuries – moved across state borders and relied on safe havens from which to strike, so that the internationalization of terrorism began well before the "modern epoch" of terrorism. What is different after 1968 is the manner in which terrorists take advantage of innovations in transportation and communication that allow them and the news of their deeds to spread globally in relatively little time. The internet, satellite phones, and other advances in communication permit attacks to be coordinated at widely dispersed places. In addition, modern-day terrorist groups can exist in multiple countries at the same time – for example,

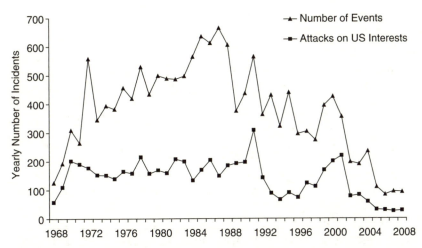

Figure 2.6. Transnational terrorist incidents: 1968–2008. *Sources*: US Department of State (1988–2004), Sandler and Enders (2004), and ITERATE for 2004–2008.

al-Qaida operates in Yemen, the United States, the United Kingdom, Saudi Arabia, Afghanistan, Iraq, and elsewhere.

Another distinguishing characteristic of the modern epoch, compared to the anarchists of the 1880s, or the anticolonialists of the 1950s and 1960s, is the extent of transnational attacks. Figure 2.6 illustrates the rapid rise of transnational terrorist incidents from 125 events in 1968 to 558 attacks in 1972. For the entire 1968–2008 period, transnational terrorist attacks averaged 377 incidents each year, with the largest number of incidents occurring during 1985–1988. Another striking feature is the comparatively large number of incidents directed at US interests. As shown in Figure 2.6, the plot of US attacks generally matches the plot of all attacks, with many matching peaks and troughs. In Figure 2.7, the proportion of transnational attacks against US interests is displayed. For 1968–2008, 38% of all transnational terrorist attacks were against US citizens or property. This focus on US interests also distinguishes the modern era of terrorism, in which the United States is a prime target, from earlier eras in which the United States was not the prime target.

In an interesting empirical study, Li and Schaub (2004) asked whether economic globalization has increased transnational terrorism. These authors used a country's openness to trade, its foreign direct investment (FDI), its portfolio investment, and its level of economic development as proxies for economic globalization. The authors tested whether these proxies affected the number of transnational terrorist incidents for a sample of

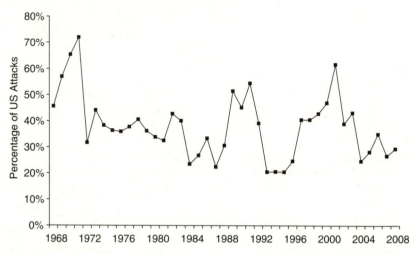

Figure 2.7. Proportion of US transnational terrorist incidents: 1968–2008. *Sources*: US Department of State (1988–2004), Sandler and Enders (2004), and ITERATE for 2004–2008.

112 countries during 1975–1997. They discovered that economic globalization by itself did not increase transnational terrorism. In fact, there was some indirect evidence that trade and FDI reduced transnational terrorism by fostering economic development. The authors did not test whether other aspects of globalization – for example, media advances or increased emigration – may have bolstered transnational terrorism.

Significant Events at the Start of the Modern Era of Terrorism

Like Hoffman (1998), we consider the 22 July 1968 hijacking of an El Al flight en route from Rome to Tel Aviv by three Popular Front for the Liberation of Palestine (PFLP) terrorists as a watershed event in the modern epoch of transnational terrorism. The PFLP terrorists commandeered the Boeing 707 with its ten-member crew and thirty-eight passengers (including the hijackers) approximately twenty minutes after the flight left the ground by threatening to explode grenades.[10] The terrorists were also armed with a pistol. This event is noteworthy for a number of reasons. First, there was clear evidence of state sponsorship *after* the plane landed in Algiers as Algerian authorities secured the hostages and held some until 1

[10] For a description of this event, see Mickolus (1980, pp. 93–4). The facts given in this paragraph come from Mickolus's account of the incident.

September 1968, when a deal was finally struck. Once the plane arrived in Algiers, the Algerian government freed the twenty-three non-Israeli passengers. Five days later, they released the Israeli women and children, but held onto the Israeli men. Second, the incident forced the Israelis to negotiate directly with the Palestinian terrorists – the one thing that the Israelis had said that they would never do (Hoffman, 1998, p. 68). Third, the media coverage showed other terrorists that such incidents could gain worldwide attention. The length of the incident – approximately forty days – meant that this single event was a major news story for weeks. Fourth, one of the terrorists helped land the hijacked plane in Algiers, marking the first time that a terrorist had flown a hijacked plane. Fifth, a $7.5 million ransom was paid by the French government to the hijackers, who were flown to a safe haven at the incident's conclusion. In addition, sixteen Arab prisoners from the 1967 Arab-Israeli War were released by Israel. The incident thus demonstrated to other would-be hijackers that this mode of attack could be financially and politically lucrative. Not surprisingly, many similar hijackings followed. Sixth, the hijacking represented a transnational externality (that is, an uncompensated interdependency among two or more countries), a common feature of modern-day terrorism. A grievance in the Middle East spilled over to Europe; ransoms paid by the French government encouraged subsequent hijackings in other countries. The presence of a transnational externality indicates the need for countries to coordinate their antiterrorism policies (see Chapter 6). Seventh, the terrorists attracted so much attention by creating a crisis situation, where one false move could result in the loss of the plane and its passengers. The incident demonstrated the need for high drama from the outset to encourage the media to allocate reporters and other assets to cover the incident. In future incidents, the terrorists often murdered a passenger or two at the incident's outset to create the necessary drama.

Such hijackings not only made the world aware of a cause, but also fostered recruitment of terrorists to the cause. The July 1968 El Al hijacking appeared to change the mindset of the terrorists by encouraging international incidents. Another important terrorist event took place on 26 December 1968 in the Athens airport, when two PFLP terrorists threw incendiary grenades and fired a machine gun at an El Al plane boarding for a flight to New York via Tel Aviv (Mickolus, 1980, p. 105). One passenger was killed, and a stewardess was wounded. Unlike the earlier El Al hijacking, this attack went awry. The event is significant because it demonstrated to the terrorists that hijackings and attacks on aircraft carry grave risks for the perpetrators.

During the late 1960s and early 1970s, there were countless hijackings in the United States to Cuba (Landes, 1978). Most of these hijackings were peaceful, with the plane landing in Cuba, the hijacker(s) being led away by Cuban authorities, and the plane and passengers returning to the United States with Cuban souvenirs. The epidemic of hijackings, inspired by the 22 July 1968 hijacking, became so severe that metal detectors were eventually installed in US airports on 5 January 1973, thereby ending the epidemic in the United States for eight years, until ways to circumvent these detectors were devised.

Another significant terrorist event, defining the modern epoch, involved the hijacking of TWA flight 840, a Boeing 707 en route from Rome to Athens on 29 August 1969 (Mickolus, 1980, p. 131). Two PFLP terrorists – Leila Ali Khaled and Salim K. Essawi – were involved in hijacking the plane that carried eighty-five passengers and twelve crew members. This incident followed the "script" of the July 1968 hijacking, with the plane landing in a country – Syria – that helped secure the hostages and protect the hijackers. Once in Damascus, Leila Khaled had the passengers and crew leave the plane before she blew up the cockpit, causing $4 million in damage to the $8 million plane (Mickolus, 1980). Syria released most of the passengers and crew but held onto two Israeli hostages until 5 December 1969, when Israel released seventy-one prisoners to Egypt and Syria. Israel also received two military pilots, captured in Egypt, in the prisoner exchange. Syria allowed the two terrorists to go free on 13 October 1969. Leila Khaled later took part in a failed hijacking on 7 September 1970 in the Netherlands (Mickolus, 1980). With flight 840, the terrorists once again captured the world's attention in a tense drama, made even more poignant by blowing up the cockpit. Thus, the terrorists raised the stakes in order to keep the media watching. Countries again made concessions to end the crisis, thereby demonstrating that terrorism could pay. Moreover, the terrorists went free.

Many other dramatic hijackings followed – for example, the hijacking of a Japan Air Lines flight on 31 March 1970 by the Japanese Red Army Faction – until metal detectors significantly decreased, but did not eliminate, hijackings (see Chapter 5). Until effective protective measures were taken and the public's interest seemed to wane, the start of the modern era of terrorism relied on hijackings. Earlier eras of terrorism involving transnational events had not relied on hijacking planes. Terrorist attacks after 1968 also included bombings against both official (for example, the 25 February 1969 PFLP bombing of the British consulate in East Jerusalem) and civilian targets (for example, the 18 July 1969 PFLP firebombing of the Marks and Spencer department store on Oxford Street, London). The modern terrorism epoch involved terrorists diversifying their attacks. As skyjackings became more difficult after 1973, terrorists shifted to kidnapping and barricade-and-hostage-taking missions (Enders, Sandler, and Cauley, 1990a).

Primary Terrorist Influences, 1968–1990

Terrorists were primarily secular during the first portion of the modern epoch of terrorism. There were two primary terrorist influences: the ethno-nationalist groups and the left-wing terrorists. The Palestinian, Latin American, Irish, and Basque terrorists epitomized the former, while the "fighting communist organizations" of Europe (for example, the Red Army Faction in West Germany, Combatant Communist Cells in Belgium, Dev Sol in Turkey, Direct Action in France, the Red Brigades in Italy, the Popular Forces of 25 April in Portugal, and 17 November in Greece) represented the latter. By far, the Palestinian terrorists were the most important influence and actually formed linkages with the Provisional Irish Republican Army (PIRA) and some leftist groups (Alexander and Pluchinsky, 1992, pp. 8–11). These linkages allowed for joint training, the sharing of operatives, and logistical support. Thus, the operation of loose terrorist networks dates back to the start of modern-day terrorism.

Many terrorist groups split off from the PLO because it was too conservative in its terror campaign for some of its members. Breakaway groups included PFLP, PFLP–General Command, Democratic Front for the Liberation of Palestine (DFLP), Palestine Liberation Front (the hijackers of the *Achille Lauro*), Black September (infamous for its attack on the Munich Olympics), and the Abu Nidal Organization (ANO). ANO was headed by Sabri al-Banna, who began forming his own clandestine group while in Iraq in 1972 (Nasr, 1997). During the late 1970s, ANO engaged in numerous assassinations, especially of PLO members[11] – for example, Said Hammami in London on 4 January 1978, and Ali Yassim in Kuwait on 15 June 1978 (Mickolus, 1980). Arguably, ANO was the most significant transnational terrorist threat from 1976 until 1991, when it assassinated Abu Iyad, second in command to Arafat in the PLO, on 14 January 1991 in Tunis.

Noteworthy ANO attacks include:[12]

- the 4 June 1982 attempted assassination of Shlomo Argov, the Israeli ambassador to the United Kingdom, at the Dorchester Hotel in London;

---

[11] The information on ANO comes from Nasr (1997) and Seale (1992).
[12] All incidents are described in detail in Mickolus, Sandler, and Murdock (1989) under the dates listed. Also see Seale (1992) on ANO and its operations.

- the 6 August 1982 machine pistol and grenade attack on the Jo Goldenberg's restaurant in Paris;
- the 16 September 1982 assassination of a Kuwaiti diplomat in Madrid, Spain;
- the 19 September 1982 armed attack on a synagogue in Brussels, Belgium;
- the 25 October 1983 assassination of the Jordanian ambassador in New Delhi, India;
- the 23 November 1985 hijacking of EgyptAir flight 648 en route from Athens to Cairo;
- the 27 December 1985 near-simultaneous armed attacks on the Rome and Vienna airports;
- the 5 September 1986 attempted hijacking of Pan Am flight 73 in Karachi, Pakistan; and
- the 6 September 1986 armed attack on the Neve Shalom synagogue in Istanbul.

These are but a tiny fraction of ANO attacks. These attacks have been singled out for a number of reasons. The 4 June 1982 attempted assassination of Ambassador Argov led to Israel's invasion of southern Lebanon. The 6 August 1982 restaurant attack illustrates the spillover of Middle Eastern terrorism to Europe, as do the September 1982 incidents in Madrid and Brussels. The 25 October 1983 incident is representative of ANO's assassination campaign against diplomats from Jordan, Israel, Kuwait, the United Kingdom, and the United Arab Emigrates (UAE). The EgyptAir hijacking left sixty-one people dead, including eight children, when a rescue mission in Malta gave the hijackers sufficient time to hurl three grenades at the passengers. The Karachi hijacking of Pan Am flight 73 also ended in bloodshed when the hijackers opened fire on the passengers (Mickolus, Sandler, and Murdock, 1989, vol. 2, pp. 452–7). At the trial, the five captured terrorists disclosed their intention to blow up the plane over an Israeli city – thus, this incident is an early forerunner of 9/11. The attacks on the Rome and Vienna airports illustrate the brutality of ANO, as does the massacre of twenty-two worshipers at the Istanbul's Neve Shalom synagogue.

Although secular, ANO was a predecessor to al-Qaida in many ways. ANO engineered the simultaneous attacks that later became the hallmark of al-Qaida. When not assassinating diplomats or PLO members, ANO engaged in "spectaculars" in order to produce ghastly images that would stay in society's collective consciousness – for example, the victims lying beside an airport snack bar in the December 1985 attacks. ANO was not concerned about collateral damage and went for maximal casualties. Like al-Qaida, ANO was organized into different committees involving military operations, political doctrine, financing, and intelligence (Seale, 1992). ANO also engaged in attacks over a geographically dispersed region.

A distinguishing characteristic of ANO was that it was state-sponsored during the era of state sponsorship in the 1980s. Sponsors of ANO included Iraq (1974–1983), Syria (1981–1987), and Libya (1987–1992). ANO ended its operations around the time that al-Qaida began its operations. Sabri al-Banna died of four gunshot wounds to his head in August 2002 while under house arrest in Baghdad, Iraq. At the time, the Iraqi government claimed that he had committed suicide.

Fundamentalist Terrorists – the "Fourth Wave"

The character of modern-day terrorism began to change as left-wing and secular terrorists began to be replaced by religious, fundamentalist terrorists. Since 1980, the number of religious-based groups has increased as a proportion of active terrorist groups: two of sixty-four groups in 1980; eleven of forty-eight groups in 1992; sixteen of forty-nine groups in 1994; and twenty-five of fifty-eight groups in 1995 (Hoffman, 1997, p. 3). The Palestinian terrorists were secular until the rise of Hamas and Hezbollah in the 1980s. The fighting communist organizations and the ethno-nationalist terrorists wanted to win the hearts and minds of a constituency, so they generally avoided casualties except those inflicted on individuals viewed as the establishment or the "enemy." The same was generally true of the PLO and PIRA. When mistakes occurred and collateral damage resulted, the secular terrorists often apologized.

Today, fundamentalist terrorist groups purposely seek out mass casualties, viewing anyone not allied with them as a legitimate target, as 9/11, the Madrid train bombings, and the London transport bombings have sadly demonstrated. Rapoport (2004) referred to religious-based terrorism as the "fourth wave" and found Islam to be at the center of this terrorist trend. In fact, today's fundamentalist terrorists are from all of the major religions (Hoffman, 1998, 2006; White, 2003); however, the primary force is Islam. The rise of fundamentalist terrorism is said to have begun in the fourth quarter of 1979, with two significant events: the takeover of the US embassy in Tehran by Islamic fundamentalist students on 4 November 1979, and the Soviet invasion of Afghanistan on 25 December 1979. Since the rise of fundamentalist terrorism, the proportion of incidents with deaths or injuries has increased greatly (Sandler and Enders, 2005). Enders and Sandler

(2000) established that a significant rise in casualties from transnational terrorism can be traced to the fourth quarter of 1979. Quarters on either side of this quarter did not display as great an increase in casualties. In recent years, an incident is almost seventeen percentage points more likely to result in death or injury compared to the earlier era of leftist and ethno-nationalist terrorism.

There are many basic differences between the left-wing terrorists who dominated terrorism in the 1970s and 1980s and the fundamentalist terrorists who have dominated terrorism in the 1990s and beyond. Table 2.3 indicates eight essential contrasts. Because they believe that they speak for God and view all nonbelievers as legitimate targets, the fundamentalists are not worried about alienating the public. For these terrorists, the death visited on their victims is sufficient payoff for their attacks. Thus, the fundamentalists do not issue advance warnings of their attacks so as to maximize the carnage. For the fundamentalists, the terrorist act is a sufficient end, particularly if it kills the nonbelievers, including women and children. The fundamentalist terrorists are less interested than the left-wing terrorists in maintaining a constituency. Frequently, fundamentalists do not feel a need to claim responsibility for their acts, performed in the name of God. In their rhetoric, these fundamentalists justify their indiscriminate killing by demonizing and dehumanizing nonbelievers. Left-wing terrorists merely degrade their enemies. Modes of attack vary between the two types of terrorists, with fundamentalists relying more on bombings and armed attacks. Left-wing terrorists resort to bank robberies and kidnappings to finance their campaigns, and engage in assassinations to limit collateral damage. In stark contrast to left-wing terrorists, fundamentalists display an interest in engaging in chemical, biological, radiological, and nuclear attacks. The differences shown in Table 2.3 result in the greater carnage per incident that characterizes recent years. As fundamentalists became the dominant terrorist influence, the number of transnational terrorist events fell, but their lethality rose (see charts in Chapter 3). Groups like al-Qaida and its associates are more interested in spectacular events with high casualty counts.

The fighting communist organizations ruled out suicide missions, while the fundamentalists have embraced them. Since 1968, a terrorist attack results in one fatality on average. A suicide attack, however, leads to twelve to thirteen fatalities on average because the suicide terrorists can choose to attack at a time when casualties will be the greatest (Pape, 2003, 2005). In Figure 2.8, we display the number of suicide terrorist attacks – domestic and transnational – per quarter for 1981–2005. There were 32 suicide attacks in the 1980s, 110 in the 1990s, 83 in 2000–2001, and 249 in 2002–2005. Suicide

Table 2.3. *Features Distinguishing between Left-Wing and Fundamentalist Terrorists*

Left-Wing Terrorists	Fundamentalists
• Secular, speak for group	• Religious, speak for God
• Selective targets, minimal collateral damage	• General targets, maximal collateral damage
• Often gave advanced warning of bombings	• Any advanced warning is of a generalized threat
• No use of suicide bombing	• Some use of suicide bombings
• Interested in a constituency	• Less interested in a constituency
• Relied on bank robberies, kidnappings, and assassinations	• Relied on bombings, armed attacks, and kidnappings
• No interest in using chemical, biological, radiological, or nuclear attacks	• Interest in using chemical, biological, radiological, or nuclear attacks
• The attack must further its goal	• The attack may be warranted if it kills nonbelievers

attacks have increased greatly over time, especially in regard to domestic terrorism and insurgencies against occupying military forces.

Attacks in the 1980s were associated with Hezbollah's campaign to remove foreign troops from Lebanon. Beginning in the 1990s, suicide attacks have corresponded to campaigns by the Liberation Tigers of Tamil Eelam (LTTE) for a Tamil state in Sri Lanka, by the Kurdistan Workers' Party (PKK) for a Kurdish homeland, by al-Qaida for the United States to vacate the Saudi peninsula, by Kashmir rebels for India to leave Kashmir, by Hamas, Islamic Jihad, Fatah, and PFLP for a Palestinian state, and by Chechen rebels for Russia to grant Chechnya autonomy. The number of victims per quarter is displayed in Figure 2.9, and has been on the rise since 9/11. The Second Intifada (2000–2006) involved many Palestinian suicide missions against Israeli targets. Although not reflected in Figures 2.8–2.9, domestic and transnational suicide terrorist attacks have plagued Iraq since the formation of the Maliki government. More recently, suicide terrorist incidents have increased greatly in Afghanistan.

Pape (2003, 2005) argued that suicide attacks possess a strategic logic and are not the random acts of deranged individuals. Figure 2.8 shows the clustering of acts in apparent campaigns, which can be verified by looking at the raw data. According to Pape, terrorists resort to suicide missions because such attacks have induced moderate concessions from liberal democracies in the past (for example, the Israeli withdrawal from Lebanon in 1985, and the US troop withdrawal from Beirut in February 1984 following the

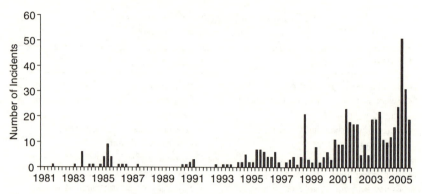

Figure 2.8. Suicide incidents: Quarterly, 1981–2005. *Sources*: Pape (2003, 2005).

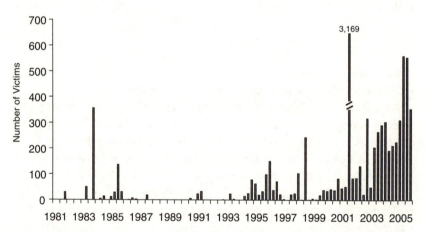

Figure 2.9. Victims of suicide incidents: Quarterly, 1981–2005. *Sources*: Pape (2003, 2005).

23 October 1983 bombing of the US Marine barracks). The *preponderance of suicide campaigns* have been *against liberal democracies*, where pressures are felt by elected officials to protect lives. Past concessions will encourage future campaigns as terrorists see that they pay.

In a follow-up piece, Moghadam (2006) challenged some of Pape's (2005) claims. Moghadam argued that Pape's suicide campaign success rate was 24% rather than 54%. The reduced success rate arises because some of Hamas's successes do not stand up to closer scrutiny. In contrast to standard definitions of terrorism, Pape (2003, 2005) included suicide attacks against military targets as terrorism. Other criticisms have been leveled against some of Pape's claims – for example, the alleged *absence* of a link between suicide terrorism and fundamentalism. In recent years, outside of Pape's sample, suicide attacks have been mostly fundamentalist-based. Despite these and other criticisms of Pape's work, it is nevertheless true that governments have conceded on occasion to suicide terrorist campaigns and that these concessions have stimulated increased use of these deadly tactics. The rising death tolls from such attacks support this view.

The motivation of the terrorists who give up their lives in suicide attacks is an important consideration. If terrorists are rational, as we believe, then there must be a rationality-based explanation for their willingness to make the ultimate sacrifice for the cause. To date, the best theoretical analysis is that of Azam (2005), who modeled suicide terrorists as altruists who highly value the well-being of the next generation.[13] Their act of sacrifice is an investment in a public good – the sought-after political change – that benefits the current and all future generations. Thus, Azam characterized suicide bombings as an "intergenerational investment." Azam argued that, since education is usually positively correlated with investment behavior, it is not surprising that one study (Krueger and Maleckova, 2003) uncovered this correlation. From a policy viewpoint, the willingness of terrorists to make the ultimate trade-off means that changes in policy that make some actions more difficult are unlikely to influence suicide attacks.[14]

CONCLUDING REMARKS

Because of their openness and their duty to protect lives and property, liberal democracies are especially vulnerable to terrorist attacks. The recent targeting of suicide terrorist attacks on liberal democracies underscores

[13] There are other grounds for suicide terrorism. For example, Wintrobe (2006) viewed suicide terrorists as being lured by camaraderie. Others indicated that suicide missions can penetrate hard targets. Recently, strategic analyses of suicide terrorism have been put forward. Rosendorff and Sandler (2010) presented a game-theoretic analysis of suicide terrorism containing three agents: the terrorist leader, a targeted government, and potential terrorist supporters. Supporters join the terrorist group if they gain more from their participation than from their economic opportunities. Proactive measures taken by the government can result in a backlash that encourages recruitment by inciting new grievances. Suicide attacks can also lead to recruitment. Also see Jacobson and Kaplan's (2007) analysis of suicide bombings and government-targeted killings in a two-agent game.

[14] That is, a policy-induced price rise need not alter a "corner" decision because some discrete changes in the constraint may have no effect. At a corner solution, the price change would have to be of a sufficient magnitude to change a choice variable. Corner decisions or solutions involve non-tangencies of the objective and the constraint at the axis or a boundary point. See a fuller analysis in Chapter 5.

this vulnerability. As liberal democracies are singled out for attack, they must decide how much in civil liberties to trade away for increased security. Clearly, terrorism presents countries with a real dilemma; they are the loser no matter how they respond. The final choice must try to minimize the losses, given society's preference for freedom versus security. In the new era of religious terrorism, when fundamentalist terrorists are bent on causing the greatest damage possible, the trade-offs are even grimmer. As attacks escalate, liberal democracies will sacrifice further freedoms as their constituencies become more willing to exchange liberties for a greater sense of security.

There are a number of unanswered questions that merit further analysis. For example, there is a need to quantify how much terrorism is exported from more autocratic regimes. Any export is motivated by the more conducive environment for terrorism in liberal democracies, including greater media coverage. Such exporting represents a negative externality. Another question concerns competition for political change among terrorist groups within the same country. Such groups may, nonetheless, have common (complementary) interests, because attacks by any group may weaken government resolve. Thus, competitive groups may form alliances in such a way that an adversarial representation fails to capture the situation.

Terrorism represents an excellent area to which to apply economic tools – theoretical and empirical. Researchers need, however, to become familiar with stylized facts associated with modern-day campaigns if theoretical models are to inform policymakers. For example, the rise of fundamentalist terrorism alters the manner in which terrorists respond to counterterrorism measures. If, for example, these terrorists are less interested in claiming responsibility, then some media bans may prove fruitless. Moreover, today's religious terrorists may view some logistical failures as successes if the body count is sufficiently high, which means that greater protective barriers may be required. Empirical models that include some countries with leftist terrorists and other countries with fundamentalist terrorists may give an average representation that is not descriptive of either set of countries. This suggests that samples should be chosen carefully so that sample countries face *similar* terrorist threats.

THREE

Statistical Studies and the Dynamics
of Terrorist Behavior

Our eyes are wonderful at detecting associations in data because our brains are wired to simplify complicated patterns and relationships. Within a few seconds, you should be able to figure out that 25 is the next number in the sequence 1, 4, 9, 16. A computer program may need to make millions of calculations just to detect a pattern in the chess pieces that is readily visible to an accomplished player. The problem is that the patterns we perceive in the data may not meaningfully characterize its actual behavior. In the same way that our brains are able to "see" elaborate paintings in the clouds, we are sometimes able to "recognize" what are spurious relationships in economic data.

This chapter will present the time plots of various types of terrorist incidents, including bombings, assassinations, kidnappings, and skyjackings. Some features of the data will be clear even to the casual observer; for example, there is no decidedly upward trend in any of the incident series. However, many other features of the data may not be readily apparent, so statistical analysis may be required to draw inferences about the data. Toward this end, the chapter uses the basic tools of spectral analysis and intervention analysis to formally analyze data of terrorist incidents. Spectral analysis enables us to estimate the cyclical patterns in the various terrorist incident series, while intervention analysis allows us to measure the effects of important structural changes on the incident series. For example, using intervention analysis we can examine the effects on skyjackings of the introduction of metal detectors in airports, and the behavior of terrorists since the attacks of 9/11.

WHY USE STATISTICAL ANALYSIS?

Statistical analysis is a way of making precise mathematical statements about the interrelationships among variables and the behavior of variables over

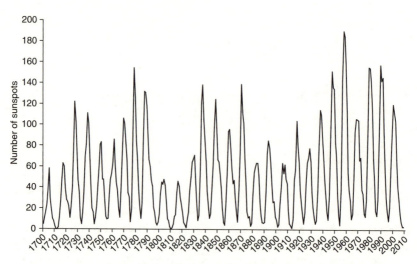

Figure 3.1. Annual number of sunspots.

time. To illustrate some of the key points, consider the data in Figure 3.1, showing the annual number of sunspots from 1700 to 2009. The number of sunspots may, at first, seem to be quite erratic; however, closer examination reveals that there appears to be a cycle of approximately eleven years in *average* duration. A cycle can be as short as the eight years from 1761 to 1769 or as long as the cycle from 1787 to 1804. What you may not see is that the cycles are asymmetric. From the low part of the cycle (that is, from a trough), it takes about four years to reach a peak and then approximately seven years to fall back to a trough.

Scientists have long used the obvious patterns in the data to forecast sunspot activity. In fact, the regularities in this particular series are such that scientists have been able to predict future sunspot activity without fully understanding the type of nuclear reaction causing the sunspots to occur. This is easily done by noting that in 2009, the last observation in the data set, there were 3.1 sunspots (some began in 2008, and others were not completed by the end of 2009). The observed patterns in the data are sufficiently clear that you should be able to predict subsequent sunspot activity. Since 2009 follows a trough of 2.9 for the year 2008, you might predict three successive increases in sunspot activity. Most people would predict about thirty-five sunspots for 2010, fifty-five for 2011, and eighty for 2012. Thereafter, most people would predict seven subsequent declines.

Of course, the forecasts will not be exact, since the series is not perfectly predictable. Some of the peaks are clearly higher than others, and the number of years from one peak to the next changes over time. For example, the first peak (58 spots) occurred in 1705, the second (63 spots) occurred in 1717, and the third (122 spots) occurred in 1727. Even though the forecasts will contain errors, the forecasts made using the observed pattern in the data should be far better than those obtained using some other method. What if you wanted to make very long-term forecasts, such as predicting the number of sunspots that will occur in the year 2400? A reasonable guess is that the number will be just equal to the sample average of fifty sunspots per year. Since the pattern does not follow a precise eleven-year cycle, a long-term forecast will not benefit from using the patterns in the data or the current value of the number of sunspots.

The discussion points out the following:

1. *An observed pattern in the data can be used for forecasting.* If sunspots have a fairly regular cycle every eleven years, this eleven-year pattern can be projected into the future.
2. *Short-term forecasts are likely to be more accurate than long-term forecasts.* Since a series will not be perfectly regular, the cumulated errors will mean that long-term forecasts will be associated with rather large errors.
3. *Mathematical methods can aid simple observation.* Some people might not recognize the fact that there are typically four years of increasing sunspot activity followed by seven years of decreasing activity. Mathematical methods applied to data (that is, statistical methods) can often find patterns that are not readily apparent. Since the movements in the data are somewhat random, any description of the data and any predictions of the future are necessarily probabilistic. Statistics is the branch of mathematics dealing with the calculation of such probabilities.
4. *A series can be forecasted without knowing why the variable changes.* As mentioned, you do not need to be an astronomer or a nuclear physicist to forecast sunspots. In the same way, we do not need to know all the details about the way terrorists operate to make predictions about their behavior.
5. *Our eyes can "see" patterns not actually present in the data.* Notice that the peaks in 1705 and 1717 are low relative to those in subsequent periods. Similarly, the peaks in 1804 and 1816 are low, as are the peaks that occur in 1883, 1893, and 1909. Do you see the episodes of relatively low sunspot activity occurring every 100 years? In addition to the eleven-year cycles, there is a second type of cycle with a duration

of 100 years or so. In actuality, there is no evidence to indicate that such cycles are real; instead, they are the result of flukes in the data that appear real. This points out the need to use statistical methods to verify (or refute) patterns suggested by casual inspection of the data.

These ideas are important for understanding the way in which social scientists apply statistical methods to the study of terrorism. In the next section, we will present some time series data on the incidence of transnational terrorism. Just as in the sunspot data, the patterns in the time series of terrorist incidents such as skyjackings, bombings, and assassinations can be investigated. The time series plot of any such series can be used to characterize the way it behaves over time for forecasting purposes. It is especially important to keep in mind that we do not need to know the actual causes of the terrorists' behavior to estimate their behavior. Remember that "eyeballing" the data may not reveal the actual patterns present in a series. Without a formal statistical model, such casual inspection may "reveal" nonexistent patterns.

THE ITERATE DATA SET

The data that we use to analyze transnational terrorist incidents are drawn from International Terrorism: Attributes of Terrorist Events (ITERATE). ITERATE uses information from the print media to construct a chronology of transnational terrorist events. ITERATE relies on a host of sources for its information, including the Associated Press, United Press International, Reuters tickers, the Foreign Broadcast Information Service (FBIS) *Daily Reports*, and major US newspapers. Mickolus (1982) first developed ITERATE for the period running from 1968 through 1977. The year 1968 corresponds to the rise in transnational terrorism resulting from the 1967 Arab-Israeli War. This data set was extended to cover 1978–1987 by Mickolus, Sandler, and Murdock (1989). More recently, Mickolus, Sandler, Murdock, and Flemming (2009) updated the data through 2008. Unless otherwise noted, the time series used in this book run through the end of 2008. The easiest way to explain the nature of the data is to consider the following excerpts drawn from the chronology by Mickolus, Sandler, and Murdock (1989, pp. 297, 300):

November 4–5, 1985 – **BELGIUM** – In early morning hours of November 4 a bomb exploded at the Brussels-Lambert Bank. Prior to the blast a car with a loudspeaker warned occupants to leave. One night watchman was shot in the arm when he emerged from the building. Property damage was described as extensive. Around 11 A.M. a second bomb caused extensive damage to the Societe Generale in

Charleroi. Leaflets of the Communist Combatant Cells (CCC) left at the bank gave the occupants 30 minutes to leave prior to the explosion. One person was slightly injured and damage was extensive.

On November 5, bombs exploded at the Manufacturers Hanover Bank in Charleroi and at the Kredietbank in Louvain. Damage was extensive, but no injuries were reported.

In a seven-page letter sent to the AGENCE FRANCE-PRESSE office in Brussels, the CCC claimed credit for the four bombs at banks, which they described as "major havens for the financial oligarchy in this country."

In December 1985 four alleged CCC members – Pierre Carette, Bertrand Sassoye, Didier Chevolet, and Pascale Vandegeerde – were arrested. The four were suspected of being the ringleaders of the CCC. On January 14, 1986, they were charged with the attempted murder of the night watchman at the Brussels-Lambert Bank.

November 5, 1985 – **GREECE** – Police discovered a bomb in a suspicious-looking cloth bag planted between the first and second floors of an Athens building at 8 Xenophon Street. The building housed the offices of Trans World Airlines. Bomb experts removed the bomb and detonated it without mishap.

November 5, 1985 – **USSR** – In Moscow, Mexican diplomat Manuel Portilla Quevedo and his domestic servant were found murdered in Quevedo's apartment. Quevedo had been shot in the neck, and the servant had been beaten to death. Quevedo had given frequent news interviews.

November 5, 1985 – **PERU** – A booby-trapped car exploded in front of the U.S. Citibank in the San Isidro neighborhood of Lima. The 10:30 P.M. blast damaged the bank's doors and neighboring buildings but caused no injuries. Slogans painted on the bank's walls attributed the attack to the Tupac Amaru Revolutionary Movement (MRTA).

November 5, 1985 – **SOUTH KOREA** – In Seoul, 14 students armed with incendiary devices occupied the American chamber of commerce for two and a half hours before being overpowered and arrested by police. One of those arrested – Kim Yong-hui – told police that the students had originally planned to occupy the U.S. embassy but changed their plans owing to the tight security. The police were seeking three others connected to the incident.

November 6, 1985 – **PUERTO RICO** – U.S. Army Maj. Michael S. Snyder, 37, was seriously injured by two .32 caliber pistol shots. The incident occurred in San Juan at 7:50 A.M. while Snyder was riding to work at Fort Buchanan. Two gunmen on a motorcycle pulled beside Snyder, who was on a motorscooter, and fired two shots hitting Snyder in the hip and side. He was listed in stable condition following surgery.

At 11 A.M. a self-proclaimed spokesman phoned the Spanish news agency EFE and took credit on behalf of Los Macheteros. A second anonymous caller claimed credit on behalf of the Volunteers for Revolution in Puerto Rico.

November 6, 1985 – **ARGENTINA** – At 1:30 A.M. a bomb damaged the Xerox Corporation branch office at the corner of Libertad Avenue and Jaramillo Street in

Buenos Aires. Windows throughout the seven-story building were shattered. No injuries were reported.

November 6, 1985 – **EGYPT** – According to Interior Minister Ahmad Rushdi, security forces thwarted an attempt by four Libyan suicide commandos to assassinate former Libyan prime minister Abdul Hamid Bakoush and former Libyan cabinet official Muhammad al-Muqaryaf. The four would-be assassins drove across the western desert after entering the country from Libya on November 2. From the time that they entered security forces put the men under surveillance. The assassination was planned for November 6 at the King Marriott Restaurant, 19 kilometers west of Alexandria. At the time of the planned assassination Bakoush dined with a group of Libyan exiles; al-Muqaryaf was out of the country. Security forces moved in and arrested the four assailants – Yusuf al-Madani (a corporal in the Libyan Jamahariyah security organization), Muhriz Muhammad 'Umar (a corporal in the same organization), Muhammad Siddiq (a sergeant in the organization), and Saqr 'Abdallah Maydun (an official in the organization) – as they sped towards the restaurant in their Toyota. Some reports said that a short-lived gun battle erupted between the security forces and the assassins, but no casualties were reported. The security forces seized four machine guns, four pistols, four silencers, eight hand grenades, and a supply of ammunition.

In November 1984 another Libyan-backed attempt on Bakoush was thwarted by Egyptian security. Minister Rushdi warned of six other commando squads trained in Libya that may be sent to Egypt.

According to the assassin's confession, each was paid 1.5 million Libyan dinars to assassinate the two men. On November 11 the four were charged with attempted murder.

There are several noteworthy features of the descriptions of these incidents.

1. Unlike the perception in the popular press that there is relatively little terrorism, many terrorist incidents occur in a single day. Although there were five separate incidents on 5 November and another five on 6 November, there were thirty-two incidents on 24 June 1993. A skyjacking or an incident with substantial property damage and many victims will be reported on the nightly news. Other intense incidents will be reported in mainstream newspapers; however, "less newsworthy" incidents will escape the attention of the general public.

2. At times, it may not be clear whether an incident is a simple crime or terrorism. Unlike the first incident in Belgium, terrorists do not always leave any hard evidence proving their involvement. The bomb found outside the Trans World Airlines (TWA) office or the assassination of the Mexican diplomat and his servant may have had nothing to do with political motives. Nevertheless, anyone constructing a complete set of terrorist incidents must make a judgment call regarding the second and third incidents.

3. The assignment of responsibility for a particular act to a specific terrorist group may be difficult. Sometimes, no one takes responsibility for having committed a terrorist act. In other cases, such as the shooting of Major Snyder in Puerto Rico, multiple groups claim credit for the same act.

4. In most instances, the date and location of a terrorist incident are recorded in ITERATE. When possible, the various attack modes (for example, bombings, assassinations, skyjackings, and shootings), the number of deaths and casualties, and other key incident characteristics are recorded.[1]

5. Some of the incidents are far more logistically complex than others. Most incidents require preparation, funds, some form of weaponry, and personnel willing to undertake a risky act. However, some incidents require far more resources than others. Placing a bomb outside of the TWA office in Athens took some careful planning: it was necessary to acquire and assemble the various parts of the bomb, gain access to the building, and plant the device without being detected. Nevertheless, it must have been far more difficult to plan the failed assassination attempt on Ahmad Rushdi and to obtain the necessary equipment, weapons, funding, and personnel.

Coders use the descriptions of the various events to construct time series data for forty key variables common to all transnational terrorist incidents from the first quarter of 1968 (denoted by 1968:Q1) to the fourth quarter of 2008 (denoted by 2008:Q4). Coding consistency for ITERATE event data was achieved by applying identical criteria and maintaining continuity among coders through the use of overlapping coders and monitors. ITERATE excludes guerrilla attacks on military targets of an occupying force and all terrorist incidents associated with declared wars or major military interventions.

For our purposes, the key variables in ITERATE are given in Table 3.1. The time and place of each incident must be known, along with the type of incident. ITERATE classifies incidents into the twenty-five different categories shown in Table 3.2. For the time period 1968–2008, there were 13,181 total transnational terrorist incidents recorded. You can clearly see that 7,372 bombings (that is, the sum of types 4, 5, 6, 7, 8, 23, 24, and 25) account for more than half of the incidents. Since logistically complex

---

[1]   ITERATE includes additional files, called Hostage and Skyjacking, containing detailed information on these two important incident types. The file called Fate contains information concerning the outcomes of the various incidents and the fate of the terrorists.

Table 3.1. *Key Variables in ITERATE*

Incident Characteristics
Date of start of incident: year, month, day
Location start: country
Location end: country
Type of incident

Victim Characteristics
Number of victims
Nationality of victims

Life and Property Losses
Total number of individuals wounded
Total number of individuals killed
Terrorists killed
Type(s) of weapon(s) used

---

incidents utilize large amounts of resources, they tend to be fewer in number. ITERATE also reports information about the victims: for example, the number and nationalities of the victims are recorded along with the number of people killed or wounded.

Before proceeding further, we need to point out that ITERATE has some shortcomings because it relies on the world's print and electronic media for its information. As a result, ITERATE is better at chronicling the actions of terrorists than in recording those of the authorities. ITERATE picks up *newsworthy* transnational terrorist incidents, so that there is some bias, which must be recognized. Given the steady increase in the severity of terrorism, some incidents (for example, the unexploded bomb in Greece on 5 November 1985, and the bombing of the Xerox office in Argentina on 6 November 1985) might not be reported in today's newspapers. Thus, ITERATE might suggest that certain types of terrorist events have declined simply because they are no longer reported. Despite these difficulties, ITERATE is suited to a wide range of empirical tasks.

THE BEHAVIOR OF THE TERRORISM TIME SERIES

As with the sunspot data, it is instructive to plot the time path of the various terrorist incident types. Although ITERATE reports the specific date for each incident, the essential features of the data are easier to visualize by using quarterly totals. Figure 3.2 shows the time paths of the quarterly totals of all transnational incidents (ALL) and bombings (BOMBINGS) contained in ITERATE. The solid line represents the ALL series, and the dashed line

Table 3.2. *Number of Incidents by Type (1968–2008): ITERATE Data*

Incident Type Code	Incident Type	Number of Incidents
1	Kidnapping	1,390
2	Barricade and hostage seizure	184
3	Occupation of facilities without hostage seizure	76
4	Letter or parcel bombing	452
5	Incendiary bombing, arson, Molotov cocktail	1,022
6	Explosive bombing	4,086
7	Armed attack involving missiles	54
8	Armed attack – other, including mortars and bazookas	1,432
9	Aerial hijacking	371
10	Takeover of a nonaerial means of transportation	61
11	Assassination, murder	1,120
12	Sabotage, not involving explosives or arson	35
13	Pollution, including chemical and biological agents	25
14	Nuclear-related weapons attack	1
15	Threat with no subsequent terrorist action	1,128
16	Theft, break-in of facilities	112
17	Conspiracy to commit terrorist action	295
18	Hoax (for example, claiming a nonexistent bomb)	323
19	Other actions	403
20	Sniping at buildings, other facilities	132
21	Shoot-out with police	48
22	Arms smuggling	92
23	Car bombing	210
24	Suicide car bombing	59
25	Suicide bombing	57
	Cumulative Total:	13,181

represents the BOMBINGS series. An examination of Figure 3.2 suggests that there are periods in which the number of incidents is quite high, and others in which it is low. For example, the number of incidents generally increased from 1968 to the early 1970s. There were forty incidents in the first quarter of 1968. By contrast, the average was ninety-three incidents per quarter from the first quarter of 1970 through the end of 1975. In the early 1980s there was another upward surge lasting until 1987. The level of terrorism remained low until the early 1990s, when a three-year wave of terrorism ensued. The number of incidents then fell until the late 1990s. The post-9/11 period ushered in a small surge in 2002 and 2003, followed by a leveling off at about twenty-three incidents per quarter beginning in 2004.

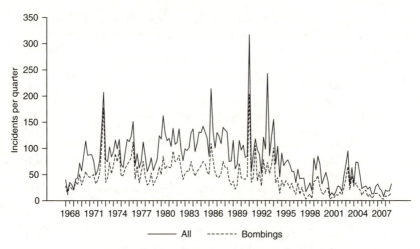

Figure 3.2. All incidents and bombings.

The seeming persistence of high-terrorism versus low-terrorism periods is helpful to social scientists trying to predict the behavior of terrorists. If any theory of terrorism is to be successful, it must capture the reasons why incidents tend to cluster. Moreover, the fact that terrorism seems to wax and wane is useful to forecasters. When the number of incidents is currently high, the number of incidents in the next period is also likely to be high. Similarly, when there is a current lull in terrorism, the number of incidents in the successive period will also tend to be low. Thus, the number of incidents in the current period can help forecast the number of incidents in the near future.

The BOMBINGS series shown in Figure 3.2 consists of various types of bombings and armed (explosive) attacks (incident types 4 + 5 + 6 + 7 + 8 + 23 + 24 + 25 in Table 3.2). This series seems to track the total number of incidents reasonably well in that the two tend to rise and fall together. Over the years, bombings have been the most common incident type, accounting for about 56% of all incidents. In many periods, bombings account for far more than half of the overall total; the large spikes in the ALL series are generally due to spikes in BOMBINGS. Terrorists can quickly increase the number of bombings, since a typical bombing incident is not logistically complex – a relatively small amount of the terrorists' resources can set off a spate of bombings – and sharp increases in bombings can therefore occur at a relatively low cost. By contrast, it is far more costly for terrorists to sharply increase incident types such as kidnappings, assassinations, and aerial hijackings (skyjackings). Notice that an interesting change in the

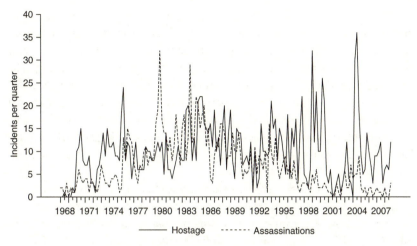

Figure 3.3. Hostage takings and assassinations.

proportion of bombings occurs shortly after 9/11. In the mid-1990s, bombings accounted for 43% of all incidents; in 2002 and 2003, the proportion was 54%. In stepping up their attacks in the aftermath of 9/11, terrorists resorted to a relatively large number of bombings.

Hostage Takings and Assassinations

Figure 3.3 shows the time series of assassinations (incident type 11) and various types of hostage takings (incident types 1 + 2 + 9 + 10). Assassinations (ASSASSINATIONS) account for about 8% of all incidents, and the constructed hostage-taking series (HOSTAGE) accounts for almost 19% of all incidents. Over the very long run, the two series seem to move together. Both start from very low levels in the late 1960s and fluctuate in the neighborhood of eight incidents per quarter in the middle to late 1970s. Notice that the ASSASSINATIONS series begins to experience a long and gradual decline in the 1990s, but the drop in hostage incidents in 1999 is quite dramatic. Unfortunately, after a large spike in 2004, the number of hostage incidents has remained at about eight incidents per quarter.

Assassinations and hostage incidents are quite resource-intensive. Nearly all assassinations and many hostage incidents require substantial amounts of planning. Victims and locations need to be chosen far in advance of the actual incident. In the case of the Mexican ambassador and his servant who were found murdered on 5 November 1985, someone had to acquire access to the apartment at a time when the ambassador was home. The timing had to be such that there was no one capable of thwarting the killing or preventing escape. Similarly, the shooting of Major Snyder may have been spontaneous, or the would-be assassins may have known that the major always rode to work on a scooter around 8 o'clock in the morning. The mechanics of staging an assassination or of capturing and holding victims can also be quite difficult. In comparison to most bombings, terrorists put themselves in great jeopardy during an assassination attempt, a kidnapping, or when holding hostages. These two incident types are logistically complex because they require large amounts of the terrorists' time, personnel, and weaponry.

Since the two incident types are similarly sophisticated, they understandably display the same long-run behavior. During short time spans, the two series can, however, move in very different ways. Notice the sharp jump in HOSTAGE incidents in 1970 and the sharp decline in 1999. During the 1990s, HOSTAGE incidents have increased while assassinations have declined. A full theory of terrorism must be able to explain the similarities in the long-run behavior of the series as well as accounting for the discrepancies in the short-run patterns.

Threats and Hoaxes

On 26 September 2001, a caller, alleged to be Adam Ray Elliott, used his cell phone to threaten that the *jihad* would destroy the US Post Office in Suwannee County, Florida. The next day, the same caller indicated that a bomb and other explosives had been placed at the base of the Buckman Bridge in Duval County, Florida. Even though *jihad* is unlikely ever to be concerned about a post office and bridge in rural Florida, the authorities must respond to such threats and hoaxes. On 21 November 2003, Virgin Atlantic flight VS010 heading for London was rerouted back to New York when a passenger found a note indicating that there was a bomb aboard. There is no question that the hoax had to be taken seriously despite the disruption in the passengers' travel schedules. On a larger scale, airport closings arising from terrorist threats are relatively costless for terrorists to issue, yet cause major disruptions to air passengers around the world. Government agencies charged with protecting the public must respond to all such incidents. After the fact, a threat or a hoax is nothing but a scare, but, until the incident is resolved, the outcome is never clear.

Figure 3.4 shows how the quarterly totals of threats (incident type 15) plus hoaxes (incident type 18) have behaved over time. Notice the dramatic spikes of sixty-three and sixty-four incidents in 1986:Q1 and 1991:Q1,

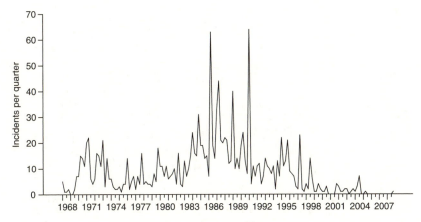

Figure 3.4. Threats and hoaxes.

respectively. Since threats and hoaxes (denoted by the THREATS series) entail few resources, such dramatic changes can occur at the will of terrorists. However, for all practical purposes, threats and hoaxes have virtually disappeared as a major weapon for transnational terrorists. There are several causes for the decline. Remember that ITERATE records specific events; the very general threats issued by groups such as al-Qaida are often too vague to be recorded as incidents. Moreover, in mid-1996, the FBIS's *Daily Reports* became unavailable to ITERATE coders, so that threats and hoaxes chronicled in the *Daily Reports*, but not in other sources, are now missed. Another reason for the decline is that the media are now less interested in reporting a threat or a hoax unless it turns out to have serious economic consequences. Over time, individuals have become less sensitive to a report of a small bomb or an unspecified attack; thus, some transnational terrorist groups feel little need to employ such tactics. Groups such as al-Qaida have been steadily intensifying their attacks by conducting incidents likely to result in large-scale property damage and deaths. As a result, most threats and hoaxes come from isolated individuals, such as the perpetrator of the Florida incidents, with no connection to a transnational terrorist group. These domestic incidents are not covered by ITERATE.

Deaths and Casualties

Obviously, some bombings are more lethal than others. Many skyjacking incidents end with no casualties; the hostages are released and the terrorists surrender. Others, including the skyjackings of 9/11, may involve great

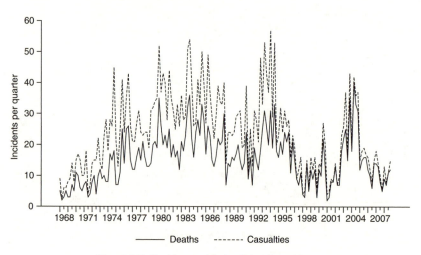

Figure 3.5. Incidents with deaths and casualties.

carnage. Hence, instead of looking at incidents by type, it is useful to look at the severity of the various incidents. The solid line in Figure 3.5 shows the time series of the number of incidents involving one or more deaths (the DEATH series). The dashed line shows the number of incidents with at least one casualty. An incident is classified as a casualty incident (CAS) if it involves at least one death or one wounded individual; hence, CAS is a more inclusive series than the DEATH series. Notice that both series rose fairly steadily from 1968 until early 1980. In the 1980s, the CAS series fluctuated around a mean of thirty incidents per quarter, and the DEATH series fluctuated around a mean of twenty incidents per quarter. For the 1980s, the exact proportion of CAS involving deaths was 61.4%. The early 1990s saw a jump in both series. Since the jump in CAS was much larger than the jump in DEATH, the proportion of DEATH to CAS incidents actually fell. However, in the mid 1990s, both incident types began to decline until the end of the decade. From this period on, there is little difference between CAS and DEATH as most incidents with a casualty involved a death, implying that the typical incident has been getting more lethal.

At the end of 2002, both series turned sharply upward, peaking in 2004:Q2 and then averaging around thirteen incidents per quarter during the remaining period. Figure 3.6 shows the proportion of incidents with deaths as a proportion of all incidents. Until the early 1970s, only 9% of the terrorist incidents in ITERATE involved a death. From the late 1970s throughout the early 1990s, DEATH incidents were about 18% of all incidents. The proportion ratcheted up to 28% in the mid-1990s and ratcheted

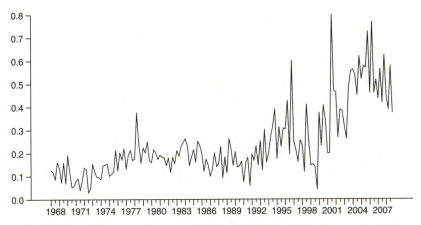

Figure 3.6. The proportion of death incidents.

up again in the late 1990s. Since 2004:Q1, the proportion of DEATH incidents seems to have leveled off at around 53% of all incidents. The evidence is consistent with the notion that terrorists have escalated the level of violence from pre-9/11 levels. As people live with terrorism, terrorists need to become more daring and sensational to attract media attention. Moreover, the rise of religious fundamentalism, discussed in Chapter 2, is associated with an increase in the number of terrorist incidents with deaths and injuries.

SPECTRAL ANALYSIS: THE ANALYSIS OF CYCLES

Time series analysis traditionally breaks down the movements in a variable into three separate parts:

Trend. The trend refers to long-run movements in the series, which is the portion of a time series that you would predict far into the future. Of course, what constitutes the long run for one data series may be very different from that for a second series. The long-run movements for the sunspot data might be a fifty- or hundred-year span. For terrorism, the long run is necessarily shorter. For example, beginning in 1993, it appears that the ALL series (see Figure 3.2) exhibited a decidedly downward trend that can be associated with the decline in state-sponsored terrorism discussed in Chapter 2.

Short-run Dynamics. Any series will temporarily diverge from its long-run level or trend. Notice how the ALL series shows a positive jump at the end of 1998 and seems to remain away from the trend for several quarters.

This type of movement is considered to be part of the short-run dynamics of the series. These short-run movements are often called *irregular* or *cyclical*.

One series might deviate from its long-run mean or trend for a substantial period of time, while another might revert back very quickly. We would hope that the lulls in terrorism are long-lasting and that high-terrorism periods are short-lived. If the nature of the short-run movements is known, the observed discrepancies from trend can be helpful in forecasting. A crucial issue for social scientists is to examine the persistence of the various terrorism series from their mean or trend. Knowledge of the persistence in a series can be helpful in predicting the number of future incidents.

For some series, the short-run movements can be quite regular. For the sunspot data, cycles are clearly present even though they are not perfectly regular. A plot of daily temperatures for Alabama would show that the highest temperatures always occur in August and the lowest in February, thus giving rise to a regular cycle. If there are cycles in the terrorism series, they are not as regular as those for sunspots or temperatures. Although not visible to the casual observer, as we will discuss later, there are reasons to believe that the various terrorist series have regular cyclical components.

Noise. This refers to the portion of a series that cannot be predicted. It is the smallest error that a forecaster can make.

Do not be dismayed if you cannot see the separate trend, irregular, and noise portions in the terrorism series. Statistical methods usually have to be employed to decompose a variable's time path into these constituent parts. Also, many people are under the misconception that the trend portion of a series is a straight line; none of the terrorism series display a linear trend. For some series, the trend is nonlinear, and for others, there is no clear trend. Whenever the form of the nonlinearity is unknown, statistical methods can be applied to capture the long-run movements in the data. To be a bit more formal, let y_t denote the number of incidents occurring during some time period t. For example, there were six transnational skyjackings in 1981:Q1 and three in 1981:Q2. For the skyjacking series, we can thus write $y_{1981:Q1} = 6$ and $y_{1981:Q2} = 3$. If we use this notation, the three constituent parts can be written as:

$$y_t = \text{trend} + \text{cyclical} + \text{noise}. \qquad (3.1)$$

Different time series display each of these components to different degrees. A series with a decided trend tends to evolve smoothly, so that its long-run movements are predictable. The sunspot data is clearly cyclical in nature. The HOSTAGE and ASSASSINATIONS series are highly volatile in that they contain large noise components. Such series are especially difficult to forecast.

A standard procedure for estimating the trend in a series is to fit a polynomial time trend to the data. Everyone is familiar with a linear time trend, and most people are aware that a quadratic time trend looks like a parabola. None of the terrorist series displays the type of sustained upward trend often implied by the media. Based on the number of incidents, the claim that terrorism is steadily increasing is clearly false. A linear trend is thus inadequate to characterize the trend in terrorism. However, a high-order polynomial trend is capable of mimicking a wide variety of functional forms. The estimation methodology involves fitting a polynomial trend in time (t) and adding successive trend terms (for example, t, t^2, t^3) until the associated coefficient is no longer statistically significant.[2] In Sandler and Enders (2004), we formally investigated the nature of trends in the various incident series and found that they were either nonlinear or nonexistent.

Cycles in terrorism can be attributed to various factors that result in the bunching of incidents on a regular basis. To the extent that these factors affect various terrorist groups concurrently, there will be wavelike patterns in the overall time series. Copycat effects are one such reason for the clustering of events. A successful event can induce others to copy the attack until the authorities devise the means and acquire the resources necessary to develop effective countermeasures. As the new antiterrorism measures become increasingly successful, new terrorist attacks will be inhibited. Terrorists learn of the government's innovation and begin to develop other types of attack modes. Similarly, other governments will incorporate the successful antiterrorism measures into their own plans. Thus, there can be extended periods when there is relatively little terrorism. During such times terrorists can form new plans, recruit new members, and acquire weapons and funding. This rebuilding of the terrorists' resources can continue until an event occurs that precipitates another round of attacks.

Economies of scale can induce particular terrorist groups to bunch their attacks. Economies of scale reduce per-incident costs by allowing terrorists to spread the fixed costs of planning and executing a campaign over a large number of incidents. The large number of suicide bomb-jackets captured from Saddam Hussein's cache is testimony to the ability to produce the weapons of terrorists in large quantities. *USA Today*

---

[2]   In much of the applied time series literature, a variable is said to be "statistically significant" if the researcher can be 95% confident that the variable's estimated regression coefficient differs from zero.

(2004) reported on a story with the headline: *Second Uzbek explosion rips bomb-making factory*:

TASHKENT, Uzbekistan (AP) – A series of bombings and attacks linked to Islamic militants, including the first known suicide missions in Uzbekistan, killed 19 people and injured 26, officials said Monday in this nation closely allied with Washington in the war on terrorism.

Bomb-making factories can turn out a large number of explosive devices all produced at the same time. The risks involved with obtaining the materials and plans for making a single bomb are similar to those for making many bombs at once. The unidentified terrorist group in the story was able to create, plant, and explode a number of bombs at various times and places around Uzbekistan.

Faria (2003) developed a theoretical cat-and-mouse model of the attack/counterattack process, where the government has many objectives, including the goal of maximizing national security by investing in enforcement. A key feature of the model is that terrorists have a budget constraint, so they cannot sustain a campaign indefinitely. Terrorists utilize weapons, financial resources, and personnel in order to plan and stage attacks. When enforcement is high, terrorists find it desirable to replenish material and financial resources, and to recruit personnel. Once there is a lull in terrorism, the public's attention begins to wane, and there is little political pressure on politicians to undertake new antiterrorism initiatives. In response to the electorate's new concerns, politicians direct their efforts to other social ills and away from antiterrorism policies. Terrorists view these lax times as ideal for launching a new round of attacks. The cycle is completed when the public demands a government crackdown on terrorists.

In a different vein, Das (2008) formulated a model that highlights the role of the public's heightened sensitivity to recent levels of terrorism. The notion is that a terrorist event may induce the public to experience a high level of distress, trauma, and fear concerning the possibility of a subsequent terrorist attack. This heightened level of duress means that it is the optimal time for a new terrorist strike. Formally, Das (2008) allowed there to be a stock of "fear" that carries over from one period to the next. This stock tends to fade (i.e., depreciate) over time because the public's memory tends to be short; however, the stock is augmented by a current successful attack. Consequently, terrorist events tend to bunch together. When terrorism has been successful, and the stock of fear is high, there tend to be additional terrorist attacks. Similarly, when the public feels calm because there have been few successful attacks, terrorists have little incentive to launch new attacks.

Such a model provides a rationale for the anthrax attacks that began exactly one week after 9/11.

Enders and Sandler (1999) and Enders, Parise, and Sandler (1992) argued that each kind of attack mode has its own characteristic cycle. Since BOMBINGS and THREATS require relatively few resources and can be initiated quickly, they should have short cycles. By contrast, logistically complex events (for example, skyjackings, hostage takings, and assassinations) are expected to have long cycles. The countermeasures taken by the authorities in response to such events may take a long time to develop. Although the business community has seen relatively little cyber-terrorism, we would expect such a process to result in rather long cycles. For example, the Technical Support Working Group (2003) is developing cyber-security projects that[3]

... focus on preventing or mitigating threats to computer networks vital to defense and transportation.... The complexity and sophistication of information technologies and widespread integration in other infrastructures increases the likelihood of unforeseen vulnerabilities. Unprecedented opportunities are created for criminals, terrorists, and hostile foreign nation-states to steal money or proprietary data, invade private records, conduct industrial espionage, or cause vital infrastructure elements to cease operations.

Such technological improvements necessarily take a long time to develop and innovate. The appropriate hardware and software need to be developed, tested, and installed on the computer networks of businesses and government agencies. Of course, once cyber-security is enhanced, we would expect terrorists to try to thwart its effects. Once terrorists develop the means to circumvent the new technology, the cycle would start to repeat itself when the authorities begin a new round of enhanced cyber-security. Thus, a testable hypothesis concerns the length of the cycles in simple events relative to complex events.

A number of variations on this theme have appeared in the literature. For example, Feichtinger, Hartl, Kort, and Novak (2001) formulated a model demonstrating the interrelationship between tourism and terrorism. The cycle begins when a tourist area develops its infrastructure to a level sufficient to accommodate large numbers of visitors. Hotels, restaurants, a major airport, and reasonable local transport all characterize most of the popular tourist destinations. As the area increases in popularity, it becomes more attractive to terrorists seeking media attention. Once terrorists target the

[3] This information was obtained from their web page: http://www.tswg.gov/tswg/ip/ip_ma.htm.

area, tourists flock to alternative destinations. There are literally hundreds of beaches with white sand and warm water in areas with a great climate. After tourists turn to these alternative destinations, investment in tourism falls. No new hotels are built or remodeled in an area with already high vacancy rates. At this point, the area is no longer strategically important for terrorists, and so the cycle repeats itself.

Spectral analysis is a statistical tool ideally suited to the study of cyclical phenomenon. The method entails removing the trend (that is, the possible nonlinear trend) from an incident series. The resulting detrended series is then examined to uncover any underlying cycles. Specifically, the researcher estimates the cyclical behavior of a series by fitting sine and cosine terms to the detrended data. These trigonometric terms are able to capture the regular increases and decreases in a series. This procedure seems perfectly natural for the sunspot data, since the series looks like a sine (or cosine) wave. Given that terrorists randomize their behavior, the cycles in the terrorist series will not be as pronounced as those in the sunspot data. Hence, in comparison to the sunspot data, a large number of sine and cosine terms with various amplitudes and frequencies must be used to capture the cyclical nature of the terrorism series. The frequency of a cycle indicates how often the cycle repeats itself. Series with long durations will have most of their variance explained by low frequencies, and series with short cycles will have most of their variance explained by high frequencies. You might find it helpful to think of the pitch of a singer's voice. Very high frequency components will dominate a soprano's voice, and very low frequency components will dominate the voice of a basso. The point is that very short cycles (high pitch) are high-frequency phenomena, and very long cycles (low pitch) are low-frequency phenomena.

The precise methodology used in spectral analysis is not reported here. Interested readers can consult Sandler and Enders (2004) for the details. Here, our goal is to update that work so as to use the data through 2009. For each series, Table 3.3 reports the proportion of its total variance accounted for by the lowest 15%, 25%, and 50% of the frequencies (in percent). Because a series with a long cycle should have most of its variation explained by the low frequencies, we expect the entries in Table 3.3 to be high for the logistically complex series. The series are listed in descending order according to the entry in the lowest 15% column.

Notice that the 15% lowest frequencies explain only 16.5% of the THREATS series. This is consistent with the notion that threats and hoaxes are relatively simple to conduct and use small amounts of terrorists' resources. The lowest 15% of the frequencies explain only 18.6% of ALL

Table 3.3. *Cyclical Properties of the Terrorist Time Series*

Series	Lowest 15%	Lowest 25%	Lowest 50%
THREATS/HOAXES	16.5	22.9	42.5
ALL	18.6	28.9	49.4
BOMBINGS	24.9	33.3	56.1
ASSASSINATIONS	28.1	45.3	64.9
HOSTAGE	34.8	41.2	63.6
DEATH	38.4	50.0	69.4
CASUALTIES	39.8	49.1	65.5
SKYJACKING	44.5	56.8	81.3

Note: The proportion of a series' total variance accounted for by the lowest 15%, 25%, and 50% of the frequencies, respectively.

and 24.9% of BOMBINGS. By contrast, almost 40% of the variance of the DEATH and the CAS series is explained by the lowest frequencies. The lowest 15% of the frequencies account for 44.5% of the variance in skyjackings, which is more than for the other series displayed. As expected, the low frequencies also explain relatively large amounts of the HOSTAGE and ASSASSINATIONS series, which is consistent with the notion that these incident types are more complicated to stage and execute than threats and bombings. It is interesting that ALL is dominated by the relatively high frequencies even though it contains series with low-frequency components. In part, this is due to the fact that bombings and threats comprise a large part of the ALL series. Also, if terrorists substitute across attack modes, we would expect that some of the series would be in the low phase of the cycle when others are in the high phase of the cycle. As a result, the low frequency components would nullify each other. The results seem to be invariant to using the lowest 25% of the frequencies or the lowest 50% of the frequencies.

INTERVENTION ANALYSIS

If you turn back to Figure 3.2, you can see that the ALL and BOMBINGS series seem to move in tandem, which should not be surprising, since bombings are the favorite attack mode of terrorists. Notice that there is nothing particularly telling around 9/11 in that both series seem to continue the upward movement that began around the first quarter of 2002. By contrast, Figure 3.3 indicates that the number of hostage incidents fluctuated around twelve incidents per quarter during the 1970s and 1980s and began to increase in the early 1990s. Suddenly in 1999, the number of incidents dropped sharply. The behavior of the series in the two figures leaves the impression that ALL incidents and BOMBINGS did not change as a result of 9/11 but that the number of hostage takings fell (see Chapter 9 and Enders and Sandler, 2005a). Notice that Figure 3.6 suggests that there have been several instances in which the proportion of incidents with deaths ratcheted up.

Intervention analysis is a statistical technique that allows us to ascertain whether these impressions are valid. The technique indicates whether an abrupt change in the pattern of a series is due to a force, such as the rise of Islamic fundamentalism in the late 1970s, or a particular event such as 9/11. Moreover, the same statistical method permits a measurement of the long-run and the short-run changes in the behavior of the various terrorist series. Essentially, intervention analysis models the cyclical (or irregular) component of a time series using its previous values. Unlike spectral analysis, which models the short-run movements in a series using sine and cosine functions, intervention analysis uses the lagged values of the series itself. If y_t denotes the value of a series in the current time period t, then y_{t-1} represents its value in the previous period, and y_{t-2} indicates its value two periods ago. The short-run dynamics of the series can be captured by fitting the lagged values of $y_{t-1}, y_{t-2}, \ldots, y_{t-p}$ to the series and retaining those lagged values that are statistically significant. In this way, the relationship between the current and past values of the series can be determined.

A typical time series model given by equation (3.1) might have the specific functional form

$$y_t = a_0 + a_1 t + b_1 y_{t-1} + b_2 y_{t-2} + \varepsilon_t, \tag{3.2}$$

where the expression $a_0 + a_1 t$ denotes a linear trend, $b_1 y_{t-1} + b_2 y_{t-2}$ represents the expression for the short-run dynamics, and ε_t stands for the pure noise. Of course, some series might have more complicated trend and/or cyclical components than those specified in equation (3.2). Nevertheless, anyone familiar with a basic regression model should have little trouble understanding the essentials of the technique.[4]

---

[4]   A regression tries to capture the relationship between a variable of interest (that is, the dependent variable) and a set of explanatory variables called the "independent variables." In so doing, the regression uses observed values to estimate how the variation of a dependent variable is explained by a linear representation of independent variables. In the process, a dependent variable is expressed as a linear equation of a constant and independent variables, whose coefficients, if significant, indicate how a change in the independent variable impacts the dependent variable.

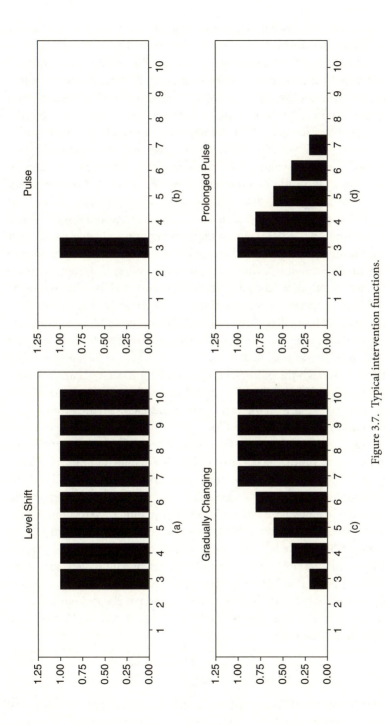

Figure 3.7. Typical intervention functions.

Intervention analysis augments equations in the form of (3.2) in that it allows for permanent or temporary breaks in the series. Panel *a* of Figure 3.7 depicts a permanent intervention, called a *level* shock (or *level* shift), where the intervention is effective during all periods after its introduction. Mathematically, we can construct a dummy variable (measured on the vertical axis) equal to zero prior to the intervention and equal to unity when the intervention is in effect. A temporary intervention, called a *pulse*, is depicted in panel *b* of Figure 3.7, where for all periods, except intervention period three, the value of the pulse is zero. A temporary tightening of airport security would be represented by a pulse, while the permanent installation of an explosive-detection device would be represented by a level shift. In either case, the airport security enhancement would result in *fewer* incidents. Similarly, if 9/11 represented a temporary change in terrorist behavior, it would be represented as a pulse. If, however, 9/11 represented a permanent phenomenon, it would be shown as a level shift. Of course, more intricate intervention variables are possible. Although a level-shift intervention will have a permanent effect on the variable of interest, the intervention variable may not immediately jump to its long-run value. Since the installation of metal detectors in airports worldwide occurred throughout the year 1973, this type of gradually increasing intervention could be represented by panel *c*. Even though the pulse is a one-time phenomenon, it can have prolonged effects on the variable of interest. Panel *d* illustrates a situation such that the effect of a pulse on the variable of interest slowly fades away.

Intervention analysis actually allows for a rich variety of interventions with various response patterns. For those of you who want to utilize the technique, the technical details are provided in Chapter 5 of Enders (2010). However, the introduction to intervention analysis provided here should be sufficient for understanding its use in the study of transnational terrorism. The key point to emphasize is that we modify equation (3.2) to allow for the various types of interventions. To take a numerical example from Enders and Sandler (2005a), we let y_t denote the values of the ALL series, D_L represent a level-shift variable for 9/11, and D_P represent a pulse. Specifically, as suggested by panel *b* of Figure 3.7, we set the variable $D_P = 1$ for 2001:Q3 and $D_P = 0$ for all other periods. As indicated in panel *a* of Figure 3.7, we also let $D_L = 0$ for all values prior to 9/11 and $D_L = 1$ thereafter. We estimated the regression equation:

$$y_t = 34.07 + 0.222y_{t-1} + 0.190y_{t-2} + 0.217y_{t-3}$$
$$- 22.66D_P - 15.31D_L + \varepsilon_t. \tag{3.3}$$

We found no significant trend in the data; the short-run dynamics are given by the expression $0.222y_{t-1} + 0.190y_{t-2} + 0.217y_{t-3}$, and the noise term

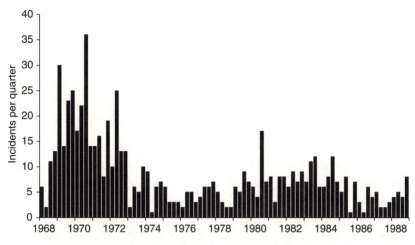

Figure 3.8. US domestic and transnational skyjackings.

is represented by ε_t. Neither the pulse nor the level intervention variables were found to be statistically significant. Thus, we can conclude that 9/11 had no statistically significant effects on the ALL series (see Chapter 9). If, however, either intervention variable happened to be significant, we would have analyzed the pattern it imparted to the data.

Estimating the Effect of Metal Detectors on Skyjackings

Aerial incidents such as the explosion of Pan Am flight 103 over Lockerbie, Scotland, on 21 December 1988 and the four skyjackings of 9/11 dominate newspaper headlines and the airwaves. Nevertheless, skyjacking incidents have actually been quite numerous. In an effort to offset a surge in sky-jackings, US airports began to install metal detectors on 5 January 1973. Other international authorities soon followed suit. The quarterly totals of all transnational and US domestic skyjackings from 1968 through 1988 are shown in Figure 3.8. Although the number of skyjacking incidents appears to take a sizable and permanent decline in January 1973, we might be interested in actually measuring the effects of installing the metal detectors.

In Enders, Sandler, and Cauley (1990a), we were interested in the effects of metal detectors on US domestic skyjackings, transnational skyjackings (including those involving the United States), and all other skyjackings. We began by viewing the installation of metal detectors as an immediate and permanent intervention. As such, we used a level-shift intervention to represent metal detectors. As suggested by panel *a* of Figure 3.7, we let the level-shift variable equal zero prior to 1973:Q1 and one in 1973:Q1 and thereafter.

Table 3.4. *Impact of Metal Detectors on Skyjackings: Intervention Analysis*

Series	Pre-Intervention Mean[a]	Impact Effect[a]	Long-Run Effect[a]
Transnational	3.03	−1.29	−1.78
US domestic	6.70	−5.62	−5.62
Other skyjackings	6.80	−3.90	−5.11

[a] Incidents per quarter.

The results of the estimations are reported in Table 3.4. Prior to 1973, the average quarter contained 3.03 transnational skyjackings. We estimated that metal detectors reduced the quarterly number of transnational sky-jackings by 1.29 incidents on impact. We also estimated the long-run effect of metal detectors to be −1.78 incidents per quarter.[5] Thus, the time path of the effects of metal detectors on transnational skyjackings looked some-thing like panel *c* of Figure 3.7. The long-run effect of the permanent inter-vention exceeded the short-run effect. Overall, metal detectors prevented about seven transnational skyjackings per year (= 4 × 1.78). As you can see from Table 3.4, the installation of metal detectors reduced each type of sky-jacking incident. The most pronounced effect was on US domestic skyjack-ings, which immediately fell by 5.62 incidents per quarter (see Table 3.4). The short-run and long-run effects were identical as domestic skyjackings immediately fell from 6.70 to the long-run value of 1.08 incidents per quar-ter. On impact, other skyjackings (that is, domestic skyjackings in countries other than the United States) fell by 3.9 incidents per quarter. The long-run effect was estimated to be 5.11 fewer incidents per quarter.

We also considered the possibility that metal detectors were only grad-ually installed in non-US airports and, even when they were installed, that enforcement was sporadic. As a check, we modeled the intervention as gradually increasing over the year 1973. Although the coefficients were nearly identical to those reported in Table 3.4, the fit of the overall regres-sions was superior when using a gradually increasing process to capture the

---

[5] On a technical note, in the absence of a time trend, it is straightforward to calculate the short-run and long-run effects of an intervention. A general model in the form of (3.3) is $y_t = a_0 + a_1 y_{t-1} + \ldots + a_p y_{t-p} + b_P D_p + b_L D_L + \varepsilon_t$. Since D_p and D_L shift from 0 to 1 at the onset of the intervention, the instantaneous (that is, short-run) effect of the intervention on the series is $b_P + b_L$. The long-run expected value of the series (y^*) is such that $y_t = y_{t-1} = \ldots = y_p = y^*$. Thus, in the long run, $y^* = a_0 + a_1 y^* + \ldots + a_p y^* + b_P D_p + b_L D_L$ or $y^* = (a_0 + b_P D_p + b_L D_L)/(1 - a_1 - \ldots - a_p)$. Prior to the intervention, $y^* = a_0/(1 - a_1 - \ldots - a_p)$, and after the intervention ($D_L = 1$ and $D_p = 0$) $y^* = (a_0 + b_L)/(1 - a_1 - \ldots - a_p)$. Hence, the long-run effect of the intervention can be calculated as $b_L/(1 - a_1 - \ldots - a_p)$.

effect of the interventions. Hence, we conclude that metal detector adoption was more gradual outside of the United States.[6]

United Nations' Conventions and Resolutions

A second aim of Enders, Sandler, and Cauley (1990a) was to examine how actions by the United Nations affected skyjackings and crimes against protected persons (for example, ambassadors, diplomats, and embassy personnel). The UN Convention on the Prevention and Punishment of Crimes Against Internationally Protected Persons, Including Diplomatic Agents (CAPP), was adopted by the United Nations on 14 December 1973 and signed into law by the United States on 20 February 1977. We chose the first quarter of 1977 as the intervention date, since most of these crimes involved the United States. The UN also took measures to reduce hostage takings. On 18 December 1985, the UN Security Council Resolution Against Taking Hostages was adopted by a 15 to 0 vote. During the period December 1969 through December 1970, several UN and international conventions against hijacking were adopted. These included UN General Assembly Resolution 2551 (XXIV): Forcible Diversion of Civil Aircraft in Flight, the Hague Convention on the Suppression of Unlawful Seizure of Aircraft, and UN General Assembly Resolution 2645 (XXV): Aerial Hijacking. After some experimentation, we settled on 1971:Q1 as a single break date for these three resolutions and conventions.

UN conventions require that a nation use its own judicial system to implement and enforce the agreement. UN resolutions, on the other hand, are simply agreements on a particular set of principles or goals. Hence, conventions are more binding than resolutions, since resolutions do not imply a commitment to enforcement. Nevertheless, the United Nations has no direct power to force a nation to abide by any of its agreements.

The key finding is that none of these interventions had a significant effect in thwarting terrorism. Specifically, we obtained the number of crimes undertaken against protected persons from ITERATE. Neither the CAPP nor the UN Security Council Resolution Against Taking Hostages had any significant effects on this series. Next, we constructed a time series of hostage events (that is, kidnappings, barricade and hostage takings, and skyjackings). Neither the CAPP nor the UN Security Council Resolution

---

[6] In Chapter 5, we consider the effects of metal detectors in a multi-equation framework. A multivariable framework allows us to simultaneously estimate the effects of metal detectors on several of the incident series.

Against Taking Hostages had any significant effect on this series. The resolutions and conventions specifically targeting aerial hijackings had no significant effect on any of the skyjacking series.

More recently, the International Convention for the Suppression of
Terrorist Bombings was signed on 15 December 1997 and was entered into
US law on 23 May 2001. We applied the methods used in Enders, Sandler,
and Cauley (1990a) to determine whether this UN convention had any
effect on bombings, deadly bombings, or the proportion of bombings relative to all incidents. Specifically, we used values of ITERATE running
through 2003:Q4 to construct time series of these three types of bombings and used 2001:Q3 as a level-shift intervention. Not surprisingly, we
found no significant effects of the convention on any of these series. As discussed in more detail in Chapter 6, without any enforcement mechanism,
nations are unlikely to change their behavior as a result of a UN convention. Moreover, after a UN agreement, terrorists still have the same resolve
and wherewithal to engage in violence. UN conventions and resolutions do
little to reduce the terrorists' resource base or to deflect terrorists toward
peaceful activities.

Estimating the Effect of the Libyan Bombing

The third aim of Enders, Sandler, and Cauley (1990a) was to consider the
effects of the US retaliatory bombing of Libya on the morning of 15 April
1986. The stated reason for the attack was Libya's alleged involvement in
the terrorist bombing of the La Belle discotheque in West Berlin. Since
eighteen of the F-111 fighter-bombers were deployed from British bases
at Lakenheath and Upper Heyford, England, the United Kingdom implic-
itly assisted in the raid. The remaining US planes were deployed from aircraft carriers in the Mediterranean Sea. We considered the effects of the
bombing on all transnational terrorist incidents directed against the United
States and the United Kingdom. A plot of this incident series showed a
large positive spike immediately after the bombing; the immediate effect
seemed to be a wave of anti-US and anti-UK attacks to protest the retaliatory strike. This spike in each of the two series is apparent in Figure 3.2
(shown previously).

We considered two possible patterns for the intervention series. We initially allowed the intervention to have a permanent effect on attacks against
the United States and the United Kingdom. Using this specification, we
obtained an estimate of the level-shift variable that was not statistically
significant. Alternatively, when we used a pulse intervention equal to 1

only in the second quarter of 1986, we found that the coefficient on the pulse term was highly significant. The fit of this second specification was far superior to that obtained when we viewed the attack as a permanent intervention. Our conclusion was that the Libyan bombing did not have the desired effect of reducing terrorist attacks against the United States and the United Kingdom; instead, the bombing caused an immediate increase of over thirty-eight attacks per quarter. Subsequently, the number of attacks quickly declined; attacks were only 12.7 incidents per quarter above the pre-intervention mean in the third quarter of 1986.

Is Terrorism Becoming More Threatening?

In Enders and Sandler (2000), we tried to determine whether transnational terrorist incidents have become more threatening. Our aim was to determine whether several intervention variables account for the behavior of the DEATH and CAS series shown in Figure 3.5. Although we had access only to data running through 1996:Q2, the results are still relevant. To be a bit more specific, we examined the effects of metal detectors, two separate bouts of embassy fortifications, the US retaliatory raid against Libya, the rise of religious fundamentalism, and the break-up of the Soviet Union on the DEATH and CAS series. We set our multiple intervention variables as shown in Table 3.5.

Although our primary focus was on the effects of the rise of fundamentalism (FUND) and the demise of the Soviet Union (POST), we included the other interventions in order to control for other possible breaks. We used all of the interventions to estimate the short-run and long-run movements in the DEATH and CAS series. Remember that the CAS series includes incidents in which individuals were killed or wounded; hence, it is necessarily broader than the DEATH series. The results are summarized in Table 3.6.

Although Chapter 5 specifically addresses the substitution between attack modes, it is interesting to note here that the installation of metal detectors actually *increased* the number of incidents with casualties and the number of incidents with deaths. The short-run impacts on CAS and DEATH were 8.33 and 5.56 more incidents per quarter, respectively. The long-run effects were even more substantial: 12.38 and 9.27 more incidents per quarter. An unintended consequence of metal detectors is that terrorists substituted out of skyjackings and into more deadly events. Skyjackings are necessarily newsworthy and, until 9/11, were not usually associated with large numbers of deaths except when a rescue mission failed. When metal detectors

Table 3.5. *Interventions*

Intervention	Description	Starting Date / Intervention Type
METAL	Metal detectors installed in US airports in January 1973, followed shortly thereafter by their installation in airports worldwide.	1973:Q1 Level shift
EMB 76	A doubling of the spending to fortify and secure US embassies beginning in October 1976.	1976:Q3 Level shift
FUND	The rise of religious-based terrorism starting with the 4 November takeover of the US embassy in Tehran, Iran. The last quarter of 1979 coincides with Soviet invasion of Afghanistan in December 1979.	1979:Q4 Level shift
EMB 85	Further increases in spending to secure US embassies by Public Law 98–533 in October 1985.	1985:Q4 Level shift
LIBYA	US retaliatory raid against Libya on 15 April 1986 for its involvement in the terrorist bombing of La Belle discotheque in West Berlin.	1986:Q2 Pulse
POST	The start of the post–Cold War era with the official demise of the Warsaw Pact on 1 July 1991 and the breakup of the Soviet Union on 20 December 1991. This date also corresponds to a decline in state sponsorship of terrorism by countries in Eastern Europe and elsewhere.	1991:Q4 Level shift

made skyjackings more difficult to initiate, terrorists substituted into similarly newsworthy events. Unfortunately, events with casualties and deaths provide the media attention desired by terrorists.

We found very different results concerning the two different attempts at embassy fortifications. The security enhancements of 1976 may have protected US embassies, but had no significant effect on the total number of CAS or DEATH incidents. The enhancements of 1985 were associated with a short-run reduction of about ten CAS incidents and six DEATH incidents. The long-run effects were even more substantial.

It is interesting that the Libyan retaliatory raid had no significant effect on either series. In light of our other estimates that the raid increased the total number of incidents directed against the United States and the United Kingdom, the overall effect of the raid was to increase noncasualty incidents, but not incidents with casualties or deaths.

The rise of fundamentalism and the demise of the Soviet Union were both associated with increases in CAS and DEATH incidents. The short-run

Table 3.6. *Effects of the Interventions (in incidents per quarter)*

Intervention	Casualties Series		Death Series	
	Short-Run	Long-Run	Short-Run	Long-Run
METAL	8.83	12.38	5.56	9.27
EMB 76	Not significant		Not significant	
FUND	7.75	10.86	4.17	6.95
EMB 85	−9.904	−13.90	−5.92	−9.87
LIBYA	Not significant		Not significant	
POST	9.90	13.89	6.77	11.12

impact of FUND was to increase CAS incidents by 7.75 per quarter and DEATH incidents by 4.17 per quarter. The long-run effects were 10.68 and 6.95 extra incidents in a typical quarter, respectively. The short-run impact of POST was to increase CAS incidents by 9.90 and DEATH incidents by 6.77. The long-run effects were 13.89 and 11.12 extra incidents in a typical quarter, respectively. Clearly, these two watershed events were associated with more threatening and more deadly forms of terrorism. In June 2000, a full fifteen months before 9/11, we stated that:

> This shift toward greater religious-based terrorism is traced to a structural change … at the time of the takeover of the US Embassy in Tehran. From this point, terrorism became more CAS prone and dangerous.…The rise in religious terrorism in which massive civilian casualties are a goal poses a potential dilemma for government counterterrorism policy. If a government responds by tightening security at official sites (embassies and government buildings) as is currently being done in the United States, its civilian targets … will become relatively less secure and attractive. (Enders and Sandler, 2000, p. 330)

When the Enders and Sandler (2000) paper was being reviewed, one reviewer strongly objected to our conclusion that transnational terrorism was posing a greater threat to society!

Are the Dynamics of Terrorism Asymmetric?

Although solar physicists cannot fully explain why sunspot cycles are asymmetric, there are solid economic reasons to expect the terrorism time series to exhibit asymmetric behavior. For simplicity, we can conceptualize two different intensity levels of terrorism campaigns. In relatively tranquil times, terrorists can "lie low" in order to replenish and stockpile their resources, recruit and train new members, enhance their funding, plan future attacks, and devise defenses against the government's counterterrorism efforts. The number of attacks remains small as the group replenishes its resources and gains strength. The level of terrorism can remain in this phase until the group's strength is sufficient to embark on a new terrorism campaign or a political shock occurs that induces terrorists to switch into a high-attack mode. Since complex attack modes utilize large quantities of the group's resources, these high-terrorism periods should be relatively short-lived as resource stocks become depleted. By contrast, low-terrorism periods can last for an extended period as the group allows its strength to grow. The point is that terror cycles should be asymmetric in that the low phase of the cycle should be more persistent than the high phase of the cycle.

A pure intervention model cannot capture this cyclical behavior adequately, since asymmetries necessitate the existence of one regime until time t and then a different regime from time $t+1$ on. Instead, a natural way to capture the asymmetric nature of terrorist campaigns is to use a threshold model that allows the series to jump back and forth across the high- and low-terrorism regimes. To formally model this type of behavior, Enders and Sandler (2005b) estimated the following equation for the DEATH series:

$$y_t = 20.90 + \varepsilon_t \text{ if } y_{t-1} > 21, \tag{3.4}$$

$$y_t = 1.86 + 0.582y_{t-1} + 0.379y_{t-2} + \varepsilon_t \text{ if } y_{t-1} \le 21. \tag{3.4'}$$

The details of estimating a threshold model are discussed in Chapter 7 of Enders (2010). The important point is that we found two different models of the DEATH series; the series behaves according to equation (3.4) when the number of death incidents is high (that is, $y_{t-1} > 21$) and according to (3.4') when the number of death incidents is low (that is, $y_{t-1} \le 21$). In a sense, the number 21 acts as a threshold value splitting the high- and low-terrorism regimes. Suppose that the number of death incidents exceeds twenty-one; from (3.4), the relevant model predicts that the subsequent incidents will be about twenty-one. If you examine Figure 3.5 carefully, you can see that the spikes in the series are quite short-lived; there is little persistence in any incident totals in excess of twenty-one. In contrast, when the number of incidents is low (that is, $y_{t-1} \le 21$), (3.4') is relevant. To take a specific example, we consider the last two observations of Figure 3.5 (that is, 2008:Q3 and 2008:Q4), which are eleven and twelve incidents. Since (3.4') is relevant, the prediction for 2009:Q1 is $1.86 + 0.582(12) + 0.379(11) = 13.013$, and the prediction for 2009:Q2 is

$1.86 + 0.582(13.013) + 0.379(12) = 13.98$. Hence, there is a substantial amount of persistence for the low-terrorism regime.[7]

We also estimated threshold models for the casualty, bombings with deaths, hostage taking, and assassinations series. All of the resultant models fit the data better than the best model in the form of (3.2). The important point is that all of these threshold models found that the high-terrorism regime had far less persistence than the low-terrorism regime. When we repeated the exercise for threats and hoaxes, we found the opposite result. This "flip-flop" in regime behavior is attributed to the fact that threats and hoaxes necessitate relatively small amounts or resources – it takes little effort to make a threatening phone call or leave a menacing note. As such, high levels of threats or hoaxes can readily be sustained, particularly if high levels of threats reinforce one another (that is, if they are complementary). Hence, there is strong evidence that terror cycles exist and are asymmetric. Not only is the asymmetry important for understanding the behavior of terrorists, it is also important for predicting the overall level of terrorism. As we stated in the article, the events of 9/11 and the subsequent "war on terror" followed what had been a low-terrorism regime. Hence, the subsequent level of terrorism could remain at a heightened level for a sustained period of time.

DOMESTIC TERRORISM DATA

There is little doubt that domestic terrorist incidents can be as horrific as transnational incidents. The 20 March 1995 sarin attack on the Tokyo subway by Aum Shinrikyo and the 19 April 1995 Oklahoma City bombing of the Alfred P. Murrah Federal Building by Timothy McVeigh were both domestic incidents. Similarly, most of the suicide attacks by the Black Widows of Chechnya, the Tamil Tigers of Sri Lanka, and the Palestinian terrorists during the Second Intifada in Israel were domestic incidents. Nevertheless, most of the empirical literature has focused on transnational terrorism because of limited data availability. Fortunately, this situation is in the process of changing as a result of the online availability of the Global Terrorism Database (GTD). Recently, the University of Maryland's National

---

[7] The data used in Enders and Sandler (2005b) ran through 2000. The coefficients in (3.4′) were not reestimated to account for the additional data. Moreover, as discussed in Enders and Sandler (2005b), it is possible to allow for the possibility of subsequent regime switches when forecasting with a threshold model.

Consortium for the Study of Terrorism and Response to Terrorism (START) (2009a) took over a data set originally collected by the Pinkerton Global Intelligence Services (PGIS). PGIS had been using the data to aid its clients interested in knowing the risk of terrorism in different countries. START now manages the data set and has recoded some of the data so that it can be used by researchers.[8]

The Need for Both Kinds of Terrorism Data

Before getting into the specifics of the GTD data set, it is useful to indicate why it is important for researchers to distinguish between domestic and transnational terrorism. In trying to ascertain the root causes of terrorism, the motives of transnational terrorists are likely to be different from those of domestic terrorists. For example, as discussed in Chapter 2, Savun and Phillips (2009) showed that democracy is a significant determinant of transnational, but not of domestic, terrorism.

When estimating the economic impact of terrorism on growth, Gaibulloev and Sandler (2008) found that, for Western Europe, the marginal costs of transnational incidents are higher than those of domestic incidents. One plausible explanation for this finding is that transnational incidents are more likely to affect foreign direct investment, international trade, and tourism decisions than purely domestic incidents. This is especially true if terrorists are known to explicitly target foreigners. Moreover, it can be more costly to defend against transnational than domestic terrorism. Transnational terrorism necessitates border defenses along with the more traditional homeland security measures. Similarly, military action may be required to root out the terrorists in their foreign bases, which entails either costly direct military intervention (for example, the assassination of Osama bin Laden in Pakistan by Navy Seals on 1 May 2011) or assistance to countries to confront their resident terrorists (for example, the recent US involvement in Afghanistan, Pakistan, and Yemen).

---

[8] Other data sets containing domestic and transnational terrorist incidents include the National Memorial Institute for the Prevention of Terrorism (MIPT) or RAND data set. However, MIPT does not code domestic attacks until 1998. Moreover, at this time the data set is not publicly available. The so-called TWEED data set, see Engene's (2007) – Terrorism in Western Europe: Event Data – records "internal attacks" for eighteen Western European countries over the 1950–2004 period. Note that TWEED's definition of internal terrorism differs from the standard definition of domestic terrorism. For example, in TWEED, if a terrorist group from country X attacks foreign tourists in X, the incident is recorded as internal instead of transnational. Note that Gaibulloev and Sandler (2008) merged ITERATE and TWEED for 1971–2004 using a consistent set of definitions.

Transnational terrorism can also be more costly than domestic terrorism because of the tendency to overspend on defensive measures when countries address a common transnational terrorist threat, such as al-Qaida. Sandler and Lapan (1988) and Sandler and Siqueira (2006) showed that defensive overspending occurs as countries attempt to divert potential attacks from their shores to others (also see Chapter 4). The analogy is to neighborhoods in which each resident has the incentive to purchase a burglar alarm. Each alarm imposes a negative externality on the other residents, in that criminals are diverted to unprotected houses, without having a significant effect on the overall level of crime. Sandler (2010) indicated that this effect does not manifest itself with domestic terrorism because all externalities associated with counterterrorism measures can be internalized by the central government.

It can be easier to maintain a no-concessions policy for domestic hostage incidents than for transnational incidents because there are no foreign pressures to concede to terrorist demands. Such pressures can arise in a transnational hostage incident owing to the presence of foreign hostages. Clearly, country Y might want country X to capitulate to the terrorists' demands, since country Y thereby does not appear weak and enjoys the release of its citizens.

The GTD Data Set

Like ITERATE, GTD records an incident's date, country location, the type of incident, the number of deaths and injuries, and other observations. Unfortunately, there are a few features of GTD that diminish the ease of its use. PGIS actually lost the raw data for 1993 – evidently a box containing the data fell off a truck. For 1993, GTD contains only an incident total, by country, without any other categorical breakdowns. Additionally, the coding conventions used for 1970–1997 do not always match those for the latter part of the data set. As indicated by Enders, Sandler, and Gaibulloev (2011), it is likely that a number of incidents were missed during the initial years of PGIS as coders were recruited and trained. By the start of the late 1970s, PGIS wanted to maintain the attention of its client base and had an incentive to be very inclusive in its classification of incidents. The point is that there is an underreporting of incidents during the early phase of data collection and an overreporting of events until START cleaned the post-1997 data.

Aside from the fact that GTD includes both domestic and transnational terrorist incidents, one difference between GTD and ITERATE involves the number of attack modes distinguished. ITERATE identifies twenty-five distinct attack modes, while GTD indicates only eight alternative attack modes. For instance, GTD combines skyjackings and nonaerial hijackings of buses, trains, and ships under the single category of hijackings. GTD puts all types of bombings (for example, explosive bombings, incendiary devices, and suicide bombings) into a single attack mode (START, 2009b).

Another important difference is that GTD contains a number of incidents (particularly assassinations) that should not be classified as terrorism. There are 82,536 "terrorist" incidents reported in GTD for 1970–2007. Although it is not necessary to discuss all of the details here, we needed to exclude some incidents that did not meet the formal definition of terrorism. In particular, each attack had to (i) have a political, socioeconomic, or religious motive; (ii) be intended to coerce, intimidate, or send a message to a wider audience than the immediate victim(s); and (iii) be beyond the boundaries set by international humanitarian law. We also purged the incidents that START classifies as "doubtful" such as many involving insurgency or guerrilla warfare, internecine conflict, mass murder, and criminal acts. This left us with the 66,382 terrorist incidents reported in the top portion of Table 3.7.

It should not be surprising that nearly half of all incidents (30,413) are bombings; on average, there are 190 bombings each quarter. By way of comparison, recall that bombings constitute 56% of all incidents in ITERATE. Clearly, both domestic and transnational terrorists find bombings to be relatively cheap and highly effective. Although ITERATE reports approximately 10% of incidents as assassinations, in the GTD data set assassinations constitute approximately 16% of the observations. It is interesting that 48.5% of the incidents in the GTD data set (32,168) involve casualties, whereas only 34% on the incidents in ITERATE involve casualties.

On Decomposing GTD into Domestic and Transnational Terrorist Events

Although GTD is an extremely rich data set, it does not distinguish between domestic and transnational incidents. In Enders, Sandler, and Gaibulloev (2011), we devised a straightforward method to break down the data into three categories: domestic, transnational, and unknown. Briefly, our procedure involved a comparison of the nationality of the victims in relation to the country in which the incident occurred. If the location of the incident is not the home country of one or more victims, the attack is clearly a transnational terrorist incident. We also coded attacks against diplomats,

Table 3.7. *Number of Incidents by Type (1970–2007): GTD Data*

	Quarterly Mean	Quarterly Maximum	Total
	All Incidents		
Assassinations	71.2	279	11,389
Armed attacks	79.3	279	12,691
Bombings	190.1	596	30,413
Hostage takings	27.3	116	4,383
Other	46.9	210	7,506
Total	414.9	1,300	66,382
Casualty incidents	201.1	608	32,168
	Domestic Incidents		
Assassinations	48.8	203	7,803
Armed attacks	61.3	223	9,802
Bombings	145.0	445	23,198
Hostage takings	2.2	30	353
Other	32.9	163	5,257
All domestic	290.1	931	46,413
Casualty incidents	145.3	571	23,245
	Transnational Incidents		
Assassinations	8.1	50	1,298
Armed attacks	8.0	40	1,272
Bombings	33.5	187	5,356
Hostage takings	21.4	110	3,424
Other	9.5	65	1,512
All transnational	80.4	296	12,862
Casualty incidents	25.9	87	4,146
	Unknown		
Assassinations	14.3	75	2,288
Armed attacks	10.1	79	1,617
Bombings	11.6	106	1,859
Hostage takings	3.8	44	606
Other	4.6	81	738
All unknown	44.4	276	7,108
Casualty incidents	29.9	117	4,777

diplomatic staff, nongovernmental organizations (NGOs), or any other diplomatic targets as transnational incidents. Clearly, terrorist attacks against US targets or those containing US victims occurring outside of the United States are transnational terrorist events. Finally, all international skyjackings are transnational terrorist events. When we used these criteria, we were able to identify 12,862 transnational terrorist incidents. By way of comparison, ITERATE contains 12,784 transnational terrorist incidents for the same time period.

Unfortunately, it was not possible to classify all of the remaining 53,521 incidents as domestic events because of missing information. Whenever the nationality of the victims or the location of the incident is missing, we coded the incident type as "unknown." In total, we had to classify 7,108 incidents as unknown. Fortunately, the post-1997 data was far more complete than the earlier data; we recorded only 376 unknown incidents after 1997. In total, 46,413 incidents for 1970–2007 are identified as domestic terrorist events. For each domestic incident, the venue country matches the nationality of the victims, and there are no diplomatic or multilateral entities involved. Moreover, US persons or property were not attacked on foreign soil.

The lower portions of Table 3.7 report the breakdowns of our identified domestic, transnational, and unknown incidents by the type of attack. Notice that there are almost four times as many domestic incidents as there are transnational incidents. Bombings account for 50.0% of domestic incidents and 41.7% of transnational incidents. These proportions are quite similar (that is, they are not statistically different from each other) and reflect the fact that a bombing is simple and effective. Domestic incidents have a greater proportion of incidents with casualties (50.0%) than transnational incidents (32.2%). Recall that the proportion of casualty incidents in ITERATE is 34.4%. The biggest difference between the two types of incidents concerns hostage takings; only 0.8% of domestic incidents involve hostages, while 26.6% of transnational incidents involve hostages. Part of the explanation for the disparity lies in the nature of the GTD data set itself. It is likely that there is some undercounting of domestic hostage events in the GTD (especially prior to 1998) because such incidents posed only a small risk to PGIS clients. Also note that the unknown category reflects GTD's tendency to count any type of assassination as a terrorist incident.

We devised a simple method to adjust the PGIS data to compensate for PGIS's proclivity to undercount incidents in the 1970:Q1–1977:Q2 period and to overcount incidents in the 1991:Q2–1997:Q4 period. Some of the details are reported in Appendix 3.1; for our purposes here, we simply apply weighting factors so as to calibrate the GTD data to the ITERATE data set. For the missing 1993 data, we recommend the interpolation method described in Appendix 3.1. Figures 3.9 and 3.10 show the time paths of the domestic and transnational casualty incident series using our modified GTD data. Except for scale, the two casualty series track one another surprisingly

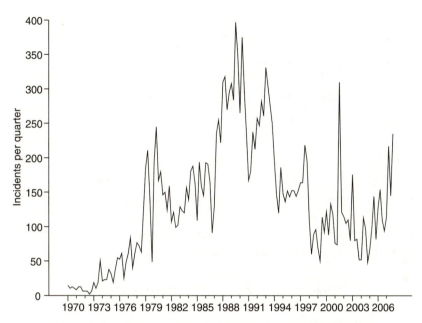

Figure 3.9. Domestic casualty incidents using the modified GTD data.

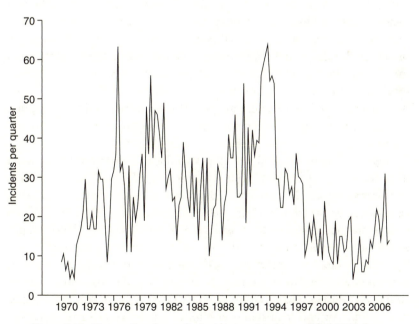

Figure 3.10. Transnational casualty incidents using the modified GTD data.

Table 3.8. *Cross-Correlations of Domestic and Transnational Incidents*

	ALL	CASUALTY	DEATH	ASSNS.	BOMBINGS
1970:Q1 to 2007:Q4	0.69	0.71	0.72	0.78	0.53
1998:Q1 to 2007:Q4	0.52	0.54	0.56	0.20	0.53

Note: Does not include incidents in Afghanistan and Iraq.

well. Both rise in the early to mid-1970s, hold reasonably steady to the mid-1980s, rise again until the early 1990s, decline with the fall of the Soviet Union, and rise around 2003. The ratio of domestic to transnational GTD casualty incidents is 1.4 through 1977:Q2, 6.5 from 1977:Q3–1997:Q4, and 8.78 thereafter. The most recent increase in the ratio of domestic incidents is the result of events in Iraq and Afghanistan.

On the Dynamic Relationship between Domestic and Transnational Terrorism

At first, it might seem surprising that the domestic and transnational series seem to move together. After all, it can be argued that domestic incidents respond to idiosyncratic events within countries, whereas transnational incidents respond to global phenomena. The tendency for the two series to move together bears a more formal examination, since the patterns that we project on the series might be spurious. One way to measure the strength of the relationships between the various types of domestic and transnational incidents is to use cross-correlations. For the ALL, CASUALTY, DEATH, ASSASSINATIONS (ASSNS.), and BOMBINGS series, Table 3.8 reports the cross-correlations between the quarterly values of domestic and transnational incidents.

There are several factors that might explain why the correlations between domestic and transnational incidents are so large. With slightly more than 150 observations, as discussed in the Supplemental Manual of Enders (2010), correlations greater than 0.15 are statistically significant at the 5% level. Of course, planned domestic terrorist incidents may result in collateral damage to foreign interests, thereby giving rise to transnational terrorist events. Similarly, domestic terrorists may seek safe havens in nearby countries; as they cross a border to attack their home country, a transnational terrorist incident ensues. However, in our view, many types of conflict begin as purely domestic and then spill over into transnational terrorism as terrorists seeks to attract greater media attention. Moreover, domestic terrorist incidents may have a demonstration effect on transnational terrorist incidents as terrorists copy each others' successful innovations. Thus, domestic terrorism cannot be treated as an isolated problem.

The important point is that domestic and transnational terrorism should not be treated as separate phenomena. Countries that are prime targets of transnational terrorism (particularly liberal democracies) must help contain domestic terrorist campaigns abroad before they spill over into transnational terrorism. A reasonable strategy might include the provision of counterterrorism-based foreign aid to countries confronting domestic terrorism.

CONCLUSION

Statistical analysis can substantiate or refute "observed" patterns in a time series plot or in patterns suggested by a particular political or economic model. Unlike the perception given by the media, there is no decided upward trend in any of the terrorism series. Instead, the ALL series and its subcomponent series vary over time in predictable ways. Spectral analysis is the specialized branch of statistics particularly well suited to analyzing cyclical phenomena. Spectral analysis indicates that logistically complex terrorist incidents (such as HOSTAGE and DEATH) have much longer cycles than less complex incidents (BOMBINGS and THREATS). Intervention analysis can be used to study how terrorists respond to particular events, such as the rise of religious fundamentalism, or to policy initiatives, such as the installation of metal detectors in airports. The statistical evidence suggests that terrorists responded to metal detectors and embassy fortifications, but not to UN conventions and resolutions. The demise of the Soviet Union and the increase in religious fundamentalism are both associated with increases in the severity of terrorism.

With the online availability of the GTD data set, it is anticipated that other researchers will begin to focus their efforts on the behavior of domestic terrorists. You can download our decomposed GTD data at www.cba. ua.edu/~wenders. We used the GTD data to indicate that the number of domestic terrorist incidents greatly exceeds the number of transnational incidents. Our decomposed GTD data suggests that domestic terrorism spills over into transnational incidents.

APPENDIX 3.1: WORKING WITH THE GTD DATA SET

The first task is to address the missing GTD values for 1993. Although Appendix 1 of the GTD codebook reports that a total of 4,954 incidents occurred in 1993, there are no breakdowns of the individual incidents by type, month, or quarter. In Enders, Sandler, and Gaibulloev (2011), we recommend modifying the missing year in GTD by an interpolation method. Moreover, because of undercounting, one reasonable strategy for users of GTD is to scale up the numbers of pre-1977:2 transnational terrorist incidents in the GTD data set by a factor of about 2.06 (= 94.67/45.93), which is the ratio of the mean number of ITERATE incidents to the mean number of GTD transnational terrorist incidents for 1970:1–1977:2. Given that the number of entries in GTD is clearly inflated for 1991:2–1997:4, we recommend deflating the numbers of transnational GTD entries from this period by a scale factor of 0.52, equal to the ratio of ITERATE to GTD incident means for this period.

Generally, counts of incidents involving deaths and casualties are likely to be more accurate than counts of all incidents that include inconsequential attacks or threats. More media reporting effort and coder care will go into recording consequential attacks. Hence, the casualty and death series will be more accurate than incident totals involving threats and hoaxes. For casualty attacks, the two adjustment values are 2.11 and 0.66. For death incidents, the values are 1.68 and 0.43.

FOUR

Counterterrorism

Counterterrorism consists of government actions to inhibit terrorist attacks or curtail their consequences. Such policies can limit attacks by confronting terrorists directly. For example, intelligence and police investigations resulted in the capture of the entire leadership of Direct Action (DA) in France between 1982 and 1987 (Alexander and Pluchinsky, 1992, p. 135; Hoffman, 1998). Italian authorities captured most of the Red Brigades after responding to a tip-off in the kidnapping of Brigadier General James Lee Dozier, the senior US officer at NATO's southern European command, who was abducted from his home on 17 December 1981. He was freed unharmed in a daring police rescue on 28 January 1982.[1] Based on state's evidence obtained from Antonio Savasta, who was captured during the raid, the police later apprehended 200 Red Brigades suspects, which resulted in further arrests and the eventual demise of the group. Other counterterrorism actions can safeguard potential terrorist targets by reducing an attack's likelihood of success or expected payoff. The installation of metal detectors in US airports on 5 January 1973 decreased terrorists' probability of success, as did the fortification of US embassies in the mid-1970s and beyond. After 9/11, the deployment of federal screeners at US airports, the reinforcement of airplane cockpit doors, and the designation of no-fly zones in Washington, D.C., and other American cities were intended to limit terrorists' success and, thereby, prevent attacks. In the extreme, counterterrorism can take the form of a military campaign against a terrorist organization. For example, the Sri Lankan army scored a decisive military victory over the Tamil Tigers on 16 May 2009, ending the group's twenty-six-year struggle for an independent state.

[1] For a detailed account of the Dozier kidnapping and its aftermath, see Mickolus, Sandler, and Murdock (1989, vol. 1, pp. 234–9), which is compiled from newspaper accounts at the time of the kidnapping.

The purpose of this chapter is to investigate and evaluate the two primary categories of counterterrorism policies – proactive and defensive. Proactive or offensive measures attack the terrorists, their resource base, or those who support them. By contrast, defensive or passive policies may erect a protective barrier around potential targets – physical or human. Such measures dissuade terrorists by decreasing their anticipated gains from attacks. This can occur if their costs are raised or their anticipated benefits are reduced. Defensive actions may also limit attacks if alternative nonterrorist actions are made more attractive. Defensive measures may involve limiting damage following a terrorist attack – for instance, enhanced first-responder capabilities or stockpiles of antidotes against chemical agents. Stiffer penalties and greater certainty of apprehension can dissuade would-be terrorists.

This chapter casts light on two puzzles. First, we explain why there appears to be a proclivity for most countries to rely on defensive rather than proactive policies when addressing transnational terrorism, and why this tendency does not appear to characterize actions with respect to domestic terrorism. Nations are quite proactive in pursuing domestic groups when they harm interests at home, either directly or indirectly through collateral damage. European action to dismantle many of the fighting communist organizations, such as the Combatant Communist Cells and the Italian Red Brigades, in the 1980s is testimony to this proactive stance with respect to domestic terrorism. Israeli aggression against the Hezbollah and Hamas leadership in recent years also underscores this orientation. Second, for transnational terrorism, we explain the tendency for the world community to rely on one or two nations' proactive responses. To accomplish these goals, we employ some elementary game theory to identify strategic differences among participants. We are particularly interested in the strategic interaction among targeted governments, which may actually work at cross purposes as they independently make policy choices.[2]

[2] The relevant literature on strategic interaction among targets includes Arce and Sandler (2005, 2007, 2009), Bandyopadhyay and Sandler (2011), Farrow (2007), Heal and Kunreuther (2003, 2005), Kunreuther and Heal (2003), Lee (1988), Lee and Sandler (1989), Powell (2007), Sandler and Arce (2003), Sandler and Enders (2004), Sandler and Lapan (1988), Sandler and Siqueira (2006), and Siqueira and Sandler (2007). Interactions between target and terrorists, when policies are decided, are addressed by Bandyopadhyay, Sandler, and Younas (2011), Bier, Oliveros, and Samuelson (2007), Bueno de Mesquita (2007), Enders and Sandler (1993, 1995), Jacobson and Kaplan (2007), Jain and Mukand (2004), Jindapon and Neilson (2009), Lapan and Sandler (1993), Rosendorff and Sandler (2004), Sandler, Tschirhart, and Cauley (1983), Siqueira and Sandler (2006), and Zhuang and Bier (2007).

Both this chapter and the next focus on counterterrorism. A common conclusion in both chapters is that an inappropriate level of antiterrorist action from counterterrorism measures often results especially when addressing *transnational* terrorism, because countries do not account for the costs and benefits that their independent choices imply for other countries. There is a marked tendency to engage in too much defensive action and not enough proactive measures. This follows because defensive measures frequently transfer the attack to softer targets abroad. Chapter 5 gives an in-depth empirical treatment of this transference phenomenon. In the case of proactive policies, too little is done as countries wait for others to act. Given the suboptimality of counterterrorism responses to transnational terrorism, there is a need for international cooperation – the subject of Chapter 6.

PROACTIVE POLICIES

Proactive policies are offensive, since a government confronts the terrorists or their supporters directly. If action can curtail terrorists' resources, their finances, safe havens, infrastructure, or sponsors, then the ability of terrorists to engage in activities is curtailed. Terrorists' resources can be reduced by capturing or killing group members or destroying their non-human resources – for example, weapons, ammunition, training camps, communication networks, or safe houses.

Consider the terrorist group's resource constraint,

$$P_T T + P_N N = I, \qquad (4.1)$$

where P_T and P_N are the unit costs of generic terrorist (T) and nonterrorist (N) actions, respectively, and I is the group's income or resources for the current period. During each period, equation (4.1) indicates that the terrorist group allocates its resources between terrorist and nonterrorist activities, thereby exhausting its resources for the period. This constraint is displayed as AB in Figure 4.1, where terrorist attacks are measured along the y-axis (vertical axis) and nonterrorist attacks along the x-axis (horizontal axis). If the terrorists devote all of their resources to terrorist attacks, then they can accomplish at most I/P_T attacks, which is found by setting $N = 0$ and solving for T in equation (4.1). Thus, I/P_T represents the y-intercept of resource constraint AB. Similarly, the x-intercept, I/P_N, of constraint AB is found by setting $T = 0$ and solving for the maximal number of nonterrorist attacks in equation (4.1). To find the slope of the resource constraint, we rewrite it, by solving for T, as,

$$T = \left(\frac{I}{P_T}\right) - \left(\frac{P_N}{P_T}\right) N. \qquad (4.2)$$

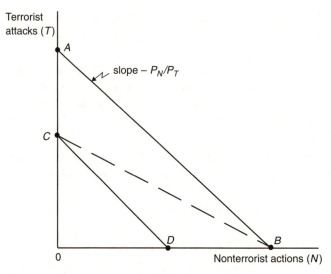

Figure 4.1. Terrorists' resource constraints.

The coefficient, $-P_N/P_T$ in front of N is the slope of the resource constraint, which indicates the change in T resulting from a unit change in N. Some proactive measures may reduce terrorists' resources, thereby shifting the resource constraint down in a *parallel* fashion to *CD*. The downward shift is parallel because a fall in I does not affect the ratio of unit costs in equation (4.2), thereby leaving the constraint's slope, $-P_N/P_T$ unchanged. Each intercept – I/P_T and I/P_N – falls by the same amount as I is reduced.

Proactive policies may, instead, raise the price of terrorist actions by making such activities more risky, thereby pivoting the resource constraint down in a nonparallel fashion to dashed line *CB*, if terrorists' resources are unaffected.[3] For example, the risk of being infiltrated by the government makes terrorist acts more costly without necessarily changing the terrorists' resource endowments. Group infiltration increases the relative attractiveness of nonterrorist acts. Finally, if the proactive measures raise the unit cost of terrorism and also reduce terrrorists' resources, then the resource constraint shifts down in a nonparallel fashion (not shown) from *AB*, so that there is a greater fall in the y-intercept compared to the x-intercept of the new resource constraint. In any of these scenarios, proactive policies reduce the terrorists' choices and may result in less of both kinds of

[3]   As P_T rises alone from the proactive policy, the intercept along the y-axis falls from A to C in Figure 4.1.

activities.[4] When the governmental policy increases the relative costliness of terrorist actions, the tendency is for terrorists to switch to nonterrorist activities. If, however, a threatened government represses freedoms and raises the unit costs of nonterrorist acts, including legitimate protests, then the government may force the terrorists to rely on terrorism to a greater extent (Frey, 2004; Frey and Luechinger, 2003; Lichbach, 1987).

Proactive policies can assume many forms, including a retaliatory raid against a state sponsor that provides resources, training, safe haven, logistical support, or intelligence to a terrorist group. An example of such a raid was the US bombing of targets in Libya on 15 April 1986 for its alleged involvement in the terrorist bombing of the La Belle discotheque in West Berlin on 4 April 1986, where 3 died and 231 were wounded, including 62 Americans.[5] Targets of the US raid included the Azizyah barracks in Tripoli, the Jamahiriyah barracks in Benghazi, the Sidi Bilal port west of Tripoli, the military side of the Tripoli airport, and the Benina military airfield.[6] The Azizyah barracks was the residence of Muammar Qaddafi. During the raid, two of his sons were seriously injured and his adopted one-year-old daughter killed. Another example of a retaliatory raid was an Israeli attack against Palestine Liberation Organization (PLO) bases in Syria in response to the Black September attack on Israeli athletes at the 1972 Olympic Games.

Another type of proactive response is a preemptive attack against a terrorist group or a country harboring it, as in the 7 October 2001 US attack on the Taliban and al-Qaida in Afghanistan. A preemptive attack differs from a retaliatory raid because the former is more sustained and intended to severely compromise the capabilities of the terrorists. During 2009–2011, the US and Pakistani military were still attacking al-Qaida leaders and members in Afghanistan and Pakistan. Israeli assassinations of Hamas leaders and operatives in 2003, 2004, and more recently also represent preemptive actions (Jacobson and Kaplan, 2007). Many past retaliatory raids merely lashed out at the terrorists or their sponsors without greatly limiting their ability to operate (see remarks in Chapter 3). As such, these raids

---

[4] The terrorists' constrained choice moves to where their indifference curve (not shown) is tangent to the lowered constraint. For parallel downward shifts, both activities are anticipated to decrease if terrorists view them as normal goods with positive income elasticities. For nonparallel shifts, one action may decrease more than another.

[5] Details of the La Belle discotheque bombing can be found in Mickolus, Sandler, and Murdock (1989, vol. 2, pp. 365–7).

[6] Details of the US raid are contained in Mickolus, Sandler, and Murdock (1989, vol. 2, pp. 373–4).

served more as a vehicle for the government to send a signal to its citizens than as punishment for the culprits.

Less drastic but effective proactive measures include infiltrating the terrorist group and gathering intelligence. Infiltration can compromise the group's security and lead to arrests. To limit such consequences in light of the Red Brigades' experience, many terrorist organizations now rely on a cellular structure, where members know little about the identity of others outside of their small cell of four to six persons. The use of bloodlines and long-term friendships limits the possibility of infiltration. Effective intelligence can identify planned attacks and allow for countermeasures – for example, the discovery of the 2006 plot in the United Kingdom to blow up transatlantic flights. Another proactive policy is to go after the financial resources of the terrorists by freezing assets. In the two years following 9/11, countries have frozen $200 million of terrorists' alleged assets (White House, 2003). At the international level, freezing assets raises problems of international cooperation addressed in Chapter 6 and by Levitt (2003) and Sandler (2005).

George W. Bush's war on terror was a broad-based action that involved both proactive and defensive measures to protect the country and its citizens at home and abroad against terrorism. There was, however, a reliance on military power and proactive measures. The motivation for this extreme response is a realization that modern-day terrorism is a form of asymmetric warfare in which the terrorists rely on unconventional, irregular, and decentralized methods to confront a superior adversary – that is, the military and police of targeted industrial nations.[7] To counter the terrorist threat, the government deploys its military to destroy terrorists' bases of operation and assets. There are criticisms leveled against a military response (see, for example, Wilkinson, 2001). By characterizing the response as a war, the proactive government gives a false impression of a possible victory where terrorism is eventually defeated.[8] Some groups or sponsors may indeed be defeated or severely compromised, but terrorism, especially transnational terrorism, remains a tactic that will be embraced by new members and groups. Any "victory" will be temporary. A military response may also result in collateral damage to innocent individuals – for example, the victims of a smart bomb that misses its mark. In addition, a

---

[7] This characterization comes from Schulze and Vogt (2003).

[8] In the case of the Tamil Tigers, military operations eventually succeeded in defeating them in May 2009. Military victory is more likely against a specific domestic terrorist group than it is against a general transnational terrorist threat.

military response may turn world opinion against the offensive country if operations appear excessive or brutal. One of the greatest drawbacks is the possibility that a military response will attract new recruits to the cause, which, in turn, could result in a wider conflict.[9]

There is also the problem of measuring success associated with military operations. Following the October 2001 preemptive strikes by coalition forces in Afghanistan, there were al-Qaida linked attacks in 2002 and thereafter – for example, the 12 May 2003 suicide truck bombings in Riyadh, Saudi Arabia, and the 16 May 2003 suicide car bombings in Casablanca, Morocco – that led critics to conclude that the Afghanistan War of 2001 did not achieve much in the long run. In 2011, al-Qaida still poses a real threat, as the attempt to blow up a Northwest Airlines flight on 25 December 2009 and other recent plots highlight. What we cannot know is how many additional attacks would have occurred had action not been taken in Afghanistan. This counterfactual problem is particularly acute in the case of military operations because of the mistaken expectation that transnational terrorism will cease. Measurement is also difficult owing to the cyclical nature of terrorist attacks; a lull may be due to a natural cycle rather than military actions taken. And fewer attacks may not even signal success if attacks become bloodier or are transferred to other countries.[10]

Proactive measures often represent pure public goods as defined in Chapter 1. A preemptive operation that reduces the capabilities of a common terrorist threat *confers nonexcludable and nonrival benefits on all potential targets.* If asked to contribute to the operation after the fact, most targets will understate their true derived benefits so as to free ride on the proactive support of others. This tendency will lead to underprovision as targets wait for others to act. At the national level, the free-rider concern is addressed by assigning the central government the authority to protect domestic targets with financing from tax revenues. When necessary, the central government coordinates the state and local jurisdictional responses. The free-rider problem is a major worry in combating transnational

---

[9] To date, there are few theoretical analyses of the process of recruitment to terrorist organizations. Recruitment can be stimulated by past incident successes or by governments' draconian measures (see, for example, Rosendorff and Sandler, 2004). To properly address recruitment, a multiperiod dynamic model is required, whereby terrorist attacks and government countermeasures influence the stock of operatives in a terrorist campaign (Faria and Arce, 2005). This stock is also affected by retirements and casualties incurred in missions. The government must be sufficiently vigilant to limit successful incidents, but not so harsh as to encourage grievances and new recruits.

[10] Based on past transnational terrorist data, Sandler, Arce, and Enders (2009) made a case that the war on terror resulted in fewer, more deadly attacks.

terrorism, because there is no supranational government that can provide a unified proactive policy *underwritten by taxes from target countries*. Since 9/11, the world community has relied on the United States to coordinate the proactive response, which other nations can voluntarily support. At the transnational level, some proactive policies may result in public bads as costs are imposed on other countries. If, for example, a proactive operation augments grievances and leads to recruitment of terrorists, then these public costs must be weighed against the public benefits in order to ascertain the net consequences (Arce and Sandler, 2010; Rosendorff and Sandler, 2004, 2010). A particularly heavy-handed operation may conceivably do more to jeopardize other countries than to safeguard them. This is particularly true when the proactive country is also hardening its own targets at home so that grievance-inducing terrorist attacks occur abroad, where other interests are impacted. The result is a "forced ride," where a nation consumes a consequence that it prefers to forego (Tanzi, 1972).

DEFENSIVE POLICIES

Defensive measures protect potential targets either by making attacks more costly for terrorists or by reducing their likelihood of success. When an attack occurs, effective defensive action also limits the losses. Many defensive policies are reactive in that they are imposed only after past incidents have revealed vulnerabilities. The installation of metal detectors to screen passengers at airports is an instance. Prior to their installation at US airports on 5 January 1973, there were on average approximately twenty-seven hijackings each year in the United States (Enders, Sandler, and Cauley, 1990a, p. 95). The installation of bomb-detecting equipment to screen luggage on commercial flights came after bombs had brought down planes – for example, Pan Am flight 103 over Scotland on 21 December 1988 and UTA flight 772 over Niger on 19 September 1989. Both metal detectors and bomb-detecting devices are examples of technological barriers, which are especially effective when authorities continuously upgrade the technology in order to stymie attempts by terrorists to circumvent the barriers – for example, the development of plastic guns and non-nitrogen-based explosives. Full-body scanners represent the latest technological barrier, which will be circumvented when terrorists place bombs in their body cavities.

Some defensive actions may involve hardening a target, such as efforts in 1976 and 1985 to fortify US embassies. Since the 19 April 1995 bombing of the Alfred P. Murrah Federal Building in Oklahoma City, barriers have been erected around other federal buildings in order to create a safety perimeter to curtail the damage from a car or truck bomb. The decision to allow fighter jets to shoot down hijacked planes that could be used to destroy buildings, as on 9/11, is another defensive policy. The deployment of sky marshals on airplanes is yet another defensive action, as are DHS terror alerts to warn the public of a heightened state of risk.

Some actions are intended to deter or hinder an attack by stiffening penalties for convicted terrorists. For example, Reagan's so-called get-tough policy on terrorism was expressed in two Public Laws (PL) passed by the US Congress and signed by President Reagan. These laws are PL 98–473 (signed on 12 October 1984) and PL 98–533 (signed on 19 October 1984). The first required up to life imprisonment for terrorists taking US hostages within or outside the United States. Penalties for destroying aircraft or airport facilities within the United States were also increased, as were penalties for acts committed with a bomb or other weapon on a US aircraft. The second bill authorized the US attorney general to pay rewards for information leading to the apprehension or conviction, inside or outside the United States, of terrorists who targeted US interests (Pearl, 1987, p. 141; Mickolus, Sandler, and Murdock, 1989).

Another defensive measure involves the stockpiling of antibiotics for biological terrorist attacks (for example, anthrax incidents) or antidotes for chemical terrorist attacks (for example, sarin gas attacks). Enhanced first-responder capabilities represent defensive measures that limit the deaths and damage following a terrorist attack. The DHS has instituted many such damage-limiting defensive measures (see Chapter 11).

At the international level, the United Nations and other multilateral bodies (for example, the International Civil Aviation Organization, the International Maritime Organization, and the Council of Europe) have passed conventions and treaties outlawing certain acts of terrorism – for example, seizure of commercial aircraft, the taking of hostages, and the use of explosive bombs. Unlike domestic laws, these international conventions suffer from the absence of an enforcement mechanism. In Chapter 6, we present an evaluation of their effectiveness.

Effective defensive measures have a publicness aspect that generally differentiates them from proactive policies. A defensive action may deflect an attack from a hardened to a softer target and, in so doing, impose a public cost on other potential targets; thus, a negative externality is associated with this transference. Unlike proactive measures, which may be undersupplied, defensive measures may be oversupplied.

For ease of reference, Table 4.1 lists many key proactive and defensive counterterrorism measures. These lists are not intended to be inclusive.

Table 4.1. *Proactive and Defensive Measures against Terrorism*

Proactive or offensive measures
- Retaliatory attack on state sponsor
- Preemptive attacks on terrorist camps and bases
- Infiltration of terrorist groups
- Destruction of terrorist infrastructure
- Limiting terrorists' financing
- Gathering intelligence on terrorists' planned operations
- Arrests of terrorists
- Eliminating terrorists' safe havens
- Assassination of terrorist leaders and operatives
- Military engagement with the terrorists

Defensive or protective measures
- Technological barriers (for example, metal detectors, full-body scanners, and bomb-detecting devices)
- Hardening of targets (for example, defensive perimeters around buildings)
- More security at potential targets
- Scrambling of fighter jets to shoot down hijacked planes
- Air marshals
- Terrorism alerts
- Stiffer penalties for terrorism
- Stockpiling of antibiotics and antidotes for biological and chemical terrorist attacks, respectively
- Enhanced first-responder capabilities
- International conventions and treaties addressing terrorist actions

GAME THEORY PRIMER

We now apply simple game theory to compare and contrast how national governments strategically interact with one another in a noncooperative framework that involves acting independently to decide their counterterrorism policies. The need for cooperative behavior for some transnational interactions then becomes apparent. A noncooperative game is fully identified by four factors: the rules of the game, the set of players, their available strategies, and the payoffs for all possible strategy combinations. To simplify the analysis, we display games in their normal or matrix form as described below.

The Prisoners' Dilemma game is relevant for many antiterrorism decisions and is thus described in detail. A story line behind the Prisoners' Dilemma game is as follows. In the vicinity of an armed robbery, two individuals in a vehicle are stopped on suspicion of being involved. Not only do

	B	
	Confess	Does not confess
Confess (A)	**2 years, 2 years**	0 years, 4 years
Does not confess	4 years, 0 years	1 year, 1 year

a. Prisoners' Dilemma in jail sentence terms

	B	
	Confess	Does not confess
Confess (A)	**2, 2**	4, 1
Does not confess	1, 4	3, 3

b. Prisoners' Dilemma in ordinal form

Figure 4.2. Prisoners' Dilemma.

the suspects appear to match eyewitnesses' vague descriptions, but a search of their car turns up an unregistered handgun. The district attorney realizes that she has insufficient circumstantial evidence to convict them of the robbery unless she can get a confession from one of the suspects. Without a confession, she can convict them only of possessing an unregistered handgun, which carries a one-year sentence. Her strategy is to separate the two suspects and offer each a deal. If just one of them confesses, then the confessor walks free, while the nonconfessor receives the maximum four-year sentence for the robbery. If both confess, then they each receive a reduced two-year sentence for cooperating with the district attorney.

In panel *a* of Figure 4.2, the relevant payoffs for the two suspects – prisoners *A* and *B* – are displayed in the four cells of the game box, where each prisoner has two strategies: confess or not confess. Given that each player has two choices, there are four possible strategy combinations for the two suspects: both confess, in the top left-hand cell; *A* confesses alone, in the top right-hand cell; *B* confesses alone, in the bottom left-hand cell; and neither confesses, in the bottom right-hand cell. In each of the four cells, the left-hand payoff or prison sentence is that of prisoner *A* or the row player, whereas the right-hand payoff is that of prisoner *B* or the column player. The payoffs in each cell correspond to those associated with the deal offered by the district attorney – for example, when both confess, they each receive a two-year term. To examine the strategic dilemma from *A*'s viewpoint, we must compare his payoffs from his two strategies. When prisoner *B* confesses, prisoner *A* gets a lighter sentence of two years by confessing, as compared to the maximum four-year sentence for not confessing. If, however, prisoner *B* does not confess, prisoner *A* is still better off by confessing, since he then is released rather than serving a one-year term for not confessing. Prisoner *A*'s payoffs in the confessing row are better than the corresponding payoffs in the not-confessing row. A strategy such as confessing, which provides a greater payoff regardless of the other player's action, is a *dominant strategy* and should be played. By the same token, a strategy whose payoffs are worse than some other strategy's corresponding payoffs is said to be a *dominated strategy* and should *not* be chosen. In panel *a* of Figure 4.2, suspect *B*'s dominant strategy is also to confess when the corresponding right-hand payoffs in the two columns are compared – that is, a two-year sentence is better than four years, and walking free is better than a one-year term. As both suspects apply their dominant strategies, the outcome is mutual confession with two years of jail time. The dilemma arises because mutual silence is better for both suspects.

The confession outcome represents a *Nash equilibrium* (with bold-faced payoffs), which is a collection of strategies – one for each player – such that no player would *unilaterally* alter his or her strategy if given the opportunity.[11] This can be seen by focusing on the confession cell in panel *a*, where both players confess. If suspect *A* (or *B*) alone changes to not confessing or withdrawing the confession, then this suspect's payoff is worsened by the addition of two years of jail time. As a consequence, the suspect will not change his or her strategy unilaterally. Of course, both suspects would have been better off had they formed an agreement from the outset to stay silent and stay with the arrangement. Even if such an agreement had been made, problems arise when the district attorney tempts them separately with the deal. Given the dominant strategy that her deal places before each suspect, neither can be sure what the other will do – promise to keep silent or no promise. Even if suspect *A* is sure that *B* will not confess, *A* is better off confessing and playing his buddy for a sucker.

An alternative representation of the payoffs in panel *a* of Figure 4.2 distinguishes the so-called Prisoners' Dilemma from myriad other payoff configurations. This is done by rank ordering the payoffs from best to worst in

---

[11] Another characterization of a Nash equilibrium is that each player chooses his or her best strategy as a counter to the other player's best response or strategy.

	B	
	Straight	Swerve
A Straight	1, 1	**4, 2**
A Swerve	**2, 4**	3, 3

a. Chicken game in ordinal form

	B	
	Does not retaliate	Retaliate
A Does not retaliate	**2, 2**	3, 1
A Retaliate	1, 3	**4, 4**

b. Assurance game in ordinal form

Figure 4.3. Chicken and assurance game.

panel *b* of Figure 4.2. The best payoff (the walk-free sentence) is assigned the highest ordinal rank of 4, the next-best payoff (the one-year sentence) is given an ordinal rank of 3, and so on. Any two-person game box that possesses precisely the same ordinal payoff array as that in panel *b* is a Prisoners' Dilemma. There are seventy-eight distinct 2 × 2 arrays of ordinal payoffs, but only one of them corresponds to the Prisoners' Dilemma. The ordinal depiction captures the essential strategic features of the game, including the presence or absence of dominant strategies and Nash equilibrium(s). In panel *b*, confessing remains the dominant strategy, since 2 > 1 and 4 > 3; and mutual confession is the Nash equilibrium, whose payoffs are bold-faced. If the columns and rows are interchanged so that confess is in the bottom row for *A* (right column for *B*), then a Prisoners' Dilemma still results with the (3, 3) payoffs switching positions with the (2, 2) payoffs along the diagonal, and the (1, 4) and (4, 1) payoffs switching positions along the off-diagonal.

Before we apply game theory to the analysis of antiterrorist policy choices, we examine two additional game forms. In panel *a* of Figure 4.3, we indicate the *chicken* game in ordinal form. The James Dean movie *Rebel Without a Cause* popularized the game's story line of two hot rods speeding toward one another from opposite directions. Each driver – *A* and *B* – has two strategies – keep driving straight or swerve to avoid a collision. The payoffs reflect the following preferences. The greatest perceived payoff derives from staying straight when the other driver swerves, because the driver who holds the course appears strong to his peers. The next best payoff occurs when both drivers swerve, which is better than swerving alone and being branded the "chicken." Of course, the worst outcome is for both drivers to hold their course and have a collision. This game has no dominant strategy: the payoffs associated with swerve are not both greater than the corresponding payoffs associated with straight, since $2 > 1$ but $3 \not> 4$. Similarly, the driving-straight strategy does not dominate swerve, insofar as $4 > 3$ but $1 \not> 2$. Nevertheless, there are two Nash equilibriums indicated in boldface, where a single driver swerves. At these equilibriums, neither player would unilaterally change his or her strategy. From an ordinal viewpoint, chicken and Prisoners' Dilemma differ by having the 1s and 2s switch positions. This small change has large strategic consequences – the failure to coordinate the proper response can be disastrous for chicken. A situation in which taking no action against a terrorist threat spells disaster may be characterized as a chicken game. In this scenario, proactive measures by one of the two threatened nations averts disaster by curtailing the terrorists' capabilities. Collective action concerns arise because the free-rider nation is better off than the nation forestalling disaster; an ordinal payoff of 4 is preferred to one of 2. How roles are assigned poses a dilemma. If one nation clearly signals that it will do nothing, then the other has no choice but to act to avoid disaster. With cardinal payoffs replacing the ordinal payoffs, the nation that engages the terrorists is likely to be the one that loses relatively more from the terrorist attack – the so-called prime-target country.

An *assurance* game is indicated in panel *b* of Figure 4.3 where two countries – *A* and *B* – must decide whether or not to retaliate against an alleged state sponsor of terrorism following some spectacular terrorist incident that creates grave losses for both countries. The ordinal payoffs in panel *b* of Figure 4.3 differ from those of the Prisoners' Dilemma in panel *b* of Figure 4.2 in one essential way: the 3s and 4s have switched positions, so that the greatest ordinal payoff comes from joint action, while the next-best payoff arises from free riding. To obtain this game, we assume that the two countries *must join forces* to get the job done – a single retaliator cannot hurt the terrorists sufficiently to outweigh the associated costs. Free riding on the country's retaliator effort is the second-best outcome because revenge, though inadequate, is better than no response by anyone. Retaliating alone is the worst outcome because it is costly without accomplishing a net positive payoff despite some political gain from taking action. The second-smallest payoff is mutual inaction.

The assurance game in panel *b* of Figure 4.3 has no dominant strategy, because the payoffs in either row (column) are not both greater than the corresponding payoffs in the other row (column). There are, however, two Nash equilibriums whose payoffs are boldfaced along the diagonal of the game box, where countries match one another's responses – either no one retaliates, or both retaliate. If one country takes the lead and retaliates, as the United States did following 9/11, then the other country is better off retaliating, since an ordinal payoff of 4 is more desirable than one of 3. The game is called the *assurance game*, since – unlike the Prisoners' Dilemma, where agreements are not honored – pledged (assured) action will elicit a like response by the other player.

The heinous nature of the 9/11 attacks and their human toll on American and British citizens at the World Trade Center altered the ordinal payoffs depicted in panel *b* of Figure 4.3. For the United States and the United Kingdom, the worst payoff was associated with no one retaliating, followed by retaliating alone. That is, the 1s and 2s switch positions in panel *b* of Figure 4.3, while the 3s and 4s remain as displayed. The resulting game matrix (not shown) has a dominant strategy for both countries to retaliate. The sole Nash equilibrium is for joint retaliatory action, which began on 7 October 2001; thus, the Prisoners' Dilemma is not always descriptive of the decision to retaliate. If a country is sufficiently hurt in a terrorist attack, retaliation may be a compelling response by those countries most damaged in the attack.

PROACTIVE VERSUS DEFENSIVE POLICIES

For a proactive policy, we consider preemption where two targeted countries must decide whether or not to launch a preemptive attack against a common terrorist threat. The preemptive strike is intended to weaken the terrorists so that they pose a less significant challenge. Suppose that each country taking the preemptive action confers a public benefit of 4 on itself and the other country at a cost of 6 to just itself. The game's cardinal payoffs are indicated in the matrix of Figure 4.4. When no one acts, so that the status quo is preserved, nothing is gained. If, say, the United States (US) preempts but the European Union (EU) does not, then the US nets -2 ($= 4 - 6$) as costs of 6 are deducted from benefits of 4, while the EU receives the free-rider benefits of 4. The payoffs in the top right-hand cell are reversed as these roles are interchanged. When both countries preempt, each gains

		EU	
		Status quo	Preempt
US	Status quo	**0, 0**	4, −2
	Preempt	−2, 4	2, 2

Figure 4.4. Two-target preemption game.

	Number of preempting nations other than nation i					
	0	1	2	3	4	5
Nation i does not preempt	**0**	4	8	12	16	20
Nation i preempts	−2	2	6	10	14	18

Figure 4.5. Six-nation preemption game.

2 as its preemption costs of 6 are deducted from the benefits of 8 (= 2 × 4), derived from the preemptive efforts of both countries. If these payoffs were ordinally ranked, then the game would be immediately identified as a Prisoners' Dilemma. The dominant strategy is to maintain the status quo (that is, 0 > −2 and 4 > 2), and the boldfaced Nash equilibrium is mutual inaction. Thus, a classic pure public good scenario emerges with nothing happening as both countries prefer to rely on the other. This outcome follows whenever the public benefit, b_i, received by the preemptor and the other threatened country is less than the cost, c_i, encumbered by the preemptor(s). Hence, the sole special property, which our illustrative numbers possess, is that $c_i > b_i$.

In Figure 4.5, we extend this same scenario to six identical countries and examine the alternative outcomes from the viewpoint of nation i, whose payoffs are indicated. The columns denote the number of nations other than i that preempt. In the top row, nation i attempts to free ride. If, say, two other nations preempt, then i receives 8 (= 2 × 4). In general, nation i gains 4 times the number of preemptors as a free-rider payoff. The bottom row displays i's payoff when it preempts. Nation i nets −2 when no other nation joins its efforts, while i receives 2 (= 2 × 4 − 6) when one other nation also preempts. In general, nation i gains $4n − 6$, where n is the number of preemptors including i.

The dominant strategy for this six-nation preemption game is not to pre-empt, because each payoff in the top row is greater than the corresponding payoff in the bottom row by 2, or the net loss from independent action. The boldfaced Nash equilibrium is where no nation preempts, as all nations exercise their dominant strategy of doing nothing. This outcome leads to a significant welfare loss to the six-nation collective. If all six nations engage in preemption, then each gains 18 for a cumulative total of 108. Thus, all-around free riding loses society 108 of potential benefits in this example.[12] As the number of nations in the scenario increases, this cumulative loss increases. For a worldwide network such as al-Qaida, these losses from inaction can be extremely large; thus, the need for international cooperation is highlighted. This example raises some interesting questions. Why is there more preemption for domestic terrorism? What explains those situations where there is preemption in light of a transnational terrorist threat?

For domestic terrorism, the target nation cannot rely on other countries, since it alone is the target of attacks. Quite simply, there are no free-riding opportunities, except among targets within the nation. A centralized response addresses any free-riding concerns within a nation. Moreover, the individual benefits from action often exceed the associated costs once the terrorist campaign surpasses some level of intensity. Thus, the net gain from acting alone is likely to be positive, not negative. As the terrorists turn up the heat – for example, the Tupamaros in Uruguay at the start of the 1970s or the Red Army Faction in West Germany in the 1970s – their enhanced brutality increases the government's perceived benefits from preemption and makes the net gain from action larger. Another factor may be the government's perceived payoff from inaction. Thus far, we have assumed it to be 0. If, instead, the government loses support by not responding, then the resulting negative payoff may transform the game into a chicken game where some action is taken.[13]

For transnational terrorism, there are at least two strategic reasons for a nation to take preemptive measures. First, the underlying game form may be something other than the Prisoners' Dilemma – for example, chicken or assurance. If the terrorist campaign is sufficiently deadly, doing nothing may be politically unacceptable (for example, following 9/11 or the train

---

[12] The social optimum does *not* correspond to the payoff of 20 in Figure 4.5 associated with *i* free riding on the other five nations. In this scenario, *i* receives 20, but each of the preemptors gains just 14 from its efforts and those of the other four preemptors (see Figure 4.5). Society nets 90 [= 20 + (5 × 14)] instead of 108.

[13] This is the case when the losses from inaction exceed in absolute value the net loss from acting alone.

	EU	
	Status quo	Preempt
Status quo	0, 0	4, –2
Preempt	**2, 4**	6, 2

US (row player label)

Figure 4.6. Asymmetric preemption scenario.

bombings in Madrid on 11 March 2004), so that the maintenance of the status quo, where terrorists attack with impunity, may have high negative political costs. This scenario gives mutual inaction the least desirable payoff, reflective of chicken. Second, the countries' payoffs may be asymmetric owing to the terrorists' targeting preferences. Consider the asymmetric preemption game in Figure 4.6 between the US and the EU. The payoffs for the EU are identical to those of Figure 4.4 – that is, it gains 4 from its own preemption or that of the US and must pay a cost of 6 when preempting. The US now gains more from its *own* preemption than it derives from EU preemption, because US action demonstrates to its citizens that it is striking back. US action still costs 6. Suppose that the US still derives just 4 in benefits from EU preemption but 8 from its own efforts. US payoffs in the bottom row are now 2 (= 8 – 6) and 6 (= 8 + 4 – 6) for acting alone and in unison, respectively. The dominant strategies in Figure 4.6 are for the US to preempt (2 > 0 and 6 > 4 for the row payoff comparison) and for the EU to do nothing (0 > –2 and 4 > 2 for the column payoff comparison).

The Nash equilibrium in Figure 4.6 involves the US preempting and the EU free riding. This example is not intended to point the finger at any country; rather, it indicates that a prime-target nation can be induced to preempt even if it has to do so alone. Only these prime targets may be sufficiently motivated to provide benefits to all potential targets by going after a common threat. This reaction is analogous to the situation where nations become more proactive domestically when attacks at home surpass a certain threshold. Despite US rhetoric prior to 9/11, it had seldom engaged in preemption, even though its interests were the target of 40% of all transnational terrorist incidents. The 15 April 1986 Libyan retaliatory raid was a short-lived operation, as were the Clinton administration's 20 August 1998 strikes on Afghanistan and Sudan for their alleged involvement in the bombing of the US embassies in Tanzania and Kenya on 7 August 1998. There is a certain irony in this preemption asymmetry. Had the terrorists treated their targets more symmetrically and not concentrated attacks on a few countries' assets, no country would have resorted to preemption. Of course, the terrorists focus their attacks in order to win over a following by trading preemption risk off against the followers' support.

When two or more target countries engage in preempting the same terrorist threat, their level of action will be negatively related because preemption is a substitute – one country's action limits the need for the other to act (Sandler and Siqueira, 2006). Thus, prime targets easy ride on the preemption of others, which implies too little preemption unless decisions are made in a cooperative framework. If, for example, one country experiences a higher level of attacks, it will increase its preemption, which will decrease the other country's efforts. This is an instance where countries work at cross purposes when deciding antiterrorist activities. Given the substitute nature of preemption, Sandler and Siqueira demonstrated that leadership by one targeted nation will result in a less optimal response by the leader, as it limits action in order to saddle the other targeted nation with more preemptive efforts. Such strategic behavior favors the transnational terrorists.

Deterrence and Other Defensive Measures

For deterrence, a nation tries to limit terrorist attacks by making potential targets less vulnerable through protective measures.[14] A symmetric two-target – US and EU – deterrence game is displayed in Figure 4.7, in which each country can do nothing or deter an attack by hardening its targets. Increased deterrence is assumed to give a private, country-specific gain of 6 to the deterring country at a cost of 4 *to both countries*. For the deterring country, costs arise from both the expense of deterrence and the increased likelihood of incurring damage to its assets abroad if the attack is deflected there. For the nondeterring country, the costs stem from the heightened risk that it assumes because it is now a relatively soft target that may draw the attack.

The payoffs in the matrix in Figure 4.7 are based on this scenario. If the US deters alone, it gains a net benefit of 2 (= 6 − 4) as its deterrence gains of 6 are reduced by the associated costs. The EU suffers external costs of 4 from attracting the attack. The payoffs are reversed when the

---

[14] We do not use "deterrence" in the Cold War context of keeping an action from occurring through a threat of punishment that is also costly to the punisher. We instead use "deterrence" in its common definitional sense of dissuading an action. This is how it has been applied in the terrorism literature since Landes (1978), where deterrence affects the terrorists' constraint.

	EU	
	Deter	Status quo
Deter	**-2, -2**	2, -4
Status quo	-4, 2	0, 0

US is the row player.

Figure 4.7. Two-target deterrence game.

roles are interchanged. If both countries deter, then each sustain a net loss of -2 [$= 6 - (2 \times 4)$] as costs of 8 from both countries' deterrence are deducted from the deterrence benefits of 6. The status quo provides no gains or losses. The game is a Prisoners' Dilemma with a dominant strategy to deter and a Nash equilibrium of mutual deterrence. If this game were extended to n countries, then all countries would choose their dominant strategy to deter. Overdeterrence results as each country does not account for the external costs associated with its efforts to deflect the attack abroad. Globalization may reduce overdeterrence somewhat by tying countries' vulnerabilities together. That is, transferring the attack abroad may hurt a country's foreign interests so that it incurs not only its deterrence expense, but also losses to its foreign interests. There may exist scenarios in which deterrence results in a net loss when a country's foreign interests are sufficiently important.

Countries' deterrence choices are usually complementary, because greater deterrence abroad encourages greater deterrence at home so as not to draw the attack. Defensive policies such as deterrence and proactive policies such as preemption may both result in a Prisoners' Dilemma when displayed as a simple game. Nevertheless, there are subtle, but crucial, differences. First, proactive decisions tend to be substitutes and undersupplied, while defensive decisions tend to be complements and oversupplied. Second, a greater variety of game forms are typically related to proactive policies (for example, Prisoners' Dilemma, chicken, assurance, and asymmetric dominance), while the Prisoners' Dilemma is typically tied to defensive policies (Arce and Sandler, 2005). Third, globalization may ameliorate the oversupply of defensive measures by making people equally vulnerable everywhere, whereas it may exacerbate the undersupply of proactive measures. Fourth, defensive measures may give rise to both negative and positive external effects. That is, deterring an attack by deflecting it abroad may result in external costs in the recipient country but external benefits to foreign residents in the deterring country. Proactive measures are typically associated with external benefits unless they create grievances, backlash, and recruitment.

The Choice between Deterrence and Preemption

We next examine the scenario where each of two targets – the US and the EU – must choose discretely between deterrence or preemption.[15] Each target now has three strategies: deter, maintain the status quo, and preempt. The scenarios for deterrence and preemption are identical to the previously described 2 × 2 games in Figures 4.4 and 4.7, respectively. Thus, deterrence provides public costs of 4 for the two targets and a private benefit of 6 to the deterrer, while preemption provides public benefits of 4 for the two targets and a private cost of 6 to the preemptor. These payoffs are illustrative – any set of public and private benefits where the private benefit of deterrence exceeds the associated costs and the private cost of preemption exceeds the associated benefits will give the outcome presented. This pattern of payoffs ensures that each component 2 × 2 game is a Prisoners' Dilemma.

The 3 × 3 game matrix is displayed in Figure 4.8, where the embedded deterrence game is captured by the northwest bold-bordered 2 × 2 matrix, and the embedded preemption game is captured by the southeast bold-bordered 2 × 2 matrix. Only the payoffs in the two cells at the opposite ends of the off-diagonal need to be derived. If one target deters and the other preempts, then the deterrer gains 6 (= 6 + 4 – 4), while the preemptor nets –6 (= 4 – 6 – 4). The deterrer earns a private benefit of 6 from its deterrence and a public benefit of 4 from the other target's preemption, but must cover its deterrence cost of 4. The sole preemptor suffers a cost of 4 from the other player's deterrence and a cost of 6 from its preemption efforts, but achieves only a private preemption benefit of 4.

The Nash equilibrium for the embedded deterrence game is for both countries to deter, and that for the embedded preemption game is for both to take no action. Which of these two equilibriums, if either, now reigns in the 3 × 3 game scenario? For the US, the dominant strategy is to deter, since its payoffs in the top row are greater than the corresponding payoffs in the other two rows. Similarly, the EU's dominant strategy is also to deter when its column payoffs (the right-hand payoff in a cell) are compared to the corresponding payoffs in the other two columns. As both targets apply their dominant strategies, the Nash equilibrium of mutual deterrence

---

[15] Material in this subsection draws from the analysis in Arce and Sandler (2005).

			EU	
		Deter	Status quo	Preempt
	Deter	**-2, -2**	2, -4	6, -6
US	Status quo	-4, 2	0, 0	4, -2
	Preempt	-6, 6	-2, 4	2, 2

Figure 4.8. Deterrence versus preemption – symmetric case.

results; thus, the deterrence equilibrium wins out. This outcome is unfortunate for two reasons. First, payoffs in the status quo outcome are higher for both targets than those in the mutual deterrence equilibrium. Second, the sum of payoffs from mutual deterrence is the *smallest* of the nine strategic combinations! Pursuit of one's self-interest by playing the dominant strategy leads to the worst social outcome in terms of total payoffs. If a nation has a choice between deterrence and preemption, deterrence often wins out – a situation reflective of nations' tendencies, when confronting transnational terrorists, to rely on defensive measures to deflect attacks rather than to go after the terrorists directly. This means that coordinating counterterrorism policies among countries can lead to significant gains. Elsewhere, Arce and Sandler (2005) examined alternative game forms – chicken, assurance, and others – when countries choose between defensive and proactive policies and demonstrated the general robustness of the tendency for targets to rely on defensive measures in *symmetric* scenarios where choices are simultaneous. They also allowed governments a fourth option to use both deterrence and preemption to varying degrees. Once again, the sole reliance on deterrence wins out.

We next permit an asymmetric response for preemption identical to the earlier analysis, so that the southeast 2×2 matrix in Figure 4.9 is that of Figure 4.6. The northwest 2×2 deterrence matrix in Figure 4.9 is that of Figure 4.7. In terms of underlying payoffs, all that changes in Figure 4.9 compared to the symmetric scenario is that the US derives 8, rather than 4, in benefits from its own preemption owing to its prime-target status. Thus, only the US payoffs in the bottom row differ from those in Figure 4.8 by being 4 larger. The EU still has a dominant strategy to deter, so that the only

		EU		
		Deter	Status quo	Preempt
	Deter	**–2, –2**	2, –4	6, –6
US	Status quo	–4, 2	0, 0	4, –2
	Preempt	**–2, 6**	2, 4	6 , 2

Figure 4.9. Deterrence versus preemption – asymmetric case.

possible Nash equilibriums must be in the first column where EU deters. Given the payoffs of the specific example, there are now two boldfaced Nash equilibriums where either both targets deter or the US preempts and the EU deters. If, however, the US receives even more benefits from its preemption, then the outcome will have the US preempting while the EU deters. After 9/11, US reliance on defensive measures would merely transfer the attack abroad, where its people and property are still targeted, thus limiting US gains from such reliance.

All of these simple games are conceptually enlightening in explaining why preferred-target countries resort to proactive *and* defensive measures against transnational terrorism, while less-targeted countries focus on defensive actions. In the latter case, the countries' assets may be hit abroad, but since their interests per se are not sought out by the terrorists, this likelihood remains small. Such countries are content to let some more at-risk country root out the terrorists and put its soldiers in harm's way in order to make the world safer. These strategic incentives bode ill for international cooperation and a united stance against transnational terrorism.

Further Remarks on Choosing between Proactive and Defensive Measures

Thus far, this choice has been based on two targeted countries simultaneously deciding proactive and defensive measures. In a recent paper, Bandyopadhyay and Sandler (2011) investigated this choice by constructing a two-stage game, in which each of the targeted countries determines the level of its proactive response in the first stage and the level of its defensive response in the second stage.[16] Each country chooses its two choice variables independently in order to minimize its costs, cognizant that the terrorists will attack the softer target. The proactive choice is cast as coming first because an effective proactive program may eliminate the terrorist threat from then on, thereby reducing the need for defensive measures. The mix between the two policies hinges on three essential considerations: the policies' cost comparisons, the countries' foreign interests, and the countries' targeting risks (that is, the tendency of the terrorists to favor attacking one country).

Surprisingly, *low proactive costs are not sufficient to determine the proactive country*, because defensive costs and/or prime-target status can overcome the influence of comparatively low proactive costs. High-cost defenders will suffer from period to period until the terrorist threat is eliminated or greatly curtailed. In addition, countries with greater foreign interests have higher effective marginal defensive costs, which favors their use of proactive measures to safeguard their assets at home and abroad. The logical candidate for providing proactive measures against a common transnational terrorist threat is a high-cost defender with significant global interests. The United States is a high-cost defender, given its long borders; it also possesses large global interests, given its huge foreign direct investments. Thus, it is no surprise that the United States has emerged as the leading proactive nation against the al-Qaida network. This role is bolstered by US interests being hit in about 40% of transnational terrorist attacks.

Even when Bandyopadhyay and Sandler reversed the stages of play – that is, defense before proaction – they found the same drivers for determining the proactive nation. These authors also showed that developments that curb the market failure associated with proactive measures also reduce the market failure associated with defensive measures. That is, there is a complementarity between the two market failures that can be ameliorated by increasing the proactive level, which, in turn, limits the need for defense.

WEAKEST-LINK CONSIDERATIONS

In some cases, risks are interdependent, so that securing one vulnerability without securing another does not achieve much (if any) safety.[17] Consider upgrades to airport screening to counter terrorists' abilities to circumvent

---

[16] Also see the related paper by Carceles-Poveda and Tauman (2011).

[17] Interdependent risk is analyzed in Heal and Kunreuther (2003, 2005) and Kunreuther and Heal (2003).

	EU	
	Status quo	Security upgrade

US	Status quo	**0, 0**	0, −6
	Security upgrade	−6, 0	**2, 2**

Figure 4.10. Weakest-link security risk.

current measures. Suppose that the screening upgrade is introduced in just one of two vulnerable airports. The risk to the flying public may not be curtailed, because the terrorists can exploit the vulnerability at the other location where the device is not installed. The security upgrade is a *weakest-link public good*, whose effective supply is measured by the smallest provision level (Hirshleifer, 1983).

Consider the game depicted in Figure 4.10, where each target has two strategies: introduce a security upgrade to its airport screening or maintain current screening devices and procedures. Further suppose that the upgrade costs 6 but provides benefits of 8 to each country only when *both* targets adopt the upgrade. Unilateral adoption implies costs of 6 with no benefits. The resulting game is an assurance game. In Figure 4.10, there is no dominant strategy, because the payoffs in either row (column) are not both greater than the country's corresponding payoffs in the other row (column). There are, however, two Nash equilibriums along the main diagonal where strategy choices are matched – either no upgrade is introduced, or both airports adopt the upgrade. Obviously, the mutual-upgrade equilibrium improves the well-being of both targets over the status quo. If the US leads and adopts the upgrade, then the EU is better off in doing the same (a payoff of 2 exceeds that of 0). Matching behavior is the hallmark of weakest-link public goods, since it is senseless to exceed the smallest level of such goods: doing so incurs extra costs with no added benefits.

Next consider the case where each of two targets must choose among five levels of upgrade (including no upgrade), where each incremental upgrade gives 8 in additional benefits to both countries only when matched by the other player. Once again, suppose that every upgrade costs 6. The resulting game can be displayed in a 5×5 matrix (not shown) where all of the Nash equilibriums are along the diagonal where upgrade levels are matched. If, for example, each country adopts three upgrade levels, then each gains a net payoff of 6 [$= (3 \times 8) - (3 \times 6)$]. Suppose that one target country has more-limited means than another. This country chooses the security level that it can afford, which may be a rather low standard of safety. The wealthier country can either match this level or subsidize the security upgrade in the other country.[18] If the level chosen by the poorer country is unacceptable to the rich country, then fostering the former's security is the logical choice. One of the four pillars of US counterterrorism policy is to "bolster the counterterrorist capabilities of those countries that work with the United States and require assistance" (US Department of State, 2003, p. xi). If, instead, two hundred countries must provide a weakest-link security activity, then shoring up the many weakest links becomes an expensive proposition that we address in Chapter 6.

For domestic terrorism, the weakest-link issue is addressed by having the central government impose and coordinate acceptable standards countrywide. The training and deployment of professional federal screeners responded to the obvious vulnerabilities at Logan, Newark, and Dulles airports demonstrated on 9/11. The creation of DHS was motivated, in part, by the goal of achieving acceptable levels of interdependent security risks countrywide.[19]

Interdependent risks abound in the study of counterterrorism. Many defensive actions involve such risks – for example, screening transferred luggage between airlines and airports, limiting the vulnerability of a network, and guarding ports of entry. Although weakest-link public goods tend to be tied to defensive measures, they may occasionally be associated with a proactive policy. For example, the least discreet intelligence-gathering operation may jeopardize everyone's efforts by putting the terrorists on notice. Moreover, efforts to freeze terrorists' assets can be severely compromised by inadequate action at some financial safe havens.

In some situations, the concept of a *weaker-link public good* may apply if efforts above the lowest add some benefits to a counterterrorist action. If, on average, more luggage is transferred at airport A, then extra measures there may compensate somewhat for lower standards elsewhere. At a few airports, efforts to rescreen all transferred luggage limit interdependent risks and provide for greater payoffs from higher levels of vigilance. With weaker-link public goods, equilibriums may include some nonmatching

---

[18] For an analysis of in-kind transfers of weakest-link public goods, see Vicary (1990) and Vicary and Sandler (2002).

[19] How well interdependent security risks are reduced in practice also depends on the screening technology given to the professional screeners. US governmental reports released in 2005 reveal that screening still has significant vulnerabilities as privacy is preserved. The same continues to be true in 2011.

policy combinations. The extent of nonmatching outcomes hinges on the degree to which extra efforts at one venue can compensate for inadequate actions elsewhere.

BEST-SHOT CONSIDERATIONS

Some counterterrorism policies are *best-shot public goods*, where the largest provision amount determines the benefits of all potential targets. Again, consider the case of transnational terrorism in which countries are confronted with a threat from the same terrorist network. The gathering of intelligence and the infiltration of the network – two proactive measures – are often best-shot public goods whose benefits depend on the greatest effort. If, for example, the group is infiltrated, its security is compromised and the group presents a reduced threat for all targets. Often the greatest effort accomplishes this outcome; additional effort by others once the group is infiltrated adds no extra benefits. Another example is the development of a security innovation, such as stun grenades or a bomb-sniffing device. The best-performing innovation will be adopted by all at-risk nations; less adequate or identical innovations offer no additional benefits.

In Figure 4.11, we display a security-innovation game where each of two targets can maintain the status quo or discover a security breakthrough that can protect both targets. Suppose that the innovation costs the innovator 4 and provides benefits of 6 to each potential target. Further suppose that a second discovery of this innovation costs the discoverer 4, but yields no further benefits. In the game box, the sole innovator nets 2, while the other target gains a free-rider benefit of 6. If both innovate, then each receives just 2, as each must cover its innovation costs. The same kind of payoff scenario characterizes infiltrating a group, because a second infiltration is costly but does not necessarily weaken the terrorist group any more than the first. The same is true of redundant intelligence.

There is no dominant strategy in the two-target innovation game, but there are two Nash equilibriums where there is a sole innovator. The bold-faced payoffs for these equilibriums lie along the off-diagonal. If the innovation scenario involves, say, twenty countries, then the equilibriums consist of just one country making the discovery and the others adopting it. The resulting game is a *coordination* game in which the countries must tacitly decide who is to expend the effort so that resources are not wasted in duplication. Often the innovation or group infiltration comes from the most threatened country. If the required effort is large enough to surpass the

	EU	
	Status quo	Innovate
US Status quo	0, 0	**6, 2**
Innovate	**2, 6**	2, 2

Figure 4.11. Best-shot security innovation.

capabilities of the prime-target country, then international cooperation and a pooling of effort may be necessary.

For domestic terrorism, the coordination is achieved by the central government orchestrating efforts to eliminate duplication. The rationale behind the creation of an intelligence czar and a single entity to coordinate the various intelligence-gathering agencies in the United States is to limit duplication and increase efficiency. The failure to identify the underwear bomber in December 2009, despite many tell-tale warnings, indicates that the US intelligence system is still deficient.

Private firms play an essential role in developing technological innovations useful to counterterrorism. At times, their research and development is subsidized by the government in order to reduce investment risk to the firm. The best technology can then be sold by the firms to governments worldwide in order to increase safety. Currently, firms are developing practical biofeedback screening devices that can identify people based on their eyes and other unique features.

TERRORISM AT HOME: WHAT TO PROTECT?

In recent years, researchers have asked how to allocate resources to protect myriad targets from terrorism.[20] Decisions must be made because even the best-funded government cannot protect every possible target. The question is especially interesting when there are two strategic (interacting) agents: the government and the terrorists. There are three considerations that determine the potential losses to a target from terrorism: the likelihood of an attack, the loss in case of a successful attack, and the vulnerability of the target. The vulnerability indicates the probability that a terrorist attack

---

[20] Important papers include Bier, Oliveros, and Samuelson (2007), Farrow (2007), Powell (2007), and Zhuang and Bier (2007). Also see Jindapon and Neilson (2009).

on the venue will succeed. As such, vulnerability can be reduced through defensive measures. The expected loss at target i is the product of the three considerations just mentioned. If, for example, there are only two targets, then one might suppose that the government should allocate its defensive measures in order to minimize its expected losses at the two targets. In a nonstrategic framework, this would work; however, with strategic terrorists, this is not the correct answer (Powell, 2007). The terrorists will favor attacking whichever target has the greater marginal expected loss, so that the marginal expected loss at the two targets must be equated in order to limit the terrorists' gain. This outcome need not occur where the government's losses are minimized. Powell broadened the analysis to include N potential targets and border defenses.

Bier, Oliveros, and Samuelson (2007) and Zhuang and Bier (2007) extended Powell's work by allowing for additional interdependencies: for example, the attacker's and defender's evaluations of the gains and losses from terrorism depend on attack efforts and target defenses at each potential target. These authors uncovered some important findings. First, terrorists and defenders may engage in escalating actions – that is, more defense induces greater attacks, so that a cease-fire may be mutually beneficial.[21] Second, the defender captures a strategic advantage by moving first so as to direct terrorist attacks to less valued, less defended targets. Third, governments should make their defensive outlays public, so that the terrorists know what has been hardened. Fourth, some targets are best left undefended because the expected losses to society are not large and defensive resources are scarce. This outcome is counter to DHS grant policy, which allocates large amounts of money to rural locations of limited value to the terrorists. Fifth, border defense must be evaluated in conjunction with individual sites, insofar as border security reduces the vulnerability of all sites. That is, border security provides a public benefit to all sites; thus, guarding borders and entry points has a high payoff.

FURTHER STRATEGIC ANALYSIS OF COUNTERTERRORISM

To keep the analysis simple, we have allowed only discrete counterterrorism decisions – that is, to preempt or not. In practice, governments can choose the level of proactive and defensive measures. This section presents the strategic analysis of such continuous choices, beginning with the level

---

[21] Terrorist network delegation, when associated with government policymaker delegation, has resulted in a similar escalation – see Siqueira and Sandler (2010).

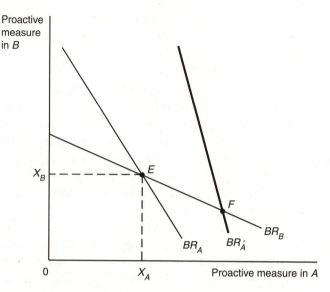

Figure 4.12. Proactive measures in two countries.

of proactive measures taken by two governments that confront the same terrorist threat.

Each of the targeted countries chooses its level of proaction, X_i, $i = A, B$, in order to minimize its costs, taking the other country's level of proaction as given. For a country, these costs usually consist of at least three components: the provision costs of proaction, the expected loss from a terrorist attack at home, and the expected loss from a terrorist attack on its interests abroad. Losses at home can be reduced through the country's own proactive measures, which weaken the terrorists. Such measures also reduce the *likelihood* of a terrorist attack at home and abroad, thereby providing purely public benefits to the other at-risk country.[22]

For each country, there is a best-response (BR_i) curve that relates a country's proactive choice to that of the other targeted country.[23] These reaction paths are downward-sloping, indicating that a country will reduce its proactive measures in response to increased proactive measures abroad. This follows because one country's proactive measures *substitute* for those in the other country. In Figure 4.12, we display the two downward-sloping

---

[22] For the mathematical details, see Arce and Sandler (2009), Sandler and Lapan (1988), and Sandler and Siqueira (2006).

[23] *A*'s best-response curve connects the minimum point of *A*'s isocost curves (not shown) for each level of *B*'s proactive efforts.

best-response curves – BR_A and BR_B. The Nash equilibrium is at E where the two curves intersect, with country A contributing X_A and country B contributing X_B. The relative slopes of the two reaction paths are consistent with a stable equilibrium, in which nonequilibrium levels of proactive efforts will return to the equilibrium.

Next, suppose that country A becomes a more favored target of the terrorists because of a foreign policy decision – say, a retaliatory raid by A against a state sponsor. This development shifts A's best-response curve out to the right to the thicker curve, BR_A', in Figure 4.12. The new equilibrium is at F, at which country A spends more on proactive measures and country B spends less on these measures, compared to expenditures at E. Enhanced risk to country A results in that country assuming a relatively greater share of the war on terror. Our analysis is entirely consistent with prime-target nations taking on the lion's share of proactive efforts against a common transnational terrorist threat. The optimal level of proactive measures involves proactive spending combinations northeast of E and F, so that both countries choose their efforts while accounting for the external benefits that they confer on other targeted countries.

Next, we consider defensive actions by two nations facing a common terrorist threat. Once again, each country minimizes the sum of its provision costs and losses from attacks at home and abroad. Provision costs now concern defensive measures at home. Unlike the proactive case, homeland defense shifts terrorist attacks abroad, thereby raising the likelihood of an attack on foreign soil. This constitutes a negative externality as one country's defensive actions impose costs on another country. In Figure 4.13, we display the two best-response paths, which are positively sloped (Sandler and Lapan, 1988; Sandler and Siqueira, 2006). Defensive measures are *complements*, because increased protection abroad makes a country a more desirable target unless it also augments its own defenses. Hence, countries that can afford to do so will increase their defenses as other countries increase their defenses. If countries have limited interests abroad, then there is a proclivity to overspend on defense. With many countries, terrorists will direct their attacks over time to those countries least able to secure their borders and take adequate defensive measures. This has been the case empirically after 9/11 with transnational attacks moving from Europe to the Middle East and Asia (Enders and Sandler, 2006).

In Figure 4.13, the Nash equilibrium is at E, with D_A defense in country A and D_B defense in country B. If, say, country A perceives a greater risk from transnational terrorism, then its best-response path will shift to the right (not shown), where country A increases its defense for each level of

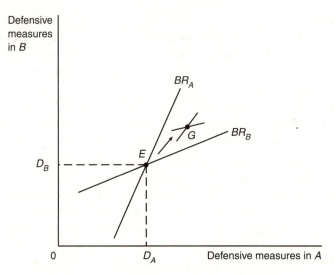

Figure 4.13. Defensive measures in two countries.

defense in country *B*. The new equilibrium involves country *A* increasing its defenses by more than the induced rise in country *B*'s defenses. Terrorists' innovations – for example, ways of circumventing technological barriers – will shift BR_A to the right and BR_B to the left. Both countries will subsequently enhance their defenses – see equilibrium *G*, where small segments of the shifted reaction paths are displayed.

Terrorists versus the Government

Best-response paths can also be applied when a terrorist group, *T*, confronts a targeted government, *G*, in the case of domestic or transnational terrorism.[24] The terrorists choose a level of attacks, *a*, while the government exerts counterterrorism efforts, *e*. In Figure 4.14, the terrorist group's best-response path, BR_T, is downward-sloping, so that the group reduces its attacks as the government increases its proactive campaign. By contrast, the government's best-response path, BR_G, is upward-sloping; increased terrorist attacks are met with greater proactive measures. The Nash equilibrium is at *E*. Thus, we have a mixed case where the two choice variables are strategic substitutes from the terrorist group's viewpoint and strategic complements from the government's vantage.

---

[24] Examples include the analysis in Siqueira and Sandler (2006, 2010).

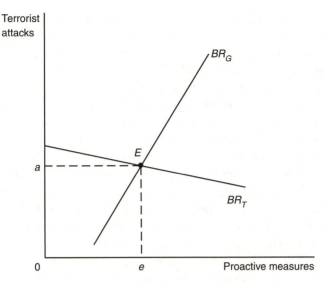

Figure 4.14. Terrorists versus the government.

Other scenarios are conceivable. For example, a weak government, with little stomach to fight the terrorists, may display a downward-sloping best-response path in which the government reduces proactive measures as the terrorist group increases its attacks. Alternatively, an audacious terrorist group may increase attacks as the government goes after the group's resources, which characterized Hezbollah's response to Israeli offensives. Many outcomes are possible depending on the resolve of the two adversaries. Shifts in the two best-response paths can come from outside influences. In Figure 4.14, state sponsorship of terrorists shifts BR_T up, while outside foreign assistance to a besieged government shifts BR_G down and to the right. The outcome of such shifts depends on the orientation of the two best-response paths – myriad outcomes are possible.

GETTING AT THE ROOTS OF TERRORISM

Another counterterrorism action is to address the grievances of the terrorists, thereby eliminating their rationale for violence. There are a number of difficulties with accommodating terrorists' demands. First, such accommodations may induce countergrievances and a new wave of terrorism by those who are harmed by the government's concessions. Second, granting concessions sends the message that violence pays and encourages more terrorism. When deciding between legal and terrorist means, a terrorist group accounts for the likelihood of success of alternative techniques. By granting concessions, the government is raising the perceived likelihood of success of terrorist tactics (see Chapter 7). Third, terrorist grievances must be well articulated if they are to be satisfied; this is often not the case for modern-day transnational terrorism. For example, the grievances of al-Qaida are not clear and appear to evolve over time. Fourth, countries' responses to terrorists' demands are apt to work at cross purposes – for example, a country that removes its peacekeepers in response to a terrorist campaign makes it more difficult for other countries to continue their missions. After the 23 October 1983 bombing of the US Marine barracks in Beirut, Lebanon, President Reagan withdrew US forces from Lebanon on 26 February 1984 and other countries (for example, France) followed suit. At the transnational level, one country's concessions create externalities for other countries as their policy options become more limited.

A more fruitful approach is to make nonterrorist activities less expensive and therefore more attractive, rather than to reward terrorist campaigns through concessions (Anderton and Carter, 2005; Frey, 2004). The latter goes against the principles of liberal democracy by allowing dissidents to circumvent the political process by extorting political change with the threat of violence. Such concessions reduce the payoffs to voting and utilizing legitimate institutions for change. By contrast, government's encouragement of peaceful dissent raises the attractiveness of legal means. Ironically, when terrorism surfaces in a country, a common governmental reaction is to limit legitimate protest, thereby inducing more terrorism. Terrorist groups with political and military wings – for example, Hezbollah, Hamas, and the ETA – pursue both legitimate and illegitimate means. Thus, actions to bolster the relative attractiveness of legitimate means can curb terrorism without compromising the ideals of a liberal democracy by rewarding terrorism.

CONCLUDING REMARKS

This chapter has applied simple game theory in order to analyze strategic differences between proactive and defensive policies. For transnational terrorism, the policy choices of a targeted government can have positive and/or negative consequences or externalities for other targeted countries. For instance, defensive measures taken by one country can deflect an attack to other, less protected countries. Following 9/11, industrial countries redoubled efforts to harden targets; these efforts coincided with more attacks in other places – for example, Kenya, Morocco, Malaysia,

Indonesia, Saudi Arabia, and Turkey – where defensive measures were not increased. At the international level, there is a real need for cooperation; otherwise, countries will work at cross purposes with a tendency to under-supply proactive measures and oversupply defensive ones. Some defensive actions are weakest-link public goods, where the smallest precaution taken determines the level of safety for all. To shore up a weakest link, wealthy nations may have to bolster the defenses of other nations. In a globalized world, a country's interests can be attacked where defenses are inadequate, so weakest-link nations are everyone's concern. Many proactive policies are best-shot public goods, where the greatest action protects everyone. For such measures, coordination is important so that actions are not dupli-cated in a wasteful manner.

In the case of domestic terrorism, the central government can account for the strategic consequences arising from proactive and defensive poli-cies. A central viewpoint allows the government to raise security to accept-able standards countrywide. The central government is motivated to pursue terrorists who target any of the countries' diverse interests. When address-ing domestic terrorism, a government is anticipated to apply the appropri-ate *mix* of proactive and defensive measures. The government understands that effective proactive spending curtails the continual need for expen-sive defense outlays. Once the terrorist threat is eliminated, government resources can be redirected to other pressing social needs.

The study of counterterrorism is a very active research area with many new topics. Recently, game-theoretic models have investigated the use of foreign aid as a counterterrorism tool.[25] After 9/11, the United States directed a sizable portion of its aid to countries that assisted in the war on terror – examples included Afghanistan, Pakistan, Sudan, Egypt, the Philippines, and Yemen (Fleck and Kilby, 2010). Aid as a counterterror-ism tool raises some important questions. What form should this aid take? Should it support education or should it bolster a recipient's ability to fight a resident terrorist group? Clearly, the form of the aid can affect the stability of the recipient country's regime. Counterterrorism-tied aid can be desta-bilizing, while general poverty-reducing aid can be stabilizing. In addition, counterterrorism aid affects the need for homeland security, because the elimination of transnational terrorist groups that target a donor nation curbs the need for defensive measures at home. Other counterterrorism issues involve the value of intelligence (Arce and Sandler, 2007, 2010) and the benefits of profiling.

---

[25] See Azam and Thelen (2010) and Bandyopadhyay, Sandler, and Younas (2011).

FIVE

Transference

Contraband such as automatic and semiautomatic machine guns, bazookas, hand grenades, suicide vests, and hand-held rocket launchers can easily fit into a ship's cargo container. The Department of Homeland Security (DHS) is understandably worried about these potential terrorist weapons reaching US shores. The Container Security Initiative (CSI) is designed to secure US ports against the importation of these and other dangerous materials (see Chapter 11 on homeland security). With the cooperation of its trading partners, US inspectors in port cities such as Rotterdam, Singapore, and Hong Kong inspect and label cargo before it reaches US shores. The CSI is predicated, in part, on the notion that terrorists make choices by taking costs and benefits into account. If it is more difficult to smuggle weapons aboard a commercial plane or by air freight, terrorists will seek out a "weaker link" or softer target. Thus, unless US ports of entry become more secure, DHS predicts that enhanced airport security will make US ports a weaker link.

The bombing of the three train stations in Madrid on 11 March 2004 is another instance of terrorists finding a weaker link. The bombs, designed to explode during rush hour, left 191 dead and injured more than 1,200 others. The coverage in the Spanish press and the effects on the Spanish psyche rivaled the influence of 9/11 in the United States. One indirect consequence of the attack was the unanticipated victory of the Socialists over the ruling Partido Popular party. Why did al-Qaida decide to attack rail passengers? One rationale given for the train station bombings was that terrorists found that skyjacking was too difficult and too risky to be successful. The main Atocha train station and the two smaller stations were softer targets.

As analyzed in this chapter, the search for weak links is an important type of policy-induced substitution. Social scientists refer to this behavior as "transference." In the two examples just mentioned, enhanced airport security resulted in a transference from airline-related crimes to those involving other forms of transportation. In a sense, the unintended consequence of many government policies designed to thwart one type of terrorist behavior is to cause an increase in another type of terrorism. As one type of attack declines, policymakers need to anticipate transference effects in order to protect the public from new attack modes.

MODELS OF RATIONAL TERRORISM

To forecast new types of terrorist attack modes, the number and severity of future incidents, or the likely behavior of terrorists in response to a shift in government policy, we must posit a rational-choice theory of terrorist behavior. If terrorists are completely irrational, there is no way of knowing how they will respond to future events. By contrast, the rational-agent model has a number of straightforward predictions that have proven to be correct. In Chapter 3, we saw that the installation of metal detectors in airports was associated with a reduction in the number of skyjackings. However, as we will consider in more detail, once skyjackings became more difficult, terrorists substituted into other, logistically similar attack modes. This transference follows directly from the assumption that terrorists are rational.

There are only two essential ingredients of rational behavior. The first is that the agent has a well-defined set of preferences, which requires that the individual is able to rank, or order, the alternative feasible choices. Consider an individual, say Justin, who has preferences over three baskets of goods, A, B, and C. For these rankings to be sensible, they must be internally consistent. If Justin prefers basket A to basket B and basket B to basket C, Justin must then prefer A to C in order for his preferences to be consistent – a condition of rationality. Unless this so-called transitivity condition is satisfied, the ordering is meaningless. The second essential ingredient of rationality is that the individual selects the most preferred of the available choices. If, therefore, Justin is presented with the equally affordable choice of A or C, then rationality requires that he selects A if he prefers A to C. Rationality does not require that we answer the question "Why does he prefer A?" or "Should he prefer A?" Moreover, a rational individual may have preferences that change over time. Some have claimed (see Caplan, 2006) that rationality requires that terrorists act in their narrow self-interest. However, as we shall see in the following discussion concerning suicide attacks, rationality allows for the possibility that terrorists act on behalf of their groups' or family members' welfare.

The rational-choice model posits that terrorists will allocate their scarce resources so as to maximize the expected value of their utility. Landes (1978) was the first to explicitly model the behavior of a potential skyjacker contemplating the forceful diversion of a commercial aircraft. To take a simplified version of his model, suppose there are three states of the world: the skyjacking is not undertaken, the skyjacking is successful, and the skyjacking fails. Landes is not especially concerned about the ultimate goals or motives of the terrorist. Simply, suppose that U^S is the terrorist's utility if the skyjacking is successful and that U^F is the terrorist's utility if the skyjacking fails. The utility of a success obviously exceeds that of a failure, so that $U^S > U^F$. A key aspect of the choice is that skyjackings have an uncertain outcome. The potential skyjacker believes that the probability of a successful skyjacking is π and that the probability of an unsuccessful skyjacking is $(1 - \pi)$.

The rational terrorist will compare the expected utility of the skyjacking to the next-best alternative. To highlight the risky nature of a skyjacking, we assume that utility in the no-skyjacking state is the certain value U^N. The decision tree for the terrorist's actions is displayed in Figure 5.1. If the terrorist chooses not to undertake the skyjacking, the payoff is U^N. If the skyjacking is undertaken, the terrorist receives U^S with probability π and U^F with probability $(1 - \pi)$. Hence, the expected utility of undertaking the skyjacking is

$$EU^{SKY} = \pi U^S + (1 - \pi)U^F, \tag{5.1}$$

where EU^{SKY} is the expected utility if the skyjacking occurs.

The skyjacking will be undertaken if the expected utility from skyjacking exceeds U^N.[1] Hence, the skyjacking will occur if

$$U^N < EU^{SKY} = \pi U^S + (1 - \pi)U^F. \tag{5.2}$$

An increase in U^N or a decrease in EU^{SKY} reduces the likelihood that the terrorist will attempt a skyjacking. A policy that reduces the utility of a skyjacking success, such as a guaranteed refusal never to concede to terrorists, reduces EU^{SKY} (see Chapter 7). If a terrorist group seeks media coverage for its cause, then government actions to limit the potential for such coverage also reduce U^S and, thus, skyjackings. A policy that reduces the utility

---

[1] Throughout, we assume that terrorists are risk-neutral in the sense that they are indifferent to taking a fair bet. Of course, if terrorists are sufficiently risk-averse (so that they would not undertake a fair bet), they might not undertake a skyjacking even if the expected utility from skyjacking exceeds U^N.

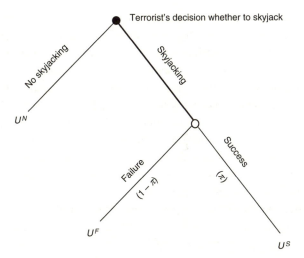

Figure 5.1. Expected utility of a potential skyjacker.

of a failure, such as longer jail sentences, reduces EU^{SKY} and skyjackings. Given that $U^S > U^F$, a policy that reduces the probability of a success, such as enhanced airport security, reduces EU^{SKY}.[2] In addition, concessions granted to a terrorist can encourage future terrorist acts by raising terrorists' perceptions of the utility associated with a skyjacking success. The concession might also induce subsequent skyjackers to perceive that the probability of success is higher. A policy that increases utility in the no-skyjacking state, such as alleviating some portion of the terrorist's grievances, reduces the incentive for terrorism.

Landes (1978) obtained US Federal Aviation Administrative (FAA) data and estimated two regression equations for US skyjackings for the 1961–1976 period. The first regressed the quarterly total of skyjackings on policy variables such as the probability of apprehension, the probability of conviction, and a measure of the severity of sentencing. Recall from Chapter 3 that a regression uses data to explain the variation in a dependent or response variable (for example, the quarterly number of skyjackings) based on the values of a number of independent or control variables. Landes's second equation regressed the time interval between skyjackings on the same set of variables. Both regressions found the length of sentence and the probability of apprehension to be significant deterrents to skyjackings. The probability

---

[2] Given that $EU^{SKY} = \pi U^S + (1 - \pi)U^F$, it follows that $dEU^{SKY}/d\pi = U^S - U^F > 0$. Hence, decreasing (increasing) π, decreases (increases) EU^{SKY}.

of conviction was only marginally significant. One of his key findings was that between forty-one and fifty fewer skyjackings occurred in the United States following the installation of metal detectors in US airports in 1973.

Enders and Sandler (1993) generalize Landes's framework to allow for substitutions between terrorist and nonterrorist activities *and* for substitutions within the set of terrorist activities. Specifically, they use the household production function (HPF) model to analyze the behavior of a terrorist group whose utility is derived from a shared political goal. This shared goal is obtained from the consumption of a number of *basic commodities* such as media attention, political instability, popular support for their cause, and the creation of an atmosphere of fear and intimidation.

Each basic commodity can be produced using a number of political strategies that include various types of terrorist and nonterrorist activities. At one extreme, the group might simply choose to turn out voters for local elections or to run their own candidates for office. Alternatively, nonterrorist acts of civil disobedience might be undertaken – protesters might block the entrance to a government building, or refuse to ride in the back of a bus in Selma, Alabama. At the other extreme, the group might resort to bombings, hostage takings, or assassinations. Some groups, such as the Irish Republican Army (IRA), simultaneously produce basic commodities using terrorist *and* nonterrorist means. The provisional wing of the IRA has engaged in numerous acts of domestic and transnational terrorism. Sinn Féin (meaning "Ourselves Alone" in Gaelic) is generally considered to be the political wing of the IRA. Under Gerry Adams's leadership, Sinn Féin has moved away from serving as a support base for the Provisional IRA to become a professionally organized political party in both Northern Ireland and the Republic of Ireland. Similarly, Hezbollah provides Lebanese Shiites with schooling, medical care, and support for agricultural production.

The point is that the group can be modeled as having a well-defined set of preferences over terrorist activities (T) and nonterrorist activities (N). Increases in terrorist activities and nonterrorist activities both augment the production of basic commodities and, hence, the utility of terrorists. We can write these preferences in the form of the utility function U:[3]

$$U = U(T, N). \qquad (5.3)$$

Terrorist activities are actually a composite good consisting of a number of different attack modes that can be substitutable if they are capable of

---

[3] An alternative way to present the model is to let the group receive utility from two basic commodities, B_1 and B_2. If the basic commodities are produced by T and N, the group's utility is an implicit function of T and N.

producing the same basic commodities. Substitution is most likely to take place between modes that are logistically similar and yield similar basic commodities. Kidnappings and skyjackings tend to be good substitutes, since both are logistically complex incident types that can result in similar amounts of media attention (see Chapter 7). Attack modes will be complements if they are essential ingredients for the production of a single basic commodity or if they reinforce each other's effectiveness. Bombings and threats tend to be complementary. In response to a bombing campaign, terrorists often make threatening calls to the media and to the authorities, since these low-cost threats heighten the tension associated with the actual detonation of the bombs.

The Resource Constraint

A terrorist group has access to resources that may include direct financial wealth, capital equipment including weapons and buildings, personnel, and entrepreneurial skills. During any period, a group's total outlays cannot exceed the total of these monetary and nonmonetary resources. The terrorist group, thus, faces the same resource allocation problems as any household because the selection of one set of activities precludes the group from selecting some other activities. The group must decide whether to produce basic commodities by terrorist or nonterrorist means, or by some combination of the two. The group must also choose among the various types of terrorist activities. For example, a group bent on attracting media attention can select between a skyjacking, a kidnapping, or a suicide bombing. Since terrorists can expend or augment their resources in the current period or "save" their resources for future attacks, rational terrorists time their attacks in order to enhance their overall effectiveness. Moreover, terrorists are able to attack domestically or abroad. From the set of activities consistent with its total resource holdings, a rational terrorist group selects the one that maximizes its expected utility.

The choices made by the group will be influenced by the prices of the various terrorist and nonterrorist activities. The full price of any particular attack mode includes the value of the resources used to plan and execute the attack and the cost of casualties to group members. The simultaneous attack on the three Madrid train stations was a high-priced incident because it required a substantial amount of planning and coordination. Certain attack modes are more likely than others to expose the group's membership to capture. The price of a suicide bombing includes the direct cost of the bomb, the cost of grooming the perpetrator to ensure that the attack takes place, and the cost of protecting the group's security in case of a failed attack. At the other end of the spectrum, threats and hoaxes typically require few inputs. The effectiveness of an attack mode is not necessarily commensurate with its price. In the months following 9/11, a number of people opened packages containing various powders disguised as anthrax. The cost of some baby powder, an envelope, and a stamp caused recipients to feel the same fear, and caused the authorities to undertake the same precautions, as if the powder had been real.

Transference occurs because the prices and payoffs faced by terrorists can be influenced by a government's antiterrorism policies. Enhanced airport security increases the logistical complexity of a skyjacking and raises its price. If, at the same time, governments do not increase security at ports of entry, attacks relying on contraband become relatively cheaper. If, similarly, immigration officials make it more difficult for terrorists to enter the United States, a terrorist group might attack US interests located abroad (for example, tourists and firms). Hence, a government policy that increases the price of one type of attack mode will induce a substitution away from that mode into other logistically similar incident types. In order to induce the group to substitute from terrorist to nonterrorist activities, policymakers must raise the price of all types of attack modes or lower the price of nonterrorist activities (for example, providing easier access to elections).

We conclude this section with the example of the 9 September 2004 car bombing outside the Australian embassy in Jakarta, Indonesia. At least 9 people were killed and more than 150 were wounded by an explosion that left a crater nine feet deep. Australia has been a strong US ally and has sent troops to support the war in Iraq. According to the *New York Times* (10 September 2004, p. A10), an Australian official stated that the al-Qaida-linked group Jemaah Islamiyah had selected the Australian embassy as a target because "it was easier to hit than the US embassy."

A FORMALIZATION OF THE MODEL

We can formalize the HPF model by combining the group's indifference curves with its budget constraint. The indifference curve labeled 1 in Figure 5.2 shows the amounts of terrorist attacks (T) and nonterrorist actions (N) necessary to produce a given level of the group's shared political goal or utility. Each indifference curve has a negative slope, since T and N both aid in the production of the basic commodity. If, therefore, T increases, then N must decrease or else the terrorist group would produce more of the basic commodity and end up on a higher indifference curve. An increased use of

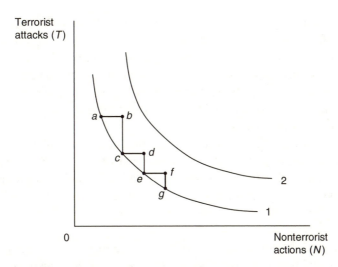

Figure 5.2. Indifference curves for terrorist and nonterrorist actions.

one type of input allows the group to reduce its use of the other input and still maintain the same utility level. If a terrorist group were contemplating increasing N by the amount ab, it could maintain the same level of utility by reducing T by bc units.

If the inputs were perfect substitutes, the indifference curves would be linear, since one unit of T could always be traded off for a fixed amount of N. All of the indifference curves in Figure 5.2 are, however, convex to the origin, because each extra unit of N has to replace ever smaller amounts of T if the terrorists are to maintain a given level of the basic commodity or utility. That is, the ability of one input to substitute for the other input diminishes as more of the former input is utilized. Notice that in moving from a to c and then from c to e, each equal increment in nonterrorist activities ($ab = cd$) releases successively smaller amounts of input from terrorist attacks, as $bc > de$. Similarly, a movement from e to g would require ef units of N but would free up only fg additional units of T. Since $ef = cd$ but $de > fg$, indifference curve 1 is convex to the origin throughout its entire range.[4]

---

[4] The convexity is consistent with the law of diminishing marginal productivity. The marginal productivity of an input diminishes if its successive application results in smaller and smaller increments of the basic commodity. Beginning on indifference curve 1, the successive application of ab, cd, and ef units of N results in smaller and smaller additional units of the basic commodity. As a result, smaller and smaller amounts of T can be withdrawn from the production process if output of the basic commodity is to remain constant.

The group's utility will increase if it can move from indifference curve 1 to indifference curve 2. If you compare the two curves, you will see that indifference curve 2 entails a greater utilization of inputs than does 1. For any point you select on indifference curve 1, there is a point on curve 2 with more T and N. Since both inputs contribute to the production of the basic commodity, the level of utility associated with indifference curve 2 is higher than the level associated with 1.

The issue for the terrorists is to choose the combination of T and N that maximizes their expected utility. Rational terrorists will combine the information contained in the indifference map with their budget constraint. As in Chapter 4, we can let the budget constraint of the terrorist group be

$$P_T T + P_N N = I, \tag{5.4}$$

where P_T and P_N are the unit costs of a generic terrorist incident (T) or non-terrorist action (N), respectively, and I is the group's income or resources for the current period.

In Figure 5.3, we superimpose the budget constraint from Figure 4.1 on the indifference map of Figure 5.2. The budget constraint, AB, is like a menu in that it indicates the feasible combinations available to the terrorists. The terrorists can allocate all of their income to terrorist attacks (producing $0A$ attacks), all of their income to nonterrorist actions (producing $0B$ units of N), or some of their income to both activities (corresponding to some point on the line AB). As shown, the optimal or best choice for the terrorist group is point R, where the group engages in $0T_0$ units of terrorist attacks and $0N_0$ units of nonterrorist activities. A few moments reflection will show why R is the optimal choice. Any movement away from R along AB (so that total expenditures are maintained) results in a lower utility level than that enjoyed on indifference curve 2, as lower indifference curves are reached. Given its budget constraint, the group would never select a suboptimal point such as S on indifference curve 1. Moreover, since the indifference curves further from the origin than curve 2 are unattainable with expenditure level I, the group can do no better than to select point R.

Now we are in a position to revisit the concept of proactive and defensive policies. Remember that defensive policies, such as the installation of metal detectors and bomb-detecting devices in airports, protect potential targets either by making attacks more costly for terrorists or by reducing their likelihood of success. Figure 5.4 illustrates the situation in which a bomb-detecting device raises the price of a terrorist act without reducing the level of the group's resources. Consequently, the budget constraint rotates from AB to BC. Notice that the original choice (R) is no longer attainable. Instead,

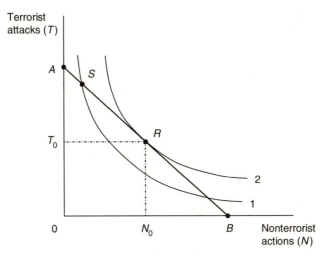

Figure 5.3. The optimal allocation.

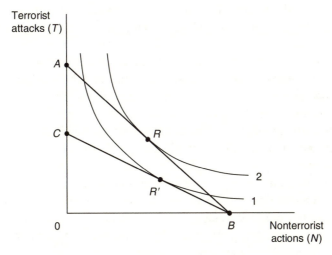

Figure 5.4. Increasing the cost of terrorist attacks.

the new rational choice for the terrorist group occurs at point R'. As drawn, the policy induces terrorists to reduce the level of terrorist attacks *and* to increase nonterrorist activities.[5]

[5] Notice that there is an ambiguity about the change in the level of N. In Figure 5.4, we could have drawn the indifference curves so that N falls. Because the relative price of nonterrorist activities decreases, there is a substitution into N and away from T. However, the group's opportunity set shifts inward from AB to BC. If we assume that T and N are

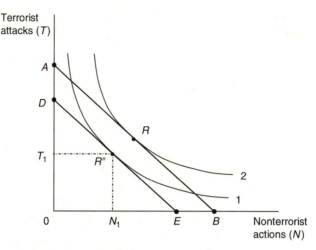

Figure 5.5. Reduction in terrorists' resources.

Some proactive policies also raise the price of terrorist actions. As mentioned in Chapter 4, an increased risk of being infiltrated by the government makes terrorist acts more costly without necessarily changing the terrorists' resource endowments. Rotating the budget constraint in Figure 5.4 from AB to BC represents such a circumstance. In that case, both a defensive and a proactive policy could induce a terrorist group to select R' instead of R. Unlike defensive measures, proactive policies can reduce the total income of the terrorist group. Certainly, the terrorists' resource holdings decline when the government captures or kills group members, cuts off the group's funding, or destroys weapons, safe havens, and infrastructure. In Figure 5.5, the reduction in the group's income is represented by the parallel shift of the budget constraint from AB to DE. The decline in total resources means that the opportunities to engage in terrorist *and* nonterrorist acts have decreased. The terrorist group now chooses point R'', engaging in T_1 units of terrorism and N_1 nonterrorist activities.

Without a careful empirical investigation, there is no simple way to determine which type of policy (proactive or defensive) is the most appropriate. The success of any antiterrorism policy depends on how successful it is in

normal goods, then the resulting negative "income effect" reduces the amounts of T and N produced. The amount of T unambiguously falls, since the relative price of T increases and the group's real income has fallen. The effect of the decrease in the relative price of N and the decrease in the group's real income have, however, opposing effects on the amount of N ultimately produced. As discussed in footnote 7, the importance of this income effect increases as the group becomes increasingly specialized in terrorism.

restricting the terrorists' choice set. The HPF approach makes it clear that policies having no effect on the group's resource constraint or preferences will be completely ineffective. Consider the United Nations' International Convention Against the Taking of Hostages that was open for signatures in 1973 (approved on 17 December 1979). The key provision of the convention is that:

Each State Party is required to make this offence [hostage taking] punishable by appropriate penalties. Where hostages are held in the territory of a State Party, the State Party is obligated to take all measures it considers appropriate to ease the situation of the hostages and secure their release. After the release of the hostages, States Parties are obligated to facilitate the departure of the hostages. Each State Party is obligated to take such actions as may be necessary to establish jurisdiction over the offence of taking of hostages. (United Nations, 2010)[6]

Although the goals of the convention are laudable, the United Nations itself has no direct enforcement mechanism; rather, it is left to each member to take "appropriate" actions to secure the release of hostages. Consequently, there may be different levels of enforcement depending on the signatories' attitudes toward terrorism. This results in an important loophole, since many nations have registered objections to one or more portions of the convention. For example, Lebanon worried that the convention's provision might compromise the means that a state can bring to bear on foreign occupiers. Given these circumstances, we might expect that the overall effect of the convention was nil, since it had no effect on terrorists' budget constraints. As mentioned in Chapters 3 and 6, past empirical tests have found no overall effect of this and similar conventions.

The model also allows for the possibility that the group fully specializes in one of the activities. If the group's preferences are such that the indifference curves are vertical (horizontal), then it will devote all of its resources to N (T). The group's indifference curves would be perfectly vertical if it received no benefit from T, and they would be perfectly horizontal if it received no benefit from N.

So far, we have considered only substitutions between terrorist and nonterrorist activities. The household production function approach also allows for substitutions among the various attack modes. Notice that little would be changed if we redrew Figures 5.4 and 5.5 using two different attack modes as the decision variables. Instead of T and N, skyjackings (Sky) might be on the vertical axis and other terrorist actions (O) on the

---

[6] This representation of the treaty's key provisions splices together statements from the convention. The treaty's text can be found in United Nations (2010).

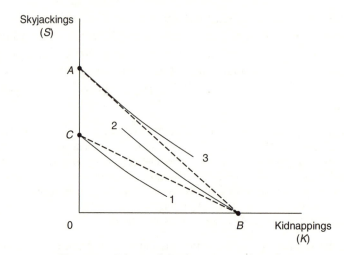

Figure 5.6. Substitutability between attack modes.

horizontal axis. Figure 5.4 would then show that an increase in the price of skyjackings would cause a substitution away from that attack mode and into other terrorist acts. The redrawn Figure 5.5 would show that a reduction in the group's expenditures on terrorist activities would be represented by a parallel shift of the expenditure line toward the origin. If both attack modes were normal, then the amount of *Sky* and *O* would decline.

Instead of being normal, some attack modes are inferior in the sense that their use is negatively related to the group's level of resources. Threats and low-level bombings tend to be used by groups with very limited resources. As groups' resource levels grow, they tend to reduce these types of attacks and engage in logistically complex actions.

A critical prediction of the HPF model is that a high degree of substitutability among attack modes reduces the effectiveness of antiterrorism policies directed to only one of the modes. Figure 5.6 depicts the trade-off between kidnappings (*K*) and skyjackings (*S*) for a hypothetical terrorist group seeking media coverage. The indifference curves are downward-sloping, since a reduction in *S* will necessitate an increase in *K* if the group is to maintain a particular level of utility from media attention. As drawn, indifference curves 1, 2, and 3 cut the horizontal and vertical axes, since neither attack mode is essential. If the group wants to spend an amount such that the budget constraint is the dashed line *AB*, then there will be a corner solution; the group selects point *A* on indifference curve 3, where it fully specializes in skyjackings. Now consider the effects of a defensive policy, such as installation of enhanced screening devices, that makes it more costly to conduct a skyjacking. In particular, suppose that the increased cost of a skyjacking is such that the budget constraint becomes the dashed line *BC*. Given its total resource endowment, the terrorist group now fully specializes in kidnappings by producing at point *B* on indifference curve 2. Total media attention falls (indifference curve 2 entails less media attention than 3), but not as much as in the case where substitutability is low. If the group could not substitute any kidnappings for skyjackings, it would necessarily produce at point *C* on indifference curve 1. Hence, when substitution possibilities are high, terrorists can readily circumvent a policy that raises the price of only one attack mode. An effective antiterrorism policy is one that raises the costs of *all* attack modes or reduces the overall resource level of the terrorists.

Enders and Sandler (1993) summarize the four main propositions of the model as follows:

Proposition 1: Relative Price Effects. An increase in the relative price of one type of terrorist activity will cause the terrorist group to substitute out of the relatively expensive activity and into terrorist and nonterrorist activities that are now relatively less expensive.

Proposition 2: Substitutes and Complements. Terrorist attack modes that are logistically similar and yield similar basic commodities will display the greatest substitution possibilities. If two or more attack modes are needed to produce a single basic commodity, then these modes are complementary. Since the effects of complementary events are mutually reinforcing, an increase (decrease) in the price of one activity will cause that activity and all complements to fall (rise) in number.

Proposition 3: Terrorist-Nonterrorist Substitutions. An increase in the price of all terrorist activities or a decrease in the price of nonterrorist activities will decrease the overall level of terrorism.[7]

Proposition 4: Income Effects. For normal goods, an increase (decrease) in the resource base will cause a terrorist group to increase (decrease) the level of terrorist and nonterrorist activities.

---

[7] As discussed in footnote 5, we are assuming that income effects associated with relative price changes do not offset the direct substitution effects. To be a bit more technical, the so-called Slutsky equation indicates that the full price elasticity of demand (ε_F) for any good is equal to the pure price elasticity (ε_P) plus the share of that good in the consumer's income (k) multiplied by the income elasticity of demand for that good (η), i.e., $\varepsilon_F = \varepsilon_P + k\eta$. Although ε_P is always negative, ε_F can be positive for goods with a positive income elasticity of demand that comprise a large share of the budget. We doubt that any attack modes are "Giffen Goods" that increase in number as their relative price rises. Note that the two elasticities are approximately equal if the share of the good in the consumer's income (k) is small.

ANALYSIS OF A "BENEVOLENCE"
COUNTERTERRORISM STRATEGY

Frey and Luechinger (2003) and Frey (2004) have championed the idea of a type of "benevolence" counterterrorism strategy. Instead of using deterrence policies (i.e., offensive or defensive policies) to restrict the terrorists' choice set, a benevolence policy actually rewards terrorists for their good behavior. The essential idea is to raise the relative price of terrorist actions by lowering the price of nonterrorist actions. In the extreme case, a terrorist could be offered a financial incentive or reduced punishment if he or she agreed to refrain from future terrorist activities. Certainly, many countries have rewarded individuals providing operable information about the inner workings of their group or of key individuals in their group. Similarly, the government could agree to engage in political discussions with a terrorist group about what actions might be necessary to alleviate their grievances or to allow the group to run candidates for political office. Frey and Luechinger (2003) point out that people with proclivities toward transnational terrorism could be invited to visit foreign universities and research institutions. By exposing such individuals to foreign culture and to new ideas, there is the possibility that they would refrain from terrorism. The Swedish Ministry for Foreign Affairs is well known for its efforts to support those who want to exit violence-promoting groups, including terrorist groups, by helping them to reintegrate into society and easing their transition into peaceful activities. All such actions lower the cost of achieving the group's aims through nonterrorist means.

Consider Figure 5.7, in which the initial equilibrium is such that the terrorists operate at point R along their budget constraint AB. As a result, the group engages in T_0 units of terrorist actions and N_0 units of nonterrorist actions. The level of utility is given by indifference curve 1 passing through points H, R, and F. Now, suppose that the government lowers the relative price of nonterrorist activities by allowing the group to participate in talks concerning their eventual emergence as a legitimate political party, allowed to run candidates for office and/or discuss their grievances in the media. Since it is now less expensive to engage in nonterrorist activities, the new budget constraint faced by the group might be depicted by AE. As such, the group's opportunity set has expanded such that it could choose to engage in a total of $0E$ units of nonterrorist activities. However, given the indifference curve shown by 1, the group will choose a point on its budget constraint somewhere in the interval FH (any other point on AE would result in a lower level of utility for the group).

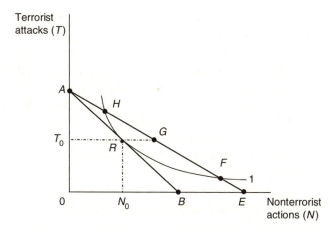

Figure 5.7. A benevolent strategy.

One possibility is that the group's indifference curves are such that it chooses to operate at point G. In this particular case, the benevolence policy increases the group's participation in nonterrorist actions without changing the overall level of terrorism. Of course, selecting G would be a coincidence, since there are other possibilities. If the highest attainable indifference curve lies in the interval FG, the benevolence policy can be deemed a success; the smaller relative price of nonterrorist acts (i.e., an increase in the relative price of terrorism) reduces the overall level of terrorism. However, there is another possibility. If the group chooses to operate somewhere on the interval GH, the benevolence policy increases the level of terrorism. To explain, the pure substitution effect associated with the increase in the relative price of terrorism means that the group engages in fewer terrorist actions. However, as demonstrated by Anderton and Carter (2005), the group's opportunity set has expanded; it can use some of this extra "income" to produce additional units of terrorism. In a sense, the benevolence policy can backfire because it may induce more terrorism.

Whether the income effects of benevolence policies dominate the substitution effect is an empirical issue. Although little is currently known about the relative sizes of the two effects, there is no ambiguity in US law. Title 18 of the US Code – 18 U.S.C. §2339B(a)(1) – makes it illegal to provide material support or resources to any organization that the US government designates as a terrorist organization. For individuals, each violation can result in a fine and a fifteen-year jail sentence. If the aid results in a death, the individual can receive life imprisonment. In a 6–3 ruling on 21 June 2010, the US Supreme Court held that the Humanitarian Law Project (HLP) was guilty of providing aid to the Kurdistan Workers Party (PKK). In the case – *Holder versus the Humanitarian Law Project, et al.* (see 130 S. Ct. 2705) – the plaintiffs were not charged with directly abetting terrorism; instead, they were charged with offering training in how to use international law to resolve disputes peacefully and "how to petition various representative bodies such as the United Nations for relief." Nevertheless, in his opinion, Chief Justice Roberts wrote that "providing material support to a designated foreign terrorist organization – even benign support – bolsters the terrorist activities of that organization." The view is that any actions by private parties that shift out the budget constraint of a terrorist organization, as in Figure 5.7, are illegal. This is true even if the group were to consume on line segment *FG* on its new budget constraint (so that the policy actually reduced the level of terrorism).

In addition to the possibility that the income effect can lead to an increase in terrorism, a benevolence policy is worrisome because it can induce rent-seeking behavior. Any remuneration resulting from past terrorist behavior might induce some to engage in a terrorist act in order to partake in the benefits of being a former terrorist. Moreover, the government needs to be careful that the payment does not appear to be a capitulation to terrorism. Frey (2004) also notes that politicians might be wary of benevolence policies because voters might view "rewarding" terrorists, who have committed a heinous act, as immoral.

SUICIDE BOMBERS AND RATIONAL BEHAVIOR

Some scholars argue that it is not possible to apply the notion of rationality to suicidal terrorist actions. Their argument is that these acts are not rash or spontaneous outbursts of emotion; instead, they are carefully orchestrated incidents that are prepared far in advance of the actual attack. While in flight training school, for example, the pilots of the 9/11 planes knew that they were preparing for a single mission. The issue is whether rational agents can carefully prepare and execute a plan of action that calls for their own demise. If such behavior is irrational, the presence of suicide missions casts doubt on the entire rational-actor framework. As illustrated by Figure 2.8 (see Chapter 2), suicide attacks are not isolated incidents.

Suicide can be rational if the utility obtained from living with the current state of affairs is less than that obtained by a life-ending action. Few would question the rationality of a person living in substantial pain asking to have a life-giving medication withheld. In the same way, a suicidal terrorist mission can be rational if the utility associated with planning and contemplating the consequences of the suicide mission is at least as great as that of living with the status quo. The issue is why certain individuals gain utility from a suicidal act. Wintrobe (2002) argues that suicidal terrorists are rational in that they engage in such acts to obtain a group "solidarity" or cohesiveness. He argues that individuals strive to belong to a group and that such solidarity is typically acquired through group-directed activity. Well-defined groups, such as gangs, cults, labor unions, political parties or movements, and religious sects, can provide this essential feeling of belonging. As terrorist group members, individuals are viewed by Wintrobe as gaining benefits from social cohesion as they adopt group-sanctioned beliefs. In a sense, there is a trade-off between being integrated into a group and a sense of self. All of us make certain sacrifices of our individual autonomy in order to be members of a well-functioning society. In some extremist groups, the belief system entails the willingness to sacrifice a few of the individual members. Wintrobe (2002) argues that for suicide attacks, there is a "corner solution" such that the individual sacrifices everything for the sake of the group.

The theory has a number of implications that seem to be borne out by terrorist groups. First, newcomers to the group are unlikely to be selected for the suicide mission – such individuals will have had scant time to bask in the camaraderie provided by group membership. Instead, the group's leadership will nurture young members, allowing them to consume the benefits of group membership. Such benefits would include the "feeling of belonging," the esteem accorded to a future martyr, and thoughts of the heavenly rewards of dying for the *jihad*. Second, a member selected for a suicide mission must be made aware that he or she will receive a strong group sanction if the attack is not carried out. Some groups will blackball, and others will harm, a member who "chickens out."

Azam (2005) argues that another motivation for suicide missions is purely altruistic. Many parents have placed themselves in harm's way in order to save their child from danger. More typically, individuals commonly sacrifice current consumption for the benefit of future family members. Actions such as the purchase of a life insurance policy, or the creation of a will or trust, indicate that members of the current generation are willing to sacrifice for future generations. Azam (2005) views suicide bombings as a form of intergenerational investment. Reducing current consumption to zero by conducting a suicide bombing is viewed as an extreme form of saving. Even in the circumstance where the bomber has no estate to pass on to descendents, the bombing can increase the probability that beneficial public goods will accrue to the next generation. In the case of Palestine, the public good might be an increased probability of an independent political state. Evidence of compensation paid to the families of suicide bombers by the Iraqi government and by members of the Saudi royal family provides some support for Azam's model. According to the BBC, during the Saddam Hussein regime a suicide bomber's family got $25,000, while relatives of militants killed in fighting received $10,000. Azam also notes that Israel punishes the suicide bombers' families by systematically destroying their houses.

Berman and Laitin (2005) provide a similar explanation. They allow a religious organization to supply social welfare benefits to members. Members of the group must adhere to group demands in order to attain the welfare benefits. They define a hard target as one that cannot be attacked without a high probability of apprehension. Suicide attacks are a favored tactic as they have the great advantage of not allowing the attacker to be apprehended, potentially exposing the other operatives.

We believe that revenge can motivate suicide attacks. On 25 August 2004, two flights left Domodedovo airport near Moscow and exploded in midair. Two Chechen women, thought to be Amanat Nagayeva and Satsita Dzhbirkhanova, detonated the explosives that blew up the aircraft. A week later, Ms. Nagayeva's younger sister set off a bomb that killed eleven people, including herself, outside a Moscow subway. On 3 September 2004, at least two (and possibly four) women were among the terrorist group that killed at least 335 children, parents, and teachers at Middle School No. 1 in the city of Beslan. According to the *New York Times* (10 September 2004, p. A1), female Chechen suicide bombers have taken part in at least fifteen suicide attacks since 1999. In the Russian media, such women are referred to as "black widows" to denote their willingness to undertake a suicide mission avenging the death of a father, husband, brother, or son.

Thwarting suicide acts is especially difficult. In terms of the Landes's (1978) model of a potential skyjacker, a person concerned about living and the quality of life in prison will have a relatively low value of U^F. However, a fanatical terrorist who does not fear death (and might even welcome it because of heavenly rewards afforded to martyrs) has a higher U^F. The point is that fanatical terrorism brings U^F closer to U^S. In the extreme, $U^S = U^F$, so that a change in the probability of success (π) has no effect on the terrorist's behavior. In the HPF model, such individuals opt for a corner solution so that they are fully specialized in suicide terrorism. Such fanatical terrorists must be apprehended or killed in order to prevent the attack.

The essential point is that suicide attacks are both cheap and effective. Hoffman (2006) argues that suicide attacks are the "ultimate smart bomb" because they kill four times as many people as other attack modes. In Israel, suicide attacks kill six times as many people and injure twenty-six times as many people as other attack modes. Such attacks are lethal because a suicide bomber can make real-time alterations to the timing and location of an attack so as to maximize the bloodshed. Moreover, suicide attacks are relatively inexpensive. In describing a suicide attack on an Israeli bus that killed twelve people and wounded more than fifty others, Hoffman (2003) calculated the cost of the bomb materials to be no more than $150. The National Commission on Terrorist Attacks Upon the United States (2004) reported that the cost of the entire 9/11 operation was less than $500,000. Other advantages of suicide attacks are that they do not require sophisticated escape plans; they ensure that the leadership is secure because the successful perpetrator cannot be questioned; they provide media coverage because of the carnage; and they serve as an important psychological weapon demonstrating the perpetrator's resolve. More importantly, as argued by Dershowitz (2002) and Pape (2005), suicide campaigns have proven to be extremely effective in promoting the terrorists' ends. The Hezbollah suicide attacks in April through December of 1983 (including the bombing of the US Marine barracks on 23 October 1983) were successful in causing the United States and France to withdraw from Lebanon. Similarly, Pape (2005) analyzed the 1995 Hamas suicide attacks against Israel. Originally, Hamas delayed attacking Israel in order to allow PLO leaders sufficient time to negotiate an Israeli withdrawal from the West Bank. When Israel seemed to renege on its timetable, Hamas began a suicide campaign that induced Israel to increase the speed of its withdrawal.

TESTS OF THE RATIONAL TERRORISM MODEL BASED ON THE TARGET OF THE ATTACKS

The discussion of intervention analysis presented in Chapter 3 described a number of empirical tests that validate the implications of the rational terrorist model. For example, Proposition 1 indicates that a change in the relative prices of alternative attack modes will induce terrorists to substitute out of high-cost incident types into relatively low-cost types. As confirmed in Table 3.4, when the US government introduced metal detectors into airports in 1973, the number of skyjackings did fall. Enders, Sandler, and Cauley (1990a) also found that terrorists substituted out of skyjackings and into other types of hostage-taking incidents. Such hostage-taking incidents are logistically complex, garner a large amount of media attention, and can be similar in scope to a skyjacking incident. Proposition 2 indicates that these comparable attack modes should offer the greatest substitution possibilities. Similarly, Propositions 1 and 4 imply that interventions such as UN conventions and resolutions that do not alter the relative prices of the incident types or the terrorists' resources should have no effect on the observed levels of terrorism. Moreover, the fact that terrorists face binding budget constraints suggests an asymmetry in the persistence of high- versus low-attack states of the world. The very notion that terrorists act irrationally or unpredictably seems to be inconsistent with these findings.

Instead of focusing on attack modes, Brandt and Sandler (2010) examined how rational terrorists substitute among four different types of targets – i.e., officials, the military, businesses, and the private sector. If a particular type of target is hardened, the HPF model predicts that terrorists should shift out of that target class into other, relatively unprotected targets. Brandt and Sandler (2010) posited the existence of four possible target regimes. The first period, 1968 through the early 1970s, saw the rise of modern transnational terrorism. Palestinian terrorists, seeking to call attention to their demands for an end to Israeli occupation, focused their attacks on airplanes and on government officials. Also during this period, left-wing groups, such as the Red Brigades and the Baader-Meinhof Gang, tried to minimize civilian casualties in order to generate sympathy for their cause. This first target regime ended in 1973 with the introduction of metal detectors in airports and embassies. As a result of their early success in curtailing skyjackings, metal detectors and other screening devices were increasingly deployed at embassies, military bases, and other high-value targets. The FAA Explosives Detection Canine Team Program began in 1973 after a bomb-sniffing dog named Brandy was brought aboard a TWA jet in order to follow up on a tip from an anonymous caller warning of a bomb. Brandy sniffed out the bomb twelve minutes before it was set to detonate on a flight from Los Angeles. The program started with forty canine teams in twenty airports and had expanded to eighty-seven teams located at twenty-seven airports by 1997. It now includes all of the large US airports. The point is that the use of these technological barriers made it relatively expensive to attack high-value targets such as the military and government officials. According to Brandt and Sandler (2010), this second regime lasted until 1979, with the rise of state sponsorship and fundamentalist terrorists. In addition to the takeover of the US embassy in Tehran in November 1979, major state-sponsored incidents during the third regime included the bombing of the US embassy in Beirut in April 1983, the bombing of the US Marine barracks in Beirut in October 1983, and the downing of Pan Am Flight 103 in December 1988. Such state-sponsored incidents were well planned and large-scale. Nevertheless, the authorities responded to these attacks by further protecting property. For example, after the truck bombing of the US Marine barracks, three-foot-high concrete barriers were placed around the White House (and later at US embassies and some airports). International corporations increased the security levels of their employees and property along with the official and military defensive measures. The demise of state sponsorship was the clear result of the collapse of the Soviet Union in 1991. During the fourth target regime, dominated by fundamentalist groups such as al-Qaida, Hamas, and Jemaah Islamiyah, terrorists are not especially concerned about maintaining a constituency in the West. Instead, they view private individuals as legitimate targets and are principally interested in large-scale attacks that draw media attention.

Fortunately, ITERATE indicates whether the target of each terrorist attack is an official, business, military (noncombatant), or a private party. Moreover, it also identifies whether the target of the attack seems to be people or property. Brandt and Sandler (2010) were thus able to determine how the hardening of airports, embassies, and military bases induced substitutions toward attacks on the civilian population. Their key finding is that, over time, the hardening of official, military, and business targets has led to an increased number of attacks against private parties. In a sense, protecting certain individuals (military and officials) and property has made the world less safe for relatively unprotected individuals. Moreover, for all target classes, attacks have shifted toward individuals and away from property.

Rather than assuming that the break dates are given, the dates were estimated along with the other parameters of the model.[8] It turned out that the officials and businesses series did not experience any statistically significant breaks prior to the early 1970s; hence, these two series never really passed from regime one to regime two. Some of the key results are summarized in Table 5.1. For the officials series, there are two statistically significant breaks, or changepoints: October 1974 and March 1993. Notice that the use of defensive measures, estimated to have its primary effect on this series beginning in September 1974, induced only a very slight change in the

---

[8]   A modification of intervention analysis such that the break dates are estimated along with the other parameters of the model is discussed in Chapter 9 and in Chapter 2 of Enders (2010). In essence, the methodology involves estimating a set of regression equations, each containing a level-shift dummy variable set for a potential changepoint. The regression containing the best fit yields a consistent estimate of the changepoint. Although the details are not important for our purposes, Brandt and Sandler (2010) actually estimated the model as a Markov-switching process. Moreover, since they used count data containing large numbers of zero and near-zero entries, the series were estimated assuming a Poisson, rather than a normal, distribution.

Table 5.1. *Target Substitution and Statistically Significant Changepoints*

Target	Regime 1	Regime 2	Regime 3	Regime 4
Officials	No significant break	to Sept. 1974	Oct. 1974 – Feb. 1993	Mar. 1993 – Dec. 2007
attacks/month	8.2	8.2	8.5	2.2
Military	to Jan. 1970	Feb. 1970 – Apr. 1979	May 1979 – Oct. 1995	Nov. 1995 – Dec. 2007
attacks/month	0.4	1.8	3.5	1.2
Business	No significant break	to Feb. 1973	March 1973 – Mar. 1990	April 1990 – Dec. 2007
attacks/month	4.8	4.8	7.2	3.4
Private parties	to Oct. 1968	Nov. 1968 – May 1973	June 1973 – May 1996	June 1996 – Dec. 2007
attacks/month	1.4	4.9	9.2	5.2

Source: Summarized from Brandt and Sandler (2010).

number of attacks against officials, from 8.2 to 8.5 attacks per month. Of course, had these defensive measures not been used, the number of attacks might have risen even more. The end of the Cold War and the rise of fundamentalism, estimated to have its primary effect on the official series beginning in March 1993, brought about a sharp decline in the monthly number of attacks against officials, from 8.5 to 2.2 attacks per month.

The more important changepoints for the military series occur in May 1979 and November 1995. During the May 1979–October 1995 period, the number of monthly attacks against military targets jumped to 3.5 (from 1.8) incidents per month. May 1979 roughly corresponds to the rise of state sponsorship. Although November 1995 follows the decline of the Cold War, it is still reasonable to conclude that the growth of the fundamentalist movements led to a reduction in the number of attacks against military targets.

For businesses, important changepoints occurred in March 1973 and April 1990. The first changepoint clearly reflects the improvements in airport security; attacks against business targets rose from 4.8 to 7.2 incidents per month. Clearly, the increased protection at airports and embassies induced terrorists to shift the focus of their attacks toward business firms. The end of the Cold War brought about a reduction in the number of attacks against businesses.

Attacks against private parties saw three important changepoints: November 1968, June 1973, and June 1996. The first changepoint, corresponding to the rise of transnational terrorism, saw a jump from 1.4 to 4.9 incidents per month. Since attacks against other target types were flat, this suggests that the growth in transnational terrorism during this period was generally directed against private parties. With the increase in defensive measures in 1973, the average number of attacks against businesses and private parties jumped (from 4.8 to 7.2 and from 4.9 to 9.2 incidents per month, respectively). Since there was little change in attacks against the other target types, it seems reasonable to conclude that defensive technologies deflected attacks toward businesses and private parties. All targets seemed to benefit from the end of the Cold War; each target class experienced a reduction in the number of attacks in the early to middle 1990s. Nevertheless, the target classes were differentially affected by this regime change, official and business targets were most affected by the end of the Cold War. The important point is that these results are quite consistent with the HPF model. As indicated by Proposition 1, the hardening of targets in the early 1970s led to more attacks against businesses and private parties. As it became more difficult to attack government officials and the military, terrorists switched their focus to relatively more vulnerable businesses and private parties.

VECTOR AUTOREGRESSIONS AND ESTIMATES OF THE SUBSTITUTION EFFECT

Vector autoregressions (VARs) have proven to be an important way to empirically measure the extent of substitution effects in transnational terrorism. You can think of a vector autoregression as a many-variable generalization of the intervention model discussed in Chapter 3. To explain VAR analysis, consider the following simplified system allowing for only two incident types:

$$Sky_t = a_{10} + a_{11}Sky_{t-1} + a_{12}Kidnap_{t-1} + \varepsilon_{1t}, \tag{5.5}$$

$$Kidnap_t = a_{20} + a_{21}Sky_{t-1} + a_{22}Kidnap_{t-1} + \varepsilon_{2t}, \tag{5.6}$$

where Sky_t (Sky_{t-1}) is the number of skyjacking incidents during time period t (period $t-1$), $Kidnap_t$ ($Kidnap_{t-1}$) is the number of transnational kidnapping incidents during time period t (period $t-1$), and ε_{1t} and ε_{2t} are shocks to each incident type that may be correlated. Since skyjackings tend to cluster, we would expect a_{11} to be strongly positive; that is, when the value of Sky_{t-1} is large, the value of Sky_t will tend to be large. Similarly, a positive value of a_{22} can capture the tendency of kidnappings to cluster. The inter-relationships between the series are captured by the values of a_{12} and a_{21}. For example, if the incident types were complements, so that an increase in skyjackings was associated with a subsequent increase in kidnappings, the value of a_{21} would be positive. Alternatively, if increases in skyjackings come at the expense of future kidnappings, the value of a_{21} would be negative. The relationship between the contemporaneous movements in the two series is captured by the correlation coefficient between ε_{1t} and ε_{2t}. If this correlation coefficient is positive (negative), the co-movements between Sky_t and $Kidnap_t$ tend to be positive (negative).

The VAR represented by equations (5.5) and (5.6) can be extended in a number of different ways. Additional lags of the variables can capture the possibility of more sophisticated dynamic linkages among the variables, insofar as more than one period may be required for a change in the number of skyjackings (kidnappings) to affect the number of kidnappings (skyjackings). Similarly, there may be interactions among a much larger number of incidents types. Increasing the number of variables used in the VAR could allow for the possibility that skyjackings, kidnappings, assassinations, and threats are all interrelated. For our purposes, a critical extension is to incorporate the effects of various intervention variables into the basic VAR. For example, the installation of metal detectors in US airports in the first quarter of 1973 (1973:Q1) can be treated as a permanent level-shift dummy variable. Suppose that the dummy variable $METAL_t$ is equal to zero for all time periods before 1973:Q1 and is equal to one beginning in 1973:Q1. After constructing such a variable, it is possible to write a VAR augmented with dummy variables as

$$Sky_t = a_{10} + b_{10}METAL_t + a_{11}Sky_{t-1} + a_{12}Kidnap_{t-1} + \varepsilon_{1t}, \qquad (5.7)$$

$$Kidnap_t = a_{20} + b_{20}METAL_t + a_{21}Sky_{t-1} + a_{22}Kidnap_{t-1} + \varepsilon_{2t}. \qquad (5.8)$$

The new VAR is similar to the original VAR except for the presence of the metal detector dummy variable. Since $METAL_t = 0$ for all periods prior to 1973:Q1, the two VARs should be identical for the pre–metal detector period. However, beginning with 1973:Q1, the value of $METAL_t$ jumps to one. Hence, for the post–metal detector period, the VAR becomes

$$Sky_t = a_{10} + b_{10} + a_{11}Sky_{t-1} + a_{12}Kidnap_{t-1} + \varepsilon_{1t}, \qquad (5.9)$$

$$Kidnap_t = a_{20} + b_{20} + a_{21}Sky_{t-1} + a_{22}Kidnap_{t-1} + \varepsilon_{2t}. \qquad (5.10)$$

Now, the difference between the VAR of equations (5.5) and (5.6) and the VAR of equations (5.9) and (5.10) is the intercept terms, so that the intervention variable acts as a change in the intercepts of the two regression equations. Prior to 1973:Q1, the intercepts are a_{10} and a_{20}; post-1973:Q1, the intercepts are $(a_{10} + b_{10})$ and $(a_{20} + b_{20})$. If b_{10} is negative (so that the new intercept for SKY_t is below a_{10}), the installation of metal detectors will have reduced skyjackings. The short-run substitution effect is captured by the magnitude of b_{20}. If b_{20} is positive (so that the new intercept for $Kidnap_t$ is above a_{20}), the installation of metal detectors is associated with an increase in the number of kidnappings. In this way, b_{10} represents the direct effect of metal detectors on skyjackings, and b_{20} represents the substitution between skyjackings and kidnappings.[9]

The long-run effects of the interventions account for the fact that lagged values of kidnappings affect Sky_t, and lagged values of skyjackings affect $Kidnap_t$. Due to the dynamic interactions between the series, the long- and short-run effects of the interventions can be quite different. Nevertheless, once the VAR equations have been estimated by a regression analysis, it is possible to shock $METAL_t$ by one unit and trace out the entire time path of the estimated effects of metal detectors on the two series. The differences between the initial mean values and the final mean values are the long-run effects of the intervention.

VAR Results on Attack Modes

Enders and Sandler (1993) used the VAR methodology to estimate the impact of important policy interventions on the attack modes used by terrorists.[10] A number of different combinations of attack modes were examined in their VAR analysis. Enders and Sandler's findings using skyjackings, *other kinds* of hostage takings (including kidnappings) (*Hostage*), attacks against protected persons, and all other attacks are especially interesting. Attacks against protected persons (*APP*) is the time series of nonhostage crimes against diplomats and other protected persons. The United Nations' definition of an "internationally protected person" includes official representatives of a head of state, diplomats, ambassadors, and all accompanying family members. Attacks are counted if they occurred in a country signing the UN convention on protected persons and involved a victim from a

[9] The statistical significance of the coefficients b_{10} and b_{20} can be tested using a standard t-test.

[10] Each regression equation of a VAR can be estimated using ordinary least squares. The details of the estimation methodology are not especially important for our purposes here. Interested readers can find a detailed discussion of VAR estimation, testing, and analysis in Chapter 5 of Enders (2010).

Table 5.2. *Description of the Intervention Variables*

Intervention	Description
METAL	The United States began to install metal detectors in airports on 5 January 1973. During the installation process, various screening techniques, including hand searches of carry-on luggage, were conducted. Other international airports worldwide followed suit shortly thereafter.
EMB76	Spending to fortify and secure US embassies was doubled beginning in October 1976. Security measures included the screening of visitors to US embassies.
EMB85	Additional resources were allocated to security in the 1980s as a result of the takeover of the US embassy in Tehran on 4 November 1979. A significant increase in spending to secure US embassies was authorized by Public Law 98–533 in October 1985.
LIBYA	On 5 April 1986, a bomb went off in the La Belle discotheque in West Berlin. It killed a Turkish woman and two US servicemen, and injured 230 people. Many of the injured were US servicemen. On the morning of 15 April 1986, the US undertook a retaliatory raid against Libya for its involvement in the terrorist bombing. At least fifteen people were killed, including the fifteen-month-old adopted daughter of leader Muammar Qaddafi. More than 100 people were injured in the raid.

signatory country.[11] The time series of all other attacks (OT) consists primarily of bombings, threats, and hoaxes. The policy interventions include the installation of metal detectors in airports, two embassy fortifications, and the retaliatory raid on Libya. More detailed descriptions of the interventions are provided in Table 5.2.

The actual quarterly incident totals of *Skyjackings, Hostage, APP*, and *OT* are shown as the dashed lines in Figure 5.8. The solid lines are the estimated time paths of the effects of the various interventions. To construct these estimated paths, we took the predicted values of *Skyjackings, Hostage, APP*, and *OT* from the estimated VAR, conditioned on the interventions alone.[12] As such, the shifts in these lines represent the effects of the interventions alone. As a visual aid, the vertical lines represent the starting dates of each of the four interventions.

[11] A complete description can be found in the United Nations (2010) Convention on the Prevention and Punishment of Crimes Against Internationally Protected Persons.

[12] As such, the predicted values are not one-step-ahead forecasts. Each series was initially set at its pre-1973:Q1 mean, and we traced out the time path of each using only the altered values of the intervention variables.

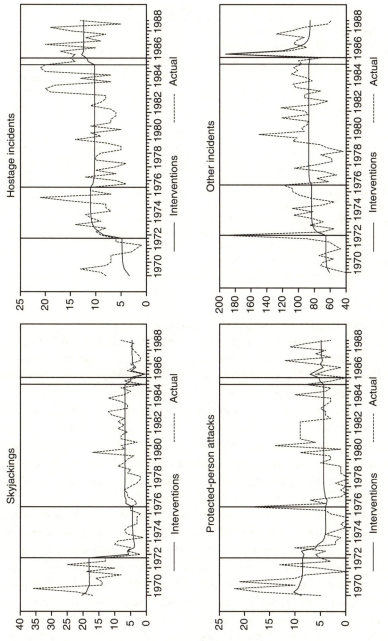

Figure 5.8. Substitutions between attack modes.

165

Table 5.3. *Results of the VAR*

Intervention	Skyjackings	Hostage	APP	OT
Short-Run Effect				
METAL	−12.20**	3.68*	0.03	12.20
EMB76	2.05	−0.44	−1.53	1.73
EMB85	−1.72	1.39	0.94	−1.48
LIBYA	−3.81	1.28	1.60	107.40**
Long-Run Effect				
METAL	−13.70#	5.21#	−4.53#	18.20
EMB76	2.32	−0.80	0.40	4.10
EMB85	−2.19	2.10	0.54	−1.30
LIBYA	NA	NA	NA	NA

** denotes statistical significance at the 5% level.

* denotes statistical significance at the 10% level.

# denotes a significant intervention or that the effect is significant through its effects on an important explanatory variable in the VAR.

All effects for Libya are temporary.

NA denotes not applicable.

From the figure with incidents per quarter on the vertical axis, one can see the abrupt changes in *Skyjackings, Hostage*, and *APP* beginning in 1973:Q1. On impact, metal detectors decreased skyjackings by 12.2 incidents per quarter. This is an important effect and is consistent with Landes's (1978) results. However, as predicted by the HPF approach, an increase in the price of a skyjacking results in substitutions into similar incident types. We found that the impact effect of $METAL_t$ was to increase hostage incidents by 3.68 incidents per quarter – see Table 5.3. Notice that *Hostage* continued to increase for several quarters following 1973:Q1. The cumulated total effect (i.e., the long-run effect) of the intervention was to increase *Hostage* by 5.21 incidents per quarter.

An important aspect of the VAR study is that the installation of metal detectors is found to decrease *APP* even though the immediate impact is almost zero (the short-run coefficient is 0.032). We found that the long-run effect of $METAL_t$ on *APP* is −4.53 incidents per quarter. The rationale is that the installation of metal detectors reduced skyjackings and that the eventual extension of the metal detector technology helped to shield protected persons at various government buildings, embassies, and military bases.

There seems to be a slight increase in *OT* following the installation of metal detectors, but this increase is not statistically significant. The embassy fortifications seemed to have no significant effect on any of the series. Other then the installation of metal detectors, the only significant intervention was the Libyan bombing, which caused the number of other incidents (*OT*) to jump sharply before falling back to the series' pre-intervention mean. Since bombings, threats, and hoaxes are usually logistically simple and utilize few resources relative to the other types of incidents, it is fairly easy to ratchet up the number of such incidents. The calculated short-run effects and the long-run effects of the four intervention variables are summarized in Table 5.3. The entries are in terms of incidents per quarter.

VAR Results on Target Substitution

In a follow-up to their 2010 paper, Brandt and Sandler (2011) used a VAR to examine the substitutability and complementarity of terrorists' target choices. Specifically, they estimated a four-equation VAR using the monthly number of attacks against government officials, the military, businesses, and private parties as the variables. Instead of estimating the break dates, as in Brandt and Sandler (2010), these authors estimated separate VARs for each of the following five time periods:

Beginning of transnational terrorism:	1968:1–1973:1
Introduction of technological barriers:	1973:2–1979:12
State sponsorship:	1980:1–1989:11
Fundamentalist terrorism:	1989:12–2001:9
Post-9/11:	2001:10–2008:12

Although these dates are slightly different than those found in Brandt and Sandler (2010), it is important to realize that the regimes are simplified descriptions of the key changes in the nature of terrorism. In reality, changes tend to occur gradually. Clearly, technological barriers were continually upgraded throughout the entire period. Similarly, fundamentalists were active during three regimes because the rise of fundamentalism can be traced back to the 1979:11 takeover of the US embassy in Tehran. The key point is that these dates should approximate the points at which any changes in the nature of terrorism are likely to be observed.

As suggested in the discussion of equations (5.9) and (5.10), the substitutability and complementarity of the target classes can be determined from the VAR coefficients. However, in a four-variable VAR containing three lags of each variable, it can be quite difficult to interpret any patterns in the coefficients. Instead, it is typical to use impulse response analysis to determine how the VAR variables covary over time. To explain, let mil_t and off_t denote the number of attacks on the military and officials, respectively, in month t, and consider the simplified two-variable, two-lag VAR system:

$$off_t = a_{10} + a_{11}off_{t-1} + a_{12}off_{t-2} + a_{13}mil_{t-1} + a_{14}mil_{t-2} + \varepsilon_{1t}, \qquad (5.11)$$

$$mil_t = a_{20} + a_{21}off_{t-1} + a_{22}off_{t-2} + a_{23}mil_{t-1} + a_{24}mil_{t-2} + \varepsilon_{2t}. \qquad (5.12)$$

After estimating (5.11) and (5.12), one can determine the dynamic relationship between officials and military targets by tracing out the effects of a one-unit shock to ε_{1t}. From (5.11), a one-unit shock to ε_{1t} increases off_t by one unit and has no contemporaneous effect on mil_t. However, it is possible to update (5.11) and (5.12) by one period and then to calculate how this change in off_t affects both off_{t+1} and mil_{t+1}.[13] Updating by another period allows the researcher to calculate the effects of these changes on off_{t+2} and mil_{t+2}. In this way, the entire dynamic paths of the two variables can be traced out and compared. If the two generally move together, then a shock to the official series induces complementary changes in the military series, and if they move in opposite directions, then a shock to the official series induces a substitution away from military targets. Finally, it is possible to repeat the exercise for a one-unit shock to military targets.

Brandt and Sandler (2011) found that the correlations of the shocks (i.e., the various values of ε_{it}) for all time periods are generally positive. Since the impulse responses between the alternative target types are almost always positive, the clear implication is that, within regimes, attacks against the various targets are complementary. However, across the various time periods, there is a decoupling of the interrelationships such that the dynamic co-movements of the variables become less pronounced.

At the same time that the impulse responses are generated, a VAR model allows the researcher to calculate the percentage of the variation of each series attributable to each of the shocks. The key finding of Brandt and Sandler (2011) is that the drivers of the various series have changed over time. During the 1968:1–1973:1 and 1973:2–1979:12 periods, attacks against officials and the military were the primary driving forces for all of the series. By the post-9/11 period, attacks on private parties and businesses were causing most of the variation in the four targets. Shocks to the officials and military series became less important, while shocks to relatively unprotected businesses and private parties became more important. The clear implication is that our defensive strategy of focusing on certain target

---

[13] With a bit of algebra, the effect of a one-unit shock to ε_{1t} on off_{t+1} can be shown to be $a_{11} + a_{21}a_{13}$, and the effect on mil_{t+1} can be shown to be a_{21}. Further details can be obtained from Chapter 5 of Enders (2010).

classes (government officials and the military) meant that rational terrorists were able to substitute away from the relatively secure targets toward the relatively unprotected targets.

CONCLUSION

Many social scientists view terrorists as rational actors who use their scarce resources to maximize their expected utility. Rational behavior is predicable and allows social scientists to formulate the terrorists' best response to any antiterrorism policy. The household production approach to terrorism indicates that an increase in the relative price of one type of terrorist activity will cause the terrorist group to substitute out of the relatively expensive activity and into terrorist and nonterrorist activities that have become relatively less expensive. Similarly, attack modes that are logistically similar and yield similar basic commodities will display the greatest substitution possibilities. Transference occurs because governments can alter the prices faced by terrorists. Even suicidal terrorists can be viewed as being rational. Unfortunately, suicidal attacks are unlikely to be deterred by a relative price change; the opportunity set of such terrorists must be reduced if suicidal attacks are to be prevented.

Transference means that the unintended consequences of government policies designed to thwart one type of terrorist behavior can induce increases in other types of terrorism. The empirical literature supports the importance of the substitution effect in transnational terrorism. Antiterrorism policies that do not constrain terrorists' behavior, such as UN conventions and resolutions, have no effect on the level of terrorism. Piecemeal policies, designed to thwart only one attack mode, are shown to induce a substitution into other, similar modes, whose unintended consequences may be quite harmful. There is strong evidence that enhanced barriers against official and military targets has led to a substitution toward attacks on private parties.

SIX

International Cooperation

Dilemma and Inhibitors

In a globalized world with a high volume of cross-border flows, transnational terrorism is a global public bad, while action to control or eliminate it is the quintessential global public good. As such, antiterrorism efforts yield nonrival benefits – enhanced security – received by all at-risk countries. The formation of far-flung terrorist networks has greatly increased the spatial dispersion of benefits derived from measures taken against these networks. The theory of public good supply teaches that as the dispersion of these measures' benefits increases, their underprovision worsens as providers fail to take account of the benefits that their efforts confer on others when deciding upon antiterrorism actions (see Chapter 4; Sandler, 1997, 2004).

The sheer volume of cross-border exchanges of all types makes it possible to monitor but a small fraction of them, thereby affording opportunities for terrorists to move personnel and equipment internationally. For example, well over a half-billion people cross US borders annually. In 2003, 130 million motor vehicles, 2.5 million rail cars, and 5.7 million cargo containers transited US borders (White House, 2004, p. 165). These transit numbers have grown annually since then. The Department of Homeland Security (DHS) has a daunting task, with 5,000 miles of Canadian border, 1,900 miles of Mexican border, and 95,000 miles of coastline to protect against terrorist and other threats (DHS, 2009, p. 70). According to DHS, 625 million airline passengers were screened in US airports in 2009. The combination of globalization and technological advances means that even the most secure borders may be penetrated by determined terrorists who utilize technologies (for example, communication advances) and apply innovative methods to circumvent security upgrades. Terrorists weigh relative risks to identify the least secure venue or weakest link at which to stage their attack against a targeted nation's assets. Thus, as we have seen in Chapter 2, most attacks against US interests occur outside the United States, where defenses are weaker. The networking of terrorists facilitates their ability to identify vulnerable targets and exploit governments' failure, except episodically, to act in unison.

The reach of 9/11 in terms of its financial consequences,[1] induced anxiety, and human toll indicates that global counterterrorism efforts are needed to fight today's terrorism. Although some coordinated actions occurred after 9/11, including the 7 October 2001 invasion of Afghanistan and some joint police operations in Europe, this coordination has waned over time. Basile (2004, p. 177) indicated that a much smaller amount of al-Qaida funds has been blocked in recent years after a great deal of success during the year immediately following 9/11. This is due in part to al-Qaida finding nations not abiding by cooperative efforts. Nations rely on unilateral counterterrorism responses to maintain their autonomy over security and to limit their transaction costs, which can be high for transnational cooperation. The US invasion of Iraq on 20 March 2003 in the name of counterterrorism and security has turned some nations away from US-led measures, which may have involved US-specific objectives – for example, the removal of Saddam Hussein. An indisputable link between al-Qaida and the Iraqi regime was never established before *or* after the US invasion. Terrorist groups, including al-Qaida, are now operating in Iraq. The 11 March 2004 attack against Spain was intended to send a warning to other nations that cooperation with the United States in its war on terror may carry additional costs. Such intimidation attacks may further hamper a united front against terrorism.

Transnational interdependencies with respect to counterterrorism policies often result in too much of some unilateral actions and too little of others. Unfortunately, terrorists are frequently motivated to address their collective action problems, while governments are not properly motivated to respond to their common concerns. As shown in Chapter 4, countries have a proclivity to rely on prime-target nations to take action against a collective terrorist threat. The associated collective action problems tend to fall into two game categories: Prisoners' Dilemma and coordination games. For the latter, the difficulty is particularly acute if a noncooperator can undo the joint efforts of the cooperators – for example, a nation that provides a secure haven for terrorists' financial assets cancels out the collective efforts of other nations to deny such a haven. Similarly, a state-sponsor country

---

[1] On these financial implications, see Chen and Siems (2004), Drakos (2004), Eldor and Melnick (2004), Kunreuther and Michel-Kerjan (2004a, 2004b), and Chapter 10.

that provides weapons and explosives to a terrorist group can nullify collective efforts to keep such supplies out of terrorist hands.

This chapter has a number of purposes. First, we explore why policy interdependencies among countries result in inefficient provision of counterterrorist action. This analysis goes beyond the presentation in Chapter 4. Second, we highlight the asymmetries between terrorists and governments in order to explain why the two adversaries achieve such different outcomes when addressing their respective collective security concerns. Third, we conceptualize some of the cooperators' dilemmas using elementary game theory – for example, the problems associated with shoring up the weakest link. Fourth, we evaluate past efforts at international cooperation. In particular, we explain why international conventions and resolutions – favored by President Reagan, Senator John Kerry, and others – have not accomplished as much as one would hope. Fifth, we review post-9/11 efforts to freeze terrorists' assets. Sixth, we evaluate the International Criminal Police Organization's (INTERPOL's) efforts, following 9/11, to coordinate national resources to fight transnational terrorism. Finally, we offer some policy recommendations regarding international cooperation.

TRANSNATIONAL EXTERNALITIES

In the fewest possible words, an *externality* is an uncompensated interdependency between two or more agents. If one nation's action or choice imposes a cost or benefit on one or more other nation(s) and no compensation is received or paid, then a *transnational externality* exists. A nation that imposes costs on another nation will not alter its behavior if doing so is costly and there is no mechanism to compel change. Thus, a nation whose electricity-generating plants create acid rain for downwind nations has no incentive to account for the external costs that it imposes on others. In fact, countries build high smokestacks for the purpose of transferring such pollutants abroad. By the same token, a country whose actions have favorable consequences beyond its borders may undersupply such actions because the associated external benefits are not supported or subsidized by recipient countries.

Proactive counterterrorism measures that reduce threats to other countries give rise to external benefits. By contrast, defensive counterterrorism actions can deflect terrorist attacks to less fortified countries, thereby generating external costs. After 9/11, the United States and many industrialized European countries instituted greater defensive actions; thereafter, there were numerous attacks on rich countries' interests in developing countries – for

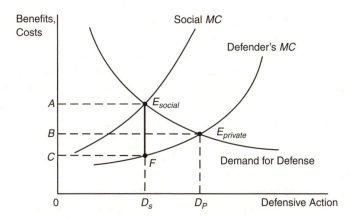

Figure 6.1. Transnational external costs.

example, the Philippines, Indonesia, Malaysia, Kenya, Morocco, Pakistan, and Saudi Arabia. Because defensive measures may also confer external benefits on other countries by protecting foreign residents, both external benefits and external costs may derive from such policies (Sandler, 2005; Sandler and Siqueira, 2006).

In Figure 6.1, we depict the case where *only* external costs arise from defensive actions that deflect an attack onto softer targets abroad.[2] The demand for these actions is downward-sloping, indicating that a country's marginal (additional) willingness to pay declines as greater defensive measures are taken. This curve's shape reflects a diminished marginal gain as security is tightened around potential targets. To provide each level of defensive measures, the country incurs costs for guards, fortifications, and intelligence. The defending country's private additional or *marginal cost* (*MC*) rises as more actions are taken. Thus, the defender's *MC* curve is depicted to rise with increased measures. In essence, this curve represents the private supply curve. When a country determines its best level of defense, it equates its demand and supply curves. In Figure 6.1, this equality occurs at $E_{private}$, where D_p defensive measures are undertaken at a marginal benefit and marginal cost of $0B$.

Social inefficiency arises at $E_{private}$ because the country's independent action does not account for the marginal costs that its defense creates for other nations through transference (see Chapters 4 and 5). These third-party costs also increase with the level of these defensive efforts – that is,

---

[2] The graph adapts the standard treatment of a negative externality – see Bruce (2001, Chapter 4) – to the case of defensive counterterrorism measures.

greater protection of home targets makes foreign targets look softer, so they attract more attacks. If these third-party costs are added to the defender's *MC* curve, then the social *MC* results. This latter curve is above the defender's *MC*, because it is the vertical sum of private *and* third-party (external) *MC*. The social optimum occurs at the intersection of the defender's demand and the social *MC* curve – that is, at point E_{social}, where D_S is the efficient level of defensive effort that accounts for costs imposed on others. As seen in Figure 6.1, independent action results in too much defensive measures, where $D_P > D_S$, as claimed at the outset of this chapter.

There are a number of ways to "internalize" or adjust for these external costs. First, the countries can bargain to level D_S – where, say, the externality recipient compensates the providing country for lowering its defense from level D_P. The recipient is willing to pay the defender *AC* per unit for reducing defensive actions from D_P to D_S as the recipient's marginal damage falls from higher levels (that is, the difference between social *MC* and defender's *MC*) to *AC*. Moreover, the defender is willing to accept *AC* because it equals the defender's unexploited marginal net gain (that is, the difference between its demand per unit and its *MC*) at D_S. A bilateral agreement, such as the US-Cuba Hijacking Pact of February 1973, in which the parties agreed to return the hijacked plane, passengers, crew members, and hijackers, attempts to internalize the associated external costs through bargaining. The bargaining solution may, however, fail when there are more than two countries involved, because the transaction costs of reaching a mutually acceptable agreement may be prohibitive.[3] Not surprisingly, nations have an easier time in framing bilateral counterterrorism agreements as compared to multilateral accords. Second, a tax of *AC* per unit can be imposed on the defender country, where this tax equals the marginal external cost at a defensive level of D_S. This "fix" is fraught with difficulties, because the international community lacks a recognized institution with the authority to tax sovereign nations for their externally imposed costs. To preserve sovereignty, nations will likely oppose setting up such an authority unless the terrorism threat is more severe. Moreover, there is an information problem in ascertaining a recipient's marginal damage. The recipient country has perverse incentives to exaggerate its damages if compensation is to follow. Third, some supranational authority can set a quota on the defender's actions at level D_S. This solution also suffers from the absence of such an authority. Fourth, nations facing a common terrorist threat will account for the external costs if they take unified actions. Except in dire times, nations

[3]   On bargaining and externalities, see Cornes and Sandler (1996, pp. 86–91).

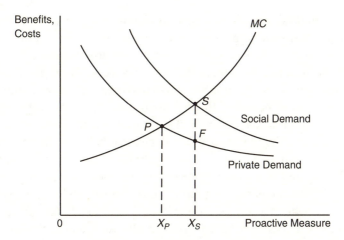

Figure 6.2. Transnational external benefits.

have insisted on maintaining independence over counterterrorism policies. Simply put, externalities are easier to conceptualize than to correct.

Transnational External Benefits

Some counterterrorism policies may give rise to transnational external benefits. For example, proactive measures that succeed in crippling or reducing the effectiveness of a terrorist group that poses a common threat to multiple countries yield external benefits to all at-risk countries. Thus, US efforts to capture or kill the al-Qaida leadership after 9/11 provided such benefits to other targeted countries. For external benefits, it is the demand curve that must be adjusted to include the marginal external gains that a nation's counterterrorism measures confer on others. Thus, the social marginal-willingness-to-pay curve or social demand curve in Figure 6.2 lies above the providing nation's demand curve by the amount of marginal external benefits. As the level of the proactive response increases, marginal external benefits decrease owing to diminishing returns; that is, the marginal gains from proactive measures are greatest when there are few such actions and decrease as more efforts are expended.

The nation's independent solution is at P, where the nation equates its private demand and MC and provides X_P. If, however, the social optimum is found, then the social demand must be equated to MC, and the optimum level is X_S, which exceeds X_P. With external benefits, independent action leads to too little of the action. Now, in order to internalize the externality, a nation must be made to include these marginal external benefits in its decision calculus. For example, a subsidy of SF per unit of proactive response to the providing nation would result in the social optimum, but requires a supranational authority that currently does not exist.

In both cases of externalities, the difference between private and social solutions increases as the number of nations receiving the externality from counterterrorism increases. This follows because the relevant private and social curves are farther apart as the external benefits or costs increase, thereby making the inefficiency of independent behavior greater. That is, X_P and X_S would lie farther apart in Figure 6.2 as the number of external benefit recipients increases. As a terrorism network expands its geographical reach, the number of targeted countries grows, and so the extent of external benefits (or costs) also increases. The al-Qaida network is more widely dispersed than earlier terrorist threats – for example, the Abu Nidal Organization (ANO) of the 1980s – so that proactive or defensive measures against al-Qaida result in more external benefits or costs than did similar actions against the ANO. As a consequence, the extent of suboptimality from the failure of nations to cooperate today is greater than in past decades. The globalization of terrorism means that the externality problem has worsened. The internet, for example, permits the terrorists to widen their network and, by so doing, enhances the inefficiency resulting from the lack of government cooperation with respect to counterterrorism against a global threat. Communication and transportation innovations will serve to worsen this concern.

In some cases, there may be both positive and negative externalities associated with counterterrorism efforts. For example, a proactive response protects other countries' interests, but may also incite anger (that is, backlash) among terrorists and their supporters, thereby motivating harsh future attacks (Rosendorff and Sandler, 2004). If these attacks are visited on soft targets outside the nation taking the proactive measures, then an external cost arises. When there are both external benefits and costs, the relative position of independent provision vis-à-vis the social optimum depends on the relative strength of the associated external benefits on social demand and the relative strength of the associated external costs on social MC.

In Figure 6.3, the case of opposing externalities for a proactive measure that generates both external benefits and costs is illustrated. External benefits arise because action against a common terrorist threat makes all at-risk countries safer, so that social demand is higher than private demand by the amount of marginal external benefits. If, in addition, proaction gives rise to new grievances and subsequent terrorist threats abroad, then marginal external costs arise, so that social MC exceeds private MC for each amount of

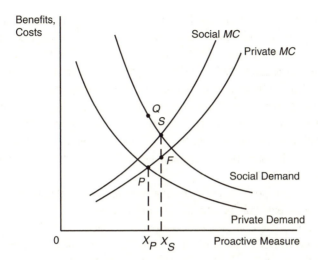

Figure 6.3. Mixed externalities.

proaction. The nation's independent solution is at P, where private demand equals private MC and X_P is provided. By contrast, the social optimum at S requires that social demand equals social MC and X_S is supplied. In Figure 6.3, the net outcome of these opposing externalities is too little provision ($X_S > X_P$) and the need for a subsidy of SF. If, instead, the external costs had been greater than private MC for each proactive effort level, then X_P may exceed X_S and a tax would be appropriate. It is conceivable, though highly unlikely, that the opposing externalities are precisely offsetting, so that no correction is needed. This is true if the social MC curve intersects the social demand curve at point Q directly above P in Figure 6.3.

Defensive measures can also generate opposing externalities. If a country's defensive efforts protect foreign investments and foreign residential workers, then there are external benefits that oppose the transference external costs. In Figure 6.1, there would be a social demand curve (not shown) above the private demand curve owing to marginal external benefits. In a globalized world, there are complex mixes of externalities that must be included when engineering the right combination of proactive and defensive measures.

Intertemporal Externalities

Externalities may also take on an intertemporal character, where action by an agent *today* may create uncompensated costs or benefits for agents *tomorrow.* A country that grants concessions to hostage takers – as France did during the 22 July 1968 El Al hijacking, or as the United States and Israel did during the 14 June 1985 hijacking of TWA flight 847[4] – creates an intertemporal externality by making terrorists believe that future hostage taking will be profitable, thus leading to more incidents (see Chapter 7). The terrorist escalation of carnage to attract media attention also creates intertemporal external costs by inducing terrorists to outdo past outrages. Thus, 9/11 means that terrorists may resort to even larger-scale events; eventually, this escalation may lead terrorists to seek weapons of mass destruction (WMD).

On the more positive side, innovations in counterterrorism can yield intertemporal external benefits to nations that can capitalize on these innovations in future operations. An excellent example occurred during the rescue mission of Lufthansa flight 181, a Boeing 737 hijacked while en route from Mallorca to Frankfurt on 13 October 1977.[5] After it was hijacked, the plane refueled in Rome and then flew on to Dubai. After a stopover in Aden, Yemen, the plane landed in Mogadishu, Somalia, on 17 October. At 2 A.M. on 18 October, West German Grenzschutzgruppe Neun (GSG-9) commandos entered the rear of the plane after creating a diversion with an ignited oil canister at the front of the cockpit. Once in the plane, the commandos exploded British stun grenades that temporarily incapacitated the hijackers. Only four of the eighty-six hostages were slightly injured in the successful rescue. Both the stun grenades and commandos' operating procedures were copied in future rescue missions.

Intertemporal externalities are even more difficult to address than standard externalities, because tomorrow's agents who benefit or are harmed by an action may not be present to bargain with the externality generator. For example, a government that applies a new procedure for freeing hostages may not have been in office when the procedure was developed years before. Moreover, the developer of the procedure may no longer be in office. Thus, intertemporal beneficial externalities will be undersupplied, while intertemporal detrimental externalities will be oversupplied not only at any given point in time, but over time.

---

[4]   A detailed description of this watershed hijacking can be found in Mickolus, Sandler, and Murdock (1989, vol. 2, pp. 219–25). On 30 June 1985, the Amal leader Nabih Berri in Lebanon released the remaining thirty-nine hostages in return for a US pledge not to launch any retaliatory strikes. Moreover, Israel agreed to release 735 prisoners from its Atlit prison. The hijackers were allowed to escape.

[5]   Based on newspaper accounts, this incident is described in detail in Mickolus (1980, pp. 734–40). The facts in our paragraph come from Mickolus's account.

ASYMMETRIES BETWEEN TERRORISTS AND GOVERNMENTS

Terrorist groups have displayed a tendency to cooperate in loose networks since the onset of modern-day terrorism (Chapter 2; Hoffman, 1998, 2006). Early terrorist networks cooperated on many levels, including training, intelligence, safe haven, financial support, logistical help, weapon acquisition, and the exchange of personnel (Alexander and Pluchinsky, 1992). For example, operatives were exchanged in the 21 December 1975 attack on the Organization of Petroleum Exporting (OPEC) countries ministerial meeting in Vienna and in the 27 June 1976 hijacking of Air France flight 139 (Mickolus, 1980). Loose ties existed among the European fighting communist organizations (FCOs), which shared a common ideology. The FCOs also had ties to the Palestinian groups, which were connected through the Palestine Liberation Organization (PLO). In addition, Euskadi ta Askatasuna (ETA) and the Provisional Irish Republican Army (PIRA) had links. In more recent years, the al-Qaida network operates in upward of sixty countries and stages its attacks worldwide. This network includes such groups as Abu Sayyaf (the Philippines), al-Jihad (Egypt), Harakat ul-Mujahidin (Pakistan), Islamic Movement (Uzbekistan), Jemaah Islamiyah (Southeast Asia), al-Qaida of Iraq, and bin Laden's al-Qaida (Afghanistan and Pakistan).

By contrast, governments detest sacrificing their autonomy over security matters and so severely limit their cooperation. An exigency such as 9/11 fosters cooperation – for example, nations participated in various capacities in the US-led retaliation on 7 October 2001 against the Taliban for harboring al-Qaida and Osama bin Laden – but this cooperation fades with time unless reignited by some new heinous terrorist attack. Why do governments have greater difficulty addressing their collective action concerns than their terrorist adversaries? There are at least three main factors at work. First, governments' strength provides a false sense of security, thereby inhibiting them from appreciating the need for coordinated action. By contrast, terrorists' relative weakness, compared to the well-armed governments that they challenge, means that terrorists have little choice but to pool resources in order to stretch limited means. Second, governments do not agree on which groups are terrorists – for example, until fairly recently, the European Union (EU) did not view Hamas, despite its suicide bombing campaign, as a terrorist organization. Although terrorist groups have different agendas and goals, these groups share similar opponents – for example, the United States and Israel – that provide a unity of purpose. Third, governments and terrorists have different time horizons. In liberal democracies, government officials' interest in the future is circumscribed by the length of the election cycle and their likelihood of reelection. Officials with one remaining term – for example, an American president in his second term – are likely to be unconcerned about the consequences of decisions beyond that term. Because governments change, agreements to combat terrorism made with leaders of other countries may be rather short-lived, and this detracts from the gains from fostering such arrangements. For example, Spanish Prime Minister Zapatero pulled the country's troops out of Iraq following his victory in the 2004 national elections. Spanish support of the US-led war on terror, which had been very strong, weakened under Zapatero. By contrast, terrorist leaders tend to be tenured for life, so they view intergroup cooperative arrangements as continual. They consequently take a long-term viewpoint and place higher value than governments on future benefits. That is, reputation matters more for terrorists than for governments. Failure of one group to honor its commitments can lead to long-run retribution by other groups in terms of withholding their cooperative action. This loss of future cooperative gains may outweigh any short-run payoff from reneging on a pact, thereby bolstering cooperation.

These three factors imply that terrorists are better able than governments to address collective concerns; in so doing, terrorists create synergistic gains. Through global networks, terrorists are able to identify and exploit a weakest link (softer target) whenever it appears. Moreover, terrorists can dispatch their best-equipped cell to this target of opportunity. The absence of sufficient intergovernmental cooperation means that these weakest links are always present (Sandler, 2003).

Other essential asymmetries distinguish governments from terrorists. Unfortunately, these asymmetries provide a clear tactical advantage to the terrorists. Governments and the nations that they protect are target-rich; terrorists and their safe havens are target-poor. Terrorists often hide among the general population in urban centers, thereby maximizing collateral damage during government raids. In other cases, terrorists reside in inaccessible places, such as the caves in Afghanistan or jungle tracts. Governments must guard everywhere, while terrorists can identify and attack the softest targets. This means that defensive measures by governments may be relatively expensive. Governments have to be fortunate on a daily basis, while terrorists have to be lucky only occasionally.[6] Hence,

---

[6] This asymmetry paraphrases what IRA terrorists said in a letter after they learned that their 12 October 1984 bombing of the Grand Hotel in Brighton had narrowly missed killing Prime Minister Margaret Thatcher. Their letter said, "Today, we were unlucky. But remember we have only to be lucky once. You will have to be lucky always." See Mickolus, Sandler, and Murdock (1989, vol. 2, p. 115).

terrorists can wait and choose the most opportune time to act, as they did on 9/11. Democratic governments are restrained in their responses to terrorists (see Chapter 2), while fundamentalist terrorists are unrestrained in their brutality. Governments are organized hierarchically, whereas today's terrorist groups are organized nonhierarchically (Arquilla and Ronfeldt, 2001; Memon et al., 2009). Given their loose networks, terrorist cells and groups can, at times, operate independently (Enders and Jindapon, 2010; Enders and Su, 2007). Infiltrators and spies can do great damage owing to the hierarchal structure of governments; by contrast, captured terrorists can provide only limited intelligence owing to the virtual autonomy of many of the network's components. Size can be a disadvantage to governments as more targets require protection and more coordination is required. The looseness of terrorist networks can make greater size an advantage as there are more resources to draw on. Also, a farther-flung network means that the terrorists can better capitalize on soft targets.

Another asymmetry involves information. Governments are not well informed about terrorists' strength, whereas terrorists can easily discover the nature and extent of the government's antiterrorist activities. In many liberal democracies, such information is a matter of public record. This asymmetry is poignantly illustrated by US estimates of al-Qaida's size as "several hundred to several thousand members," just five months prior to 9/11 (US Department of State, 2001, p. 68). Experience during the US-led invasion of Afghanistan and intelligence gathered thereafter indicated that al-Qaida had far more members than the upper bound of the US estimate. Misleading intelligence can greatly compromise the planning and success of such an invasion. In 2011, the US military is still trying to rid Afghanistan of al-Qaida and its supporters. Such misestimates inhibit the ability of a leader nation to encourage other countries to contribute to a preemptive strike. In the case of Aum Shinrikyo, Japanese authorities had no idea until after their raids in 1995 what a formidable threat this group posed.

In Table 6.1, we have gathered together the asymmetries for ready reference. The irony of these asymmetries is that they reverse the roles somewhat by transferring the advantage from the strong (the governments) to the weak (the terrorists). The only way to minimize the disadvantage that some of these asymmetries create for the governments is for them to rely less on security autonomy and to start cooperating more fully with their counterparts. Other asymmetries – for example, response restraint, the need for luck, and size considerations – derive from adversarial roles associated with terrorism. Because such factors favor the weak, they resort to terrorism, which levels the playing field.

Table 6.1. *Essential Asymmetries between Terrorists and Targeted Governments*

Terrorists	Targeted Governments
• Target-poor	• Target-rich
• Weak relative to adversary	• Strong relative to adversary
• Take a long-term viewpoint when interacting with other terrorist groups	• Take a short-term viewpoint when interacting with other governments
• Agree on common enemies	• Do not agree on common enemies
• Address their collective action concerns	• Do not address their collective action concerns
• Can be restrained or unrestrained in their response	• Restrained in their response
• Nonhierarchical organization	• Hierarchical organization
• Size furthers interests	• Size may hamper interests
• Luck needed on occasion	• Luck always needed
• Reasonably well informed about government's strength	• Not well informed about terrorist's strength

GAME-THEORETICAL ISSUES

We begin with an explanation, using some elementary game theory, of why the short and *fixed* time horizon of government officials hampers international cooperation among governments. We purposely construct the example to minimize computational complications. Suppose that two governments confronting the same terrorist threat must decide whether to preempt the terrorists through an attack on their base or sponsors. Unlike the analysis in Chapter 4, we further suppose that the two governments in our example can interact for only *two* periods owing to election-term considerations.

The procedure for solving such a game is to examine the Nash equilibrium for the second period and then to *condition* the Nash equilibrium solution for the first period on the solution value found for the second period. In technical parlance, this gives a *subgame perfect equilibrium* in which the players would not unilaterally change their strategies during the current *or* future period. This solution strategy is found by solving the game backward, starting at the last period. As we did in Chapter 4, we assume that the preemption game is a Prisoners' Dilemma. In Figure 6.4, we display the 2 × 2 game matrix for the two players – nation 1 (the row player) and nation 2 (the column player) – viewed from the standpoint of the second and last period of the two-period game. Recall that the left-hand payoff in each cell

	nation 2	
	Preempt	Status quo
Preempt	6, 6	–2, 8
Status quo	8, –2	**0, 0**

nation 1

Figure 6.4. Prisoners' Dilemma viewed from period two of two-period game.

is that of nation 1, and the right-hand payoff is that of nation 2. The payoffs are based on the following assumptions. During each period, a preemptor confers a benefit of 8 on each of the two players at a cost of 10 to itself. If, therefore, only one country preempts, then the preemptor nets –2, while the free rider gains 8. If, however, both countries take action, then each receives 6 (= 2 × 8 – 10) as cumulative benefits of 16 from two preemption actions are reduced by the country-specific provision costs of 10. When no one acts, there are no benefits. This is a classic Prisoners' Dilemma (see Chapter 4) with a dominant strategy of status quo, where the payoffs are greater than the corresponding payoffs of preempting (that is, 8 > 6 and 0 > –2). As each nation exercises its dominant strategy, the second-period Nash equilibrium, whose payoffs are boldfaced in Figure 6.4, is achieved with no nation taking measures against the terrorists.

We now use the second-period solution's payoffs to view the first-period game. This is done by adding the Nash equilibrium payoffs of 0 to each player's first-period matrix, whose payoff array is identical to Figure 6.4 prior to this addition. Because we are adding 0 to each payoff, the first-period matrix augmented by the second-period Nash payoffs stays identical to that in Figure 6.4 and so is not displayed. If, say, the Nash payoffs in the second period had been 2 for each player, then *every* payoff in the first-period matrix would be greater by 2 than those in the second-period matrix. Whether 0 or some other constant is added to every payoff of the first-period matrix, *the dominant strategy will not change and remains for each nation to maintain the status quo.* Thus, the subgame perfect equilibrium for the two-period repeated interaction is for each government to maintain the status quo during each period – hence, the absence of action or cooperation against a common terrorist threat.[7]

---

[7] If preemption during the first period degrades the terrorists and, thus, reduces the benefits from action during the second period, then one would have to allow for different contingent matrices during period two depending on first-period actions. This complication need not change our conclusion, because the net benefits to a preemptor during the

Suppose that the government officials in the two countries have any number of *known* periods to interact. The game is solved in the same way, starting at the last period as in Figure 6.4 and finding the Nash equilibrium at mutual inactivity with payoffs of 0. These zero payoffs are then added to every payoff in the 2 × 2 matrix for the next-to-last period. The Nash equilibrium of the augmented next-to-last-period matrix is again mutual inactivity, as it is for the next-earlier period, and so on. In short, the game is "folded back" period by period to show that the subgame perfect strategy is to maintain the status quo during each and every period. The same result follows if there are more than two interacting governments (Sandler, 1992). Limited office terms inhibit cooperative arrangements among governments when addressing a threat of transnational terrorism.

There are only two instances where cooperation develops: when the officials' number of terms in office is *unknown* (that is, when the officials can be elected for an indefinite number of terms) or when the officials are tenured for life. In either instance, the officials know that reneging on a cooperative arrangement may have repercussions as their counterpart punishes their misbehavior.[8] Because the last office period is not known with certainty, there is no point at which cheating would necessarily go unpunished during the ensuing period. The presence of future periods is precisely what motivates a terrorist group with tenured leaders to honor its commitments to other groups. Quite simply, terrorists are interested in the future because failure to abide by understandings has consequences for future interactions. Reputation matters.

Coordination Games

Many alternative game forms can reflect countermeasures against transnational terrorism (see Chapter 4; Arce and Sandler, 2005; Sandler and Arce, 2003). An important game form for certain counterterrorist policy choices is a "Stag Hunt" coordination game, where both nations are better off taking identical measures. When one nation takes the measure alone,

---

second period *will remain negative* if preemption benefits have declined due to first-period actions. The transformed game stays a Prisoners' Dilemma during the second period, with a Nash equilibrium of no action. In fact, no action is also anticipated during the first period owing to the Prisoners' Dilemma.

[8]   This assumes a tit-for-tat strategy, where a nation cooperates during the first period and then matches its counterpart's strategy of the preceding period. If, therefore, nation 1 does not preempt during some period, then nation 2 will withhold preempting until nation 1 preempts. For more on repeated games, see Sandler (1992) or any game theory text.

nation 2

	Freeze	Status quo
Freeze (nation 1)	**F, F**	B, E
Status quo (nation 1)	E, B	**A, A**

$F > E > A > B$

Figure 6.5. Freezing assets: Coordination game.

this nation receives the smallest payoff, and the nation that fails to act earns the second-greatest payoff. This kind of scenario is descriptive of a host of counterterrorism policies where two or more nations must act in unison for the best payoffs to be achieved. Instances include freezing terrorist assets, denying safe haven to terrorists, sharing intelligence about a common threat, and staying with a no-concession policy. Even a sole defector can spoil the policy's effectiveness for all nations abiding by the policy. We use agreements to freeze terrorists' assets to illustrate such games.

For illustration, we assume just two nations – 1 and 2 – and a situation in which each can either freeze the assets of the terrorists or take no action (status quo). In Figure 6.5, the highest payoff, F, results from mutual action, followed by a payoff of E from doing nothing when the other nation freezes assets. This scenario implies that the nation that does not join the freeze can profit by providing a safe haven for terrorists' funds. The nation may be so inclined if it does not view its own people and property as likely targets. Nevertheless, F exceeds E because this nation may risk negative ramifications if discovered. Moreover, the noncooperator cannot be positive that its people and property will never be attacked, which limits the size of E. The third-lowest payoff, A, is from mutual inaction, while the worst payoff, B, is the "sucker" payoff of acting alone. This follows because the sucker bears the costs and gains no added safety, because the terrorists can still safeguard their assets through the other nation's duplicity.

The game in Figure 6.5 has three Nash equilibriums. If both nations freeze terrorists' assets, this is a Nash equilibrium because neither nation would switch strategies on its own, insofar as $F > E$. Another Nash equilibrium is for both nations to do nothing. Once again, neither nation will unilaterally change strategies, because $A > B$. Obviously, there is no dominant strategy. These first two equilibriums are known as pure-strategy Nash equilibriums, because a nation exercises the same strategy all of the time. A third Nash equilibrium involves mixed strategies in which each pure strategy is played in a probabilistic fashion. For example, nation 1 may freeze assets p percent of the time and do nothing $(1 - p)$ percent of the time, while nation 2 may freeze assets q percent of the time and do nothing $(1 - q)$ percent of the time. To identify this mixed-strategy equilibrium, we determine nation 2's q probability for freezing assets that makes nation 1 *indifferent* between freezing terrorist assets and doing nothing.[9] Similarly, we can determine nation 1's p probability for freezing assets. These probabilities identify the mixed-strategy equilibrium. For example, p represents the uncertain belief that nation 2 has of the likelihood that nation 1 will freeze assets; similarly, q denotes the uncertain belief that nation 1 has of the likelihood that nation 2 will freeze assets. If nation 2 (nation 1) believes that there is a greater than p (q) chance that its counterpart will freeze terrorists' assets, then nation 2 (nation 1) will follow suit. Anything that reduces these "adherence probabilities" serves to make cooperation more likely, because a nation has to be less certain of action by its counterpart in order for the nation to freeze assets. For example, an increase in the gain from mutual action, F, or a smaller mutual status quo payoff, A, promotes coordination by reducing the required adherence probabilities. An increase in the payoff, B, associated with unilaterally freezing terrorists' assets promotes cooperation, while an increase in profitable opportunities, E, from hiding terrorists' assets serve to inhibit cooperation. Although the mathematics appear complicated, these outcomes are quite intuitive.[10]

A fascinating extension, which we will not show analytically, is to allow for more nations. Suppose that all n nations are required to freeze assets so that the terrorists cannot merely circumvent the restriction through some safe haven. The greater the number of required adherents for effectiveness, the larger the adherence probabilities required by each nation to participate. Even for a relatively small number of nations, near-certain adherence is

---

[9] The calculation for q (or p not shown) goes as follows:

$$qF + (1 - q)B = qE + (1 - q)A,$$

so that nation 1's expected gain from freezing assets, based on nation 2's uncertain action, equals nation 1's expected gain from not freezing assets, again based on nation 2's uncertain action. This equality indicates nation 2's indifference. This equation yields:

$$q = (A - B)/[(F - B) + (A - E)].$$

This expression and an analogous one for p give the influences described in the text. See Sandler (2005) for details of further calculations.

[10] These outcomes follow from taking the partial derivative of the mixed strategy q or p with respect to a given payoff – for example, F. If this partial derivative is negative (positive), then the adherence q or p is smaller (larger) and cooperation is more (less) likely.

required, which is not an encouraging result.[11] Hence, nations will not join freezes unless the actions of others can be guaranteed. This is of particular concern for freezing assets, because even one nonadherent nation can be the spoiler when one realizes that the 1993 World Trade Center bomb cost only $400 but caused over $500 million in damage (Hoffman, 1998). Terrorists' operations are fairly inexpensive, so money flows must be stopped almost completely if large-scale terrorist incidents are to be avoided.

Counterterrorism actions that require only a small subset of nations – for example, a bilateral treaty to punish hijackers or a bilateral agreement to incarcerate local terrorists – can be successful, even as coordination games, because limited adherence probabilities may apply. Unfortunately, transnational terrorists can greatly stifle cooperation by involving more countries and seeking an accommodation with the weakest country. For domestic terrorism, the central government can coordinate a unified response, so that terrorists cannot play one region off against another. Failed or failing states cannot always provide this coordination.

Weakest-Link Problems

In Chapter 4, we introduced weakest-link security considerations where the overall level of the associated public good hinges on the smallest provision effort. Consider the case of man-portable anti-aircraft missiles (MANPADs) that can shoot down commercial aircraft. Planes are especially vulnerable to MANPADs on takeoff and landing, when a terrorist on the ground near an airport can fire a heat-seeking missile at a plane. Currently, the US Department of Homeland Security (DHS) appears committed to having MANPAD defenses, which fire flare decoys, installed on US planes at the cost of billions of dollars for the entire US fleet. In August 2006, DHS issued contracts to Northrop Grumman, BAE Systems Electronics, and Integrated Solutions to develop a Counter-Man Portable Air Defense System for commercial airliners (Sieff, 2006). It may be two decades before such systems are installed on the entire US fleet. If US planes are protected and other countries do not follow suit, then terrorists bent on using MANPADs will merely travel to a country where planes are not so equipped and try to shoot down a foreign plane full of Americans. The additional safety derived from MANPADs depends on the least efforts taken. The need for international

---

[11] This assumes that each nation's likelihood of freezing terrorist assets is independent of those of the other nations. If, however, these likelihoods are positively correlated, then the prognosis is better (Sandler and Sargent, 1995).

cooperation, so that all air carriers equip their planes with similar security methods, is evident.

Because countries have different capacities to respond owing to income considerations, there is a need in the case of MANPADs and other security upgrades (for example, full-body scanners) to consider "*shoring up*" the defenses of some countries. A prime-target nation, such as the United States, may be expected to help bolster the defenses of some of these weakest links (Sandler, 2004, 2005). There are, however, a number of problems with this fix. First, the United States does not have sufficient resources to shore up all of the weakest-link situations, particularly when its own antiterrorism budget has grown so fast since 9/11 (see Chapter 11). Second, there is a proclivity for other countries to free ride on any nation so inclined to shore up weakest links, because this action provides purely public benefits for all countries. Third, nations that take on the lion's share of this effort can be expected to have an agenda – that is, the assistance may involve conditions, such as a demand for military bases or political concessions. Fourth, there is a moral hazard problem because the recipient country may not use the money as intended unless the providing country supplies the assistance in kind.

To shore up weakest links requires coordinated international action directed by some multilateral institution such as the United Nations. This institution would need to pass an assessment resolution, requiring member nations to share in the funding needed to shore up the weakest links in a system similar to UN assessment accounts for underwriting peace-keeping expenditures.[12] Assessment would be based on member nations' ability to pay based on gross domestic product and benefits derived. For benefit-based assessments, those developed countries attracting the most terrorist incidents – say, over the last ten-year period – would have the greatest assessment shares of expenditures to cover. To avoid the moral hazard problem, this institution would need to provide the actual security upgrades and train the country's personnel. Of course, nations would have to agree to such an assessment arrangement, and the recipient country must also consent to the assistance.

INTERNATIONAL ACTIONS TO ADDRESS
TRANSNATIONAL TERRORISM

In Table 6.2, global and regional conventions and treaties relating to controlling international terrorism are displayed. The table is set up as

---

[12] On UN assessment accounts, see Durch (1993) and Mills (1990).

follows: the convention/treaty is named in the first column; the supporting institution is given in the second column; the date and place of framing are listed in the third column; and its entered-in-force date is indicated in the fourth column. Global conventions are listed first, followed by regional conventions. Only conventions are given in Table 6.2; there are myriad international resolutions – for example, UN General Assembly Resolution 2551 on the Forcible Diversion of Civil Aircraft in Flight (12 December 1969) and UN General Assembly Resolution 2645 on Aerial Hijacking (25 November 1970).[13] A resolution typically expresses a declared position or intended action, while a convention indicates a mandated, but usually unenforced, response. We focus on the latter because resolutions are weaker and are often later enacted as a convention if deemed important.

To date, there are thirteen international conventions and nine regional ones that forbid a wide range of terrorist activities, from bombings to hostage taking. International conventions prohibit actions against diplomatic missions, aircrafts, ocean platforms, nuclear power plants, and ships. A 1998 convention makes terrorism more difficult by tagging plastic explosives in order to identify perpetrators, and another convention seeks to suppress terrorist financing. The most recent UN international convention banned acts of nuclear terrorism; this convention went into force within months of its initial framing. In contrast to their international counterparts, regional conventions outlaw all forms of terrorism that meet the convention-approved definition. Some regional conventions took time for ratification as parties argued over the definition of terrorism.

These conventions have been reactive, responding only after a spate of attacks. For example, the adoption of the International Civil Aviation Organization (ICAO) conventions followed numerous hijackings and bombings of commercial airlines in the 1960s. The UN convention outlawing crimes against diplomats and other protected persons was approved only after many such attacks in the late 1960s and the beginning of the 1970s. The recent antinuclear terrorism convention was ratified after evidence, gathered from the US-led invasion of Afghanistan in 2001, indicated al-Qaida's efforts to acquire nuclear weapons. The presence of terrorist groups in India and Pakistan, which might someday possess nuclear weapons, makes the world understandably concerned. All conventions rely on

---

[13] During 1992–1993, the UN Security Council issued a series of resolutions (Resolutions 731, 748, and 883) condemning Libya for its role in the downing of Pan Am flight 103 and UTA flight 772. These resolutions asked that Libya extradite two accused nationals and end its sponsorship of terrorism.

Table 6.2. *Global and Regional Conventions and Treaties Relating to Controlling International Terrorism*

Convention/Treaty	Supporting Institution	Date/Place Signed	Entered into Force
Global Conventions			
• Convention on Offences and Certain Other Acts Committed on Board Aircraft	International Civil Aviation Organization (ICAO)	14 September 1963 Tokyo	4 December 1969
• Convention for the Suppression of Unlawful Seizure of Aircraft	ICAO	16 December 1970 The Hague	14 October 1971
• Convention for the Suppression of Unlawful Acts Against the Safety of Civil Aviation	ICAO	23 September 1971 Montreal	26 January 1973
• Convention on the Prevention and Punishment of Crimes against International Protected Persons, including Diplomatic Agents	UN General Assembly	14 December 1973 New York	20 February 1977
• International Convention against Taking of Hostages	UN General Assembly	17 December 1979 New York	3 June 1983
• Convention on the Physical Protection of Nuclear Material	International Atomic Energy Agency	3 March 1980 Vienna and New York	8 February 1987
• Protocol for the Suppression of Unlawful Acts of Violence at Airports serving International Civil Aviation	ICAO	24 February 1988 Montreal	6 August 1989
• Convention for the Suppression of Unlawful Acts against the Safety of Maritime Navigation	International Maritime Organization (IMO)	10 March 1988 Rome	1 March 1992

• Protocol for the Suppression of Unlawful Acts against the Safety of Fixed Platforms Located on the Continental Shelf	IMO	10 March 1988 Rome	1 March 1992
• Convention on the Marking of Plastic Explosives for the Purpose of Detection	ICAO	1 March 1991 Montreal	21 June 1998
• International Convention for the Suppression of Terrorist Bombings	UN General Assembly	15 December 1997 New York	23 May 2001
• International Convention on the Suppression of Financing of Terrorism	UN General Assembly	9 December 1999 New York	10 April 2002
• International Convention for the Suppression of Acts of Nuclear Terrorism	UN General Assembly	13 April 2005 New York	7 July 2005
Regional Conventions			
• Arab Convention on the Suppression of Terrorism	League of Arab States	22 April 1998 Cairo	7 May 1999
• Convention on Combating International Terrorism	Organization of the Islamic Conference	1 July 1999 Ouagadougo, Burkina Faso	7 November 2002
• European Convention on the Suppression of Terrorism	Council of Europe	27 January 1977 Strasbourg, France	4 August 1978
• Convention to Prevent and Punish the Acts of Terrorism Taking the Form of Crimes against Persons and Related Extortion That Are of International Significance	Organization of American States	2 February 1971 Washington, D.C.	16 October 1973

(*continued*)

Table 6.2 (continued)

Convention/Treaty	Supporting Institution	Date/Place Signed	Entered into Force
• Convention on the Prevention and Combating of Terrorism	African Union	14 July 1999 Algiers	6 December 2002
• Regional Convention on Suppression of Terrorism	South Asian Association for Regional Cooperation	4 November 1987 Kathmandu	22 August 1988
• Treaty on Cooperation among the States Members of the Commonwealth of Independent States in Combating Terrorism	Commonwealth of Independent States	4 June 1999 Minsk	In force for Tajikistan, Kazakhstan, Kyrgyzstan, Moldova, Armenia, Belarus, and Russian Federation as of 25 January 2009
• Inter-American Convention against Terrorism	Organization of American States	3 June 2002 Bridgetown, Barbados	10 July 2003
• ASEAN Convention on Counterterrorism	ASEAN	13 January 2007	Not yet in force

Sources: United Nations (2002b, pp. 17–18; 2003; 2009; 2010).

the ratifying countries to implement the stipulated prohibition or institute the required action using their own laws and resources. Essentially, conventions are a means of bolstering antiterrorist policy by coordinating national action through set guidelines. Varying levels of adherence are consequently anticipated, especially since none of these conventions possesses an enforcement mechanism and nations have different counterterrorism capacities, resources, and interests. Conventions involving a weakest-link public good are particularly problematic because success may be compromised by inadequate response by nonratifiers or by ratifiers with limited capacity. Terrorists will take advantage of such vulnerabilities. For example, plastic explosives may not be traced following a bombing if terrorists acquire them in a country where the convention is not effectively implemented. For many international conventions, a single compliance failure can severely jeopardize the safety of all potential targets in a globalized world. Such noncompliance greatly limits the usefulness of the convention. For some conventions, universal ratification and implementation are necessary, but never attained.

To investigate the effectiveness of some of these international conventions, Enders, Sandler, and Cauley (1990a) applied intervention analysis to various terrorist events. In the case of crimes against diplomats and other protected persons, they compared the pre-convention mean of the series for such attacks with its post-convention mean and *uncovered no significant differences*, suggesting that this convention was ineffective. For skyjackings, these authors performed the same test for the UN Security Council resolution of 1985 and earlier antihijacking resolutions and conventions (for example, the Hague Convention on seizure of aircraft and the UN General Assembly convention against taking hostages), and again found no significant impact on the mean number of hijackings. In Chapter 3, we performed a test on the effectiveness of the 23 May 2001 International Convention for the Suppression of Terrorist Bombings and found no impact. Ironically, bombings as a proportion of terrorist incidents have been rising since about the time that the convention entered into force. Simply condemning a type of terrorist event is not going to hold any sway over individuals consumed by a purpose and willing to sacrifice themselves for the cause.

Regional conventions typically prohibit all forms of terrorism. These all-purpose condemnations are unlikely to lead to anything concrete, especially when the underlying definition of terrorism permits exceptions for campaigns of national liberation or other motives. Many regional conventions provide for cooperation among states confronting a common terrorist threat, usually in terms of sharing intelligence and other information about

the terrorists (for example, preferred targets). On the surface, this cooperation should improve the situation, but this may not be the case if other policy decisions are not shared as well. Nations independently decide which
targets to harden and determine their own budgets for deterring attacks.
Shared intelligence may exacerbate nations' working at cross purposes
as they spend even more money on deterrence after they learn terrorists'
strengths and targeting predispositions from shared intelligence (Chapters
4–5; Enders and Sandler, 1995). This is a classic "second-best" problem
where cooperating on only one of two choice variables may reduce the well-
being of everyone, as noncooperation on the second policy option more
than offsets any gain achieved from the partial cooperation.

Nations' insistence on making most security decisions on their own
is highlighted by the wasted resources spent on maintaining commando
squads for individual nations rather than developing a single network that
can respond quickly to a terrorist crisis anywhere. Such a network, if constituted, would save not only on equipment, but also on manpower. The
networked commandos would be deployed more often than those from
individual countries and, thereby, acquire more experience and expertise.
Deployment to specific incidents would be determined in part geographically in order to speed deployment, so that nations would preserve some
autonomy. The proposed network could provide "surge capacity" when
a large-scale lengthy incident occurs (for example, the four-day Mumbai
armed attacks in November 2008) or when multiple incidents are staged.
In addition, the network could shore up weakest-link nations that do not
possess commando or crisis-management forces.

COLLECTIVE ACTION AGAINST TERRORIST FINANCING

Successful efforts that limit terrorists' resources curb their ability to engage
in all forms of terrorism. Unlike antiterrorism policies that harden targets,
actions that reduce terrorist resources do not merely change the terrorist
attack mode from, say, hijacking to kidnapping. Since 9/11, select nations
have tried to be more attentive to tracking the money trail as a way of inhibiting terrorist operations. In September 2003, the US Treasury reported that
$135 million of alleged terrorists' assets had been frozen worldwide after
9/11 (*The Economist*, 2003). In February 2004, the White House (2003)
increased this figure to $200 million. More recently, the amounts frozen
have not been reported.

In Table 6.3, some of the international initiatives targeting terrorist funds
are highlighted, starting with the creation of the Financial Action Task

Force on Money Laundering (FATF), established in 1989 by the G-7 countries. FATF issues recommendations aimed at limiting terrorists' and drug cartels' ability to move funds internationally. Key recommendations include freezing assets, adopting international conventions, generating accurate originator data on wire transfers, reporting suspicious transactions, fostering greater international cooperation, reviewing laws regulating nonprofits (including charities), registering businesses active in international remittances, and criminalizing the funding of terrorism (Levitt, 2003, p. 62).

Another development in stemming the funding of terrorism came with the creation of Financial Intelligence Units (FIUs) in November 1996. At the national level, FIUs monitor money transactions in order to spot and eliminate those supporting crimes, including terrorism. International cooperation and information exchange among the FIUs are bolstered by the Egmont Group, which began its efforts to link FIUs starting in June 2001. Because it is not a worldwide network, the Egmont Group leaves terrorists plenty of avenues (that is, weak links) to escape FIU surveillance. Moreover, the Egmont Group has no means to compel cooperation or universal participation.

Even before 9/11, the International Monetary Fund (IMF) and the World Bank pledged greater anti–money laundering activities in April 2001. IMF complements FATF's activities by providing technical assistance to countries needing enhanced capacity to cope with terrorist financial flows (IMF, 2001b). Primarily, IMF fosters the exchange of information among countries whose institutions are working to reduce terrorist and criminal money transfers. At the same time, the World Bank Executive Board indicated that it will work with the IMF to reduce money laundering while bolstering countries' ability to address the problem. Following 9/11, UN Security Council Resolution 1373 called for global cooperation to combat terrorism and formed the UN Counterterrorism Committee to serve in an advisory role to member states that seek its advice. Resolution 1373 also implored UN members to ratify and implement the international conventions, including the International Convention on the Suppression of Financing of Terrorism, which eventually came into force in April 2002.

INTERPOL added its own expertise and forged links with the FIUs and IMF to curb terrorist financing. To bolster its efforts to limit terrorist funds, INTERPOL conducts training workshops and conferences for its 188 member countries' law enforcement personnel. In addition, INTERPOL works with the World Customs Organization to gather information and best practices on addressing cross-border flows of laundered money and terrorist financing. The most important asset that INTERPOL brings to the problem

Table 6.3. *International Efforts against the Funding of Terrorism*

Action/Date Established	Description
Financial Action Task Force on Money Laundering (FATF), 1989	This intergovernmental body, created by the G-7 countries in 1989, issues recommendations for reducing terrorist funding. It can merely make suggestions. Currently, FATF is chaired by the Netherlands and consists of thirty-three countries and two regional organizations.
Financial Intelligence Units (FIUs), November 1996	FIUs are national bodies established to limit money flows for illicit purposes, including terrorism.
Egmont Group and FIUs, June 2001 (Egmont Group established in 1995)	Through the exchange of intelligence, the Egmont Group promotes cooperation among FIUs to reduce money laundering and the financial resources of terrorists.
International Monetary Fund (IMF) Actions, April 2001	Bolster efforts at curbing money laundering by working with the major international anti–money laundering (AML) groups. Provide technical assistance to countries whose AML capacity is limited. Promote international cooperation and information exchange to reduce terrorist funding.
World Bank Executive Board, April 2001	In partnership with IMF, the Bank agreed to limit money laundering and funding for terrorism. The Bank also promised to implement the recommendations of FATF.
UN Security Council Resolution 1373 and UN Counterterrorism Committee (CTC), November 2001	The resolution calls for global efforts to combat terrorism. It mandates three primary actions: to curb terrorist finances, to stop state sponsorship of terrorism, and to cooperate with other states' antiterrorist actions. The resolution instructs all nations to sign and implement the twelve international antiterrorist conventions. The CTC serves an advisory role for those countries actively seeking to curb terrorist funding.
International Convention on the Suppression of Financing of Terrorism, April 2002	Requires states to take appropriate actions to detect and freeze terrorist finances. The convention provides for no enforcement mechanism.
INTERPOL's Working Group on Money Laundering and Terrorist Financing, September 2004	Provides outreach to FIUs. Conducts training workshops and conferences. Links police and customs administrations in addressing terrorist financing. There is a long-run plan to develop a database on currency seizures and air passengers that will be available on INTERPOL's I-24/7 secure communication network for member countries' law enforcement agents to access.

Sources: IMF (2001a, 2009), Levitt (2003), Organization of Economic Cooperation and Development (2003), United Nations (2002a, 2003), United Nations Security Council (2001).

is its expertise in developing a comprehensive database on currency seizures, air passenger information, and terrorist watchlists. INTERPOL also possesses a secure communication network – I-24/7 – that its members can access for its databases. INTERPOL has extensive databases on stolen and lost travel documents (SLTDs), DNA and fingerprints, and terrorist groups. These databases may prove helpful in identifying suspicious persons at border crossings in the search for funds intended to support terrorism.

A Leaky Bucket

At first, efforts by the world community to go after terrorists' finances as reported in this chapter appeared impressive, but actions have waned compared to those in the year immediately following 9/11 (Basile, 2004, p. 177). All such efforts rely on nations to rigorously enforce standards of vigilance and best practice endorsed by FATF. As long as some countries lack the capacity or will to institute FATF's recommendations, terrorists will find ways to finance their heinous acts.

There are numerous means for al-Qaida and other terrorist networks to circumvent international efforts to freeze their assets.[14] First, terrorists can hide their financial assets in nations that are noncompliant to agreements. Second, they can transfer their money in small transactions – under $5,000 – because only suspicious transfers above this ceiling must be reported under current guidelines. Multiple small transfers can fund most terrorist operations, including spectaculars – the 1993 World Trade Center bomb cost just $400, and the 9/11 attacks cost less than a half-million dollars (*The Economist*, 2003, p. 45). Third, terrorists use the *hawala* system of informal cash transfers, where bookkeeping balances are held and settled among a network of balance holders at a later time through a wire transfer or an exchange of commodities. This serves to disguise who is making the transfer to whom and the exact amount of the transfer (Basile, 2004, p. 176). Fourth, terrorists can convert their financial assets to precious commodities, such as diamonds, to underwrite operations. Fifth, terrorists can disguise their financial dealings through legitimate and illegitimate business transactions. Sixth, terrorists can rely on contributions to charitable organizations for some of their finances. The initial success in freezing terrorist assets came as the terrorist networks were caught unprepared. Since then, terrorists have found new means and venues to bypass restrictions.

[14] This paragraph derives, in part, from the research of Basile (2004) and Levitt (2003).

An Assessment

Articles by Basile (2004) and Levitt (2003) suggested ways to address the problems with freezing terrorists' assets – for example, applying pressure on Saudi Arabia to control its charities, bringing more nations under FATF guidelines, lowering the limits on reporting money transfers, and monitoring the *hawala* system. Although implementing such policy recommendations would temporarily improve efforts to freeze terrorists' assets, their long-run effectiveness is very limited. As loopholes are closed, the terrorists will innovate and find new ways to transfer funds used to finance their relatively inexpensive operations. Freezing terrorists' assets is a moving target, and so the authorities must anticipate the next loophole. Additionally, international efforts will never involve a universal compliance to freezes; terrorist networks will always be able to counter some (much) of the collective efforts of others owing to the strategic (Stag Hunt) nature of the underlying interaction. Some nations will not go along with a freeze simply because they know its effectiveness is limited by nonuniversal subscription. Such freezes may prove an annoyance to terrorists, but freezes by themselves will not greatly curb terrorism, no matter what loopholes are closed. Freezes are not a panacea to terrorism, since the bucket will always leak by the very nature of the problem.

INTERPOL AFTER 9/11

In the fight against transnational terrorism, there is a marked tendency for nations to undersupply proactive measures – for example, apprehending terrorists. After 9/11, INTERPOL's Secretary General Ronald Noble made a decision to redirect some of the organization's modest resources to assist member countries in their counterterrorism activities. INTERPOL supplies this assistance through its secure communication system (I-24/7), its databases, its investigative resources, its dissemination of best practices, its bioterrorism program, its workshops, and its weapons and explosives tracking system. Its greatest counterterrorism assistance comes from the use of I-24/7 to issue Red Notices for the arrest of suspected criminals, including terrorists. In addition, "diffusions" can be initiated by member countries asking other countries to arrest a suspected criminal or terrorist. INTERPOL–UN Security Council Notices are issued to limit the activities (that is, international travel, possession of firearms and explosives, and funds transfers) of al-Qaida and Taliban members and affiliates.

It is essential to emphasize that INTERPOL does not deploy agents to make the requested arrests. Rather, INTERPOL makes its resources and linkages available to facilitate the arrest of suspected terrorists, made by law enforcement agents from member countries. In a recent study, Sandler, Arce, and Enders (2011) used standard benefit-cost methods to compute the likely returns from INTERPOL resources assigned to counterterrorism in 2006 and 2007. INTERPOL gave these researchers cost figures for the two years, broken down by the various INTERPOL assets assigned to counterterrorism. In 2006, this cost was a mere $13.5 million; in 2007, it came to $16.6 million. These expenditures are dwarfed by the thirty to forty billion dollars spent each year on homeland security just in the United States (see Chapter 11).

The difficult calculation involves translating the number of suspected terrorists arrested owing to Red Notices and diffusions into a benefit measure. Such a computation hinges on a counterfactual – that is, how many more terrorist incidents would there have been had these individuals not been arrested. Because the counterfactual exercise is based on the number of INTERPOL-assisted terrorist-related arrests, there is an implicit assumption that these arrests would not have occurred during that year without the use of INTERPOL's resources. In 2006, there were 74 such terrorist-related arrests; while in 2007, there were 104 such arrests.

To lend credence to their counterfactual computation of benefits, the authors presented twelve scenarios to show the robustness of their benefit-cost estimations. Moreover, they always erred on the side of underestimating benefits and overestimating costs whenever judgments were required. Their counterfactual calculations were driven by two key assumptions: the arrest of a suspected terrorist results in one fewer terrorist incident, and the arrest of an average-size terrorist attack force (usually four to six persons) results in one fewer terrorist incident. The authors translated the hypothesized fewer attacks into reduced deaths and injuries by using historical incident averages, drawn from ITERATE event data. Deaths and injuries avoided were then matched with dollar values based on payments made by the US government to the families of 9/11. In addition, the authors estimated a value for the saved gross domestic product (GDP) that resulted from the reduced number of terrorist incidents. Their benefit-cost ratios averaged from 40 to 200 over the twelve counterfactual scenarios. The larger figure applied when benefits included the gains from fewer casualties *and* higher GDP.

Their exercise shows that each dollar of INTERPOL counterterrorism spending returns from $40 to $200. This suggests that the efforts of a multilateral agency, and of INTERPOL in particular, can result in huge gains from international cooperation in the war on terror. This type of analysis should be applied to assess other forms of international counter-terrorism cooperation. Given the anticipated undersupply of such proactive efforts, the high return is credible.

CONCLUDING REMARKS

Networked terrorists present a formidable threat to a globalized and tech-nologically sophisticated world where target nations act largely inde-pendently to curb transnational terrorism. Our analysis of transnational externalities associated with counterterrorism demonstrated that there will be too few of some actions and too many of others so long as nations con-tinue to preserve their autonomy over security. The cooperation asymmetry between terrorists and target governments, whereby terrorist groups coop-erate while governments do not, permits terrorists to exploit government vulnerabilities. Watershed events – 9/11 and the 3/11 Madrid train bomb-ings – foster cooperation temporarily until countries become complacent about the terrorist threat or else encounter a political disagreement (for example, over the US invasion of Iraq).

Although difficult to achieve, international cooperation will not only save on resources but also make for a more effective resource allocation, as demonstrated by the INTERPOL example. If international cooperation is to work, then an enforcement mechanism is needed, and that is unlikely at this time. Past resolutions and conventions have been shown to have little real impact in outlawing specific terrorist modes of attack. Recent efforts to freeze terrorists' assets have waned over time as terrorists find and exploit loopholes. More thought is required to engineer international cooperative arrangements on a par with those that have characterized terrorist networks since the late 1960s. Unless nations universally view the benefits from such arrangements as sufficient to support their efforts, noncompliant nations can play the role of spoiler by offsetting cooperative gains. As long as the terrorists do not pose a threat to all countries, international cooperation will remain partial and of limited effectiveness.

SEVEN

Hostage Taking

"He has pulled a hand-grenade pin and is ready to blow up the aircraft if he has to. We must land at Beirut. No alternative." These are the frantic words of pilot John L. Testrake to the control tower at the Beirut International Airport on 14 June 1985 during the hijacking of TWA flight 847 (Mickolus, Sandler, and Murdock, 1989, vol. 2, p. 219). Testrake's plea came after Lebanese officials had blocked the runway with fire trucks to keep the Boeing 727–200, with less than fifteen minutes of fuel remaining, from landing.[1] Flight 847 was hijacked en route from Athens to Rome with 145 passengers (including the two Lebanese hijackers) and 8 crew members. The hijackers, armed with a chrome-plated pistol and two hand grenades, stormed the cockpit and took over the plane ten minutes after takeoff; thus began a hijacking that would last until 30 June as the plane flew back and forth between Algiers and Beirut. In total, the plane made three landings in Beirut and two in Algiers. During the first three days of the incident, hostages were released sequentially in exchange for fuel and other demands. From 16 June until the end of the incident, the plane remained on the ground at Beirut, where most of the remaining hostages, but not the three-member crew, were hidden throughout the city to inhibit a rescue attempt. As the incident dragged on, the number of terrorists increased, thereby indicating state assistance. The world's media provided nonstop coverage of the seventeen-day ordeal, which captured the world's attention. In the end, the hijackers succeeded in pressuring Israel to release 735 prisoners from the Atlit prison. Moreover, the United States had to reaffirm its support for the sovereignty of Lebanon and agree not to retaliate against the Amal

---

[1] The information in this paragraph is derived from Mickolus, Sandler, and Murdock (1989, vol. 2, pp. 219–25), where the incident is described in detail from a variety of news sources.

militia that had aided the hijackers in Beirut. The hijackers were allowed to read a statement and then escaped. Flight 847 reflects the type of media coverage that only a few hostage-taking missions have achieved.

On 1 September 2004, roughly 25 Chechen and other terrorists held over 1,000 people hostage in a school in Beslan, Russia, for 52 hours.[2] Once again, the world's attention turned to Beslan, given the large number of children being held as hostages and the apparent ruthlessness of the terrorists. The outcome of past incidents involving Chechen rebels – for example, the October 2002 seizure of a Moscow theater – gave the world ample reason to be apprehensive. At 1 P.M. on 3 September, the incident ended horribly as emergency personnel were being allowed by the terrorists to retrieve the bodies of dead hostages. Apparently, the hostage takers mistakenly thought that a rescue mission was under way and began firing. Fire was returned by security forces and the townspeople as bedlam broke loose. Terrorist-planted bombs in the school also began going off. By the time the shootings and explosions had stopped, 340 people had perished and hundreds were injured.

Hostage-taking incidents come in four varieties: kidnappings, skyjackings, the takeover of nonaerial means of transportation (for example, a bus or a ship), and barricade and hostage-taking mission (henceforth, referred to as *barricade missions*). The last type involves the takeover of a building or venue and the seizure of hostages, as in the Beslan incident. The riskiness of hostage-taking incidents differs by type: typically, kidnappings are the least risky, because the authorities often do not know the kidnappers' location or that of their hostages. As a kidnapping drags on, the authority's ability to learn the kidnappers' location increases. The other three types of hostage-taking events pose much greater risks to the terrorists, insofar as their location and that of their hostages are known from the outset (Wilson, 2000). Skyjackings became more dangerous after the installation of metal detectors in January 1973, because would-be hijackers now must get their weapons past security barriers unless the ground crew can plant them on board the plane. The same is true of an embassy takeover, but may not be true of occupying other buildings.

This chapter has five purposes. First, the strengths and weaknesses of past theoretical approaches to the study of hostage taking are reviewed. Second, we evaluate the feasibility of a no-concession policy to limit hostage taking, which is one of the four pillars of US counterterrorism action

---

[2]   The facts in this paragraph are drawn from *The Economist* (2004, pp. 23–5).

(US Department of State, 2003).[3] Third, we investigate past empirical tests of bargaining theory based on terrorist hostage-taking events. Data on hostage-taking incidents afford researchers an opportunity to test propositions regarding bargaining in intense situations. For example, does an increase in the number of dimensions over which the negotiations are conducted augment the likelihood of a negotiated success, as bargaining theory suggests? Moreover, do disagreement amounts (that is, payoffs in the absence of an agreement) and relative bargaining strengths make a difference in hostage negotiations? Fourth, we investigate the dynamics of hostage-taking incidents. In particular, we inquire how past concessions in hostage events have encouraged the taking of more hostages. Fifth, we suggest some directions for future research. In the course of the chapter, we conclude that a game-theoretic analysis of hostage taking is particularly appropriate, given the intense interaction between the terrorists and the targeted government. The effectiveness of a no-concession policy depends on many unstated assumptions that may not hold in practice, thus leading governments to renege on their pledge in practice. The outcome of the TWA flight 847 hijacking indicates that the Reagan administration along with the Israeli government made some concessions to the hostage takers – a situation that often encourages more hostage taking. In kidnappings and skyjackings, past concessions have encouraged the capture of more hostages; however, government rescue missions have not discouraged future kidnappings (Brandt and Sandler, 2009).

WHY HOSTAGE TAKING?

Terrorists can resort to many alternative attack modes – for example, ITERATE identifies twenty-five types of attacks – and new types may arise in the future. Hence, one must wonder why terrorists use hostage-taking missions that are not only logistically very complex, but also costly in terms of resource expenditure and associated risks. Terrorists will be drawn to such actions provided that the expected payoffs – taking into account the probability of success – equal or exceed the expected costs. Thus, the terrorists must perceive there to be a reasonable chance of large gains in terms of media exposure and potential concessions if they are going to engage

---

[3] The four pillars are as follows: (i) make no concessions to terrorists; (ii) bring terrorists to justice; (iii) make states end their sponsorship of terrorism; and (iv) bolster the counterterrorist capabilities of target countries that require assistance.

in such costly attacks. Since the rise of modern terrorism in the late 1960s (see Chapter 2), terrorists have viewed hijackings and other hostage-taking events as having the potential for huge gains. Based on ITERATE data for 1968–2008, just 15.5% of all terrorist attacks were hostage-taking missions. The individual percentages corresponding to each type of hostage-taking event are: 10.65%, kidnappings; 2.94%, skyjackings; 1.42%, barricade missions; and 0.46%, takeovers of nonaerial means of transportation. These percentages indicate that terrorists choose the type of hostage-taking event by responding to risks, because the least risky kind of hostage operation represents just over two-thirds of all such operations. The higher percentage of skyjackings as compared to barricade missions can be explained by the greater difficulty of ending a skyjacking as compared to the takeover of a building. In a skyjacking, it is often difficult for the rescuers to approach the plane unseen. Moreover, in the confined space of an airplane, hostages are in great peril during rescue missions. The capability of the terrorists is aptly illustrated by their relatively high level of logistical success – 75.7% (1,350 of 1,784) of all hostage missions ended in the terrorists securing one or more hostages.[4]

A much smaller percentage of hostage-taking missions end in a successful negotiation where one or more demands are met. In a study using US government data on 549 transnational hostage events from July 1968 to July 1984, Sandler and Scott (1987) found that 87% of such attacks resulted in logistical success, while only 27% ended in successful negotiation. The lower percentage of successful negotiations is understandable for two reasons: an event must first be logistically successful in order to move into the negotiation phase; and governments realize that giving in to terrorists' demands encourages more hostage taking.

Despite the difficulties and risks posed by hostage operations, terrorists have good reason to turn to them some of the time. Hostage-taking missions can stay in the news longer than other types of events, with the sole exception of "spectacular" attacks like those of 9/11 and 3/11 in which there were massive casualties and widespread fallout. Hostage-taking attacks not only receive media coverage during the drama, which can be drawn out, but also after it is over. Even a failed attempt to take hostages or to negotiate a concession will receive a good deal of news coverage. By contrast, a massive bombing is over in seconds and receives coverage only in its aftermath. Hostage taking may yield concessions that augment the terrorists' prestige, cause, recruitment, and resources. Other kinds of terrorist events

---

[4]   This percentage is based on ITERATE data for 1968–2003.

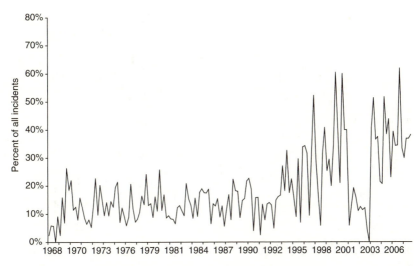

Figure 7.1. Percentage of hostage-taking missions.

seldom result in concessions. If the media are properly exploited by the terrorists, hostage-taking events can yield a great deal of publicity for the terrorist cause. During the hijacking of TWA flight 847, the terrorists used the media on several occasions to make their grievances and concerns known. As explained in Chapter 2, the Popular Front for the Liberation of Palestine (PFLP) takeover of an El Al flight on 22 July 1968 resulted in the Israelis having to recognize and negotiate with the Palestinians. The drama of hostage-taking events may be more efficient than most other terrorist events in creating an atmosphere of fear, where the public feels more vulnerable than the true underlying probabilities warrant. The need for screening the flying public is a constant reminder of these risks.

Figure 7.1 depicts the quarterly percentage of hostage-taking missions for 1968–2008, based on ITERATE transnational terrorism data. As mentioned earlier, the overall mean is 15.5% of all events. From July 1968 until 1970, the percentage of hostage-taking incidents increased greatly owing to the success of the PFLP hijacking of the El Al flight. Thereafter, the percent of hostage-taking events displays a cycle where a successful event yields an upturn in the percentage owing to a demonstration effect, followed by a downturn as terrorists either experienced a failure or have to accumulate resources for future events (Sandler and Enders, 2004). From 1992 until the end of 2000, hostage-taking events display a heightened presence and greater variability. After 9/11, the number of hostage events drop precipitously in percentage terms (see Chapter 9 and Enders and Sandler, 2005).

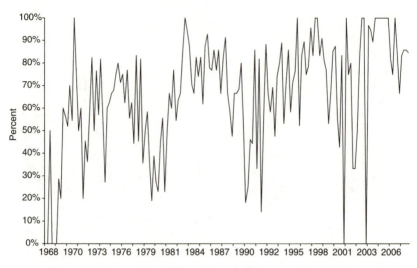

Figure 7.2. Proportion of kidnappings to all hostage-taking missions.

After 2003, hostage-taking missions followed the pre-9/11 pattern with an increased presence and high variability. As al-Qaida and its affiliates found new safe havens and sources of funds, complex hostage-taking missions grew in prominence. At first, this hostage-taking reemergence was stimulated by the kidnappings of foreigners in Iraq following the Abu Ghraib prison-abuse revelations in April 2004.

Figure 7.2 displays kidnappings as a proportion of all transnational hostage-taking attacks. When the percentage is 100, all hostage-taking incidents are kidnappings. The diagram shows how kidnappings as a share of hostage-taking missions have varied over time. At the start of the modern era of transnational terrorism in 1968–1971, there was greater reliance on skyjackings and barricade missions as transnational terrorists used such missions to grab headlines. This was also true during two subperiods: 1979–1981 and 1989–1991. During the first subperiod, there were numerous skyjackings to Cuba prior to Castro's adopting a tough stance; during the second subperiod, there were numerous skyjackings in the Soviet Union prior to the end of the Cold War. Generally, kidnappings have been more favored by terrorists since 1981. During 1968–1981, 54% of all hostage-taking incidents were kidnappings; during 1982–2008, 75% of all hostage-taking incidents were kidnappings. Kidnappings gained favor over time as more countermeasures were installed at airports and buildings, especially embassies and other government buildings, to prevent hostage seizures. A similar pattern characterizes domestic hostage incidents.

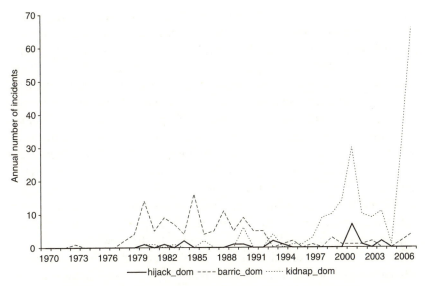

Figure 7.3. Annual number of domestic hostage-taking missions.

In Figure 7.3, we display the annual number of domestic hijackings (hijack_dom), domestic barricade missions (barric_dom), and domestic kidnappings (kidnap_dom), based on the Global Terrorism Dataset (GTD). After 1997, kidnapping is the hostage-taking operation of choice, given its ability to generate funds for terrorist organizations. We believe that GTD undercounts kidnappings prior to 1998. Hijacking, which includes the takeover of any means of transportation in GTD, is not a prevalent form of hostage taking domestically. Barricade missions have declined over time with enhanced security at potential target venues.

PAST INCIDENTS

In Table 7.1, we display some key transnational hostage-taking incidents prior to 1986, beginning with the PFLP hijacking of the El Al flight in July 1968. For each of the nine incidents listed, we provide the incident date, the terrorists responsible, the incident's nature, and its outcome. These hostage-taking incidents are chosen because they are watershed events; the list is, however, highly selective and ignores many other watershed incidents. The July 1968 incident demonstrated to other terrorists worldwide the publicity value of the hijacking of an international flight and resulted in numerous copycat events. Because of this hijacking, terrorists realized the benefit of bringing their struggle to the world stage through transnational terrorism. As such, this one event gave rise to the modern era of transnational terrorism, where many local struggles motivated terrorist events in distant venues (see Chapter 2). The August 1969 hijacking, also carried out by PFLP, showed that a nation could aid and abet the terrorists during the incident. In particular, Syria exploited the incident and engineered a prisoner exchange involving itself, Israel, and Egypt. This exchange underscored the idea that even the staunchest supporters of the no-concession policy may make an exception and concede if the cost of holding firm is too high. Such deals mean that terrorists will be less inclined to believe a government's stated policy never to concede to the demands of terrorists.

The 1972 Munich Olympics incident, where nine Israeli athletes were taken hostage, represents the first true terrorist "spectacular" that captured the attention of the world's viewing audience. The drama was especially poignant because satellite technology meant that it could be broadcast live to the global community. The Munich Olympics etched transnational terrorism in everyone's mind; the world lost a good deal of innocence with this event. Even though the terrorists failed to secure any of their demands, this incident led to many recruits for the Palestinian cause (Hoffman, 1998). It also motivated governments to improve their commando forces in order to manage such crises.

The infamous Maalot incident of 15 May 1974, where ninety schoolchildren were taken hostage, is an instance in which Israeli Premier Golda Meir appeared willing to negotiate with terrorists. Apparently, the government agreed to swap the requested prisoners held in Israeli jails for the children. Kozo Okamoto, the sole surviving Japanese Red Army terrorist from the Lod Airport massacre (30 May 1972), was among the prisoners to be exchanged (Mickolus, 1980). The prisoners had been taken out of their Israeli cells and were on a bus on their way to the exchange when the Israeli commandos sensed something wrong and stormed the school. Twenty-one children died in the raid. This incident again illustrates that if the "right" hostages are captured, then concessions may ensue. The Maalot takeover has many parallels with the Beslan school incident three decades later.

Another important hostage-taking event was the seizure of eleven Organization of Petroleum Exporting Countries (OPEC) ministers in Vienna on 21 December 1975. The PFLP terrorists were led by Illich Ramirez Sanchez ("Carlos"), who was involved in many high-profile terrorist attacks during the 1970s and 1980s. A large ransom – reputed to be $5 million – was paid to the terrorists (Mickolus, 1980, pp. 570–3). This incident sent two disturbing messages: almost anyone can be taken hostage, and capturing high-value hostages can lead to media coverage and money for future operations.

In a much less successful event, the PFLP hijacked Air France flight 139, with 257 people aboard, on 27 June 1976. This event is noteworthy because Israeli commandos eventually freed the hostages at the Entebbe Airport in Uganda. The rescue mission, known as "Operation Thunderbolt," required the Israeli commandos to fly from Israel to Uganda in a troop transport plane that landed on the darkened runway. In a complex and dangerous mission, the commandos managed to kill all of the terrorists and many of the Ugandan troops who had been providing cover for the terrorists at the Entebbe Airport. This incident indicated that a government could execute a successful hostage rescue in a distant venue. Operation Thunderbolt resulted in little loss of life to the hostages. Another daring rescue characterized Egyptian efforts to free 103 hostages on an EgyptAir flight while it was on the ground for refueling in Luxor before it was to fly to Benghazi, Libya (Mickolus, 1980, pp. 639–40). The commandos gained access to the plane disguised as mechanics – a ploy that would be copied in other rescue missions. Media reports of this tactic in this and subsequent rescue missions rendered it useless over time. In the Egyptian operation, the hostages were freed with hardly any injuries.

Another watershed event was the seizure of the US embassy in Tehran, Iran, by 500 radical Moslem students on 4 November 1979. Although the takeover appeared to be spontaneous and not orchestrated by the Iranian government, the latter quickly stepped in to protect the students and began negotiations with the United States on ending the barricade mission.[5] At first, the United States used economic, diplomatic, and legal channels in an effort to end the crisis. Thus, President Carter froze Iranian assets, expelled Iranian diplomats, and ended the US purchase of Iranian oil. The US government also sought international condemnation of the embassy takeover. On 7 April 1980, the United States broke off diplomatic relations with Iran and began an economic embargo that banned all exports to Iran except food and medicine. On 24 April 1980, the United States launched a rescue mission, which had to be aborted when a helicopter collided with a transport plane in the Iranian desert, some distance from Tehran. The remaining hostages were finally released after 444 days of captivity on the Inauguration Day of President Reagan. This incident illustrated not only state sponsorship, but also the difficulty of a hostage rescue in a distant venue. Operation Thunderbolt is not easy to copy. Following this embassy takeover, there

[5] The facts in this paragraph come from Mickolus (1980, pp. 880–5).

Table 7.1. *Select Key Hostage-Taking Incidents Prior to 1986*

Date	Terrorists	Incident	Outcome
22 July 1968	Popular Front for Liberation of Palestine (PFLP)	Hijacking of El Al Boeing 707 en route from Rome to Tel Aviv. Plane flown to Algiers.	Negotiated settlement: ransom paid by France and Israel released some prisoners. Algeria aided the hijackers in Algiers.
29 Aug. 1969	PFLP	TWA flight 840 with 113 people aboard was hijacked after leaving Rome. Plane flown to Damascus, Syria.	After letting passengers and crew off of the plane, the terrorists blew up the cockpit. Two Israeli passengers held by Syria. On 5 Dec., they were released in a prisoner exchange involving Syria, Israel, and Egypt.
5 Sept. 1972	Black September	Seizure of nine Israeli Athletes at the Munich Olympics.	All hostages killed when the West German police shot at the terrorists at Fürstenfeldbruck Military Airport as preparations were being made to fly the terrorists and hostages to Egypt.
15 May 1974	Democratic Front for Liberation of Palestine	Seizure of ninety schoolchildren and some adults at a school in Maalot.	Negotiated deal arranged but never consummated when Israeli commandos stormed the school. Twenty-one children died.
21 Dec. 1975	PFLP	Seizure of seventy hostages, including eleven Organization of Petroleum Exporting Countries (OPEC) ministers, in Vienna.	Ransom paid and ministers released.
27 June 1976	PFLP	Hijacking of Air France flight 139 with 257 people aboard, en route from Athens to Paris. Flight originated in Tel Aviv.	Hostage-freeing mission at Entebbe Airport, Uganda. Israeli commandos stormed airport in Operation Thunderbolt. All terrorists killed, along with a few hostages. Mission was a success.

23 Aug. 1976	Three hijackers	Hijacking of EgyptAir flight with ninety-six people aboard, en route from Cairo to Luxor.	Egypt mounted a successful commando raid in which all hostages were released unharmed.
4 Nov. 1979	500 radical Moslem students	Seizure of over 100 hostages at the US embassy in Tehran, Iran.	Ended after 444 days with the release of the remaining hostages. A US rescue mission was aborted following a helicopter crash. Iran aided the terrorists.
14 June 1985	Lebanese and Amal terrorists	Hijacking of TWA flight 847 with 153 people aboard, en route from Athens to Rome. Plane diverted to Beirut and then to Algiers. From Algiers, it went back to Beirut. The plane was flown back to Algiers before returning for a third time to Beirut. During the incident, one hostage was killed and dumped on tarmac. Also, hostages were released sequentially.	A negotiated settlement was reached between the United States, Syria, and Israel on 30 June. The United States released a statement guaranteeing Lebanon sovereignty. Israel released 735 Lebanese prisoners some time after the incident.

Sources: For incidents prior to 1980, the source is Mickolus (1980). For TWA flight 847, the source is Mickolus, Sandler, and Murdock (1989).

was a rise in fundamentalist and state-sponsored terrorism. This incident also highlighted the fact that a hostage incident, perceived as being poorly handled, could lose an elected leader his or her office. Thus, high-profile terrorist incidents may have significant political repercussions even when concessions are not granted.

The final watershed event in Table 7.1 is the one with which we began the chapter – the hijacking of TWA flight 847. The incident is noteworthy because of the media attention that it received and the concessions made by the United States and Israel to the terrorists' demands. During this hijacking, the terrorists operated not only with impunity but also with the help of the Amal militia in Beirut and supporters in Algiers. After this incident, there were six additional hijackings in 1985 and another five in 1986; clearly, a successful hijacking stimulates future incidents.

These incidents illustrate a number of lessons:

- The Palestinian terrorists were the first to exploit international hostage taking for political advantage.
- A successful hostage mission spawns additional incidents.
- Some watershed hostage incidents can affect the nature of terrorism.
- Governments have not been consistent in adhering to their no-concession policy, especially when high-value hostages are secured.
- Successful hostage-taking missions push governments to develop effective defensive and crisis-management techniques. Such techniques motivate terrorists to devise effective countermeasures.
- In some major incidents, state sponsorship has lengthened the incident and provided cover for the terrorists.
- Hostage-taking incidents can have large payoffs or large losses for the terrorists.

These messages also characterize key hostage-taking incidents in the 1990s and beyond. For example, the hijackings on 9/11 illustrate that hostage-taking missions can alter the future of transnational terrorism: passengers are less apt to be passive, and some governments are prepared to shoot down a hijacked plane. The hijacking of Indian Airlines flight 814 on 24 December 1999 shows that a government may still protect the terrorists during their mission. This flight was hijacked by five members of Harkul ul-Mujahideen, an Islamic group opposed to Indian rule in Kashmir.[6] The plane was commandeered after it left Kathmandu International Airport with 186 people aboard. After stops in Amritsar (India), Lahore (Pakistan),

---

[6] The description of this incident derives from Silke (2001).

and Dubai, the plane landed in Kandahar, Afghanistan, where it remained surrounded by Taliban militia until a deal with the Indian government was reached on 30 December 1999. The terrorists gained the release of a comrade jailed in India and were allowed safe passage to Pakistani-controlled Kashmir. The Taliban government of Afghanistan did nothing to end the incident and permitted the hijackers to escape. Moreover, by surrounding the plane in Kandahar, the Taliban made a rescue mission impossible.

Kidnappings

Kidnapping has been, and remains an important terrorist tactic. The potential political consequences of kidnapping are aptly illustrated by a domestic terrorist event: the kidnapping of former premier Aldo Moro on 16 March 1978 by twelve members of the Italian Red Brigades (Mickolus, 1980, pp. 780–2). At the time of his abduction, Moro was the leader of the ruling Christian Democrats, and it was anticipated that he would be elected to lead Italy in the next election. At 8:15 A.M., the terrorists ambushed Moro's car and the accompanying police car – in the ensuing mayhem, 710 shots were fired and 5 policemen killed. An unharmed Moro was taken hostage and driven away. On 6 May 1978, his bullet-riddled body was discovered in the trunk of a car parked in central Rome, not far from the headquarters of the Christian Democrats. This kidnapping determined the leadership of the Italian government and enraged the authorities, which eventually brought the kidnappers to justice.

More generally, terrorists rely on kidnappings to generate ransoms that can be used to finance operations. This was true of the left-wing European terrorists in the late 1970s and 1980s. In Latin America, unprotected foreign businessmen and dependents make inviting targets for today's ransom-hungry leftist terrorists. In some cases, kidnappers demand the release of an imprisoned comrade or the publication of a political statement.

At times, kidnapping campaigns have been used to gain political concessions. Islamic fundamentalists – Hezbollah (Islamic Jihad) – relied on kidnappings in Beirut during 1982–1992 to obtain ransoms and political concessions. Table 7.2 lists some of the most noteworthy hostages captured during this period, along with the nationality, position, abduction date, and final status of each. A number of insights can be gleaned from the table. First, Westerners were a desired target. Second, the terrorists went for soft targets: academics, journalists, and businessmen were favored. Third, hostage releases were often followed by the taking of more hostages. For example, the release of Rev. Benjamin Weir, Rev. Lawrence Jenco, and

Table 7.2. *Select Hostages Captured during 1982–1992 Lebanon Hostage Crisis*

Hostage	Nationality/Position	Capture Date	Final Status[a]
David Dodge	American, acting president of American University of Beirut (AUB)	19 July 1982	Released, 21 July 1983
William Buckley	American, CIA officer	16 March 1984	Murdered
Rev. Benjamin Weir	American, Presbyterian minister	8 May 1984	Released, 14 Sept. 1985
Peter Kilburn	American, librarian, AUB	3 Dec. 1984	Murdered, 17 April 1986
Rev. Lawrence Jenco	American, Catholic Relief Services	8 Jan. 1985	Released, 26 July 1986
Terry Anderson	American, Associated Press, Middle East bureau chief	16 March 1985	Released, 4 Dec. 1991
Marcel Fontaine	French, diplomat	22 March 1985	Released, May 1988
Marcel Carton	French, diplomat	22 March 1985	Released, May 1988
Alec Collett	British, journalist working with UN Relief and Works Agency	26 March 1985	Murdered, April 1986
Jean-Paul Kauffman	French, journalist	22 May 1985	Released, May 1988
Michael Seurat	French, researcher, French Center for Studies of Contemporary Middle East	22 May 1985	Murdered, 6 March 1986
David Jacobsen	American, directed Medical School, AUB	28 May 1985	Released, 2 Nov. 1986
Thomas Sutherland	American, dean, AUB	9 Jan. 1985	Released, 18 Nov. 1991
Albert Molinari	Italian, businessman	11 Sept. 1985	Presumed murdered
Do Chae-sung	South Korean, diplomat	31 Jan. 1986	Released, 31 Oct. 1987
Jean-Louis Normandin	French, TV journalist	8 March 1986	Released, 27 Nov. 1987
Brian Keenan	Irish, educator, AUB	11 April 1986	Released, 24 Aug. 1990
John McCarthy	British, TV reporter	17 April 1986	Released, 8 Aug. 1991

214

Frank Reed	American, director of Lebanese International School	9 Sept. 1986	Released, 30 April 1990
Joseph Ciccipio	American, comptroller, AUB	12 Sept. 1986	Released, 2 Dec. 1991
Edward Tracy	American, writer	21 Oct. 1986	Released, 11 Aug. 1991
Roger Augue	French, photojournalist	13 Jan. 1987	Released, 27 Nov. 1987
Rudolf Cordes	West German, businessman	17 Jan. 1987	Released, 7 Sept. 1988
Terry Waite	British, Church of England, envoy	20 Jan. 1987	Released, 18 Nov. 1991
Alfred Schmidt	West German, engineer	21 Jan. 1987	Released, Sept. 1987
Robert Polhill	American, educator, Beirut University College (BUC)	24 Jan. 1987	Released, 28 April 1990
Allan Steen	American, educator, BUC	24 Jan. 1987	Released, 3 Dec. 1991
Jesse Turner	American, Educator, BUC	24 Jan. 1987	Released, 22 Oct. 1991
Mithileshwar Singh	Indian with US resident status, educator, BUC	24 Jan. 1987	Released, Oct. 1988
Charles Glass	American, journalist	17 Jun. 1987	Escaped, 18 Aug. 1987
Ralph Schray	West German, businessman	27 Jan. 1988	Released, March 1988
Lt. Col. William Richard Higgins	American, Marine Corps	17 Feb. 1988	Murdered

[a] Exact dates are given when known.
Sources: US Department of State (1987–1992) and Mickolus, Sandler, and Murdock (1989).

David Jacobsen was followed by the capture of Robert Polhill, Allan Steen, and Jesse Turner. Thus, three American academic hostages replaced the three Americans who had been released.[7] This replacement was highly publicized when it became known that the Reagan administration had traded arms for hostages to obtain the release of Weir, Jenco, and Jacobsen (Islam and Shahin, 1989; Mickolus, Sandler, and Murdock, 1989, vol. 2). A fourth American hostage – William Buckley – had been murdered by the terrorists before the trade could be made. The action of the Reagan administration became known as "Irangate" and again illustrated that governments may go against their stated no-concession policy for a valued hostage. Apparently, Buckley's status as a Central Intelligence Agency (CIA) officer, stationed at the US embassy in Beirut, first motivated the Reagan administration to negotiate with the hostage takers. Once the terrorists realized that gains could be made, they replenished their supply of hostages upon negotiated releases.

In April 2004, a new and even more ominous kidnapping campaign emerged in Iraq, undertaken by radical Islamic fundamentalists as a means to pressure foreign governments and nongovernmental organizations (NGOs) to pull their people out of Iraq. Table 7.3 lists some select hostages captured in this campaign during 2004. These hostage-taking incidents began shortly after the abuse of prisoners by US service personnel at Abu Ghraib prison became known. The situation took an especially grisly and repulsive turn when the beheading of Nicholas Berg was video recorded and posted on the internet. Terrorists again exploited modern technology to heighten the public's anxiety. A group called Tawhid and Jihad, once headed by Abu Masab al-Zarqawi,[8] claimed responsibility for Berg's abduction and murder. Credit for subsequent kidnappings has been claimed by various groups, including Tawhid and Jihad, Holders of the Black Banners, Islamic Army in Iraq, Ansar al-Sunna Army, and the Green Brigade of the Prophet (Lexis Nexis, 2004). Favored hostages have included security guards, construction workers, truck drivers, aid workers, and journalists. In some cases, governments have given in to demands – for example, the Philippine government withdrew its troops in order to secure the release of Angelo de la Cruz, a truck driver threatened with beheading. Such concessions imply negative externalities on other governments as terrorists reap rewards for their actions and are encouraged to

---

[7]   A fourth hostage – Mithileshwar Singh – was abducted with the three American academics at Beirut University College.

[8]   Abu Masab al-Zarqawi was killed in a US Air Force bombing raid on his safehouse on 7 June 2006. His Tawhid and Jihad group later became known as al-Qaida of Iraq.

Table 7.3. *Select Hostages Captured during 2004 in Iraq*

Hostage	Nationality/Occupation	Capture Date	Final Status
Eight hostages	South Korean/ missionaries	8 April 2004	Released, 9 April 2004
Nicholas Berg	American/businessman	9 April 2004	Murdered, 8 May 2004
Keith Mopan	American/soldier	9 April 2004	Murdered, 28 June 2004
Thomas Hamil	American/truck driver	9 April 2004	Escaped, 2 May 2004
Elmer Krause	American/soldier	9 April 2004	Murdered, 23 April 2004
Seven hostages	Chinese/construction workers	11 April 2004	Released, 12 April 2004
Fabrizio Quattrocchi	Italian/security guard	12 April 2004	Murdered, 14 April 2004
Salvatore Stefio	Italian/security guard	12 April 2004	Released, 8 June 2004
Umberto Cupertino	Italian/security guard	12 April 2004	Released, 8 June 2004
Maurizio Agliana	Italian/security guard	12 April 2004	Released, 8 June 2004
Hussein Ali Alyan	Lebanese/construction worker	10 June 2004	Murdered, 12 June 2004
Sun-Il Kim	South Korean/translator	17 June 2004	Murdered, 22 June 2004
Georgi Lazov	Bulgarian/truck driver	27 June 2004	Murdered, 15 July 2004
Ivaylo Kepov	Bulgarian/truck driver	27 June 2004	Murdered, 22 July 2004
Angelo de la Cruz	Filipino/truck driver	7 July 2004	Released, 20 July 2004
Abdurrahman Demir	Turkish/truck driver	31 July 2004	Released, 4 Aug. 2004
Sait Unurlu	Turkish/truck driver	31 July 2004	Released, 4 Aug. 2004
Durmas Kumdereli	Turkish/truck driver	14 Aug. 2004	Murdered, 17 Aug. 2004
Mustafa Koksal	Turkish/truck driver	14 Aug. 2004	Released, 18 Aug. 2004
Anzo Baldoni	Italian/journalist	20 Aug. 2004	Murdered, 27 Aug. 2004
Scott Taylor	Canadian/journalist	7 Sept. 2004	Released, 11 Sept. 2004
Jack Hensley	American/civil engineer	16 Sept. 2004	Murdered, 21 Sept. 2004
Eugene Armstrong	American/civil engineer	16 Sept. 2004	Murdered, 20 Sept. 2004
Kenneth Bigley	British/Civil Engineer	16 Sept. 2004	Murdered, 8 Oct. 2004

Source: Lexis Nexis (2004) at http://web.lexis-nexis.com/universe.

take more hostages from other countries.[9] The table clearly shows that the release of hostages is quickly followed by the capture of new hostages – for example, the release of de la Cruz on 20 July was followed by the abduction of two Turkish truck drivers on 31 July. Their later release on 4 August, after their company withdrew employees, was followed by the kidnapping of two more Turkish truck drivers on 14 August. Unless nations devise a way to keep from conceding to kidnappers' demands, such campaigns will continue to increase in scope. This required international coordination is extremely difficult to achieve, thereby bolstering the terrorists' efforts as nations act independently (see Chapter 6).

Hostage taking of foreigners in Iraq continued in a much abated form after 2004. Some abductions occurred – for example, Peter Moore, a British citizen, was kidnapped in May 2007 and released in 2009. The epidemic of kidnappings of foreigners subsided as potential victims took better precautions and NGOs limited their personnel in Iraq. Terrorists then switched to abducting Iraqis, who became the softer target. In addition, the terrorists turned their attention to car bombings and other modes of attack in order to increase the body count.

NON-GAME-THEORETIC ANALYSIS OF HOSTAGE TAKING

To date, there have been three analytical non-game-theoretic analyses of hostage taking – two have been theoretical and one empirical in nature. All three have used an expected utility approach, where the likelihood of each possible outcome (that is, each state of the world) is determined and then multiplied by the associated value to give an expected value of the outcome. The sum of these expected values over all possible states is the associated *expected utility*, *EU*. In Chapter 5, we found the expected utility of a skyjacking by computing

$$EU^{SKY} = \pi U^S + (1 - \pi) U^F, \qquad (7.1)$$

where U^S is the gain from a successful hijacking; U^F is the payoff from a failed hijacking; π is the probability of success; and $(1 - \pi)$ is the probability of failure. Probabilities must sum to one so that all possible outcomes are included. The analysis can be expanded by allowing for more states of the world. The *net expected payoff* is then found by subtracting the expected cost of hijacking, EC^{SKY}, from EU^{SKY}. If this net expected payoff is positive,

---

[9]   A negative externality results because one country's action creates costs for another country, one not party to the transaction.

then the terrorists may decide to abduct hostages. Anything that increases the associated expected utility – for example, a greater probability of success or the presence of more desirable hostages, such as diplomats, aboard the plane – or decreases the expected costs of the operation makes skyjacking more desirable.

The analysis can allow for alternative hostage-taking missions involving skyjackings or other kinds of hostage taking. Suppose that terrorists must choose between a skyjacking and a kidnapping. The terrorist group compares the net expected payoff from the skyjacking with that of the kidnapping and picks the operation with the largest net expected payoff. This decision can be made more interesting by allowing the payoff *or* the probabilities to depend on the decision variables or policy parameters of the government. Thus, the government decision to install metal detectors in airports induced terrorists to choose kidnappings over skyjackings more often by lowering the latter's probability of success. Government actions must reduce the net expected payoffs associated with all kinds of hostage-taking missions in order to sway terrorists to turn to non-hostage-taking operations. If, for example, the prison sentences for all hostage taking are increased, then this may reduce the number of such incidents.

Islam and Shahin (1989) constructed an expected utility model to conceptualize how a government's past willingness to negotiate may influence terrorists' future hostage taking. Three states of the world characterize their situation from the hostage takers' viewpoint: the targeted government takes no action, valued at W, with probability p; the targeted government concedes a gain, G, to the terrorists, with probability q; or the targeted government takes a punitive action, L, with probability $1 - p - q$. This last may involve a raid on the terrorists' hideout in a rescue mission. The expected gain, EU^H, to the terrorists is then

$$EU^H = pW(n,m) + qG(n,m) + (1-p-q)L(n), \qquad (7.2)$$

where n is the number of hostages and m is the media manipulation by the hostage takers. The net expected payoff to the hostage takers is the difference between EU^H and the associated cost of hostage taking. Under various assumptions on the W and G relationships, the authors analyzed whether an increase in the likelihood of negotiation, q, would increase hostage taking.[10] Alternative cases were identified, including cases where

---

[10] Islam and Shahin (1989) used the first-order conditions of the objective function in equation (7.2) to compute comparative-static changes such as $\partial n/\partial q$ – that is, the change in the optimal number of hostages for a change in a government's likelihood to concede.

concessions may increase hostage taking. However, this result does not account for reputational effects, in which terrorists raise their perceived likelihood, q, of government concessions. If the government's reputation for toughness suffers from giving in to terrorists' demands, then this favors taking more hostages in the future. Islam and Shahin did not provide for such intertemporal consequences.

Such analytical models have not been part of the standard terrorism literature. We agree with Silke's (2001) argument that such models could have a real role to play in shaping government policy if the model is appropriately formulated. Models allow a researcher to simplify a complex reality in order to discover insights not apparent without such simplification. The trick is to simplify while maintaining key ingredients so that the skeleton relationship provides useful insights. The trouble with the nongame analyses of hostage taking is that the interplay between the adversaries is missing. For example, the government's likelihood of punitive action depends on the hostage takers' choice of n, and vice versa. The media represent an important missing player, one whose decisions impact both the terrorists' and the governments' payoffs and actions (Rohner and Frey, 2007). Non-game-theoretic models ignore such essential interactions.

This same criticism applies to the other two non-game-theoretic models of hostage taking by Shahin and Islam (1992) and Landes (1978). In the former, the authors showed that in some cases a policy mix of penalties and rewards to hostage takers leads to a superior result when compared to just punishment *or* reward. Reward involves a positive payoff to terrorists who release their hostages and then engage in legal activities. In a true interactive framework, hostage takers will view rewards as an inducement for grabbing more hostages – a frequent outcome, as shown in Tables 7.2 and 7.3. Shahin and Islam tried to eliminate this likely outcome by assuming that the reward is used sparingly and appears unanticipated. This assumption is, however, inconsistent with the way in which expectations are formed – that is, past concessions condition would-be hostage takers to anticipate a greater likelihood of future concessions (Sandler, Tschirhart, and Cauley, 1983). Even if the original hostage takers "go straight" because of the reward, the reward sends a signal to other potential hostage takers that such actions pay. By assuming a response *not in keeping* with the anticipated actions of adversaries, the authors greatly limited the usefulness of their model. The strategic interactions of adversaries must be part of a hostage-taking analysis. In the Shahin-Islam framework, there are really three active participants – the hostage takers, the government, and the media – that should make choices in an interactive fashion. To simplify, the modeler may have the government control the media's decisions. Alternatively, the modeler can use a multistage game to allow for three active agents.

The Landes (1978) article also suffers from the lack of a strategic framework, because the only choice modeled was that of the skyjacker who faces three states of the world: a successful hijacking and freedom in another country; apprehension and no conviction; and apprehension and conviction. Once again, a true interactive scenario between the hijacker and the government is not analyzed. This is, however, less problematic for the Landes study because his main goal was to ascertain the *empirical* impact of government actions on the number of hijackings or the time interval between hijackings. If government policies are effective deterrents, then the number of hijackings should fall, and/or the time interval between hijackings should lengthen (also see our remarks in Chapter 5). Using data on US hijackings from 1961 to 1976, Landes (1978, p. 12) found that an increase in the probability of apprehension had a negative and highly significant influence on the number of hijackings, a reduction of 1.1 to 2.2 hijackings per quarter. Other important deterrents included a higher probability of conviction and longer prison sentences. Landes found that a greater probability of apprehension, a greater likelihood of conviction, and longer prison sentences also lengthened the time interval between successive hijackings. A greater chance of being killed during the hijacking also deterred hijackings. Finally, increases in unemployment made for more frequent hijackings, a finding consistent with fewer opportunities in the host country.

As mentioned in Chapter 5, Landes's (1978) evaluation of metal detectors failed to account for the motivation of terrorists to substitute from the now more costly skyjackings into less costly kidnappings and other kinds of attacks. Enders and Sandler (1993) uncovered clear evidence of such substitutions following actions by the government to prevent skyjackings through the installation of metal detectors. This shortcoming of Landes's (1978) important study is a consequence of his failure to account for strategic interaction among adversaries.

GAME THEORY AND HOSTAGE TAKING

There have been five game-theoretic analyses of hostage-taking events by Atkinson, Sandler, and Tschirhart (1987), Gaibulloev and Sandler (2009a), Lapan and Sandler (1988), Sandler, Tschirhart, and Cauley (1983), and Selten (1988).[11] We focus our remarks on the Lapan and Sandler study,

---

[11] Browne and Dickson (2010) published a related game-theoretic paper about making statements "not to talk to terrorists" as a strategic move that may, at times, increase the denouncer's ability to consummate an agreement owing to audience costs. This interesting analysis is about reaching negotiated solutions with an adversary. It is not about hostage negotiations per se; nevertheless, the analysis can be applied to hostage negotiations.

which investigated the practicality of a policy that commits governments never to concede to hostage takers' demands. The conventional wisdom hinges on the notion that if terrorists know ahead of time that they have nothing to gain, then they will never abduct hostages. As we show, the success of this policy depends on some unstated assumptions that may not always hold in practice. Our earlier examination of real-world incidents identified cases where governments reneged on their stated no-concession policy. We explain the pitfalls of this policy and what can be done to keep governments true to their pledge.

The underlying game tree is displayed in Figure 7.4, where the government goes first and chooses a level of deterrence that determines the likelihood of a logistical failure by the terrorists – that is, the probability, θ, that the terrorists will fail to secure their intended hostage(s). Given their perceived likelihood of logistical success or failure and also their perceived likelihood of negotiated success or failure, the terrorists decide whether or not to take hostages. If there is no hostage incident, the game ends. If the terrorists attempt to take hostages, then either the terrorists fail and the game ends, or they succeed and secure hostages. In the latter case, the government must then decide whether or not to capitulate to the terrorists' demands. Terrorists perceive the capitulation probability to be p.

For each of the four possible end points of the game, the government's payoff is listed on top, and the terrorists' payoff is underneath. In every contingency, the government must cover deterrence cost, which is like an insurance premium that must be paid regardless of the outcome. If the terrorists attempt an incident but fail, then the cost to the government is $D(\theta)$ plus a. The latter represents any expenditure incurred from putting down the incident – for example, resources spent to stop the incident in the planning stage. When an incident succeeds, the government incurs an additional expense of h if they capitulate and an expense of n if they do not capitulate. The relative values of h and n depend, in part, on the value of the hostage(s) taken. The government is motivated to choose D in order to minimize its cost. From the terrorists' viewpoint, they receive nothing if they do not attack. A failed attack gives them c. If they abduct hostages, then they get m for a negotiated success and s for a negotiated failure. Obviously, the payoffs are ordered as follows: $m > s > c$. Moreover, c is typically negative, while s may be positive or negative depending on how the terrorists value publicity for their cause. Media attention may, at times, provide a net benefit for the cause even if negotiations are unsuccessful. This was true for the Palestinian cause following the 1972 Munich Olympics incident, when recruitment increased despite the terrorists' failure to obtain any concessions.

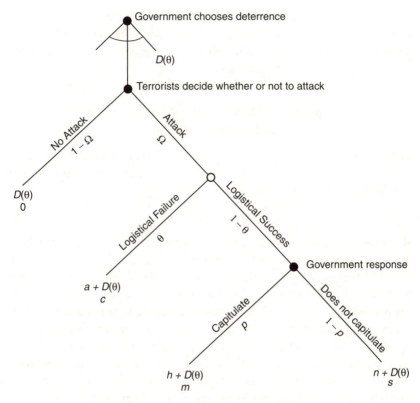

Figure 7.4. Game tree for hostage event.

Given the game in Figure 7.4, the terrorists will take hostages provided that they perceive there to be an expected benefit. This occurs if the following inequality holds:

$$(1-\theta) \times [pm + (1-p)s] + c\theta > 0. \qquad (7.3)$$

In (7.3), the expected gain from a logistical success exceeds the expected cost of a logistical failure. The former is made up of the expected payoffs from either a negotiated success or a negotiated failure.[12] From (7.3), the likelihood of an attack increases as either the probability of a logistical success, $(1 - \theta)$, or the perceived likelihood of government capitulation, p, rises,

---

[12] In Figure 7.2, Ω corresponds to $\int_0^{c^*} f(c)dc$, where $f(c)$ is the probability density for c, which reflects the unknown resolve of the terrorists, where $c^* = [(1-\theta)/\theta] \times [pm + (1-p)s] > -c$.

since $m > s$. An increase in the level of concessions, m, or a decrease in the consequences of a logistical failure, c, also augments the chances of a terrorist action by raising the left-hand side of the inequality, thereby increasing the chances that it will be positive.

Conventional Wisdom about Not Conceding to Terrorists' Demands

Suppose that the government pledges never to negotiate *and* its pledge is believed by the terrorists, so that $p = 0$. In this scenario, the terrorists will take hostages *only* when

$$(1-\theta)\, s + c\theta > 0. \tag{7.4}$$

If, moreover, the terrorists gain nothing from a failed negotiation, in which the government does not concede, then $s < 0$. Because c is also negative, the terrorists will perceive no gain from hostage taking and refrain from taking hostages. When, alternatively, deterrence makes $\theta = 1$, so that logistical failure is a certainty, no attacks ensue provided that $c < 0$. These are the implicit assumptions consistent with the conventional wisdom that hostage taking stops in the face of a pledge by the government never to capitulate.

If, however, the government's pledge is not believed by the terrorists, then $p > 0$ and the relevant inequality is (7.3), which exceeds the left-hand side of (7.4) by $(1-\theta)(pm-ps)$. When the expected payoff from a successful negotiation, $(1-\theta)pm$, is large, the government's pledge is not a sufficient deterrent. Next, suppose that the terrorists view a failed negotiation or even a logistical failure as having a positive payoff, so that $s > c > 0$. The latter may hold when a fanatical terrorist group considers self-sacrifice – martyrdom or imprisonment – to be a positive payoff. In this scenario, inequality (4) holds, and hostages are abducted despite the government's pledge *even when it is fully credible.*

Because this is an interactive framework, we must next examine what the government is going to do in those cases when the terrorists are not deterred from capturing hostages. First, suppose that the costs of capitulation, h, or of not capitulating, n, are known with certainty and that $h > n$. In this scenario, the government will stick by its pledge because it is more costly to do otherwise. If, however, n or h is not known beforehand because the identity of the hostage(s) is not known, then the outcome may be different. When the revealed value of n exceeds h, the government will renege on its pledge. Thus, the right hostage(s) (for example, a CIA agent, schoolchildren, soldiers, or a member of parliament) may induce the government to give in to the terrorists. The terrorists' task is to abduct hostages that make the government's pledge too costly to maintain.

The game representation can be made more realistic by allowing multiple periods and reputation costs. A government concession to hostage takers during one period makes terrorists raise their expectations about future concessions. As the perceived p increases for future periods,[13] more hostages will be taken, so that there is an added cost to conceding during any period. This cost is denoted by R for loss of reputation, and results in the capitulation cost to the government becoming $h + R$. Even when reputation cost is included, conceding is not eliminated as a possible outcome unless $h + R$ exceeds n for all its possible realizations. Such a scenario may be achieved through the institution of rules that do not allow the government to have any negotiating discretion. Only when these rules impose sufficiently severe punishments on conceding to terrorists' demands will the government not go back on its word. The Irangate hearings were intended to keep future administrations from making covert deals.

In summary, the never-concede policy hinges on at least five implicit assumptions: (i) the government's deterrence is sufficient to stop all attacks; (ii) the government's pledge is fully credible to all potential hostage takers; (iii) the terrorists' gain from hostage taking derives only from fulfillment of their demands; (iv) there is no uncertainty concerning the costs to government of having hostages abducted; and (v) the government's costs from making concessions always exceed those of holding firm. Our analysis clearly demonstrates that a game-theoretic framework is required to explain why such pledges do not necessarily work. The strategic interaction between adversaries must be taken into account.

EMPIRICAL TESTS OF BARGAINING IN HOSTAGE INCIDENTS

The ITERATE data set records observations in hostage-taking events that include demands made, concessions granted, length of the incident, deadlines that passed uneventfully, sequential release of hostages, rescue missions, terrorists killed or wounded, nonterrorists killed or wounded, and negotiated outcome. Terrorists' demands along multiple dimensions – ransoms, prisoner release, safe passage, and propaganda statement – are also indicated in the data. Thus, data are available that can be used to analyze hostage-taking incidents in light of bargaining theory.

---

[13] The first analysis of this dependency of p on past concessions is found in Sandler, Tschirhart, and Cauley (1983).

Three papers – Atkinson, Sandler, and Tschirhart (1987), Sandler and Scott (1987), and Gaibulloev and Sandler (2009a) – have done so. We focus on the results contained in the first and third papers.

An Application of the Cross Theory of Bargaining

Atkinson, Sandler, and Tschirhart (1987) tailored the Cross (1969, 1977) theory of bargaining to a scenario where the terrorists (government officials) are viewed as maximizing the present value of their perceived net benefits from negotiations over hostages. A bargaining framework is a game-theoretic framework in which strategic interactions among agents are part of the analysis. For Cross, the *duration* of the incident is an essential consideration, because the longer one must wait for the payoff, the smaller will be the present value of the payoff. Each party perceives this duration to equal the difference between current demands and concessions divided by the concession rate of the opponent. An impatient negotiator displays a greater concession rate. In choosing demands (concessions) during each period, the terrorists (officials) can trade away large (small) values of demands (concessions) at the expense of a longer incident with its concomitant greater costs and reduced present value of an eventual payoff. The greater the difference between initial demands and initial concessions offered, the longer the negotiation phase of the incident. The more impatient side in the negotiation is at a bargaining disadvantage. If, for example, terrorists are wounded, then they are more inclined to reach an agreement with smaller concessions. An incident concludes with a settlement once demands match concessions.

In their analysis, Atkinson, Sandler, and Tschirhart (1987) tested three hypotheses that emerged from the Cross model:

1. Increases (decreases) in bargaining costs to the terrorists induce them to decrease (increase) their demands owing to the opportunity costs of waiting. Similarly, increases (decreases) in bargaining costs to the government cause it to raise (reduce) concessions.
2. Increases (decreases) in bargaining costs to either side will shorten (lengthen) the duration of the incident.
3. Bluffing will diminish a party's payoff, since exaggerated demands lead to a faster concession rate, which induces the opponent to hold firm.

Greater terrorist demands are anticipated to make for greater payoffs and longer incidents. Bluffing can show up in the form of allowing a deadline to pass uneventfully – for example, a threat to kill a hostage that is not executed. These authors hypothesized that such bluffs will reduce the final ransom and will shorten the incident by signaling a lack of terrorist resolve. The number of hostage nationalities involved in an incident should, however, increase the cost to the government, which then results in greater concessions. Actions by the terrorists to sequentially release hostages indicate a willingness on the part of both parties to negotiate, and this should lead to greater ransoms being paid and a longer incident. The incident's duration is anticipated to be longer if it is a kidnapping (owing to its unknown location) or involves US hostages. In addition, the larger the final payment, the longer the incident. Finally, the greater the number of terrorists wounded in the incident, the shorter the incident, because such injuries raise the terrorists' cost of holding firm.

Atkinson, Sandler, and Tschirhart (1987) ran two regressions using ITERATE data to ascertain the importance of some of these bargaining variables. In particular, they examined 122 hostage incidents from 1968 to 1977. First, they made ransom paid the dependent variable and determined the significant influences on this variable. Second, they presented a "time-to-failure" investigation, where the duration of the hostage incident in hours is the dependent variable. The significant determinants on incident duration were tested for numerous independent variables. In the top portion of Table 7.4, the significant variables are indicated for ransom paid and for duration. The authors' priors are largely confirmed by the empirical results. For example, bluffing (i.e., allowing a deadline to pass uneventfully) reduced ransoms received. Sequential release of hostages, a larger number of hostage nationalities, and greater ransom demands resulted in larger ransom payments. The influences on the duration of the incident are also confirmed in many cases – wounded terrorists reduced the incident's duration, while the presence of US hostages increased the incident's length. In addition, kidnapping incidents were longer in duration. Larger ransom demands and larger concessions paid resulted in longer incidents.

Two-Stage Model of Hostage Taking

Gaibulloev and Sandler (2009a) formulated a two-stage hostage-taking model to derive some hypotheses that they subsequently tested using ITERATE hostage-taking data for 1978–2005. These authors characterized hostage-taking attacks as first involving a logistical stage, where the mission is planned and the hostages are then abducted. If hostages are secured, then a negotiation stage ensues, in which terrorists seek concessions in return for

Table 7.4. *Significant Determinants of Various Aspects of Hostage Incidents*

Ransom paid[a]

Significant variables	*Influence*
Terrorists allowed sequential release of hostages	Greater ransom
Ransom demanded	Greater ransom
Number of nationalities of the hostages	Greater ransom
Terrorists allowed a deadline to pass uneventfully	Smaller ransom

Duration of incident[a]

Significant variables	
Terrorists allowed sequential release of hostages	Greater duration
Kidnapping incident	Greater duration
Ransom demanded	Greater duration
Ransom paid	Greater duration
US hostage	Greater duration
Number of terrorists wounded	Smaller duration

Logistical success[b]

Significant variables	
Number of terrorists in attack force	+0.7%
Number of terrorist casualties	−(49−55)%
Number of terrorist nationalities	−(18−22)%
Number of hostages (square root)	2%
Kidnapping incident	37−47%
Protected persons	−15%
Attack force/high-powered weapon	1−2%

Negotiated success[b]

Significant variables for nonkidnappings	
Number of hostages (square root)	4−5%
Number of terrorist casualties	−(29−35)%
Number of nonterrorist casualties	−(26−31)%
Two or more demands	32%
Hours	0.06%
Demand for money	−(35−50)%
Protected persons	−24%

Significant variables for kidnappings	
Number of hostages (square root)	9−10%
Number of terrorist casualties	−(24−28)%
Number of nonterrorist casualties	−(18−19)%
Two of more demands	Not significant
Days (square root)	1−2%
Demand for money	25%
Protected persons	Not significant

[a] Results are from Atkinson, Sandler, and Tschirhart (1987), which examined 122 hostage-taking incidents during 1968–1977.

[b] Results are from Gaibulloev and Sandler (2009a), which examined 413 hostage-taking incidents during 1978–2005; also see Sandler and Scott (1987) for a study not separating kidnappings and nonkidnappings for negotiation successes. This latter study examined 549 hostage-taking incidents during 1968–1984.

the hostages. These stages were displayed earlier in Figure 7.4. Because the data set includes kidnappings, the negotiations may involve private parties, unlike Figure 7.4.

In the first stage, the authors related the probability of logistical success to two sets of variables that correspond to the resources of the terrorists and the vulnerability of the targeted hostage(s).[14] The terrorists' logistical success – that is, their ability to secure one or more intended hostages – increases with their resources, which include the size of their attack forces, the presence of high-powered weapons (that is, automatic rifles, shotguns, explosives, or incendiaries), or a combination of the two. For example, a larger attack force can more easily secure hostages and keep would-be inter-veners at bay. A larger attack force provides more operatives to overcome defenses. Multiple terrorist nationalities on the attack force may dilute their resources, given the concomitant problems arising from language, goal, and cultural diversity. Multiple nationalities may also imply that the terrorists have less time to train as a team, thereby limiting the effectiveness of the terrorist resources in achieving a logistical success.

More vulnerable hostage-taking targets are conducive to logistical suc-cess. The likelihood of logistical success is anticipated to be higher for kid-nappings relative to other hostage missions, because the terrorists are able to choose the safest venue to nab the hostage(s). Obviously, skyjackings and barricade missions leave less discretion on venue. In the case of skyjackings, this is especially true if airport screening and security measures abide by the same standards. A larger number of intended hostages may increase the vulnerability of a hostage target and, thus, increase the terrorists prospects of logistical success. When the terrorists target a large number of hostages, logistical success may be achieved even though some intended hostages escape. In a large hostage grab, the authorities may be more reluctant to use lethal force, thereby making such targets more vulnerable at the abduc-tion stage. Target fortification limits vulnerability, thereby reducing logis-tical success. Protected persons (that is, diplomats, military officials, and government personnel) are apt to have bodyguards, armor-plated cars, and other protections that decrease their vulnerability. Guarded venues are also less vulnerable and may result in terrorists sustaining casualties at the initial stages of the operation.

After hostages are secured, the likelihood of negotiated success becomes germane. Gaibulloev and Sandler (2009a) viewed terrorists as being suc-cessful in their negotiations if they get away with *some* of their demands.

---

[14] Their logistical-stage analysis modified a model in Berrebi and Lakdawalla (2007).

Terrorists may negotiate over several dimensions. Some of the determinants of negotiated success will differ from those of logistical success. For instance, once hostages are secured, the size and diversity of the attack force are not relevant for the outcome of negotiations. High-powered weapons are not required for negotiated success in kidnappings and skyjackings.

These authors derive their hypotheses from a Nash bargaining model, where two parties negotiate over a fixed amount (Dixit and Skeath, 2004; Nash, 1950). If the negotiations fail, then each party walks away with its disagreement value. The party with the relatively greater disagreement value is anticipated to fare better in the negotiation. When, for example, salary is negotiated, the prospective employee with a higher alternative offer will gain a higher salary. Bargaining outcomes are also dependent on the two adversaries' bargaining strengths. The bargaining literature shows that the more patient adversary possesses the greater relative bargaining strength and the better prospects for success.

A large hostage seizure reduces the government's disagreement value, because negotiation failure means that the government is then responsible for more lives lost. A large hostage pool also provides the terrorists enhanced leverage or bargaining strength as hostages can be traded sequentially for food and other comforts during negotiations. Terrorist casualties work against the terrorists by reducing their bargaining strength as they become impatient for a resolution. These casualties also lower the terrorists' disagreement value because their human resources have been depleted. Nonterrorist casualties decrease the government's disagreement value as fewer lives may hang in the balance.

The authors distinguished between nonkidnapping and kidnapping negotiations. This follows, in part, because the negative influence of nonterrorist casualties on negotiated success can be more marked in nonkidnappings, where the fate of hostages, bystanders, and the police are in full view of the public during negotiations. Bargaining over two or more demands promotes negotiated success by increasing the size of the negotiation set. This may be particularly important for nonkidnappings, where the government does not want to be seen as paying ransom. Insofar as kidnappings often involve private parties – families or corporations – money ransom may be more conducive to a negotiated agreement. Given governments' pledges not to concede to terrorist demands, the presence of protected persons among the hostages may reduce the likelihood of a negotiated success in a nonkidnapping, because the government does not want to appear to be reneging on its pledge in order to gain the freedom of one of its own. As a hostage incident drags on, pressures mount on the government in nonkidnappings or on private parties in kidnappings to concede some demands. Incident length favors the terrorists as their relative bargaining strength increases as pressure for a resolution mounts.

Gaibulloev and Sandler (2009a) identified the significant determinants of terrorist logistical success for all types of hostage missions, along with the key determinants of terrorist negotiated success for nonkidnappings and kidnappings, respectively. These authors examined 413 hostage-taking incidents during 1978–2005. Their findings are displayed in the bottom portion of Table 7.4, where the marginal influences on the probability of a logistical or a negotiated success are indicated. The size of the attack force and the number of hostages increased the likelihood of a logistical success at the margin by just 0.7% and 2%, respectively. During the operation, terrorist casualties reduced the likelihood of a logistical success by 49 to 55%. As the number of terrorist nationalities in the attack squad increased by one, the probability of a logistical success decreased by 18 to 22%. A kidnapping incident increased the likelihood of a logistical success by 37 to 47% as compared to other types of hostage missions. Going after protected persons reduced the marginal probability of a logistical success by 15%. Finally, the marginal impact of the size of the attack force interacted with high-powered weapons was a gain of 1 to 2%.

For negotiated success, Gaibulloev and Sandler's (2009a) results also conform to their hypotheses. We first focus on nonkidnappings. A larger hostage pool raised the marginal probability of a negotiated success by 4 to 5%. Terrorist casualties, nonterrorist casualties, and making money demands lowered the marginal probability of successful negotiations by 29 to 35%, 26 to 31%, and 35 to 50%, respectively. Abducting protected persons decreased this marginal likelihood by 24%. Making two or more demands had the greatest favorable impact on gaining concessions; there was a 32% marginal gain in success. Incident length had a tiny influence on the marginal likelihood of a negotiated success.

Some of the results are similar for kidnapping negotiations. The main differences involve making multiple demands, demanding money, and abducting protected persons. Unlike the result for nonkidnappings, making multiple demands did not significantly affect the marginal probability of a negotiated success in kidnappings. Demanding money bolstered the marginal probability of a successful negotiation by 25% in kidnappings. Holding protected persons did not significantly influence the marginal probability of a negotiated success in kidnappings. For the other determinants of a negotiated success, the magnitude of the marginal probabilities differed between the two types of events.

A number of policy insights may be gleaned from the Gaibulloev and Sandler study. First, negotiation strategies must be tailored to the two classes of hostage events, since the impacts of negotiation variables differ. The results here can inform negotiators not only on strategy, but also on the likely outcome of negotiations given the actions of the terrorists. If, for example, negotiations are likely to fail, then the authorities can focus on finding the ideal time to launch a rescue mission, especially for non-kidnappings. Second, when choosing operational parameters (for example, the size of the attack force or the number of hostages) at the execution stage, terrorists choose near-optimal amounts where the marginal impact is almost zero. This implies that terrorists will react to government responses in a predictable fashion in order to undermine such actions. Thus, government efforts to harden one type of potential hostage target will induce the terrorists to abduct a less guarded individual. Such policy-induced terrorist responses must be anticipated. Third, in nonkidnapping hostage-taking events, governments appear resolute, as pledged, not to concede to terrorists when protected persons are captured. Less strict adherence to such pledges is associated with kidnappings, where private parties are being extorted. This difference should result in terrorists engaging in a larger proportion of kidnappings, which appears to characterize Figures 7.2 and 7.3. Fourth, even though kidnappings greatly foster logistical success, the authorities must remain vigilant to nonkidnappings, because the large potential payoffs may warrant the greater associated risks from the terrorists' viewpoint. Fifth, the ability of governments to inflict casualties on the terrorists significantly reduces their success at both stages of hostage incidents. Sixth, longer incidents are somewhat conducive to terrorists achieving some of their demands; hence, waiting out the terrorists has a downside from the authority's viewpoint.

Silke (2001) criticized bargaining studies as coming to different conclusions.[15] Moreover, Silke (2001) applied the hypotheses of the bargaining model to three hostage events – the hijacking of Air France Flight 8969 on 24 December 1995; the barricade siege of the Japanese embassy in Lima, Peru, on 17 December 1996; and the hijacking of Indian Airlines flight 814 on 24 December 1999 – with diverse outcomes. In evaluating the two studies from 1987, one must remember that different things were being tested. That is, Atkinson, Sandler, and Tschirhart (1987) examined the significant

---

[15] His criticism was applied to Atkinson, Sandler, and Tschirhart (1987) and Sandler and Scott (1987). Gaibulloev and Sandler (2009a) is a much improved update of Sandler and Scott (1987).

influences on the *duration* of a hostage incident, while Sandler and Scott (1987) and, subsequently, Gaibulloev and Sandler (2009a) studied the significant influences on a *logistical* success. These variables relate to different phases of a hostage incident: logistical success concerns the period when the hostages are initially being abducted, while the duration involves the period *after* the hostages are secured. There is no reason for these influences to be the same. Even the negotiation variable – ransom paid and the probability of a negotiated success – differs between the studies. A negotiated success may not imply that a ransom is paid, because the negotiation may involve a prisoner release, a media statement, or an escape to a safe haven. A paid ransom, however, implies a negotiated success. Also, the samples for the three studies are vastly different, and this is expected to influence the results.

Silke's (2001) dismissal of bargaining models because of their failure to give consistent predictions for three *specific* hostage incidents indicates a fundamental flaw in reasoning that one sees in some criticisms of quantitative studies. A theory is *not* intended to explain every case; instead, it is meant to explain a large portion of instances. The ability to find select hostage missions that do not abide by a theoretical prediction does not refute the theory. If, however, the empirical analysis of a sufficiently large sample does not conform to the theory, then there is ample reason to develop a new theory.

DYNAMICS OF HOSTAGE TAKING

Brandt and Sandler (2009) investigated the dynamics of hostage-taking incidents using advanced time series methods. Based on data for 1968–2005, they quantified how many new hostage-taking incidents were generated from a successful negotiation. Although the conventional wisdom indicates that concessions given to hostage takers lead to more incidents, no one had previously tested this wisdom using past incidents. Brandt and Sandler separated hostage-taking incidents into kidnappings, skyjackings, and others (that is, barricade missions and nonaerial hijackings), because they believed that the dynamics associated with these time series would differ.

For kidnappings, each successful negotiation resulted in 2.62 additional incidents, while for skyjackings, each successful negotiation resulted in 0.6 additional incidents. Successful negotiations had no significant effect on generating additional barricade events or nonaerial hijackings. The findings for kidnappings and skyjackings showed that a longer-term harm came from giving in, which is particularly true for kidnappings. Unfortunately, it is quite difficult to maintain a no-concession response by families and corporations when the lives of loved ones or valued employees are at stake. Brandt and Sandler (2009, pp. 768–71) also tested the response of hostage takers to an incident that ends violently in a government raid to free the hostage(s). A violent end dissuaded 0.29 future skyjackings; however, a violent end encouraged 1.18 more kidnappings. This surprising result may follow because kidnappers reason that better efforts to keep their location secret will prevent a shoot-out with authorities even if a recent incident has concluded in this way.

These authors also investigated the correlations among the three hostage-taking time series. They found kidnappings and skyjackings to be negatively correlated, indicative of substitutes, and skyjackings and others to be positively correlated, indicative of complements. The identification of substitute and complement modes of hostage taking is essential to informed and effective policymaking. Policymakers must anticipate that actions to reduce one type of hostage-taking mode will be somewhat offset by a greater reliance by terrorists on a substitute hostage-taking mode. Thus, the authorities must also have the foresight to protect against this anticipated substitution. For complementary modes, a single policy intervention is apt to reduce both forms of hostage taking. If hostage modes are uncorrelated (for example, kidnappings and others), then a policy intervention aimed at one mode is unlikely to have repercussions on the other attack modes.

Brandt and Sandler (2009) also identified important changepoints for the three hostage-taking time series. They employed advanced techniques that allow the data to identify the points at which the associated series alter their behavior in a statistically significant way. Earlier tests specified the changepoints – for example, 5 January 1973 for metal detectors – and then ascertained the significance of the changepoint. Such pre-specification can bias the results. If the installation of metal detectors is truly a significant influence on skyjackings, then a significant changepoint for skyjackings should appear during the first part of 1973. This novel technique is apt to identify unanticipated changepoints.

In Table 7.5, the twenty-two changepoints of the Brandt-Sandler analysis are displayed. The first column numbers the changepoint; the second column identifies the median date of the change; the third column indicates the direction of the change; and the fourth column lists the likely precipitating event. There are a few things to highlight. First, each type of hostage-taking event has different changepoints. The more risky the event, the fewer the number of changepoints, so that kidnappings have the most and other

Table 7.5. *Hostage-Taking Changepoints for Transnational Terrorism*

Kidnappings

Changepoint	Median Date	Direction	Event
1	17 February 1970	rise	Rise of transnational terrorism
2	25 October 1977	fall	Unknown
3	27 July 1983	rise	Lebanon MNF, Middle East kidnappings
4	27 July 1988	fall	Fall in Middle East kidnappings
5	22 May 1993	rise	Algerian/Turkish kidnappings
6	9 January 1998	fall	Fall in transnational terrorism
7	21 December 1998	rise	African/Latin American kidnappings
8	14 October 2000	fall	Pre-9/11 fall
9	5 April 2004	rise	Abu Ghraib revelations
10	6 November 2004	fall	Reduction in Iraqi kidnappings

Skyjackings

Changepoint	Median Date	Direction	Event
1	2 August 1969	rise	PFLP skyjackings – demonstration effect
2	17 April 1973	fall	Metal detectors
3	2 January 1980	rise	Cuban skyjackings
4	24 November 1981	fall	Castro's forty-year sentences
5	29 April 1990	rise	Soviet skyjackings
6	2 January 1991	fall	End of Cold War
7	3 September 1996	fall	Low terrorism year
8	23 April 2003	fall	Heightened airport security

Barricade and Hostage Events and Nonaerial Hijackings

Changepoint	Median Date	Direction	Event
1	26 June 1972	rise	Post-Israeli occupation
2	1 October 1979	rise	Transference into other hostage events
3	10 February 1985	fall	Embassy fortification
4	10 June 1993	fall	Post–Cold War reduction

Source: Brandt and Sandler (2009).

hostage events have the least. Innovations or shocks are less prevalent for risky, complex events. Second, the installation of metal detectors reduced skyjackings during the first third of 1973 – the median date is 17 April 1973, after installation in January 1973, because these devices were introduced gradually worldwide during the first half of 1973. Third, some policies or actions – for example, the Lebanon Multinational Force (MNF) and the Abu Ghraib abuses – had unintended negative consequences that generated a wave of kidnappings. Fourth, changepoints may follow from explicit policies, political events, or terrorism hot spots. Political events include the end of the Cold War, backlash against the alleged Armenian genocide, and changes in the overall level of transnational terrorism.[16] Terrorism hot spots are associated with Africa and Latin America during the late 1990s and the Soviet Union prior to its collapse. Previous studies that focused on counterterrorism policies missed many such changepoints.

CONCLUDING REMARKS

Although hostage-taking missions involve a relatively small portion of terrorist attacks, these operations have had a disproportionately large influence and have included some of the most noteworthy terrorist incidents of the last forty or more years. Despite pledges never to concede to terrorist demands, governments have not always honored such declared commitments, particularly when high-value hostages are abducted. This commitment is essential because empirical findings show that conceding to hostage takers' demands leads to more kidnappings and skyjackings. We have applied game theory to explain such policy inconsistencies. Because past concessions by countries influence terrorists' perceptions of how other governments may behave, there is an interdependence among governments' negotiations that must receive greater recognition. Hostage-taking incidents involve a strategic interdependence between terrorists and the target government that can only be understood using game theory. Moreover, the strategic interdependence among targeted governments involves game-theoretic notions, as does the bargaining process between terrorists and officials once hostages are taken.

There are numerous future directions. First, there is a need to build better bargaining models to represent negotiations in hostage-taking events. Differences in negotiations between domestic and transnational incidents

---

[16] The end of the Cold War resulted in less state sponsorship and fewer terrorist incidents of all kinds. The backlash against the Armenian genocide led to Turkish kidnappings.

have not been adequately explored. We would anticipate that pledges not to concede are more apt to be honored in domestic than in transnational incidents, because the consequences of being inconsistent (that is, of conceding to demands) in a domestic incident are borne solely at home and are not shared by all countries. Second, there is a need to construct multistage and multiperiod models of negotiations that better account for the importance of reputation. Third, data sets are needed that are richer in terms of observations on the actions of governments during negotiations. We typically know more about the responses of terrorists than about those of government officials. Unless we have the latter observations, we cannot develop the best practice for the field during hostage crises. Fourth, there is much more data on hostage incidents now than when the two initial bargaining studies were done in 1987. Gaibulloev and Sandler (2009a) and Brandt and Sandler (2009) are the first subsequent studies to use this expanded data set on hostage-taking events. Other studies are needed.

EIGHT

Terrorist Groups and Their Organization

Terrorist groups vary greatly in terms of their longevity, structure, and evolution. The longest-lived groups in recent years include Euskadi ta Askatasuna (ETA), established in 1959; Revolutionary Armed Forces of Colombia (FARC), established in 1964; National Liberation Army of Colombia (ELN), established in 1964; Palestine Liberation Organization (PLO), established in 1964; Popular Front for the Liberation of Palestine (PFLP), established in 1967; Provisional Irish Republican Army (PIRA), established in 1969; and the Moro National Liberation Front (MNLF), established in 1970. Most terrorist groups are more ephemeral; the median duration of transnational groups is between 1.7 and 3 years (Blomberg, Engel, and Sawyer, 2010, p. 319). In fact, there is a preponderance of terrorist groups that strike only once, called "one-hit wonders" by Blomberg, Engel, and Sawyer (2010). Terrorist groups are generally driven by one of four orientations: left-wing, nationalist/separatist (henceforth, nationalist), religious, and right-wing. Many single-issue groups – for example, animal rights or environmental protection – can be placed into one of these four categories. Nationalist, left-wing, and religious terrorist groups correspond to the second, third, and fourth waves of modern terrorism, respectively.

Terrorist groups have used many alternative organizational structures. At first, terrorist groups tended to be hierarchical organizations with a clear chain of command and many linkages among members. Terrorists discovered that hierarchical, densely linked structures are vulnerable, because the arrests of one or two terrorists could result in the entire group being compromised. A vivid example of this vulnerability was the Italian Red Brigades. In the aftermath of the General Dozier kidnapping in 1982,[1] Red

[1] General James Lee Dozier was kidnapped from his home by members of the Red Brigades posing as plumbers on 17 December 1981. At the time, he was the senior US officer at

238

Brigades member Antonio Savasta turned state's evidence, which led to the arrests of 200 suspected group members (Mickolus, Sandler, and Murdock, 1989, vol. 1, p. 237). In fact, the bulk of the Red Brigades was captured and tried. Although sporadic terrorist incidents claimed by the Red Brigades occurred in subsequent years, the group ceased to be much of a threat after the massive arrests.

Learning from the mistakes of the Red Brigades, many terrorist groups adopted a nonhierarchical cellular structure, in which members knew only the identity of the other cell members.[2] As such, the terrorist group would not be compromised by the arrest of one or more members. After 9/11, this switch to nonhierarchical, loosely linked networks became even more imperative as the United States and other prime-target countries took a more proactive approach against the terrorists (Enders and Su, 2007). In particular, the USA PATRIOT Act (see Chapter 11) expanded the authorities' power to intercept wire, oral, and electronic communications, while reducing congressional oversight. This act also allowed for domestic and foreign law enforcement agencies to share findings from criminal investigations into suspected terrorists. Enhanced interrogation methods and redoubled efforts to infiltrate groups put terrorist groups at greater peril. Other at-risk countries enacted emergency measures that expanded efforts to break up terrorist groups. These actions induced terrorist groups to redesign their organizational structure in order to make the groups less connected and, thus, less vulnerable to penetration.

In recent years, there has been a growing interest in the study of terrorist groups and their organizational structure. An understanding of terrorist group structures can expose their weakest links, against which counterterrorism efforts can be more effective. If, for example, a terrorist group ties each member to all other members (i.e., an all-channel network), then the capture of a single member can yield intelligence on the entire group. It is, however, essential to remember that terrorists are resourceful and

---

NATO southern Europe ground forces command base in Verona, Italy. He was also the deputy chief of staff for logistics and administration at the base (Mickolus, Sandler, and Murdock, 1989). Dozier was freed unharmed on 28 January 1982, following a rescue mission by a special police squad in Padua.

2   Some terrorist groups that maintained a hierarchical structure later suffered a fate similar to that of the Red Brigades. Prime examples include Aum Shinrikyo in Japan and the Revolutionary Organization of 17 November in Greece. Both of these groups were annihilated, once compromised by the authorities. For 17 November, a failed bombing in June 2002 resulted in the critically injured terrorist providing information that led to the capture of the entire group. Such group failures underscored the hazards of tightly connected terrorist groups.

will adapt their networks to counterterrorism policy. Thus, we are skeptical about studies that advocate strategies for disabling terrorist groups through a minimal number of arrests that sever all links between the leadership and the "foot soldiers" – see, for example, Farley (2003). Such analysis can inform policymaking only if terrorist group structures are known (McGough, 2009) and if terrorists do not respond to counterterrorism measures by altering their institutional forms. Gaining information about terrorist groups presents formidable challenges. Governments' estimates about such basic things as group size have been notoriously inaccurate in the past. If intelligence cannot get a group's membership correct, then one cannot be sanguine that a group's structure will be known.

The purpose of this chapter is to investigate myriad aspects of terrorist organizations. First, we present a brief historical perspective for 1970–2007 of the twenty most active terrorist groups for each of the four main categories, based on the Global Terrorism Database (GTD).[3] Second, we identify some factors that determine terrorist groups' longevity. Third, we investigate the organizational structures of terrorist groups in light of post-9/11 counterterrorism policy. This investigation not only highlights the trade-off between connectivity and security, but also shows how this trade-off influences large-scale sophisticated events. Fourth, we distinguish component parts of terrorist groups – for example, political and military wings, and hard-line and moderate members. These component interests can result in splintering or factions – for example, Black September and the PFLP splintered from the PLO. Fifth, we examine how asymmetric information and differing preferences within terrorist organizations give rise to a difficult control problem that defies standard remedies and can greatly curtail a group's efficiency. Finally, we consider dynamic issues, including recruitment, associated with the evolution of terrorist groups. Terrorist organizations can alter their structure over time and involve multiple generations of members. In examining all of these topics, we are particularly interested in the implications for counterterrorism policy.

TERRORIST GROUPS BY TYPE

In Table 8.1, we display the twenty most active terrorist groups during 1970–2007 for the four primary motives or orientations. In each category, the groups are listed in descending order by their total number of terrorist

---

[3]   GTD data is compiled by the National Consortium for the Study of Terrorism and Response to Terrorism (START) (2009a). GTD is event data on domestic and transnational terrorist events for 1970–2007.

incidents, as recorded in GTD. The first column indicates the group; the second column records the total number of incidents; the third column lists transnational terrorist incidents; the fourth column counts domestic terrorist incidents; and the fifth column denotes the group's longevity. This longevity corresponds to the number of years between the group's first and last incident as found in GTD; it does not necessarily correspond to the years since its founding.

In the leftist category, Shining Path (SL) of Peru is by far the most active group in the table with 3,713 terrorist incidents, 95% of which are domestic attacks. The second-most active leftist group is the Farabundo Marti National Liberation Front (FMLN) of El Salvador, which, until the peace accords in 1992, served as the umbrella group for five terrorist groups in the country. FMLN primarily engaged in domestic attacks; 96% of its 1,932 terrorist attacks are domestic. The third- and fourth-most-active leftist terrorist groups are the Revolutionary Armed Forces of Colombia (FARC) and the National Liberation Army of Columbia (ELN). These groups engaged in a larger share – 19% and 28%, respectively – of transnational terrorist attacks. The Manuel Rodriguez Patriotic Front (FPMR) in Chile is the fifth-most-active leftist group, while the New People's Army (NPA) in the Philippines is the sixth-most-active leftist group. South and Central America contain some of the most active leftist terrorist groups, which represent guerrilla movements. In Europe, the three most active leftist groups are Del Sov in Turkey, the Red Brigades, and the First October Antifascist Resistance Group (GRAPO) in Spain. Of the listed European leftists, only Dev Sol still conducts attacks. GRAPO ceased its operations in 2006. With the exception of Montoneros in Argentina, the left-wing terrorists engaged mostly in domestic terrorist incidents.

For nationalist groups, the ETA, PIRA, the Liberation Tigers of Tamil Eelam (LTTE), Kurdistan Workers' Party (PKK), and the Corsican National Liberation Front (FLNC) are the top five active groups for the sample period. PIRA and LTTE are no longer active. Compared to the leftists, the nationalist groups display a greater reliance on transnational terrorist attacks. The FLNC, the Armenian Secret Army for the Liberation of Armenia (ASALA), FLNC–Historic Channel, and Resistenza Corsa conducted more transnational than domestic terrorist attacks. The PKK, the Ulster Freedom Fighters (UFF), Mujahideen-I-Khalq, and PFLP have a relatively high proportion of transnational terrorist attacks. PFLP has been active throughout the sample period and is credited as an instigator of the modern age of transnational terrorism, with some high-profile skyjackings starting in 1968 – see Chapters 2 and 7.

Table 8.1. *Major Terrorist Groups by Motive and Number of Attacks*

Group	Total	Transnational	Domestic	Longevity
Left Wing				
Shining Path (SL)	3,713	189	3,524	30
Farabundo Marti National Liberation Front (FMLN)	1,932	80	1,852	17
Revolutionary Armed Forces of Colombia (FARC)	1,051	204	847	33
National Liberation Army of Colombia (ELN)	1,004	282	722	35
Manuel Rodriguez Patriotic Front (FPMR)	730	54	676	14
New People's Army (NPA)	675	86	589	32
Tupac Amaru Revolutionary Movement (MRTA)	462	79	383	14
M-19 (Movement of April 19)	344	81	263	13
National Union for the Total Independence of Angola (UNITA)	325	37	288	25
Movement of the Revolutionary Left (MIR) (Chile)	295	11	284	19
Dev Sol	244	54	190	18
(Italian) Red Brigades	177	25	152	17
First of October Antifascist Resistance Group (GRAPO)	173	24	149	26
Popular Liberation Army (EPL)	166	47	119	33
Simon Bolivar Guerrilla Coordinating Board (CGSB)	152	18	134	18
Khmer Rouge	137	54	83	10
Sandinista National Liberation Front	126	28	98	27
Montoneros (Argentina)	110	71	39	10
People's Liberation Forces (FPL)	110	13	97	15
United Popular Action Movement	103	36	67	12
Nationalist				
Euskadi ta Askatasuna (ETA)	1,590	294	1,296	38
Provisional Irish Republican Army (PIRA)	1,242	376	866	37

Group	Total	Transnational	Domestic	Longevity
Liberation Tigers of Tamil Eelam (LTTE)	760	77	683	29
Kurdistan Workers' Party (PKK)	759	252	507	22
Corsican National Liberation Front (FLNC)	525	387	138	34
African National Congress (South Africa)	524	14	510	21
Hamas (Islamic Resistance Movement)	209	21	188	18
Armenian Secret Army for the Liberation of Armenia (ASALA)	175	136	39	23
United Liberation Front of Assam (ULFA)	147	20	127	20
Corsican National Liberation Front–Historic Channel	128	123	5	9
Muttahida Qami Movement (MQM)	126	2	124	13
Ulster Freedom Fighters (UFF)	101	36	65	36
Al-Aqsa Martyrs Brigade	100	16	84	8
Free Aceh Movement (GAM)	92	8	84	29
Mujahideen-I-Khalq (MK)	91	35	56	30
Popular Front for the Liberation of Palestine (PFLP)	91	40	51	38
Resistenza Corsa	79	78	1	14
Fuerzas Armadas de Liberacion Nacional (FALN)	76	16	60	13
Bodo Liberation Tigers (BLT)	74	2	72	11
Palestine Liberation Organization (PLO)	66	18	48	26
Religious				
Taliban	447	119	328	13
al-Gama'at al-Islamiyya (IG)	248	19	229	8
Armed Islamic Group (GIA)	144	22	122	13
Moro National Liberation Front (MNLF)	140	37	103	33
Moro Islamic Liberation Front (MILF)	137	20	117	22
Islamic Salvation Front (FIS)	135	10	125	3

(continued)

Table 8.1 *(continued)*

Group	Total	Transnational	Domestic	Longevity
Hezbollah	127	64	63	26
Abu Sayyaf Group (ASG)	96	30	66	15
Lord's Resistance Army (LRA)	74	11	63	14
al-Qaida in Iraq	69	29	40	4
Lashkar-e-Taiba (LeT)	64	4	60	9
al-Qaida	62	29	33	10
Jewish Defense League (JDL)	54	40	14	17
Hizbul Mujahideen (HM)	50	4	46	18
Salafist Group for Preaching and Fighting (GSPC)	35	1	34	9
Pattani United Liberation Organization (PULO)	24	0	24	27
Jemaah Islamiyah (JI)	19	10	9	6
Jaish-e-Mohammad (JeM)	18	2	16	7
Muslim United Army (MUA)	18	18	0	1
Jama'atul Mujahideen Bangladesh (JMB)	17	0	17	5
Sipah-e-Sahaba/Pakistan (SSP)	17	4	13	17
Right Wing				
Mozambique National Resistance Movement (MNR)	150	33	117	21
Recontras	48	15	33	7
Argentine Anticommunist Alliance (AAA)	19	7	12	5
Anti-terrorist Liberation Group (GAL)	18	13	5	7
United Self Defense Units of Colombia (AUC)	18	1	17	4
Spanish Basque Battalion (BBE) (rightist)	9	3	6	5
People Against Gangsterism and Drugs (PAGAD)	8	2	6	2
Mano Blanca	5	3	2	11
Spanish National Action	5	1	4	1
Ku Klux Klan (KKK)	4	0	4	19
Aryan Nation	3	0	3	1

Group	Total	Transnational	Domestic	Longevity
Boere Aanvals Troepe (BAT)	3	0	3	1
Charles Martel Group	3	2	1	7
Secret Army Organization	3	0	3	1
White Legion (Georgia)	3	1	2	2
Actiefront Nationalistisch Nederland	2	0	2	1
Anti-Zionist Movement	2	0	2	1
Clandestini Corsi	2	2	0	1
Fatherland and Liberty Nationalist Front (Frente Nacionalista Patria y Libertad) (FNPL)	2	1	1	1
New Order	2	0	2	8
Secret Organization Zero	2	2	0	2

Source: National Consortium for the Study of Terrorism and Responses to Terrorism (START) (2009a) database.

The five most active religious terrorist groups include the Taliban in Afghanistan and Pakistan, al-Gama'at al-Islamiyya (IG) in Egypt, the Armed Islamic Group (GIA) in Algeria, the Moro National Liberation Front (MNLF) in the Philippines, and Moro Islamic Liberation Front (MILF) in the Philippines. The spiritual leader of IG is Omar Abdel-Rahman, the cleric who is now jailed for his part in the 26 February 1993 bombing of the World Trade Center. Other noteworthy religious fundamental groups include Hezbollah, Abu Sayyaf, al-Qaida in Iraq, Lashkar-e-Taiba, al-Qaida, Jemaah Islamiyah, and Jaish-e-Mohammad. Geographically, the most active religious terrorist groups are primarily based in North Africa, the Middle East, and Asia; however, these groups can execute attacks throughout the world. With a few exceptions, the most active religious terrorist organizations conduct both domestic and transnational terrorist incidents. Even al-Qaida engaged in more domestic than transnational terrorist incidents. Counterterrorism measures imposed by prime-target countries following 9/11 have curbed terrorist mobility somewhat, resulting in more attacks at home (Enders and Sandler, 2006). The longevity of religious terrorist groups is shorter than that of leftists and nationalists, because the rise of fundamentalist terrorism is generally traced to the last quarter of 1979 (Enders and Sandler, 2000; Hoffman, 2006).

The most active right-wing terrorist groups include the Mozambique National Resistance Movement (MNR or RENAMO), Recontras, Argentine Anticommunist Alliance (AAA), Anti-terrorist Liberation Group (GAL), and United Self Defense Units of Colombia (AUC). Some of these right-wing groups are supported by governments in order to target leftists and nationalists – for example, GAL in Spain targets ETA members, and AUC targets leftist insurgents. Other right-wing groups include hate groups, such as the Ku Klux Klan (KKK), Aryan Nation, Anti-Zionist Movement, and New Order. Of the four classes of terrorists, right-wing groups conduct the fewest attacks and are generally very short-lived. Moreover, right-wing groups favor domestic terrorism.

Some crucial lessons can be drawn from Table 8.1. First, important terrorist groups engage in both domestic and transnational terrorist attacks. Thus, studies concerning terrorist groups' behavior and duration must include more than just transnational terrorist attacks. When more than a third of its attacks are transnational in nature, a group is best classified as a transnational terrorist group. Second, geography is a consideration in the dispersion of the most active terrorist organizations by motive. Many leftist groups are located in Latin America, while active nationalist groups show a wider geographical dispersion, including Europe, the Middle East, North Africa, and Asia. Religious groups are concentrated in the Middle East, North Africa, and Asia, while right-wing groups can surface anywhere. Because counterterrorism measures differ by the groups' four motives,[4] geography thus plays a role in designing such measures. Third, international cooperation is essential for addressing religious terrorism owing to the prevalence of transnational terrorist incidents. For nationalist terrorism, international cooperation can be more on a regional basis – for example, ETA attacks mainly affect French and Spanish interests. Fourth, the longevity of nationalists and leftists reflects the timing of the second and the third waves of terrorism preceding the fundamentalist wave. Fifth, right-wing terrorism is more of a domestic concern and does not necessarily require international cooperation. Sixth, for the entire GTD sample, the terrorist groups are represented as follows: leftist, 55%; nationalist, 35%; religious, 8.5%; and right-wing, 1%. The comparatively recent appearance of religious groups explains their small percentage. Leftist group numbers

---

[4]   The alternative mix of domestic and transnational terrorist attacks requires differing combinations of defensive and offensive counterterrorism measures. Terrorist motives leading to a greater share of transnational attacks may, for example, necessitate foreign aid as a counterterrorism tool. Because religious groups favor attacks with greater carnage than leftists and others, there is a greater need for intelligence and first-responder capacity.

are high because they have been around since the late 1960s and often use new names for some cells.

Why Is There a Mix of Attack Types?

Terrorist groups often start with domestic attacks and then escalate to transnational terrorist incidents in order to gain greater exposure for the cause. Thus, terrorist groups of all persuasions may hone their tactics at home before targeting foreign interests or moving some attacks abroad. This was true for many of the European left-wing groups. ETA started to target tourist resorts in the 1980s in order to gain heightened publicity and hurt the lucrative Spanish tourist trade. At other times, a domestic terrorist event becomes a transnational terrorist event owing to random factors such as when a foreigner becomes an unintended victim. Terrorists may gravitate to transnational terrorist attacks as they seek soft targets of opportunity. When terrorists obtain safe havens abroad, some of their attacks will be transnational as they cross back to their home country to wage attacks. Transnational terrorism allows terrorists to locate targets in countries where governments are the least vigilant or least equipped to react. Since transnational terrorism requires more logistical support than domestic terrorism, it is understandable that transnational terrorist groups still conduct a relatively large proportion of domestic terrorist attacks. As border protection increased following 9/11, it is not surprising that Muslim fundamentalist terrorists increasingly killed Muslims in their base countries of operation – for example, in Iraq, Egypt, and Saudi Arabia – even though such operations turned away potential supporters.

A terrorist groups' longevity may increase with a judicious mix of transnational and domestic terrorist attacks, as the group gains greater visibility (and recruitment) and takes advantage of more opportune targets. The geographical migration of terrorist groups' bases of operation and their targeting decisions in response to counterterrorism trends also hold research potential. Another question of interest concerns how the mix of domestic and transnational terrorist incidents responds to changing counterterrorism measures.

DETERMINANTS OF TERRORIST GROUPS' LONGEVITY

In a recent article, Blomberg, Engel, and Sawyer (2010) utilized ITERATE transnational terrorist event data (Mickolus et al., 2009) to analyze the determinants of terrorist groups' duration. Blomberg and his colleagues applied a time-to-failure or hazard model that relates the duration or survival of a terrorist group, as the dependent variable, to a host of independent variables, including regime type, population, and income per capita. These authors also investigated whether the current level of violence of a terrorist group influenced its survival in a positive or negative fashion.

Blomberg, Engel, and Sawyer (2010) found that a large number of terrorist groups engaged in just a single attack – thus, they called such groups "one-hit wonders." Groups that attacked more than once were called recidivists. Almost half of the sample included these single-attack groups. The authors ran two sets of hazard models – those with all groups and those with only recidivists – and showed that:

- When one-hit wonders are included with recidivists, terrorist groups are more likely to survive as their age increases. If, however, only recidivists are included, then the survival rate decreases as the group ages.
- The venue countries' income per capita and population affected terrorist groups' survival in a positive manner – that is, terrorist groups survive longer when they operate in rich, populated countries.
- More violent terrorist groups display longer life spans.
- Terrorist groups survive longer in regions that have poor counterinsurgency capacity – for example, sub-Saharan Africa and the North Africa–Middle East region.

The first bullet suggests that once groups make it past their first couple of terrorist attacks, they initially have a favorable prognosis for survival. For recidivists, the authors found that these groups' reduced survival rate diminished over time, leading Blomberg, Engel, and Sawyer (2010) to argue that a few long-lived terrorist groups came to monopolize or dominate transnational terrorism over time – for example, the PLO. Some evidence of this domination is presented. The authors also showed that the median life span for recidivists is 5.2 to 7.3 years.

The Blomberg, Engel, and Sawyer's (2010) worthwhile article is the first data-driven analysis of group survival. The basic shortcomings of their study are the absence of a clear theoretical framework and the reliance on transnational terrorist incidents. As previously displayed in Table 8.1, most groups engage in a large share of domestic terrorist attacks. Inclusion of these events not only increases the number of sample groups but also permits groups to choose an appropriate portfolio of attacks in order to trade off risk factors. An interesting theoretical hypothesis is related to terrorist groups' share of transnational terrorist attacks. Groups with a *smaller* share of transnational attacks are likely, other things constant, to have a longer life span. Transnational terrorist incidents are more risky than domestic attacks as personnel and supplies often must cross guarded borders. Moreover, transnational terrorist campaigns encourage other countries, whose interests are targeted, to come to the assistance of the venue country. For some prime-target countries, this has resulted in counterterrorism foreign aid – for example, US aid to Pakistan, Yemen, Sudan, and the Philippines – that can jeopardize terrorist groups' survival. Other terrorist groups' tactics (for example, the diversification of attacks) may affect their survival. Diversification is apt to bolster groups' longevity as frequent switching of attack modes and targets keeps authorities guessing. The groups' ideology may also play a role – for example, religious groups may have better survival prospects owing to greater support by the population.

Other such theoretical hypotheses need to be formulated and tested, so that terrorist groups' life spans can be better understood. This understanding can yield essential policy insights for effective steps that can shorten a group's survival.

ORGANIZATIONAL STRUCTURE: TRADE-OFF OF CONNECTIVITY AND VULNERABILITY

In response to enhanced risks, mentioned in the introduction, terrorist groups have adopted flatter structures, where the chain of command is less hierarchical (Arquilla and Ronfeldt, 2001). In addition, terrorist organizations are more loosely knit in order to limit outside monitoring and infiltration. Unfortunately for terrorist groups, the enhanced security from such organizational restructuring comes at a cost in terms of functionality. Network gains or externalities, conferred by one network member on other members, can dissipate as members become more loosely linked (Enders and Jindapon, 2010).

Some Basic Network Definitions

We begin our brief study of terrorist networks with some basic definitions, drawn from graph theory. A terrorist network consists of *nodes*, representing the individual terrorists, and *edges*, connecting two or more nodes (terrorists). These edges or links permit joined terrorists to communicate. Nodes that are not joined cannot communicate and are *disconnected*.

Figure 8.1, taken from Enders and Jindapon (2010), can be used to illustrate essential graph-theoretical concepts. The top left-hand network consists of three disconnected two-terrorist cells, where the nodes or

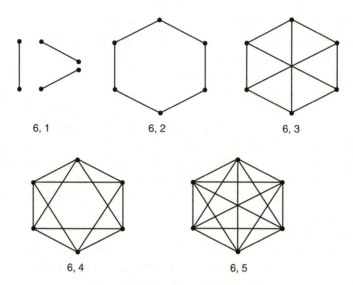

6, 1   6, 2   6, 3

6, 4   6, 5

Figure 8.1. Regular networks (n, r).

terrorists are the points. Each two-person cell cannot communicate with the other two cells, so the three cells must work independently. This disconnection provides security to the other two cells, but none of the cells possesses sufficient manpower for a sophisticated terrorist operation. The other four six-member structures in Figure 8.1 represent ever-increasingly linked networks. In the bottom right-hand network, each of the six members is linked to all of the other five members. Such a structure is a *complete* or *all-channel* network because every member can directly communicate with the other members. Information flows are complete, and there is no entropy, since messages are not transmitted through intermediaries. In the other three connected networks, communications between some members must be via indirect linkages, mediated by other members. In the top middle graph, each member can communicate directly with two other members; in the top right-hand graph, each member can communicate directly with three other members. The bottom left-hand graph has each member joined to four other members. The *neighbor* of node i consists of all nodes directly tied to node i. The *degree* of node i is the number of other nodes joined to it and is denoted by n_i. If the degree of every node in a network is the same, then the network is *regular* with $n_i = r$. In Figure 8.1, the five graphs are regular networks (n, r) with $n = 6$ and $r = 1,\ldots,5$ as indicated.

When r increases, the network becomes more operational, but it also becomes more vulnerable. For the $(6, 4)$ network, five-person teams can pull

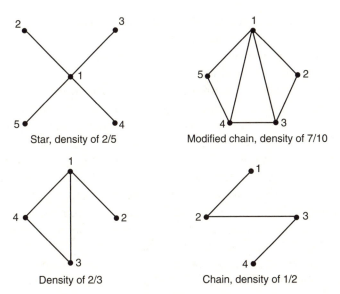

Figure 8.2. Nonregular networks and their densities.

off more complex missions than the three-person teams associated with the (6, 2) network. The three successful 9/11 hijackings were accomplished by the five-member cells, while the only failure was by the four-member cell. Vulnerability increases with the degree of the network, because each member can directly compromise more members. Thus, there is a clear trade-off between connectivity and vulnerability. Counterterrorism measures can directly impact this trade-off, as shown below, thereby motivating terrorists to alter their network structure.

Next, we consider some nonregular networks, where each node is not linked to the same number of other nodes, so that the degree of every node is not the same. This is illustrated for four networks in Figure 8.2, drawn in part from Enders and Su (2007). In the top left, a *star* network is displayed where individual 1 is linked to the other four members, but each of them is linked only to central individual 1. The other three networks are *chains*. The bottom right-hand network is a simple chain or path where members are linked in a particular order. Individuals 2 and 3 are each linked to two other members, while individuals 1 and 4 are linked to just one other individual. In the top right, the chain can also be called a ring. Individual 1 is linked to everyone else as in a star, while individuals 2 and 5 are directly linked to two other members. Individuals 4 and 3 are directly tied to three other terrorists. This modified chain can be divided into three-, four-, and five-person cells;

hence, a lot of communication and flexibility is provided by this particular network. The nonregular chain in the bottom left of Figure 8.2 involves fewer people and fewer communication possibilities.

A useful measure of communication flows within a network is the *density* measure, which is the number of links in the network divided by the maximum number of possible linkages. For an n terrorist network, the maximum number of links is $(n)(n-1)/2$. Consider the star network with $n = 5$. The maximum number of possible links among five members is ten, so that the density of the star in Figure 8.2 is $4/10 = 2/5$. The other three networks in Figure 8.2 have densities of $7/10$, $2/3$, and $1/2$. The modified chain possesses the greatest information flows and the greatest vulnerability of the four networks displayed. Individuals 2 and 5 can compromise just two individuals, while the other three members can compromise three or four others. Woo (2009) indicated that the IRA's use of a very small cell to bomb the Brighton Hotel on 12 October 1984 allowed the plot to remain secret despite the intent to kill Prime Minister Margaret Thatcher and her cabinet. The immediate capture of Patrick Magee, who planted the bomb, did not compromise the IRA, because this cell was disconnected from other cells. Woo (2009) pointed to some large post-9/11 plots that were foiled because the authorities tapped into information flows from large denser networks.

Returning to Figure 8.1, the bottom right network has a density of 1, since all possible links are utilized in an all-channel network. The other densities in the figure can be computed by dividing the number of links by fifteen – the maximum number of links for a six-member network. The density increases as the degree of these regular networks increases: network $(6, 2)$, density of $6/15$; network $(6, 3)$, density of $9/15$; network $(6, 4)$, density of $12/15$; and network $(6, 5)$, density of 1. As the density increases, the police have more opportunities to intercept communications, and captured terrorists can compromise more of the network.

Centralized versus Decentralized Networks

Enders and Jindapon (2010) formulated an interesting analysis of regular terrorist networks that displays network externalities and the trade-off between connectivity and vunerability. Most important, these authors allowed the terrorists to adjust the connectivity or degree of the network in response to counterterrorism policy. In so doing, they combined graph theory with microeconomic optimizing principles. We merely sketch the key features of their analysis, encouraging the interested reader to seek out their article for further details.

Terrorist i's satisfaction, u_i, depends on the network's output $q(v_i)$ net of cost, where $q(\cdot)$ is the production function, which depends on aggregate effort, v_i. From i's viewpoint, this total effort equals

$$v_i = e_i + \delta \sum_{j \in N_i} e_j, \qquad (8.1)$$

where e_i is i's effort and e_j is the effort of some *other* network member, represented by j. These other members are denoted collectively by set N_i, which excludes i. For a regular network, there are r members in N_i for every i. The δ weight represents the spillover or network externality that i gains from the efforts of others. This δ varies between 0 (no network externality) and 1 (full network externality). When $\delta = 1$, each member's effort is a perfect substitute for one's own effort, which is analogous to contributing to a pure public good. To simplify, we assume symmetry so that everyone is identical. This lets us rewrite aggregate effort as

$$v = e(1 + \delta r), \qquad (8.2)$$

where subscripts are no longer needed.

Following Enders and Jindapon (2010), we assume that the government infiltrates a single terrorist node, but that destroying, say, node i may affect other, neighboring nodes. The vulnerability of neighboring nodes is denoted by π, which varies between 0 and 1. When π is 1, the destruction of node i takes down the entire cell. If, however, π is 0, then neighboring nodes are not at risk. For simplicity, we hypothesize that each node faces infiltration with equal probability $1/n$, the inverse of the size of the network or cell. The likelihood that one of i's neighbors is compromised through i is π/n.[5] Given these assumptions, i's probability of annihilation is $p = (1 + \pi r)/n$. An increase in the network size or its density puts i at greater peril from counterterrorism measures that influence π. This simple representation captures the feature that network size and density (connectedness) increase terrorist vulnerability. Node i survives to benefit from its attack with probability $1 - p$.

The expected utility of a representative terrorist is

$$u = \left(1 - \frac{1 + \pi r}{n}\right) q(e + e\delta r) - ce, \qquad (8.3)$$

where ce is the total cost of effort, with c being the constant marginal cost. In equation (8.3), terrorist benefits come from the expected output

---

[5] For simplicity, we do not allow node i to be infiltrated through one of its neighbors.

(e.g., damage and deaths for some groups) that is derived from the aggregate effort. A central planner for the terrorist group chooses effort, e, and connectivity, r, to maximize aggregate welfare, W,

$$W = \left(1 - \frac{1 + \pi r}{n}\right) nq(e + e\delta r) - cne, \qquad (8.4)$$

where both expected benefits and costs of a representative terrorist are scaled up by group size owing to group symmetry.

Counterterrorism can influence the central planner's objective through three avenues: raising the vulnerability, π, of nodes; lowering network externalities, δ; or increasing the marginal cost of effort, c. Proactive measures to monitor or infiltrate terrorist networks increase vulnerability, while proactive efforts to make sophisticated operations more difficult reduce net externalities. Defensive actions that harden potential terrorist targets raise the marginal cost of effort. An interesting exercise is to investigate the influence of effort and connectivity, associated with each of these three counterterrorism actions, on the planner's equilibrium choice. This is accomplished by maximizing aggregate welfare with respect to effort and connectivity and then differentiating these optimal choice variables with respect to each of the counterterrorism policies.[6] In economics, the effect of such policy variables on equilibrium choices is known as comparative statics.

Under a set of realistic assumptions, policy-induced enhanced vulnerability has the effect of reducing terrorist effort and limiting network connectivity. The central planner responds to more precarious linkages stemming from proactive measures by reengineering networks in order to have fewer ties among terrorists. However, this response by terrorist leaders limits the ability of their networks to engage in complex missions such as 9/11. In light of those enhanced proactive measures, terrorist efforts to execute complex missions are apt to lead to failure at the planning stage due to leaks (Woo, 2009). Thus, the optimizing response of the terrorist leader does not undo the benefits derived from the authorities' countermeasures. Action by the government to reduce network externalities generally results in fewer terrorist efforts and smaller network connectivity. If terrorists gain less from the efforts of others, then there is less motive to be connected and to assume the associated risks. Finally, augmented marginal cost also

---

[6] Technically, we find the two first-order conditions and then differentiate them to find $\partial r^*/\partial \pi$, $\partial e^*/\partial \pi$, etc., where the asterisk denotes optimal value. These partial derivatives are complicated expressions that require some additional assumptions to derive unambiguous signs – see Enders and Jindapon (2010, pp. 269–72).

reduces the amount of effort and curtails network connectivity. The basic message is that terrorist leaders do not keep their networks static, but are constantly adjusting them to government actions. This readjustment limits the threat that these networks present.

Enders and Jindapon (2010) compared the centralized network, just described, to a more decentralized structure. In the latter, the planner selects connectivity in stage 1, while the terrorist members choose their effort levels in stage 2. The choice variables for this network are solved by backward induction starting with stage 2, where the optimal effort level is ascertained. In stage 1, the planner then chooses connectivity based on the optimal effort levels of terrorist members in stage 2. This is a complex problem whose comparative statics must be analyzed using simulations for different values of the three counterterrorism policies. The comparison of the two types of networks yields some interesting findings. First, since the centralized form can always mimic the two-stage decision process, it is a less constrained institutional form than the decentralized form. Consequently, centralized output and aggregate welfare must be at least as large as that of the decentralized network. Thus, greater centralization pays, which is also true for governments confronting a common terrorist threat (see Chapters 4 and 6). Second, the centralized terrorist network responds more fully to the three counterterrorism policies, compared to the decentralized network. That is, the centralized network is better able to offset the policy effectiveness of the government. Third, there is less ambiguity in these responses for the centralized form. These findings indicate that government actions that force terrorist groups to allow their operatives to act more independently limit the effectiveness of the terrorist groups. This is very good news.

Other Network Questions

There is a lot of recent work on how best to compromise terrorist networks. This work typically tries to identify the minimal set of nodes that must be compromised in order to destroy a network. We have three difficulties with this line of thinking. First, it assumes knowledge about a terrorist network's structure that governments often do not possess. Second, a minimal-cut strategy does not account for terrorist leaders taking evasive action to adapt the form of their network. Third, lesser actions than those aimed at destroying the network may be more cost effective.

Another line of reasoning asks how terrorists organize their networks in order to minimize risks and maximize output – see, for example, Lindelauf, Borm, and Hamers (2009) and McGough (2009). This work unites graph theory and optimization techniques. Lindelauf, Borm, and Hamers (2009) showed that the riskiest operations should be assigned to parts of the terrorist network least connected to the rest of the network. This follows because if these parts are compromised, then there are fewer subsequent arrests. These authors also investigated when star networks are preferable to chains and other formations. In particular, the star is more desirable when exposure is uniform – all nodes face equal risks – and there is a relatively high possibility of detection. Stars are less desirable when the detection possibility of central operatives is high. Although this work is interesting, one must wonder whether these insights aid the terrorists more than the authorities. Similar work designed optimal structures that are more resilient to infiltration. McGough (2009) examined when terrorist networks profit from multiple leadership that offers an alternative to the hierarchical top-down form.

MILITARY VERSUS POLITICAL WINGS

Up to this point, we have treated terrorist networks as a single entity, devoid of parts serving distinct functions. This is often not the case – terrorist organizations may contain parts that plan attacks, recruit individuals, finance operations, seek political support, or address the media. Some terrorist groups allocate resources to providing for the social needs of the population – for instance, Hamas and Hezbollah – as a way of building a political base.

Drawing from Siqueira (2005), we assume just two distinct parts to the terrorist organization – a military wing and a political wing. Examples include the ETA and Batasuna; the PLO and Fatah; the IRA and Sinn Féin; and the Islamic Resistance and Hezbollah. These wings may work in conjunction or in opposition. Siqueira (2005) characterized wings with mutually reinforcing actions as supplying strategic complements. By contrast, wings with mutually interfering actions provide strategic substitutes. In Figure 8.3, we display the case of strategic complements. BR_m and BR_p represent the military and political wings' best responses, respectively, to the actions of their counterpart. For example, the positive slope of BR_m indicates that the military wing increases its efforts in tandem with those of the political wing. The same holds for the positively sloped best-response path for the political wing. For the solid best-response paths, the Nash equilibrium is E, where the equilibrium effort levels of the two wings can be read by dropping perpendiculars to the two axes. These best-response paths come from the solutions to two companion constrained optimization problems, in which each

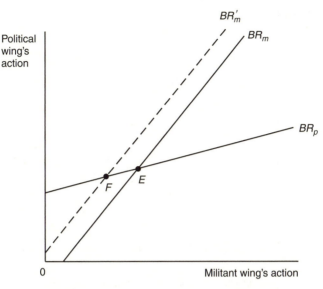

Figure 8.3. Terrorist wings' actions as complements.

wing chooses its efforts given the effort levels of the other wing.[7] If the government increases its countermeasures against just the military wing, then its best-response path shifts left to the dashed path, BR_m', so that there is less military effort for each level of political action. In Figure 8.3, the new Nash equilibrium is at F, where both levels of activities fall. With strategic complements, counterterrorism can be piecemeal – targeted against one wing – and yet reduce both types of terrorist activities. The greatest fall will characterize the targeted wing. Hezbollah is an excellent example of complementary wings, because both wings are directed by the same leadership and, thus, act to reinforce the same goals. Another case is al-Qaida prior to 9/11, where the leadership controlled both military and political actions.

The case of substitute activities for the two wings is illustrated in Figure 8.4. Consider the two solid best-response paths, which are downward-sloping insofar as each wing's efforts replace the need for the competitive efforts of the other wing. The substitute scenario may relate either to the intense

[7] Each wing maximizes its perceived utility, which depends on its efforts and the aggregate (weighted) efforts of the two wings. The latter is analogous to the aggregate effort of nodes in the previous section. These utility functions are constrained by resource constraints. The interplay between the two wings shows up in how each wing attracts resources through its activities. In particular, each wing's generation of resources depends on its own action and that of the other wing. The signs of the direct and cross-partial derivatives determine the presence of substitutes, complements, or a mixed case – see Siqueira (2005).

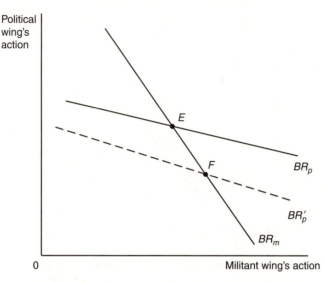

Figure 8.4. Terrorist wings' actions as substitutes.

rivalry between the PLO and Hamas, or to the rivalry between Sinn Féin and radical militant elements of the IRA in the 1980s. The best-response path shows that each wing reduces its own efforts as the other wing increases its actions. The Nash equilibrium is initially at E. If, however, the government cracks down on the political wing, so that its best-response path shifts down to BR'_p in Figure 8.4, then the new equilibrium is at F. This crackdown has the undesirable outcome of ratcheting up military operations as political efforts fall. To reduce both kinds of terrorist activities, the government must target both wings – piecemeal policy is not effective. If, however, a democratic government is more concerned about curtailing violence and possesses limited resources, then targeting the military wing alone (shifting BR_m to the left) is a more sensible piecemeal policy, because violent attacks will decrease. The resulting increased political activity may provide a greater political presence for the terrorists' views, so that some kind of political resolution may follow.

There are also two mixed cases, not illustrated diagrammatically. One mixed case has the political wing's efforts supply external resource-recruiting benefits to the militant wing, so that the latter's best-response path is upward-sloping. By contrast, the militant wing's actions provide external resource-reducing costs to the political wing, so that the latter's best-response path is downward-sloping. In this scenario, the militant wing operates in conditions that favor it over the political wing. The government must choose its piecemeal counterterrorism policies with care. Government efforts to limit militant actions will raise the level of political activities; however, government efforts to reduce terrorist access to the media can shift down BR_p and decrease *both* militant and political activities. Unfortunately, such action also compromises some of the principles of a free press, associated with a democracy. This first mixed scenario may apply to the Palestinian terrorists – Hamas and Palestinian Islamic Jihad (PIJ) – during the Second Intifada, when supporters favored militant acts of carnage and suicide bombings (Bloom, 2005), so that BR_m was upward-sloping.

The second mixed case favors the political wing, so that militant actions result in greater resources for the political wing. However, political efforts reduce resources for the militant wing. There is a positive externality conferred on the political wing and a negative externality conferred on the military wing. The political wing's best-response path is upward-sloping, while the militant wing's best-response path is downward-sloping. Piecemeal counterterrorism efforts to limit the militant wing will reduce both the military and political actions of the terrorists and is more advisable than such efforts directed at the political wing.

Factionalism

A related topic has to do with terrorist group splintering or factionalism. Factions involve interests within the terrorist group that have different viewpoints – for example, hard-line and moderate – that may eventually lead to the division of the group into distinct entities. The PIRA splintered from the IRA; the Continuity IRA and the Real IRA later splintered from the PIRA (Bueno de Mesquita, 2008). Important groups splintered from the PLO, including Black September, PFLP, and the Abu Nidal Organization (ANO). In fact, other groups subsequently split from the PFLP – for example, the PFLP–General Command. The PIJ and Hamas divided from the Muslim Brotherhood. Myriad other examples of factionalism exist.

In an early analysis of factions, Sandler and Arce (2003) formulated a simple game where the government is ill-informed about the composition (proportion) of hard-liners and moderates in the terrorist group. The government must decide what to offer to placate some or all of the group members. An offer that satisfies the hard-liners will placate both factions and provide a rent to the moderates, who would have accepted less. An adverse-selection problem arises when the government satisfies just the moderates, thereby leaving a more extreme element of the terrorist group to be confronted in future attacks. The likelihood of this adverse selection increases as hard-liners' demands rise or as the portion of hard-liners fall. The adverse-selection outcome is less likely as the anticipated violence increases, because the government will then make an offer that satisfies hard-liners. In a subsequent analysis, Bueno de Mesquita (2005a) examined this adverse-selection problem.

Bueno de Mesquita (2008) tailored methods from the median voter model from public choice to examine factionalism in terrorist groups. In particular, he allowed the leader of the original group to choose an ideal position on a moderate-to-extreme preference scale. Bueno de Mesquita's highly specialized model permits potential factions to choose more extreme positions than the original group in the hope of attracting a constituency. If a segment of the population possesses preferences nearer to the more radical position of the splinter group, then it will gain a support base and members. When a potential faction gains a sufficient following, it will splinter from the main organization.

A key limiting assumption of Bueno de Mesquita's (2008) analysis is that a splinter group must identify a more extreme position. There are many instances where a faction put forward a more moderate position – for example, the Justice Commandos of the Armenian Genocide (JCAG) offered a less radical orientation than ASALA. JCAG advocated assassinations of Turkish diplomats and targeted killings, while ASALA wanted more indiscriminate attacks, culminating in the Orly Airport bombing on 15 July 1983 (Hoffman, 2006, pp. 71–4). Bueno de Mesquita (2008, p. 405) found that the original faction will assume a fairly radical position in order to discourage factionalism. If this is the case, then a more moderate faction could gain a large constituency, but this was not allowed in his model. Given his assumptions, Bueno de Mesquita (2008) found that "an improvement in the economy increases the extremism of the original faction, decreases the probability of a splinter faction forming, and conditional on a splinter forming, increases the extremism of the splinter faction" (p. 408). These findings are driven by his assumption that only more extreme groups can splinter. A much richer, and more realistic, set of results would follow from dropping this assumption. In fact, economic improvements are apt to deradicalize some of the population, thereby opening up the opportunity for more moderate groups. With less constrained factionalism, we anticipate that extreme factions will form when events make a distribution of supporters come to possess bimodal preferences with one mode in the extreme part of the spectrum. If, however, the distribution of preference for the population is single-modal, then factions' positions may be less distinguishable as they vie for the median.

UNITY OF PURPOSE?

We have already seen that military and political wings may possess conflicting goals or tastes. Supply-side externalities may exacerbate the competitiveness of these wings, thereby hampering their ability to generate resources. We have also seen that diverse views within terrorist groups may divide them into competing factions that may work at cross purposes. After leaving the PLO, ANO waged a murderous war against the PLO and its leadership. Hence, the conventional view that terrorist groups act with a unity of purpose does not hold up to closer scrutiny.

Shapiro and Siegel (2007) have questioned this unity of purpose by raising a control problem within a terrorist organization that may plague its efficiency. Like any organization, terrorist groups are hampered by asymmetric information, because the leader is not able to view the actions of his underlings. A terrorist cell assigned to a mission may waste some resources on its aggrandizement – for example, alleged nightclub visits by some hijackers prior to 9/11 – at the expense of the collective. A terrorist financier may siphon off money to his or her own purse, thereby leaving less for operations (Shapiro, 2007, p. 59).

The terrorist group's leader observes the outcome of missions but cannot necessarily discern whether intervening factors have influenced the outcome. That is, a high level of effort by the terrorist cell may still result in failure owing to random factors beyond the cell's control – for example, a faulty fuse or an unexpected change in the night watchman's routine. Similarly, low effort by the terrorists may still result in success owing to luck or randomness – for example, the lack of attention of a metal detector screener at an airport. The increased orientation of terrorist networks to cellular structures, as described earlier, worsens the control problem because terrorist leaders have little oversight over their operatives, who can then pursue their own interests. There is also an adverse-selection problem that confounds the control problem, because terrorists with the longest service assume key management positions. Their long-term survival may reflect the fact that they are less accepting of risk and, thus, less committed to the goals of the organization. The same adverse-selection concern may characterize terrorists in relatively safe, but crucial, finance and planning roles.

The standard fixes for this principal-agent problem in other organizations – firms and governmental institutions – is to institute more controls on the agents or to reward good outcomes, so that a high level of effort becomes the dominant strategy despite the random factors and the gains from shirking.[8] These fixes are difficult or inadvisable for a covert terrorist organization because they increase the organization's vulnerability (Shapiro, 2007; Shapiro and Siegel, 2007). Enhanced monitoring and auditing can compromise the terrorists and their handlers if the group is infiltrated. This lesson was learned by the Red Brigades in Italy (Mickolus, Sandler, and Murdock, 1989). The use of incentive-based compensation schemes requires enhanced record keeping, which jeopardizes the terrorist group's security. This is also true of punishment of nonperforming middlemen, whose loyalty may wane with harsh treatment. Obviously, instituting tighter ties between the leadership and middlemen also exposes the organization to greater risk.

Shapiro and Siegel (2007) drew some interesting policy recommendations from this control problem. Most important, the level of counterterrorism can be somewhat curtailed because terrorist organizations are inefficient with lower attack levels. In fact, there is evidence that terrorist leaders have limited funds for missions owing to control worries, thus inhibiting operations (Shapiro and Siegel, 2007). In the 26 February 1993 bombing of the World Trade Center, less than $1,000 was spent on the bomb, which did not have the intended effect of toppling the north tower or poisoning the victims (Mickolus and Simmons, 1997). In fact, two cash-strapped terrorists went to collect the deposit on the Ryder truck days after the explosion, which resulted in their arrest and important intelligence on other group members. Another counterterrorism implication of the control problem is that law enforcement agents should anticipate more small-scale attacks and fewer sophisticated attacks as terrorist groups adjust to the control problem. We should add that the war on terror has exacerbated the control problem and, in so doing, has limited the ability of terrorist organizations to engage in complex incidents.

In a different study, Siqueira and Sandler (2010) investigated an alternative control problem that arises between a general terrorist organization (GTO) or network and its component terrorist groups in the field. A GTO determines the nature and level of terrorist attacks in each country indirectly through its choice of the representative associated with the local terrorist group. A GTO may strategically opt for a local terrorist group that is more or less extreme than itself in order to respond optimally to its perceptions of the local government's toughness and the local supporters'

---

[8]   Even though good outcomes can arise by chance from low effort, these outcomes are more apt to come from high effort. Thus, sufficient rewards for good outcomes will stimulate high effort.

commitment. In their game-theoretic model, the GTO delegates responsibilities to local terrorist groups in n countries. There are four sets of players: the GTO, local terrorist groups, governments, and terrorist supporters. In stage one, the GTO chooses its n representatives to head the local terrorist groups; in stage two, the local terrorist group chooses its attacks, and the local government picks its counterterrorism level in battleground countries; and in stage three, terrorist supporters determine their level of participation. The GTO is interested not only in maximizing its global net gains from the terrorist campaign, but also in maximizing the support that it receives. By contrast, the local terrorist representative maximizes his or her net benefits from terrorism while ignoring local supporters. Thus, the GTO has the responsibility of trying to internalize the associated supporters' externalities by choosing the appropriate local representative for the cause.

This analysis casts light on some interesting recent puzzles. For instance, why did al-Qaida-affiliated groups engage in heinous attacks in Iraq, Jordan, and Egypt that alienated supporters? In particular, three suicide bombings on Western hotels – the Grand Hyatt, Radisson SAS, and Days Inn – in Amman, Jordan, on 9 November 2005 that killed many Muslims resulted in public condemnation throughout the region (Mickolus, 2008). Siqueira and Sandler (2010) showed that when the GTO perceives the host government as weak (that is, reducing counterterrorism as terrorist campaigns grow in strength) and supporters as committed, the GTO will place more extreme representatives into the field. If, however, the host government becomes tougher or the terrorist supporters' fervor wanes, then the GTO may come to regret its deployment decision. Thus, al-Qaida came to lament its deployment of al-Zarqawi to Iraq in the aftermath of the three Jordanian hotel bombings (Brachman, Fishman, and Felter, 2008). Once terrorist representatives are in the field, it is nearly impossible to recall them. Another change in government response came in Saudi Arabia after a series of attacks against Western interests during 2003–2005. When these extremists started to attack the country's pipelines and oil industry, which is the lifeline of the economy, the government grew tough on terrorism, taking its local terrorists by surprise.

Yet another government's about-face involved the Maliki government in Iraq. Following the US-backed surge, the Maliki government began to increase its counterterrorism measures as attacks escalated. Moreover, the local tribes lost favor with the terrorists and allied themselves with US troops (Siqueira and Sandler, 2010). This realignment came after al-Qaida in Iraq had increased its attacks on the local population. Thus, the strategic advantage of the GTO can be reversed when outside assistance increases or the local population has a change of heart.

Siqueira and Sandler (2010) investigated two-way delegation, where both the GTO and the local government can delegate. In the government case, it can delegate its counterterrorism measures to a tougher policymaker, who places more weight on reducing risk. Two-way delegation can, under certain circumstances, harm both delegators – the GTO and the local government – if the local government is perceived by the terrorists as weak. If, however, the government is tough, it comes to possess a strategic advantage as attacks decline and the need for countermeasures also declines (Siqueira and Sandler, 2010, pp. 250–1). Their study highlights that the interface and control of the component parts of the terrorist organization are important for the appropriate policy decisions. Unlike earlier analyses, control involves every level of the terrorist organization, as well as its efforts to gain a strategic advantage through delegation. Future principal-agent studies of terrorist groups need to account for multilevel decision making, as in the industrial organization literature.

DYNAMICS OF TERRORIST GROUPS

A relatively unexplored aspect of the study of terrorist groups concerns their development over time. Feinstein and Kaplan (2010) investigated how a terrorist group's choice of mission scale over a two-period planning horizon influences the group's evolution over time and the proper counterterrorism response. The terrorist group is permitted to conduct two types of operations: a small-scale attack requiring a single-period horizon and a large-scale attack requiring a two-period horizon. The small mission has low fixed cost and relatively high marginal cost; the large mission has high fixed cost and relatively low marginal cost. Obviously, successful large missions provide greater resources for the terrorists during the subsequent period than successful small missions. Although the analysis is very stylized, it does capture an important campaign choice that terrorism groups must make over time, which tends to affect their evolution. These authors' decision-theoretic model allows terrorist groups to expand over time propelled by their natural and induced growth rates. The latter is a consequence of the mix of attacks and success.

Feinstein and Kaplan (2010) established that a terrorist group must surpass a resource threshold before engaging in large-scale attacks. Novice organizations typically do not have the necessary war chest to go for spectacular attacks. A less obvious finding is that terrorist group size increases at an increasing rate with successful attacks and acquired resources, so that governments must be vigilant to destroy groups early in their tenure. This finding accords with the empirical duration study of Blomberg, Engel, and Sawyer (2010) in which terrorist groups become harder to counter after their initial successful attacks. Moreover, long-lived groups come to monopolize terrorist attacks owing to their size. The authors also showed that terrorist campaigns fall into well-ordered regimes – for example, small-scale attacks often precede large-scale attacks. This outcome and others in their study can inform policymakers.

There are a number of directions to extend their interesting work. The model can be made strategic by allowing the terrorists and the government to react to one another's choices. Currently, the government is a passive agent on the sidelines; thus, the government is not reacting to the terrorists' choices. More periods can be added to the study so that a more dynamic interactive game (known as a differential game) analysis is presented. Finally, equations should be derived from the study that can be empirically tested based on the data on terrorist groups in GTD and ITERATE, where terrorist groups' operations have been tracked for almost forty years.

Faria and Arce (2005) presented a dynamic model that links terrorist activities to the support of the terrorists through a recruitment mechanism. Their model derives from the study of group dynamics associated with guerrilla warfare. In particular, public support depends on past terrorist attacks, while terrorist recruitment today hinges on contemporaneous public support. Finally, current terrorist attacks increase with today's recruits and the surviving recruits from earlier periods; however, current terrorist attacks decrease with the government's counterterrorism policy. Using a linear model, Faria and Arce found the steady-state level of terrorists (where their numbers remain constant over time) for the organization as a function of some policy variables – for example, information (antiterrorist propaganda), terrorist income levels, political repression, and law enforcement levels.

Faria and Arce (2005) found two stable long-run equilibriums: one with no terrorism and one with a pervasive level of terrorism. The second equilibrium is the one of interest, because the first generally characterizes one-hit wonders, which disappear on their own owing to insufficient support or recruitment. This disappearance can be accelerated by a swift counterterrorism response. After specifying the requirements for equilibrium stability, these authors investigated some comparative dynamics where changes in the equilibrium level of terrorist attacks are tied to counterterrorism policies. In all instances, counterterrorism decreases the long-run level of terrorism. In particular, improvements in economic conditions and enhanced antiterrorism propaganda reduce terrorism. Increased political freedom (less repression) also curtails terrorism.

Some nondynamic studies have cautioned against severe proactive counterterrorism actions that can create a backlash (Rosendorff and Sandler, 2004). The Faria-Arce model did not permit this possibility owing to its linearity. To keep the dynamic model tractable, Faria and Arce had a simple relationship between terrorist recruitment and economic conditions. In some recent static studies, the wage rate or economic conditions did not necessarily decrease terrorism owing to other considerations (Bueno de Mesquita, 2005b; Siqueira and Sandler, 2010). To date, the empirical literature has not conclusively related improved economic conditions to a decrease in terrorism.

In a subsequent exercise, Gutfraind (2009) formulated a dynamic model of a terrorist group, where its strength, S, is

$$S = mL + F, \tag{8.5}$$

which is a weighted sum of the group's leaders, L, and foot soldiers, F. Leaders are more important for strength, so that $m > 1$.[9] The dynamics of the composition of the terrorist organization hinges on

$$\dot{L} = \psi F - \alpha L - b, \tag{8.6}$$

and

$$\dot{F} = \rho \left(mL + F \right) - \alpha F - k. \tag{8.7}$$

The overhead dots indicate a time derivative – that is, $\dot{L} = dL/dt$, and $\dot{F} = dF/dt$. In equation (8.6), ψ is the promotion rate of foot soldiers to leaders; α is the defection rate for leaders; and b denotes counterterrorism-induced losses of leaders. In equation (8.7), ρ is the recruitment rate of foot soldiers, which is applied to the group's strength; α is the defection rate of foot soldiers; and k indicates counterterrorism-induced losses in foot soldiers. By setting the two time derivatives to zero and solving, we find the steady-state equilibrium values of leadership and foot soldiers in terms of the parameters. The set of dynamic equations – (8.6) and (8.7) – also permits the construction of a phase diagram, which displays the trajectories for different initial values of foot soldiers and leaders. The phase diagram also distinguishes stable from unstable equilibriums.

---

[9]   This is becoming less true for today's loose network, in which m approaches a value of 1.

If the steady-state equilibrium is unstable, then an efficacious counterterrorism policy is to reduce the levels of leaders and foot soldiers to levels at which the group can no longer sustain itself. Moreover, the analysis indicates when attacks on the leadership – for example, targeted killings – is preferable to attacks on the members. These assassinations are preferable when the promotion parameter is low and the other parameters are high. This was not the case for the Israeli assassinations of Hamas leaders – Ahmen Yassin on 22 March 2004 and Abdel Aziz al-Rantissi on 18 April 2004 – which were met with the immediate designation of new leaders, some of whom were more ruthless than their predecessors. Counterterrorism policies can also influence α, ψ, ρ, and m. Concessions to the terrorist cause can raise defections, α, while antiterrorism propaganda can reduce recruitment, r, for each level of strength. Media blackouts can also reduce recruitment.

Like Faria and Arce (2005), Gutfraind treated the government as a passive player, whose policies are mechanically added to the equations. Dynamic studies of terrorist group evolution will become more intriguing and useful in a game framework, where both the terrorists and the government are strategic players who are choosing *a plan of action over time*. The inchoate study of the evolution of terrorist organizations needs much further work.

CONCLUDING REMARKS

There is now a long-term data set – GTD – that records both domestic and transnational terrorist incidents according to the perpetrating group. These data are essential to the proper study of terrorist groups because few groups execute transnational (domestic) terrorist attacks to the exclusion of the other kind of attack. Table 8.1 on major terrorist groups underscores this insight.

To date, there have been relatively few empirical or theoretic studies of terrorist groups. Many of the studies reviewed here have appeared in the last few years. This dearth of investigations needs to be corrected because an understanding of terrorist groups – their membership, campaigns, recruitment strategies, and evolution – would greatly inform policymaking. If, for instance, the authorities can discover the tipping point of a terrorist group, at which smaller membership or leadership is not sustainable, then the authority will know when to redouble its offensive to weaken the group. If feasible through intelligence, knowledge of a network's most vulnerable and essential nodes would allow counterterrorist agents to get the largest payback from their operations until the group reorganizes.

There are some essential caveats to remember. First, network and dynamic treatments of terrorist groups presuppose knowledge of a terrorist group that is seldom available unless it has been infiltrated. Even when it is infiltrated, only segments of the network may be uncovered. Since 9/11, terrorists have responded to proactive government measures by instituting looser networks with disconnected segments. Second, terrorists rapidly adapt their networks to counterterrorism policies – terrorist groups are not static structures, ripe for attack. Counterterrorist action must be swift and must anticipate optimal readjustments to the network. Third, dynamic analysis of terrorist groups must allow the government to be a strategic player like the terrorists. Although they are a useful start, the current one-sided models in the literature do not tell us enough. Fourth, theoretic models of terrorist groups must be used to derive testable hypotheses so that the theory can be evaluated and adjusted.

NINE

Before and After 9/11

In February 1998, Osama bin Ladin and Ayman al Zawahiri published a signed statement declaring a *fatwa* against the United States. Bin Laden, al Zawahiri, and the other signatories of the statement called for retribution against the United States because it had "declared war against God."[1] The statement went on to claim that it was the individual duty of every Muslim to murder any American anywhere on earth. Three months later, in an interview on ABC-TV, bin Laden stated: "We believe that the worst thieves in the world today and the worst terrorists are the Americans. Nothing could stop you except perhaps retaliation in kind. We do not have to differentiate between military and civilian." As we now know, the *fatwa* resulted in the unprecedented 9/11 attack against the United States.

As we discuss in subsequent chapters, the tragedy of 9/11 was a defining moment for the United States, other Western nations, and the Islamic nations in many profound ways. Chapter 10 focuses on the economic costs of terrorism, including the direct and indirect costs of 9/11. Chapter 11 evaluates homeland security, and Chapter 12 speculates on the future of terrorism. In this chapter, we report the results of several studies that quantify the ways in which the type, location, and nature of terrorist incidents have changed since the *fatwa* and in the aftermath of 9/11. We also discuss how 9/11 affected our collective psyche and how it has made us feel more aware of and more vulnerable to terrorism.

BEFORE 9/11: WHAT DID WE KNOW
AND WHEN DID WE KNOW IT?

Given the call for a *fatwa* against the United States and the growing severity of al-Qaida's attacks, many observers hypothesized that the 9/11 attacks

---

[1] All quotations in this paragraph use the translations from the National Commission on Terrorist Attacks Upon the United States (2004, p. 47), *The 9/11 Commission Report*.

could have been anticipated and possibly prevented. The issue culminated in a debate in front of the 9/11 Commission when Richard Clarke (former national coordinator for security, infrastructure protection, and counter-terrorism), claimed that the Bush White House had overlooked the obvious al-Qaida threat because it was obsessed with the possibility that Saddam Hussein possessed weapons of mass destruction. George Tenet (former CIA director) further fueled the controversy when he testified, "We didn't recruit the right people, ... We didn't integrate all the data we had prop-erly, and probably we had a lot of data that we didn't know about that if everybody'd known about maybe we would have had a chance."

In defense of the White House, US National Security Adviser Condoleezza Rice testified, "I don't know what a sense of urgency – any greater than the one that we had – would have caused us to do differently." She also described a number of measures the Bush administration used to heighten the terror-ism alert, including: "all fifty-six FBI field offices were also tasked in late June to go to increased surveillance and contact with informants related to known or suspected terrorists in the United States." The issue is still contro-versial; at the very end of its term on 17 December 2008, the Bush White House issued a fact sheet detailing how it "Kept America Safe."

One way to ascertain whether 9/11 could have been prevented is to deter-mine whether the then-existing data could have provided any statistical evi-dence indicating a change in al-Qaida's behavior immediately following its *fatwa* against the United States. Toward this end, Lee, Enders, and Sandler (2009) asked whether there was a structural change in the terrorism data at or after February 1998, but prior to July 2001. The idea was to determine whether an analyst examining the terrorism data would be able to make a real-time assessment that an attack on the scale of 9/11 was pending. A pos-itive finding might suggest that the authorities could have used this statisti-cal evidence to bolster US counterterrorism efforts before the 9/11 attacks.

To explain our methodology, we consider the simplified intervention model of the type discussed in Chapter 3,

$$y_t = a_0 + a_1 y_{t-1} + \alpha_1 D_L + \varepsilon_t, \tag{9.1}$$

where y_t is the series of interest and D_L is a *level-shift* dummy variable repre-senting the date of a possible structural break. For y_t, we constructed three principal series. The ALL series, shown in Figure 9.1, consists of all types of transnational terrorist incidents having a US victim. Since the actual monthly values are quite erratic, the figure reports quarterly values. We did not extend the sample past 9/11 because our hypothetical analyst would not have had access to such data. We also constructed a time series for the

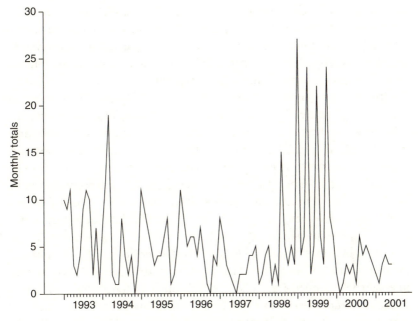

Figure 9.1. All incidents with US victims.

number of attacks with a US casualty (CAS) and a time series for all trans-national deadly bombings (BOMB) with a US victim – these time series are not displayed here.

Temporarily assume that the dummy variable is such that $D_L = 1$ if $t \geq$ 1998:M2 (the date of the announcement of the *fatwa*), where M2 denotes the second month, and $D_L = 0$ otherwise. Thus, in equation (9.1), the magnitude of α_1 indicates the initial impact of the break, and the rate of decay is determined by the magnitude of a_1. In point of fact, the actual break date (if any) is unknown to us and needs to be estimated. Hence, it might be possible to estimate a model in the form of equation (9.1) for every possible break date during the interval 1998:M2 through 2001:M6. The model containing the best fit would then yield a consistent estimate of the break date. Unfortunately, the issue is a bit more complicated insofar as it is necessary to control for other breaks, such as the rise of fundamentalist-based terrorism and the demise of the Soviet Union. We therefore used the Bai-Perron (1998, 2003) procedure, which allows for the estimation of multiple structural breaks when the number of breaks and their dates are unknown. Bai and Perron (1998) derived the appropriate statistical distribution to test the null hypothesis of no breaks against the alternative hypothesis of an arbitrary number of breaks. Thus, we can use the Bai-Perron (1998, 2003) methodology to obtain point estimates of the break dates and to form confidence intervals around the estimated dates. Our particular interest was to determine whether there is a statistically significant break date such that a 95% confidence interval contains February 1998.

Although the sample used in Lee, Enders, and Sandler (2009) began in 1968:M1, for clarity, Figure 9.1 shows the ALL series for the eight years prior to 9/11. There is an apparent jump in the monthly totals sometime in mid-1998. To an analyst examining the data, this jump would probably signal an important ratcheting up of the number of attacks with US victims following the *fatwa*. However, as should also be clear from the figure, the ALL series fell precipitously in late 1999. Thus, the hypothetical analyst could easily have been lulled into believing that the level of terrorism had declined as the *fatwa* played itself out.

To be a bit more formal, we found two statistically significant breaks in the ALL series. The first break date of February 1991 had a 95% confidence interval that spanned December 1989 through October 1992. The mean of the ALL series fell from 11.72 to 6.08 incidents per month; hence, the demise of the Soviet Union apparently led to a nearly 50% reduction in the number of attacks with a US victim. The second break, in September 1999, was estimated to occur about nineteen months after the announcement of the *fatwa*. The break could have occurred as early as July 1999. The key point is that this break was associated with a *reduction* in the number of incidents with a US victim preceding 9/11. The mean number of monthly incidents fell from 6.08 to 4.14. It could be argued that the decline in the number of incidents actually signaled that al-Qaida was hoarding resources for the upcoming 9/11 attacks. Nevertheless, any analyst would be hard-pressed to make the point that this small (albeit statistically significant) decline actually signaled that al-Qaida was preparing for the largest terrorist attack in history. Given the overall volatility of the ALL series (recall that the values prior to 1995 are not shown in the figure), we did not find a statistically significant third break near 1998. Even though we did find breaks in the CAS and BOMB series, none of them corresponded to the announcement of the *fatwa*. Consequently, we concluded that there was no clear-cut time-series evidence that could have been used to predict 9/11.

THE COMPETING FORCES: REDUCED STRENGTH VERSUS ENHANCED SENSITIVITY

Even though Lee, Enders, and Sandler (2009) found little evidence of a sizable structural change just before the 9/11 attacks, many changes have occurred since. Within two years of the US-led war on terror, about two-thirds of al-Qaida leaders had been either killed or captured. The rank-and-file membership was reduced as 3,400 al-Qaida suspects were arrested and many of its operatives were lost during the Afghan War in 2001 (Gerges and Isham, 2003). Additionally, the White House (2003) reported that more than $200 million of the al-Qaida network's assets had been frozen following 9/11. More recently, the White House (2008) indicated that enhanced intelligence capabilities were responsible for foiling attempts to bomb fuel tanks at JFK airport, blow up airliners bound for the East Coast, destroy a Los Angeles skyscraper, kill soldiers at Fort Dix, and blow up the Sears Tower in Chicago. Enhanced intelligence, along with al-Qaida's losses in manpower, leadership, and finances should limit the network's ability to engage in logistically complex modes of attack such as hostage taking. Even though al-Qaida and its affiliated groups have been able to find additional recruits and volunteers willing to assume leadership positions, such attrition should severely limit the amount of entrepreneurship that al-Qaida's highest echelon can display.

Although the terrorists' abilities to conduct attacks may have been weakened, any given attack is now likely to produce a greater feeling of fear and insecurity than during the pre-9/11 period. The events of 9/11 have sensitized the public in such a way that terrorist actions are likely to have enhanced effects on the electorate's psyche. Graham (2001) indicated that stress-related illnesses are more likely to result from events caused by deliberate violence than from natural disasters. Had the World Trade Center been destroyed by an off-course airplane approaching New York's LaGuardia Airport, the amount of post-traumatic stress disorder would have been markedly reduced. Graham also noted that the fear of the unknown often has profound psychological consequences on individuals already having problems struggling with the problems of daily life. When people are afraid of something specific, they can find ways to avoid the source of their anxiety. For some, a generalized fear of a future attack at some unspecified place and date can be debilitating.

In November 2001, Gallagher (2003) surveyed the directors of eighty-two university and college testing centers. The intent of the survey was to determine how college students had been affected by 9/11. Eighty-eight percent of the counseling centers reported a considerable increase in their caseloads after 9/11, an increase averaging 21% for schools located on the Eastern seaboard and 15% for schools elsewhere. Both numbers are underestimates, since more than two-thirds of the respondents reported that the increase in caseloads was so sudden that many students had to be placed on a waiting list before seeing a counselor. Respondents also indicated that their student clients directly linked their problems to 9/11. Students suffered from nightmares, depression, sleeplessness, anxiety attacks, and an inability to focus on their studies. Notably, the attacks themselves did not cause the psychological problems; rather, the students' problems resulted from the general climate of "fear and vulnerability that followed 9/11." Perhaps the most worrisome part of the survey is that the majority of center directors believed that the problems experienced by these students may be quite long-lived.

In another study, Wolinsky and colleagues (2003) surveyed 291 older adults who participated in an ongoing longitudinal study regarding coronary artery disease. Since the original study had started before 9/11, they were able to measure pre- and post-9/11 attitudes about personal stress, mental health, and a sense of self-control. The study is also interesting because social gerontologists believe that older adults are most vulnerable to stress-related disorders. Each patient was interviewed three times before and three times after 9/11. The study's participants reported a reduced sense of control over their personal lives that was heightened among higher-income individuals and those reporting greater religiosity.

More recently, Metcalfe, Powdthavee, and Dolan (2011) analyzed a longitudinal survey of approximately 10,000 UK households. Since 1991, the British Household Panel Survey has been administered annually in such a way that a significant number of the interviews take place in September of each year. Interestingly, the respondents provide a measure of their subjective well-being (SWB) that involves such factors as how often during the last four weeks they have lost sleep over worry, felt strain, experienced difficulties, and/or felt depressed. Thus, it was possible to compare the SWB of UK households during the periods right before and after the 9/11 attacks. The results indicated that 9/11 did have a significant detrimental impact on the SWB of female, but not of male, respondents. Splitting the sample by age indicated that the attacks had a larger psychological effect on individuals over thirty-five. Of course, diverse groups may differ in their candor in revealing actual stress levels; for example, men and young people might not want to indicate that they experienced fear. The survey also revealed that the greatest impact of the attacks were found to have been felt a few weeks after the attacks and to have dissipated by December 2001. The delayed response might be due to persistent images of 9/11 shown in the worldwide media. The key insight is that the fear and intimidation induced by 9/11 clearly transcended international borders.

One further unknown is the "recruitment" factor. Faria and Arce (2005) argued that each terrorist success makes it easier for groups such as al-Qaida to recruit new members. To the extent that recruitment has been enhanced by 9/11 and by the recent events in Iraq, the composition of terrorist groups will shift from older and experienced members to new recruits. The way in which terrorists respond to these simultaneous changes by altering the number, targets, locations, and types of attacks is clearly an empirical issue.

CHANGES IN THE TYPES OF ATTACK MODES

As a consequence of the reduction in its leadership (including the assassination of bin Laden on 1 May 2011), resource base, and connectivity, the al-Qaida network and its affiliates can be expected to turn to logistically simple, but deadly, bombings. Such bombings can also be more attractive than assassinations or hostage takings, which can be logistically complex and yield just a few victims. Given the events following 9/11 and the preferences of many of today's terrorist groups for carnage, we anticipate a smaller reliance on hostage-taking events and assassinations and a greater reliance on deadly bombings.

This substitution from logistically complex into relatively simple attack modes is illustrated by the recent incidents staged by al-Qaida in the Arabian Peninsula (Aqap). For example, the Aqap attack undertaken by the so-called underwear bomber, Umar Farouk Abdulmutallab, caused no serious injuries, but led to the installation of full body scanners in US airports. Moreover, Aqap claimed responsibility for placing bombs inside ink cartridges sent from Yemen that were addressed to a Chicago synagogue. In an article in its *Inspire* magazine, Aqap indicated that the cost of the so-called Operation Hemorrhage was only $4,200. Nevertheless, these small-scale operations made headlines around the world. The article further indicated that the intent was not to cause mass carnage. Instead, the goal of Aqap was to "stage smaller scale attacks that involve less players and less time to launch." Aqap promised "Death by 1000 Cuts" rather than large-scale operations such as the attacks on the World Trade Center and the Pentagon.[2]

A model illustrating the rationale behind this substitution into a "1000 Cuts" strategy is provided by Enders and Su (2007). The central idea is that an optimizing terrorism network can be expected to reduce its connectivity in response to government's enhanced ability to intercept its wire, oral, and electronic communications. As indicated in Chapter 8, highly connected groups can conduct logistically complex attacks (such as simultaneous

---

[2]   Much of the information from this paragraph is discussed in further detail by Gartenstein-Ross (2010).

embassy bombings). but are subject to infiltration. In a *complete* or *all-channel* network, every member can directly communicate with the other members. As potential information flows are complete, all group members can plan and coordinate their activities without the need to transmit messages through intermediaries. Nevertheless, this network structure is the least secure in that a single infiltrator can bring down the entire network. At the other extreme, in the chain network structure, each individual can communicate with only two others. Teams of two or three cannot conduct very complex operations, but are the most secure because contact with the leadership is minimized.

Once the communication links within the network become less secure, a rational group will economize on the number of communication links within the organization. As a result, the group's density declines *and* the group tends to substitute into tactics that are not intensive in communication links (that is, tactics that are less logistically complex). In contrast to a coordinated set of attacks such as 9/11, a bomb placed in a printer or ink cartridge is a very secure attack mode because it involves few individuals and because the authorities have little means to trace the bomb back to the network's leadership.

In Enders and Sandler (2005a), we wanted to determine whether changes in the mode of attack are statistically significant, whether they pertain to other classifications of incident types, and whether they are specifically related to 9/11. We extracted eight primary time series from ITERATE in order to determine how the number of attacks and the attack modes have changed since 9/11.[3] The ALL series includes quarterly totals of *all* types of transnational terrorist incidents; the most important component of this quarterly series is BOMBINGS, accounting for over half of all annual terrorist attacks on average. The BOMBINGS series combines seven types of events: explosive bombings, letter bombings, incendiary bombings, missile attacks, car bombings, suicide car bombings, and mortar and grenade attacks. The HOSTAGE series includes quarterly totals of kidnappings, skyjackings, nonaerial hijackings, and barricade and hostage-taking missions, whereas the ASSASSINATIONS series consists of politically motivated murders. Two additional primary series are: (i) a quarterly DEATH series, recording the number of terrorist incidents in which one or more individuals (including terrorists) died; and (ii) a more-inclusive CAS series, recording the quarterly total number of incidents in which one or more individuals were injured or died. We further broke down the BOMBINGS

---

[3] The series were previously described in Chapter 3.

series by identifying the quarterly number of bombings with one or more deaths and the number of bombings with one or more casualties.

To test for a structural break at 9/11, we estimated an intervention model of the form described earlier. Consider the simplified intervention model

$$y_t = a_0 + a_1 y_{t-1} + \alpha_1 D_P + \alpha_2 D_L + \varepsilon_t, \tag{9.2}$$

where y_t is the series of interest and D_P and D_L are dummy variables representing 9/11. In equation (9.2), D_P is a dummy variable such that $D_P = 1$ if $t = 2001\text{:}Q3$ (third quarter of 2001) and $D_P = 0$ otherwise. This type of *pulse* variable is appropriate if the 9/11 attacks induced an immediate change in the series lasting for a single quarter. The magnitude of α_1 indicates the initial effect of 9/11 on y_t, and the rate of decay or residual effect in subsequent quarters is determined by the magnitude of a_1. To allow for the possibility that 9/11 had a permanent effect on the level of the time series of terrorist events of a particular type, the second dummy variable in equation (9.2) is such that $D_L = 0$ prior to 9/11 and $D_L = 1$ for 2001:Q3 and thereafter. The impact effect of the *level* dummy variable on the time series is given by α_2. We began by estimating the ALL series with both *pulse* and *level* breaks. The key features of the estimated equation were such that the estimated coefficients for the *level* and *pulse* variables are both negative. This might seem to imply that both series fell as a result of 9/11; however, you can see in Figure 9.1 that the ALL series actually began its downward movement prior to 9/11. Even though the ALL series seems to decline around 9/11, the issue is whether these coefficients are spurious. The *level* and *pulse* variables are not statistically significant; hence, there are no statistically significant short-run or long-run effects on the behavior of the ALL series resulting from 9/11. Since bombings (also shown in Figure 3.2) comprise the majority of incidents, it is not surprising that we found similar results for the BOMBINGS series. In particular, bombings are also quite persistent, but the total number of bombings was not affected by 9/11.

When we examined the other series, none of the *pulse* dummy variables were significant at conventional levels. The *level-shift* dummy was significant only for the HOSTAGE series. The short-run effect is such that hostage incidents are estimated to fall by about six incidents in 2001:Q3. Given the persistence in the series, a low number of incidents is expected to be followed by other low-incident periods. We calculated the long-run effect to be a decline of approximately nine incidents per quarter. However, even this finding is problematic because a careful inspection of the HOSTAGE series (see Figure 3.3) shows that the sharp drop in hostage incidents actually started in 1999.

We also examined how the composition of the ALL series changed over time. Specifically, we estimated an intervention model in the form of equation (9.2) for the ratio of each incident type to ALL. The *pulse* dummy variable was statistically significant for incidents with a death as a proportion of all incidents (P_DEATH) and for incidents with a casualty (that is, a death or injury) as a proportion of all incidents (P_CAS). Immediately following 9/11, the proportion of incidents with deaths rose by fifty-four percentage points and the proportion of incidents with casualties rose by forty-eight percentage points. The *level* dummy variables were, however, not significant at conventional levels; hence, the jumps in the P_DEATH and P_CAS were not permanent.

The *level* dummy variable was, however, highly significant for the proportion of hostage incidents (P_HOSTAGE) and the proportion of deadly incidents due to bombings (P_DEATH_B). The proportion of hostage takings was approximately 13% of all incidents prior to 9/11. As a result of 9/11, the short-run change in the P_HOSTAGE series was estimated to fall to just 4% of all incidents. In the longer run, the proportion of hostage incidents was near zero. We also found evidence of a significant sixteen-percentage-point decline in assassinations as a proportion of all incidents. In contrast, the P_DEATH_B series rose by twenty percentage points.

We concluded that the US-led offensive against al-Qaida and its network has taken a toll on al-Qaida's leadership and finances by compromising al-Qaida's ability to direct complex operations. The ALL, DEATH, and CAS series *have not changed following 9/11*. The main influence of 9/11 has been on the composition of the ALL series. In particular, hostage-taking incidents have fallen after 9/11 as terrorists, bent on carnage, have substituted into deadly bombings. As a consequence, the proportion of deadly incidents due to bombings has increased as the proportions of hostage-taking and assassination attacks have decreased. The net result is that al-Qaida has substituted away from logistically complex attacks (for example, hostage takings and assassinations) into logistically simpler bombings.[4]

DISTRIBUTION OF TERRORIST INCIDENTS BY COUNTRY AND REGION

Post-9/11 actions to augment security in wealthy nations may have unintended negative consequences by inducing terrorists to stage their attacks in

---

[4] We also utilized a number of other methods, including one that allowed us to search for the most likely break dates.

countries less able to afford widespread defensive measures. Thus, the new emphasis on homeland security in the United States and throughout the European Union (EU) may merely displace terrorist attacks to softer venues where people and property from prime-target countries are attacked abroad (Enders and Sandler, 1993, 1995; Sandler and Enders, 2004). The point is that rational terrorists weigh the costs, risks, and benefits when choosing the venue for an attack. Hence, attacks may be displaced from high-income countries (HICs) to low-income countries (LICs) as some HICs deploy enhanced security measures that make attacks more difficult and costly for terrorists to accomplish.

Geographic transference will occur as attack venues shift across regions (for example, from Europe to the Middle East or Asia). A geographical shift may also be motivated by the ability of the terrorists to blend in and establish a support system, especially for religious fundamentalist terrorists. If terrorists attack foreign interests closer to home, then they do not have to cross borders that are more closely guarded in some regions since 9/11. In the 1980s, there was a significant "spillover" of Middle Eastern terrorism throughout Europe – for example, there were forty-three terrorist incidents of Middle Eastern origin in Europe in 1987 (US Department of State, 1988, pp. 16, 18). Given the increased scrutiny given to Middle Easterners in Europe following 9/11, more incidents staged in the Middle East are anticipated.

In Enders and Sandler (2006), we used intervention analysis to determine whether terrorists have shifted their venues based on target countries' income and/or regional location in response to 9/11. To accomplish this task, we partitioned countries into income categories based on the World Bank's classification of countries into low (LIC), middle (MIC), and high (HIC) per capita income countries.[5] In constructing our time series, we took account of the fact that individual nations may switch among the three income groups. As a result of economic growth, the number of nations included in the HIC group generally increased, thereby working against a possible transnational terrorism substitution from HICs into LICs. For

---

[5] The groupings are described in detail in each issue of World Bank's (various years) *World Development Report*. For 2000, LICs had per capita Gross National Income (GNI) of $755 or less; MICs had per capita GNI greater than $756 and less than or equal to $9,265; and HICs had per capita GNI in excess of $9,265. Country codes from ITERATE for location start of incidents allow us to associate terrorist event's location to the country's income classification. When matching countries to terrorist attacks and income classes, we also had to adjust for changes in the political map of Eastern Europe, Africa, and elsewhere over the entire sample period.

instance, Algeria and Mexico moved from the LIC group to the MIC group, whereas Israel, Portugal, and Spain switched from the MIC group to the HIC group owing to high per capita income growth. In the late 1980s, Poland moved in the opposite direction, from the class of MICs to the LICs, at a time when it was a transition economy, but returned to the MIC group in the mid-1990s.

In order to take account of the most recent events, we update the study through 2008. In order to illustrate the key changes since 9/11, we present the series starting from 1990:1 in Figure 9.2. Panel 1 shows that from 1990 to about 1998, the proportion of transnational incidents occurring in the LICs fluctuated around 70%.[6] The proportion fell through 2002 and has since accelerated to unprecedented levels. Panel 2 shows that the proportion of LIC incidents with a US victim has been rather stable. Although there was a sharp drop during the 1999–2001 period, in recent years the proportion has fluctuated around 85%. Overall, transnational terrorism has shifted to the low-income region, which has the highest proportion of incidents with US victims. As shown in panel 3, except for 2001, the proportion of incidents in the HICs has steadily declined. Moreover, in contrast to the LICs, the proportion of HIC incidents with US victims during the 2004:Q1–2008:Q4 period averaged 8.4%.

We also wanted to determine the change in the distribution of terrorist events by geographic region. Toward this end, we applied the six regional classifications given in the US Department of State (2003) *Patterns of Global Terrorism*. These regions are the Western Hemisphere (North, Central, and South America), Africa (excluding North Africa), Asia (South and East Asia, Australia, and New Zealand), Eurasia (Central Asia, Russia, and the Ukraine), Europe (Western and Eastern Europe), and the Middle East (including North Africa). This partition of countries locates most of the Islamic population in the Middle East, Eurasia, and Asia. Although this geographical division differs from the income taxonomy, there is likely to be some similarity between the two classification schemes.

Figure 9.3 depicts the casualty series for four of the major geographical regions. Clearly, there has been a substitution away from the Western Hemisphere and Europe. In part, countries comprising this composite region tend to fall into the MIC and HIC groups. Nevertheless, it is likely the case that enhanced post-9/11 security measures in these areas have

---

[6] Because the proportions can be quite erratic, we smoothed each series using a two-period lead and lag moving average.

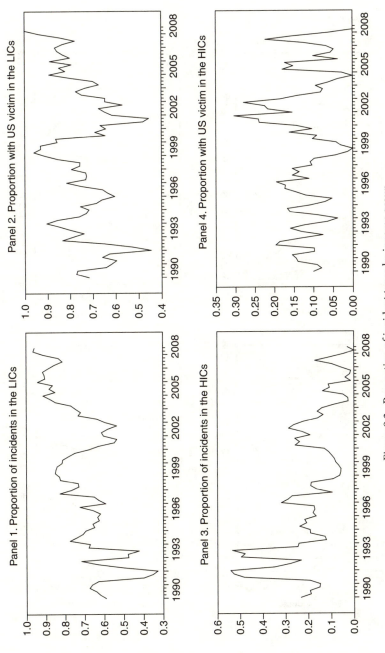

Figure 9.2. Proportion of incident types by income group.

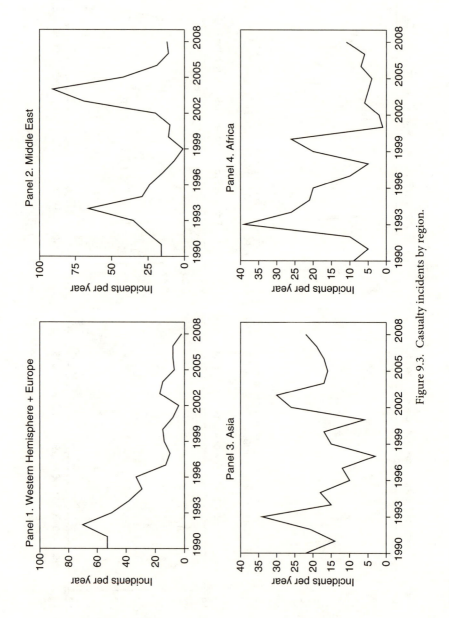

Figure 9.3. Casualty incidents by region.

dissuaded terrorists from operating in the countries comprising these two geographic areas. Probably the most striking feature of Figure 9.3 is the sharp upward trend in the number of Middle Eastern incidents immediately following 9/11. It appears that the jump was transitory in that many of the incidents were associated with attacks against noncombatants in Iraq. The values for the latter years are reasonably close to the numbers for the early 1990s. The region showing the most striking permanent change since 9/11 is Asia. As shown in panel 3, a permanent jump in the number of incidents staged in the Asian countries started in 2002. There is also a small upward trend in casualty incidents in Africa following 9/11 – see panel 4.

Overall, the changes in the venues of transnational terrorist attacks necessitated a modification of the view (see Chapter 2) that liberal democracies foster terrorism; instead, it seems that most attacks occur in low-income countries and in areas that could be called failed states. The lack of governance in these areas affords terrorists the same freedoms of speech and association found in liberal democracies. Nevertheless, as evidenced by the data shown in panel 2 of Figure 9.2, the targets of transnational terrorists remain the citizens and the property of liberal democracies such as the United States.

THE RELATIONSHIP BETWEEN TERRORISM AND POVERTY

Today's large-scale terrorist organizations operate differently than groups like the Front de Libération Nationale (FLN) in Algeria, the Red Army Faction, and the Italian Red Brigades, because the leadership does not generally directly participate in the attacks. Instead, individuals need to be recruited and trained. Economic theory suggests that it would be easier to enlist low-income or unemployed individuals, since they have a relatively low opportunity cost of time. Moreover, people who believe that their prospects have been limited by other members of society may have grievances that could attract them to terrorism. The fact that most transnational attacks are staged in the LICs raises the question of whether poverty causes terrorism. After all, if poverty does breed terrorism, then it would follow that a fruitful counterterrorism strategy could involve raising living standards in terror-prone regions. The media and our politicians seem to believe that there is a direct causal relationship between terrorism and poverty. Although it is hard to find common ground between US Presidents Bush and Obama, consider their response to the 9/11 attacks. In a speech before the United Nations Financing for Development Conference in Monterrey, Mexico, President Bush stated,[7]

We fight against poverty because hope is an answer to terror.... We will challenge the poverty and hopelessness and lack of education and failed governments that too often allow conditions that terrorists can seize and try to turn to their advantage.

Similarly, on 19 September 2001, page 4 of the *Hyde Park Herald* quoted then Illinois State Senator Obama as stating,

The essence of this tragedy, it seems to me, derives from a fundamental absence of empathy on the part of the attackers: an inability to imagine, or connect with, the humanity and suffering of others.... Most often, though, it grows out of a climate of poverty and ignorance, helplessness and despair.

Nevertheless, the causal relationship between the two is not as straightforward as it might appear. Sageman (2004) assembled biographical information on approximately 400 Salafi Mujahedin terrorists using publicly available information. Approximately 75% of the terrorists came from upper-class or middle-class backgrounds, and 63% had attended college. Sageman (2004) provided corroborating evidence by comparing the economic characteristics of murdered Hezbollah and Palestinian terrorists with those of Palestinians from a similar population demographic. More than 50% of all Hezbollah suicide bombers had more than a high school education. The Palestinian terrorists were twice as likely to have attended college compared to other Palestinians, and 94% held some form of employment. In contrast, only 69% of the Palestinian population held jobs.

Krueger and Maleckova (2003) found little relationship between the lack of market opportunities and terrorism. They began by analyzing a public opinion poll of 1,357 Palestinians aged eighteen or older living in the West Bank and Gaza Strip, conducted by the Palestinian Center for Policy Survey Research. The results of the survey are quite striking in that at least 72% of every educational and occupational group supported (or strongly supported) armed attacks against Israeli targets. The percentage supporting such attacks did not decrease with income or educational levels. In fact, support was especially strong among students and lowest among the unemployed. Krueger and Maleckova (2003) went on to test the relationship between terrorism and poverty, and estimated the following regression equation:

$$T_i = -5.78 + 0.42 \log P_i + 0.75 D_1 + 0.36 D_2 + 0.17 D_3, \qquad (9.3)$$

[7] The full text of the speech is available at http://www.un.org/ffd/statements/usaE.htm, accessed 4 January 2011.

where T_i is the number of transnational terrorist events in country i over the 1997–2002 period, P_i is the population of country i, and D_i ($i = 1, 2,$ and 3) are dummy variables indicating whether country i's real per capita GDP is in the lowest, second, or third quartile for all countries.

Only the intercept, the population variable, and the dummy for the lowest GDP quartile were statistically significant at conventional levels. Hence, in accord with the conventional wisdom, large countries with low levels of real per capita GDP tend to have the highest levels of terrorism. However, Krueger and Maleckova (2003) made the point that the poorest countries tend to be those with the lowest levels of civil liberties. When they included a measure of civil liberties in the regression equation, all of the GDP dummy variables become statistically insignificant. Thus, they concluded that it is the lack of political freedom, and not poverty, that spawns terrorism. According to the authors, terrorism is not a response to economic circumstances, but a reaction to frustrated political aspirations and feelings of indignity.

In a related study, Abadie (2006) measured terrorism using a data set that included both domestic and transnational incidents. Since the number of domestic incidents far exceeds the number of transnational incidents, the relationship between terrorism and poverty might best be captured using this broader terrorism measure. Instead of measuring terrorism using the number of incidents, Abadie (2006) used the World Market Research Center's Global Terrorism Index (WMRC-GTI). For 186 countries, the index attempts to measure the motivation, presence, scale, efficacy, and prevention of terrorism within each country. Note that the index ranges from 10 to 100, with higher values representing a greater risk from terrorism. For our purposes, the interesting regression equation is

$$T_i = -0.095\log(GDP_i) + 0.297R_i - 0.030(R_i)^2, \tag{9.4}$$

where T_i = log of the WMRC-GTI for country i, GDP_i = per capita GDP in country i, and R_i is the Freedom House measure of political rights (high scores indicate a lack of rights). All three variables are statistically significant at the 5% level. Hence, both economic and political variables appear to be associated with terrorism.

Since the terrorism and income variables both appear in logarithmic form, a one percent increase in *GDP* reduces terrorism risk by 0.095 percent. Do not be misled into thinking that this figure is exceedingly small – the income levels of the high-income countries can be several hundred percentage points more than those of the low-income countries. The effect of political freedom on terrorism is nonlinear. Abadie's (2006) nonlinear relationship indicated that countries with many (liberal democracies) or few (authoritarian regimes) political freedoms displayed low levels of terrorism. An intermediate level of political freedoms was most conducive to terrorism. Nevertheless, the overall results were mixed because the relationship between income and terrorism was not robust to other specifications. For example, after controlling for ethnic fractionalization and geographic variables (for example, elevation), income was not significantly associated with terrorism.[8]

CONCLUDING REMARKS

The attacks of 9/11 and the associated copycat anthrax attacks created a heightened state of anxiety among citizens desperately looking for security. In a climate of intimidation and fear, each new attack has the potential for enhanced benefits to the terrorists, so there is little reason to suppose that terrorism will decline. At the same time, the 9/11-motivated increases in homeland security in some high-income countries and the terrorists' hunt for soft targets are expected to change the types and locations of terrorist incidents. Our findings suggest that changes in al-Qaida's top leadership positions and finances have induced a substitution away from logistically complex hostage takings and into simple deadly bombings. In Figure 9.2, for incidents with US casualities, we find a strong substitution of attack venues from rich to poor countries. When countries are classified into six regional groups, there is evidence of shifting venues based on geography. For casualty incidents, in Figure 9.3, we find a clear transference after 9/11 away from the Western Hemisphere and Europe and into the two regions with the largest Islamic populations (that is, the Middle East and Asia). This substitution into the Middle East ended around 2005. Thus, today's fundamentalist terrorism is shifting to Asia, where large support populations exist and terrorists do not have to transcend fortified borders in order to attack US and Western interests.

Overall, there appears to be a shift in venues away from liberal democracies, which once provided a more supportive environment to terrorists, and into failed states, which have little control over lawless elements. Upgrades

---

[8] In another statistical study, Blomberg, Hess, and Weerapana (2004) estimated the relationship between economic conditions and the level of transnational terrorism using a panel of 127 countries over the 1968–1991 period. Using this older data set, they found that terrorism occurs less frequently in high-income countries; however, business cycle contractions act to increase the level of transnational terrorism. Hence, they argued that it is sudden unanticipated reductions in income levels that generate terrorism.

in antiterrorism activities in the liberal democracies are, in part, behind this shift in terrorist venues to regions where terrorists can operate relatively freely. Nations that are not able to check terrorists' behavior because of a lack of political will and weak law-enforcement mechanisms are today's safe havens for terrorist groups.

Augmented homeland security seems to have made Americans safer at home, while placing them at greater risk when abroad. This vulnerability should also apply to the people and property of other countries that have assisted the US agenda in the Middle East. Current US policy is to assist certain LICs in their efforts to fight terrorism. Given the changing post-9/11 pattern of transnational terrorism aimed at US targets, this policy is somewhat misdirected, since soft targets can exist anywhere. Countries such as Saudi Arabia and the Philippines are not LICs, but are located in areas that experienced greater levels of religious-based terrorism immediately following 9/11. Government's *ability to track* the shifting patterns of transnational terrorist attacks and the interests targeted is absolutely essential for allocating support to other countries. Future homeland security measures in the United States and elsewhere will continue to alter terrorism patterns. Nevertheless, the very notion of "1000 cuts" means that it is almost impossible to prevent every type of terrorist attack. The clear implication is that defensive measures alone cannot significantly reduce a nation's vulnerability to terrorist attacks.

TEN

The Economic Impact of Terrorism

On 12 October 2000 in Aden, Yemen, a small motorboat full of explosives rammed the USS *Cole* while it was in port for a refueling stop. Seventeen sailors died and another thirty-nine were injured by the explosion, which ripped a forty-foot by forty-foot hole in the ship's side. On 13 December 2000 the USS *Cole* returned to the United States, carried aboard a transport ship, for repairs that lasted fourteen months. Two years later (6 October 2002), Yemeni terrorists attacked the French tanker *Limburg* while it was readying to receive its cargo of crude oil from an offshore terminal. Although Yemen is ideally located as a major Middle Eastern port because it borders the Red Sea and the Arabian Sea, the combined attacks on the USS *Cole* and the *Limburg* crushed Yemen's shipping industry. A US Department of State (2002) fact sheet indicates that a 300% increase in insurance premiums led to ships routinely bypassing Yemen for competitive facilities in Djibouti and Oman. As a result of a 50% decrease in port activity, Yemen expects to lose $3.8 million per month as a result of the attacks.

The incidents in Yemen illustrate the direct and indirect costs of terrorism. The direct costs can be calculated by summing the replacement costs of damaged goods, equipment, structures, and inventories. Despite the difficulty of measuring the cost of a human life or the cost of pain and suffering, such calculations are now routine, using either lost earnings or the value of a statistical life. The indirect costs, such as the decline in Yemeni shipping revenues, are more difficult to measure. How much of the actual decline is due to insurance costs rather than to the military activities associated with the Iraq War or to higher oil prices is difficult to gauge. Beyond these lost revenues, Yemen faces increased security costs as it decided to purchase additional patrol boats and helicopters to guard its waters. Calculating the associated costs of any attack is difficult, since, unlike traditional crimes, terrorism is designed to create a general and ongoing atmosphere of intimidation and fear. Terrorists are most successful when they lead the public to expect future attacks. Because the psychological effects of the two Yemeni attacks were mutually reinforcing, they increased the "risk premium" necessary to compensate insurers for the potential damage of future attacks.

These episodes also illustrate one of the essential lessons of this chapter. The effects of terrorism are likely to be greatest in small, undiversified economies facing sustained terrorist campaigns. When shipping became risky in Yemen, alternative port facilities in nearby countries were found, and the entire Yemeni economy suffered. In large market economies, terrorism is more likely to cause a substitution from sectors vulnerable to terrorism into relatively safe areas; prices can quickly reallocate capital and labor to the sectors where they have the greatest marginal product. This reallocation can limit the economic impact of terrorism in diversified market economies.

Although terrorism can cause a vast amount of damage, the costs of conducting terrorist attacks are relatively small. The 9/11 Commission reports that the full cost of the 11 September 2001 attacks was between $400,000 and $500,000. Of this total, $270,000 was spent by the nineteen hijackers while staying in the United States. The remaining costs included travel to obtain passports and visas, expenses incurred by Khalid Sheikh Mohammed and Mohammed Atta while outside the US, and the expenses of those who did not directly participate (such as the so-called twentieth hijacker, Mohamed al-Kahtani). CBS News (2010) estimated that Faisal Shahzad, the Times Square car bomber, spent a grand total of $2,100 on a used Nissan Pathfinder, gasoline canisters, alarm clocks, fertilizer, and other equipment used in the attack. His indictment indicates that he received only $16,000 from his co-conspirators and the Pakistani Taliban. The Madrid train bombings are estimated to have cost no more than £36,000 (or about $56,000), obtained mostly from the drug dealings of the group's operational leader, Jamal Ahmidan (see the *Guardian*, 2007).

MEASURING THE IMPACT OF 9/11

The largest terrorist incident in the largest market economy is the unprecedented attack of 9/11. The Bureau of Economic Analysis (BEA) (2001) reported that damage to structures and equipment (including the destruction of the World Trade Center) amounted to $16.2 billion. As a result of work disruptions, layoffs, and a two-day partial work stoppage, wages and salaries of private sector employees fell by $3.3 billion. This loss was partially offset by wage gains of $0.8 billion by state and local government employees (primarily police and firefighters). Clean-up costs, estimated to be $10 billion, are not included in the BEA measure of direct losses because they are a component of government spending that appears elsewhere in the gross domestic product (GDP) calculations. Moreover, the indirect costs of the attack (such as a reduction in GDP growth or a decline in inflation) are not included in the BEA totals insofar as they could not be separately identified.

In addition to the loss of physical capital, human capital was destroyed on 9/11. Even though many people have difficulty with the concept of pricing a human life, we all place an implied value on our own lives every day. Suppose you dash across a busy intersection to save two minutes. Also suppose that you value your time at $45/hour but that the maneuver exposes you to a 1 in 1,000,000 chance of being in a fatal accident. You thus save $1.50 (= 2 × $45/60) worth of your time against a one-in-a-million chance of being killed, so that the implicit price you place on your life is no more than $1.5 million ($1.50 multiplied by one million). Navarro and Spencer (2001) actually placed the value of a human life at $6.67 million; if we use this figure, the economic value of the approximately 3,000 people killed on 9/11 is about $20 billion.[1] Given that US GDP was almost $10 trillion in 2001, the total direct losses of $48.7 billion represent about 0.5% of total annual output.

These cost estimates are in line with reports that the insurance industry lost about $18.8 billion (or $22.7 billion in constant 2009 dollars) as a result of 9/11. Some care must be used in comparing the insurable losses of various catastrophic incidents because many types of risks are not insured.[2] Nevertheless, as shown in Table 10.1, the insured losses of 9/11 far exceed those of any other terrorist attack. Although these direct costs are staggering, they are overshadowed by the indirect costs of 9/11.

Lost Output

The full macroeconomic cost of 9/11 is difficult to measure, since the attacks occurred while the economy was in the midst of a recession that had begun

---

[1] Navarro and Spencer (2001) used the preliminary figure of 6,000 deaths from 9/11. The numbers in the text have been adjusted to account for the more accurate measure of fatalities.

[2] For example, the January 2010 earthquake in Haiti was estimated to cause approximately $8 billion in overall losses even though the insured losses totaled only $150 million. Note that insurance company losses include compensation for loss of life and property damage. Hence, to avoid "double counting" we should not add these losses to the direct costs of 9/11.

Table 10.1. *Insured Losses from Terrorist Attacks and Disasters*

	Disaster	Insured Loss
Sept. 1989	Hurricane Hugo	$6.6 billion
March 1989	Exxon Valdez oil spill	$ 7.0 billion
Aug. 1992	Hurricane Andrew	$22.2 billion
Jan. 1994	Northridge earthquake	$17.1 billion
Sept. 2008	Hurricane Ike	$12.6 billion
Sept. 2004	Hurricane Ivan	$8.1 billion
Aug. 2005	Hurricane Katrina	$45.1 billion
	Terrorist Attack	Insured Loss
Feb. 1993	World Trade Center bombing	$758 million
Aug. 1993	Bishopsgate bombing (London)	$1.1 billion
April 1995	Oklahoma City bombing	$176 million
Sept. 2001	World Trade Center/Pentagon	$22.7 billion
July 2005	London 7/7 attacks	$57 million
Nov. 2008	Mumbai, India	$102 million

Sources: Various tables from the Insurance Information Institute, http://www2.iii.org/features/ factsandstats/index.cfm. Last accessed 14 September 2010.

in March 2001. Navarro and Spencer (2001) estimated the cost of the two-day partial work stoppage and the associated loss of productivity to be $35 billion. The Bureau of Labor Statistics (2003) reported that at least 145,000 workers were laid off for thirty days or more as a result of the 9/11 attacks. The unemployment rate jumped by almost one percentage point in the quarter following 9/11. Overall, Navarro and Spencer estimated the total output loss at $47 billion. As discussed in the next section, there is reasonable evidence to support the view that the overall macroeconomic effects of the attacks were short-lived; nevertheless, certain sectors of the economy, such as the transportation and tourism industries, experienced persistent problems. For example, immediately following 9/11, income from passenger fares plummeted by $1.5 billion and the hotel industry suffered losses estimated to be $700 million. Ito and Lee (2005) estimated that the heightened, albeit temporary, fear of flying reduced airline demand by more than 30%, while other factors, such as increased passenger screening and security checks, caused a permanent 7.4% decline in airline demand.

Lost Stock Market Wealth

The difference between stock prices on 10 September 2001 and those prevailing at the end of the first week of trading after the attack can be readily calculated. Navarro and Spencer (2001) reported declines in the prices of shares selling on the New York Stock Exchange (NYSE), Nasdaq, and Amex markets of 11.24%, 16.05%, and 8.10%, respectively. The total market value of these declines equals $1.7 trillion! We must, however, be careful to avoid the double counting of some losses. Because the value of the four planes lost in the 9/11 attacks was $385 million, airline stocks should have declined to reflect this tangible loss of physical capital. Given the estimated loss of structures and equipment of only $14 billion, most of the $1.7 trillion decline reflects shareholder estimates of lost future profits and a higher risk premium. When the economic environment stabilized following 9/11, stock prices regained much of their value. How much of the decline in stock prices was permanent and how much was a temporary reaction to increased market uncertainty remains unclear.

Victim Compensation Fund

To stem a flood of lawsuits arising from potential liability issues, the federal government established the Victim Compensation Fund.[3] The explicit goal of the fund was to provide a no-fault alternative to compensate individuals who were injured or whose relatives were killed as a result of the 9/11 attacks. Individuals were compensated for economic as well as noneconomic losses in order to make the awards commensurate with those obtainable through the court system. Compensation for noneconomic losses, such as pain and suffering, were set at $250,000 for each deceased victim plus an additional $100,000 for the victim's spouse and each dependent. Some individuals received far more than others, because the economic loss to any individual included the present value of the estimated stream of future earnings. The average amount of compensation paid to date to the 7,407 families of those who died in 9/11 is $2,082,128. Individual death compensation amounts ranged from $250,000 to $7.1 million. The fund also settled 2,682 personal injury claims for amounts reflecting the nature of the injury, the long-term prognosis, and the ongoing pain and suffering. To date, awards have ranged from a low of $500 to a high of over $8.6 million. Including the payments received from

---

[3]   Information for this section was taken from the website of the Department of Justice (2004).

insurance companies and charities, the payouts to those who were injured or whose relatives were killed in 9/11 totaled $38.1 billion. However, the establishment of the fund raised a number of controversial questions: Was it appropriate that families of high-income individuals received more than those of low-income individuals? Should 9/11 victims have been treated differently from victims of other attacks, such as the Oklahoma City bombing? At the time of 9/11, families of US military personnel killed in active duty typically received a single tax-free $100,000 lump-sum payment. If another terrorist attack occurs, should a similar victim compensation fund be established?

There are no clear answers to these questions. A full nine years after 9/11, policymakers finally passed the James Zadroga 9/11 Health and Compensation Act (H.R. 847) on 2 January 2011. The act, named after an NYPD detective who died of respiratory problems resulting from 9/11, would provide an estimated $7.2 billion to treat first responders and community residents for health conditions related to the World Trade Center attacks. It would also reopen the original Victim Compensation Fund so as to provide additional payments to those physically injured in the 9/11 attacks and to those injured in the process of debris removal or in their efforts as first responders.

Long-Term Costs

The long-term indirect costs of terrorism clearly include the higher expenditures for security. Becker and Murphy (2001) hypothesized that if the time of a typical air traveler is valued at $20 per hour, then increased airline security costs are $10 billion per year, which is in addition to the Congressional Budget Office (2004) estimate of $20 billion in increased security costs for the year 2002. As detailed in Chapter 11, since its inception in 2003, the Department of Homeland Security's budget has risen from about $31.1 billion to $56.3 billion in 2011. To put these figures into perspective, in 2009, the Office of Management and Budget (2010) reported that outlays of the US Department of Defense were $636.5 billion and outlays of the US Department of Education were $32.4 billion.

Moreover, terrorism-induced risk may be viewed as a long-term tax on the economy. Even though it is possible to insure against an attack, terrorism-prone sectors bear the largest share of the costs. Obviously, consumers want to avoid activities exposing them to possible injury or death. Rational investors will substitute out of high-terrorism activities in order to avoid potential losses. As consumers and investors move out of risky activities, there is a long-run reallocation of resources such that terrorism-prone sectors contract and others expand. This makes it difficult to measure the total output or employment loss resulting from terrorism, since one sector's loss may be another's gain. If, for example, a family decides to drive rather than fly to a tourist destination, some of the lost airfares accrue to gasoline companies and roadside motels.

Comparison to the Costs of the Madrid 3/11 Bombings

Busea and colleagues (2007) estimated the direct costs of the 11 March 2004 (henceforth, 3/11) rush hour attacks on Madrid's commuter railway system. As in 9/11, damage to infrastructure (5.3 million euros) and the value of lost working hours (2.4 million euros) were only a small part of the direct cost of the attacks. The costs of rescue and first aid for the victims were about 2.2 million euros. The subsequent health care costs of the victims and the approximately 4,500 first responders were 2.17 million and 10.1 million euros, respectively. The 134.1 million euros paid as compensation to the families of the deceased and to those with physical disabilities can be viewed as the lost value of human capital. Interestingly, one of the larger direct costs involved the resulting demonstrations in support of the victims of 3/11. One day after the attacks, an estimated 2.3 million people flooded the streets of Madrid. Streets were blocked, and work in much of the city was suspended for half a day. Busea and colleagues (2007) estimated that 40% of the demonstrators were workers and that the cost of their lost wages was another 57.4 million euros. Table 10.2 shows how to make this total more comparable to the other values in Table 10.1. Multiply by the 2009 average US dollar price of the euro (equal to $1.39/€) and by the Spanish price level in 2009 relative to 2004 (equal to 1.14) in order to obtain $335.1 million. These total direct costs of the 3/11 attacks were only a small percentage (0.03%) of Spain's GDP. Nevertheless, as with 9/11, the direct costs of 3/11 were only a modest portion of the total direct and indirect economic, political, and social costs of the attacks.

MACROECONOMIC EFFECTS OF TERRORISM

Contrary to the views often expressed in the media, many economists and political scientists believe that the US macroeconomy should experience only small effects from terrorism. The justification for this view is that relatively few attacks are staged in the United States and that the US economy is sufficiently diverse to absorb the impact of an attack by shifting activities to

Table 10.2. *Direct Costs of 3/11 in Constant 2009 US Dollars*

	Cost (Millions)
Damage to infrastructure	5.3 euros
Lost working hours on 3/11	2.4 euros
Victim's rescue and first aid	2.2 euros
Health care	10.1 euros
Death and disability	134.1 euros
Lost wages due to demonstration	57.4 euros
Total	211.5 euros
Exchange rate $1.39/€	
Price index 1.14	
Total × 1.14 × 1.39 =	$335.1

unaffected sectors. According to Robert Shapiro (2004), a former undersecretary of commerce in the Clinton administration, the immediate costs of a terrorist act such as a kidnapping or an assassination are localized, so that an act of terrorism resembles an ordinary crime. Instead of affecting the entire macroeconomy, terrorism causes a substitution away from sectors vulnerable to terrorism and into relatively safe areas. If airlines become risky, factors of production will quickly leave the airline sector to find gainful employment in now relatively less risky areas. "Modern economies regularly absorb greater losses from bad weather and natural disasters – for example the 1988 heat wave that took the lives of more than 5000 Americans or the 1999 earthquake in Izmit, Turkey, that killed 17,000 – without derailing" (Shapiro, 2004).

A similar argument was made by Becker and Murphy (2001). They compared terrorism to the Kobe earthquake of 1995 that killed over 6,000 people, destroyed over 100,000 buildings, and resulted in estimated total losses exceeding 2% of Japan's GDP. Part of the reason that Kobe rebounded so quickly was that the earthquake did not represent an ongoing threat. By contrast, terrorists try to create long-term fear and intimidation. Nevertheless, Becker and Murphy argued that modern economies can readily adjust to ongoing threats with the same resilience that was shown during the oil price shocks of the 1970s. They noted that the precipitous rise in oil prices during the 1970s increased the total cost of oil imports by 1% of GDP. The total ongoing costs of terrorism (that is, security costs, loss of life, loss of property, and reduced GDP growth) are estimated to be in the neighborhood of 0.3% of GDP.

This representation is in stark contrast to the situation in small economies in which terrorism is prevalent, such as Colombia, Israel, and the Basque

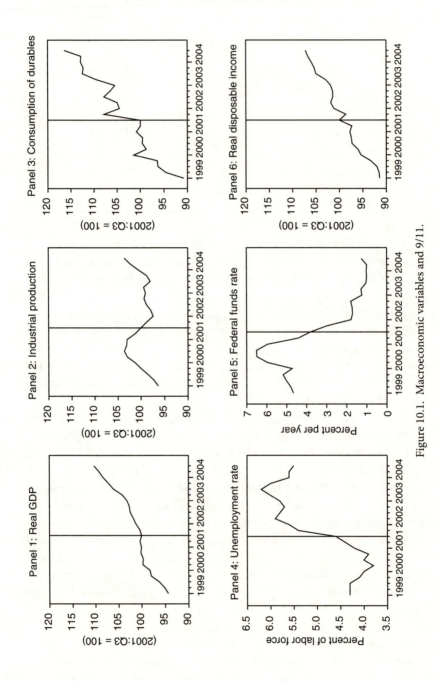

Figure 10.1. Macroeconomic variables and 9/11.

region of Spain. For these areas, terrorism depresses economic growth and development. Protracted terrorism leads to the expectation of future terrorist events. The fear of future violence leads to high risk premiums in terrorism-prone activities. There are few available avenues for diversifying the risk in small economies.

Some evidence for the view that the US economy quickly rebounded from 9/11 is provided in Figure 10.1. Each of the six panels of the figure shows the time path of an important US economic variable during the period surrounding 9/11. The vertical line in the center of each panel represents the third quarter of 2001 (i.e., 2001:Q3). Panel 1 shows that real GDP had been stagnant throughout the year 2000 and fell slightly in the first and third quarters of 2001. Notice that real GDP began a sustained upward trend beginning in the fourth quarter of 2001. Panel 2 shows that industrial production had been falling for several quarters prior to 9/11. At the beginning of 2002, industrial production reversed direction and began to increase. The strong growth of consumption helped to bolster real GDP and industrial production. As shown in panel 3, the consumption of durables, the most volatile component of total consumption, jumped in the fourth quarter of 2001. Panel 4 shows a somewhat contradictory picture. The unemployment rate was rising prior to 9/11, but jumped dramatically as a result of the attack. However, since the unemployment rate is a lagging indicator of economic activity, what would have happened had 9/11 not occurred remains an unanswered question.

Macroeconomic Policy Responses to a Terrorist Attack

There is an overwhelming consensus that well-orchestrated macroeconomic policymaking cushioned the blow from 9/11. As a result of 9/11, bond market trading was suspended for a day, and stock market trading did not resume until 17 September. The attacks damaged much of the physical infrastructure of the markets; the communication and computer systems at the world's largest settlements bank – the Bank of New York – were severely damaged. Most firms in the New York financial district took several days to operationalize their backup systems. Risk-averse asset holders did not want to be caught holding financial instruments for which the resale market had been severely damaged. In times of uncertainty, investors usually flock to highly liquid assets. With 9/11, the demand for liquidity surged to unprecedented highs. As shown in panel 5 of Figure 10.1, the Federal Reserve reacted to this increased demand by sharply cutting the federal funds rate (the interest rate that banks charge each other for very short-term loans).

Liquidity was also increased when the Federal Reserve encouraged banks to borrow at the discount window (the mechanism by which banks directly borrow from the Federal Reserve). Such borrowing, including repurchases, jumped from an average daily level of $24 billion to a total of $61 billion on 12 September.

Fiscal policy played an important role as well. Fortuitously, the first tax cut since 1985 was signed into law in May 2001, months before 9/11. As shown in panel 6 of Figure 10.1, after an initial drop, real disposable income (the after-tax income of households) grew sharply in 2002:Q1. On 14 September, Congress approved a $40 billion supplemental appropriation for emergency spending for such items as search-and-rescue efforts at the four crash sites and tightened security. Not only did this spending provide disaster relief, but it also served as a direct stimulus to aggregate demand. Such crisis management played an important role in restoring consumer and business confidence. Although consumer confidence fell by about 20% at the onset of the attacks, this measure of anticipated economic activity exceeded its pre-9/11 level by the end of 2001.

Studies on Terrorism and the Macroeconomy

Due to its extraordinary scale, it is not possible to draw parallels between 9/11 and other terrorist incidents. Moreover, the costs of terrorism borne by the United States are likely to be different from those borne by the global economy, since countries vary in size, confront different terrorism risks, and possess diverse institutional structures.

It is tempting to think that it is possible to measure the overall costs of terrorism by aggregating the costs borne by the individual subsectors of the economy. The problem is that many of the losses also entail a redistribution of income toward other sectors. Part of the reason why air travel declined immediately after 9/11 was that substantial numbers of tourists decided to vacation within driving distance of their homes. The resultant gains in roadside motel revenues, gasoline sales, and car rentals need to be considered as well. Property values rose in resort destinations near large metropolitan areas at the same time that property values and occupancy rates fell in terror-prone areas such as downtown Chicago and New York. The London Chamber of Commerce and Industry (2005) reported that the taxi industry and cycle shops were direct beneficiaries of the 7 July 2005 (7/7) Underground bombings. Due to the difficulty of using a sector-by-sector approach, a number of researchers measured the total cost of terrorism using macroeconomic aggregates such as real GDP growth. After all, pure redistributions of income have no direct effect on GDP, since one sector's gain is another's loss.

The Growth Costs of Terrorism

Blomberg, Hess, and Orphanides (2004) provided a formal test of the relationship between terrorism and economic growth using a sample of 177 countries from 1968 to 2000. Of course, not all of the countries have a complete set of data for all of the periods; nevertheless, they provide over 4,000 total observations. Consider the following regression equation:

$$\Delta y_i = -1.200 \ COM_i - 1.358 \ AFRICA_i - 0.461 \ln y_0 \\ + 0.142 \ I/Y_i - 1.587 \ T_i, \tag{10.1}$$

where Δy_i is country i's per capita average growth rate over the entire sample; COM_i is a dummy variable equal to 1 for a nonoil commodity exporter; AFRICA is a dummy variable equal to 1 for an African nation; $\ln y_0$ is the log of the initial value of GDP; I/Y_i is country i's per capita average rate of investment's share of GDP over the entire sample; and T_i denotes the average number of years in which there was at least one transnational terrorist event in country i. All variables are statistically significant at the 1% level.

This baseline regression has a number of interesting implications. Nonoil commodity exporters and African nations are associated with low levels of economic growth. On average, the nonoil commodity exporters have growth rates that are 1.2 percentage points lower than those of other nations. African nations have growth rates that are 1.358 percentage points lower than those of other countries. The effect of initial GDP on growth is such that high-income countries tend to have lower growth rates than other nations.[4] As expected, large amounts of investment relative to GDP (so that I/Y_i is large) enhance economic growth. For our purposes, the main result is that terrorism is associated with a reduction in economic growth. If a country experiences transnational terrorist incidents in each year of the sample, per capita growth falls by 1.587 percentage points. Thus, Blomberg, Hess, and Orphanides (BHO) (2004) argued that the costs of terrorism can be sizable for a country experiencing at least one incident per year. Since T_i is the average number of years in which there was at least one terrorist event in country i, a country with multiple incidents across all thirty-three years

---

[4] The initial value of GDP (y_0) is included because high-income countries tend to grow at lower rates than low-income countries. Including the initial level of GDP controls for this "convergence" phenomenon.

of the sample period would suffer a 1.587-percentage-point reduction in its growth rate. If transnational terrorists struck in one year only, the drop in the growth rate would be 1.587 percentage points divided by 33 (or 0.048% less growth in that year).

The BHO results are quite robust to alternative specifications. When they use the per capita number of incidents in a country, rather than the number of years with at least one incident, the results do not change in any meaningful way. Moreover, when the terrorism variable is replaced by a measure of internal conflict, terrorism has a larger effect than the conflict variable. The use of data panels, instead of the cross-sectional regression represented by equation (10.1), also indicates a modest effect of terrorism in inhibiting economic growth.

BHO went on to examine one of the channels through which terrorism affects growth. Toward this end, they estimated another set of regressions indicating that terrorism redirects economic activity toward government spending and away from investment spending. The essential insight is that terrorism induces new government expenditures directed at homeland security. This increase in government spending acts to crowd out private sector capital formation and so inhibits long-term economic growth.

Sandler, Arce, and Enders (2009) used BHO's estimates from equation (10.1) to calculate the worldwide loss of income resulting from terrorism. They substituted each nation's real per capita GDP, population, and terrorism level into equation (10.1) to obtain that nation's growth cost of terrorism. After aggregating across all nations, they arrived at a worldwide growth cost of terrorism for the year 2005 equal to $19.4 billion. This figure was quite robust to alternative measures of terrorism and to Blomberg's (2009) argument that the full costs of terrorism include the costs of other terrorism-induced conflicts. Note that $19.4 billion is comparable to the insurable losses from Hurricane Andrew and from the 9/11 attacks.

Tavares (2004) used a data set and methodology similar to those of BHO. When aggregating across all types of countries and controlling for additional determinants of growth – such as inflation, the degree of trade openness, currency crises, and primary goods exports – Tavares found that the coefficient on the terrorism variable is negative, but statistically insignificant. Hence, terrorism does not appear to affect a nation's growth rate. However, Tavares (2004) went on to compare the costs of terrorism in democratic versus nondemocratic countries. For our purposes, the key part of his regression equation is

$$\Delta y_{it} = 0.261\Delta y_{it\text{-}1} - 0.029T_{it} + 0.121(T_{it} \times R_{it})$$
$$+ \text{ other explanatory variables,} \qquad (10.2)$$

where Δy_{it} is country i's rate of growth of per capita GDP in year t; Δy_{it-1} is country i's rate of growth of per capita GDP in year t-1; T_{it} is the number of terrorist incidents in country i during year t; and R_{it} is a measure of political rights in country i (scaled between zero and unity) such that increases in R_{it} imply increased levels of political freedom.

Notice that equation (10.2) is a dynamic specification for which current-period growth is affected by growth during the previous period. In contrast to Tavares's original specification, which ignored political rights, all of the coefficients reported in equation (10.2) are statistically significant. The coefficient on T_{it} means that a single terrorist incident in country i in year t reduces its annual growth rate for that year by 0.029 percentage points. Since the model is dynamic, this growth effect is persistent. Nevertheless, the results are not that different from those of BHO because the cost of a typical terrorist attack is found to be quantitatively small. The interesting result concerns the positive coefficient on the interaction term $T_{it} \times R_{it}$, for which the effect of a typical terrorist attack decreases as the level of political freedom increases. The implication is that democracies are better able to withstand attacks than countries with other types of governmental structures having less flexible institutions. Yet another interpretation is that democracies are better able to withstand terrorist attacks because they are more likely to rely on markets to allocate resources.

Domestic versus Transnational Terrorism

In order to analyze the differential effects of transnational versus domestic terrorism on economic growth, Gaibulloev and Sandler (2008) combined Engene's (2007) data set, Terrorism in Western Europe: Events Data (TWEED), with ITERATE to obtain the number of domestic and transnational incidents occurring in Western European countries over the 1971–2004 sample period. Consider the regression model

$$\Delta y_{it} = b_1 T_{it} + b_2 (I/GDP)_{it} + \text{other explanatory variables,} \tag{10.3}$$

where, for country i during period t, Δy_{it} is the growth rate of real per capita GDP; $(I/GDP)_{it}$ is the ratio of investment to GDP; and T_{it} is the number of terrorist incidents per million persons.

When only transnational terrorism was used as an explanatory variable, the estimate of b_1 was −0.374, indicating that each transnational terrorist incident per million persons reduces a nation's growth rate by slightly more than one-third of a percentage point. Pooling domestic and transnational incidents resulted in an estimate of −0.153, and when only domestic incidents were used, the estimate was −0.095 (and was not statistically significant at any conventional level). Thus, there is strong evidence that transnational incidents have a greater growth cost than domestic incidents.

Even though domestic terrorism seems to have no direct effect on growth, it would be incorrect to conclude that domestic incidents have no growth effects at all. Gaibulloev and Sandler (2008) went on to show that terrorism (both domestic and transnational) significantly increases the share of government spending as a proportion of GDP and significantly decreases the share of private sector investment relative to GDP. Since the coefficients for the domestic and transnational terrorism variables are virtually identical, it appears that in selecting the level of counterterrorism spending, governments do not discriminate as to the target of the terrorist attack. Their finding is similar to that of BHO, since terrorism leads to a reduction in growth because government spending replaces real private sector capital formation. As indicated by equation (10.3), any reduction in $(I/GDP)_{it}$ leads to a significant reduction in per capita income growth. However, as we will discuss in detail later, the overall growth effect of transnational terrorism is larger because transnational attacks also affect the level of foreign direct investment, tourism, and international trade.[5]

Case Studies

Instead of pooling countries with different institutional structures and levels of terrorism, we believe that it is preferable to examine the effects of terrorism on a case-by-case basis. One possible problem with a purely cross-sectional model, such as the BHO model, is that the regression equation cannot capture the dynamic interrelationship between terrorism and economic growth. Moreover, panel studies that average the growth costs across widely disparate economies may not be appropriate. Also, the effects of terrorism in high-terrorism nations may be quite different than the effects in a nation experiencing only one or two events. As was the case in Yemen, the effects of multiple attacks can be mutually reinforcing.

---

[5] The effects of terrorism on growth are not robust across all nations. In a follow-up study, Gaibulloev and Sandler (2009b) applied a similar methodology to study the effects of terrorism on the growth rates of the developed and the developing countries in Asia. For the developing nations, each additional terrorist incident per million people reduces per capita GDP growth by 1.5%. They do not find a significant effect of terrorism on the growth rates of the developed Asian nations. For fifty-one African countries, Gaibulloev and Sandler (2011) found that transnational, but not domestic, terrorism has a significant effect on growth. It may be that domestic terrorism is such an everyday occurrence that people learn to live with it. Domestic terrorist incidents far outnumbered transnational terrorist incidents. For other grounds for the insignificance of domestic terrorism in Africa, see Gaibulloev and Sandler (2011).

Eckstein and Tsiddon (2004) used the vector autoregression (VAR) methodology introduced in Chapter 5 to study the effects of terrorism on the macroeconomy of Israel. They used quarterly data from 1980 through 2003 to analyze the effects of terrorism on real GDP, investment, exports, and consumption of nondurables. Their measure of terrorism is a weighted average of the number of Israeli fatalities, injuries, and noncasualty incidents. Interestingly, they find that the initial impact of terrorism on economic activity lasts for as little as a single quarter. Moreover, the effect on exports and investment is three times larger than that on nondurable consumption and GDP; thus, the sectoral effects of terrorism are much larger than the overall effect.

Next, Eckstein and Tsiddon (2004) used their VAR estimates to calculate the counterfactual time paths of the four macroeconomic variables under the assumption that all terrorism ceased at the end of 2003:Q4. In this counterfactual experiment, real per capita GDP is forecast to grow at a rate of 2.5% from the beginning of 2003:Q4 to 2005:Q3. If, however, terrorism holds steady, then the estimated VAR predicts a zero rate of growth of real per capita GDP. Thus, continued terrorism would cost Israel all of its real per capita GDP growth. Finally, if terrorism in Israel were to continue its upward trend, real per capita GDP would decline by about 2%. The figures for investment are even more dramatic, since, in this third scenario, investment would fall by 10% annually.

In another set of experiments, Eckstein and Tsiddon (2004) estimated the costs of the *intifada*. They relied on their data to estimate the VAR through 2000:Q3 (the beginning of the *intifada*) and forecast real GDP for the quarters 2000:Q4 through 2003:Q4. Forecasts were conducted assuming no subsequent terrorism and terrorism at the levels that actually prevailed over the 2000:Q4 through 2003:Q4 period. The difference in the forecasts is such that the terrorism cost of the *intifada* was about $1,000 per capita by the end of 2001, $1,700 per capita by the end of 2002, and $2,500 per capita by the end of 2003. By comparison, per capita GDP in Israel was just under $18,000 in 2003.

Abadie and Gardeazabal (2003) focused on the macroeconomic cost of terrorism in the Basque region of Spain. They noted that the Basque Country was the third-richest region of Spain prior to any terrorist conflict. With the onset of Basque terrorism in the early 1970s, the region dropped to sixth place in terms of per capita GDP. After more than thirty years, other factors might be responsible for the decline in the relative position of the Basque region. After controlling for these factors, Abadie and Gardeazabal estimated a 10% loss in per capita GDP due to terrorism. For example, per capita GDP in the Basque region was approximately $10,000 in real US dollars in 1997, but had terrorism ceased, it would have been about $11,000.

As further evidence of the costs of terrorism, Abadie and Gardeazabal were able to construct two different portfolios of common stock. The portfolio consisting of companies with sizable business dealings in the Basque region was found to increase by 10.14% when a credible cease-fire was announced by the Euskadi ta Askatasuna (ETA) in late 1998. The same portfolio fell by 11.21% when the cease-fire collapsed fourteen months later. The non-Basque portfolio did not experience any noticeable movement corresponding to the cease-fire announcements.

MICROECONOMIC EFFECTS OF TERRORISM AND TRANSFER FUNCTION ANALYSIS

Although the overall effects of terrorism are best measured using aggregate variables, such as GDP, the costs of terrorism are not uniformly distributed throughout the economy. Daniel Prieto (2005) reported that one-third of all terrorist attacks target transportation systems, and these attacks have the highest casualty rates. The typical attack against a land-based transport system creates more than double the casualties of a typical attack on an aviation target (for example, 191 killed and 1,500 injured on 3/11; 52 killed and 700 injured on 7/7; and 40 killed and 100 injured in the 29 March 2010 Moscow Metro bombings). Moreover, in terms of fatalities per incident, aerial and land-based transport attacks, along with attacks on tourist targets, are the most deadly. Transportation systems are especially vulnerable to terrorists because they involve high volumes of people and are difficult to secure without causing disruption.

Clearly, those sectors of the economy that rely on the transport of people and/or material are likely to be most affected by terrorism. Thus, it should not be surprising that researchers have tried to measure the costs of terrorism on the aviation and tourism industries, the volume of international trade, and the level of foreign direct investment (FDI). For example, in July 1996, at the height of the Spanish tourist season, an ETA bomb exploded at Reus airport in Tarragona, injuring twenty British vacationers. As might be expected, the number of tourists visiting Spain sharply declined for many months after the bombing. Transfer function analysis is especially well suited to estimate the short-term and long-term effects of such an attack. A transfer function generalizes the intervention model discussed in Chapter 3 by replacing the dummy variable(s) with an explanatory or "independent" variable.[6] A very simple transfer function for the effect of terrorism on Spanish tourism might be

$$y_t = a_0 + b_1 y_{t-1} + c_0 x_t + \varepsilon_t, \tag{10.4}$$

where y_t is the number of tourists visiting Spain during period t; x_t is the number of terrorist incidents in Spain during period t; and ε_t is the error term. Equation (10.4) simply states that the number of tourists visiting Spain during any period, y_t, is affected by its own past, y_{t-1}, as well as the number of terrorist events in Spain, x_t. Because periods with high versus low levels of tourism tend to cluster, we expect b_1 to be positive; a large value of y_t tends to follow a large value of y_{t-1}. The magnitude of c_0 measures the contemporaneous effect of a terrorist incident on tourism. If c_0 is negative, the number of tourists declines in response to an increase in the number of incidents. To illustrate the point, suppose that $c_0 = -2$ and that there are three terrorist incidents during a particular period (so that $x_t = 3$). The contemporaneous effect of terrorism on tourism is then -6. If the unit of measure is a thousand, then there are six thousand fewer tourists. Since there is persistence in the system (so long as b_1 is not equal to zero), the effects of terrorism could be long-lasting.

The central feature of equation (10.4) is that it can be used to estimate the indirect effects of terrorism. To perform the desired counterfactual analysis, a researcher would estimate equation (10.4) to obtain the magnitudes of a_0, b_1, and c_0. Once these magnitudes are known, one can calculate what each value of y_t would have been if all values of x_t had been zero. The difference between this counterfactual value and the actual value of y_t is due to the effect of terrorism.

Moreover, equation (10.4) can be generalized to allow for the possibilities (i) that additional lagged values of the dependent variable (i.e., y_{t-2}, y_{t-3}, ...) affect the current value of y_t, and (ii) that current and past values of the x_t series affect the dependent variable y_t. For example, a generalization of (10.4) could be

$$y_t = a_0 + b_1 y_{t-1} + b_2 y_{t-2} + c_1 x_{t-1} + \varepsilon_t, \tag{10.5}$$

where both the first and second lagged values of tourism affect the current value of y_t. Because the lagged value of x_{t-1} appears in the equation, it takes

---

[6] If x_t is a pulse or a level-shift dummy variable, equation (10.4) is nothing more than the intervention model discussed in Chapter 3. You might want to refresh your memory by rereading the sections on intervention analysis in Chapter 3 and on VAR analysis in Chapter 5. Further details of the properties of transfer functions can be found in Enders (2010).

one period for terrorism to begin to affect tourism. We note that the transfer function analysis assumes that x_t is the independent variable and that y_t is the dependent variable. If terrorism is affected by tourism, then there is reversed causality, so that a regression equation in the form of equation (10.4) or (10.5) does not show the effect of terrorism on tourism.

THE EFFECTS OF TERRORISM ON TOURISM AND TRADE

Enders, Sandler, and Parise (1992) used transfer function analysis to analyze the economic impact of terrorism on tourism. Tourists are viewed as rational consumers allocating their resources among various goods and services, including tourist trips. An increase in terrorist activities in country i places tourists at risk, which is especially true when terrorists explicitly target tourists. The higher risk to tourists induces a substitution away from that country and into other countries. The overall prediction is that terrorism in a country reduces tourism in that country and increases tourism in close substitute tourist venues.

Enders, Sandler, and Parise gathered total tourism receipts over the 1970:Q1–1988:Q4 period for twelve countries: Austria, Canada, Denmark, Finland, France, West Germany, Greece, Italy, the Netherlands, Norway, the United Kingdom, and the United States. The estimated transfer function for Greece is

$$y_t = -0.00165 + 0.70851y_{t-1} - 0.00638x_{t-3}, \qquad (10.6)$$

where y_t is the seasonal change in Greece's share of revenues relative to those for all twelve countries, and x_t is the quarterly number of transnational terrorist incidents in Greece. Since y_t is a logarithmic change, it can be interpreted as the percentage change in Greece's share of tourism revenues. The transfer function shows a three-quarter lag (nine-month lag) before a terrorist incident in Greece will affect Greek tourism revenues. This type of lag may be expected, because it takes time for tourists to revise their plans; bookings on airlines and cruise ships cannot be cancelled without sizable penalties. The implication is that existing plans are generally honored, but new bookings to Greece are curtailed. The "memory" in the system is given by the coefficients of y_{t-1} and x_{t-3}. Thus, the interpretation of the transfer function is straightforward: a terrorist incident during period t has a direct negative effect on the growth rate of Greece's share of tourism revenues three periods hence of -0.00638. Approximately 71% of the direct effect persists for a quarter owing to this memory.

Going from the change in the log-share of Greece's tourism revenues to the actual value of revenue losses is not so straightforward. The effect of an incident lasts for a number of quarters, and the number of incidents differs for each period. Nevertheless, using a 5% real interest rate, Enders, Sandler, and Parise calculated the cumulated sum of all tourism losses for Greece arising from terrorism to be about $575 million. This total was equal to 23.4% of the annual tourism revenues for 1988.

Similar calculations were performed for Greece, Austria, and a number of other continental European nations. The Austrian case is particularly interesting because Austria is rather small and experienced a number of brutal attacks that attracted substantial media attention. The first wave of Austria's terrorist attacks was directed against Jewish interests during 1979 and 1980. Another wave of incidents occurred during the 1985–1987 period, including the infamous Abu Nidal attack on tourists at the Vienna airport on 27 December 1985. As a result, the cumulated sum of all tourism losses for Austria was $3,474 million, or 40.7% of the country's annual tourism revenues for 1988. By contrast, Italy lost only the equivalent of 6% of its 1988 tourism revenues. France's tourism losses from terrorism were statistically insignificant. The sum of the effects for all of continental Europe was greater than the sum of the individual country's effects, thereby implying a strong transnational externality. Terrorism in one European nation – say, France – may not have a particularly strong effect on France, but may deter tourists from visiting Europe in general.[7]

Drakos and Kutan (2003) extended the Enders, Sandler, and Parise (1992) methodology to explicitly allow for cross-border and regional effects. The essential insight is that terrorism in a country will lead to a decrease in tourism for that country but may increase tourism elsewhere. Drakos and Kutan, however, considered only the shares of Greece, Italy, Turkey, and Israel. They disaggregated terrorist attacks in a number of interesting ways: that is, they looked at the particular geographic location (rural versus urban) of the attack and the intensity of the attack (measured by the number of fatalities). In its simplest form, their transfer functions is

$$G_t = a_0 + b_1 G_{t-1} + c_0 x_{Gt} + c_1 x_{It} + c_2 x_{Tt} + \varepsilon_t, \qquad (10.7)$$

where G_t denotes Greece's share of tourism revenues relative to those of the four-country composite; x_{Gt} represents terrorist attacks in Greece during

---

[7] In terrorism research, it is not clear how to properly measure the level of terrorism. Pizan and Fleischer (2002) showed that the number of terrorist acts occurring during a period is more important than the severity of incidents in explaining tourist demand in Israel.

period t; x_{It} indicates terrorist attacks in Israel during period t; and x_{Tt} depicts terrorist attacks in Turkey during period t.

Terrorist attacks in Turkey will not affect Greek tourism revenues when $c_2 = 0$. If $c_2 > 0$, tourism in Greece and Turkey are substitutes, so that a Turkish terrorist attack will increase Greek tourism. If, however, $c_2 < 0$, tourism in Greece and Turkey are complementary, and a Turkish terrorist attack will decrease Greek tourism. Tourists will thus avoid the region altogether. Drakos and Kutan (2003) used monthly data for the period January 1991 to December 2000. Their estimates of the memory for each country are very similar to those of Enders, Sandler, and Parise in that about 70% of the direct effect persists for three months for all countries except Greece.

Attacks of low and medium levels of severity have a significant negative effect on Greek tourism. High-intensity attacks (those with three or more deaths) have an immediate impact on tourism revenues. Overall, the own-effects of terrorism on tourism are a loss of 5.21% in Turkey's share of revenues. Drakos and Kutan also found significant spillover effects – low-intensity terrorist attacks in Israel increased Greek tourism revenues, but high-intensity terrorist attacks in Israel reduced Greek tourism revenues. The overall regional effects are negative.

Sloboda (2003) also used transfer functions to analyze the effects of terrorism on tourism revenues for the United States. The estimated transfer function is such that a terrorist incident aimed at US interests has immediate and lagged direct effects on US tourism revenues. The wave of anti-US terrorism that began with the start of the Gulf War in 1991 was calculated to have caused a total decline in US tourism revenues of over $56 million.

Fleischer and Buccola (2002) provided an interesting example of why terrorists often choose to target tourist areas. They estimated the price elasticities of demand for Israeli hotel rooms by foreigners and by Israelis. Foreigners' demand for Israeli hotel rooms displays substantial price responsiveness and is quite sensitive to the number of terrorist attacks. This reflects the fact that international tourists have a wide variety of travel options and can alter their plans when prices change and/or when the risk of terrorism increases. By contrast, Israeli demand is very inelastic and, because Israelis regularly face terrorist attacks, is quite unresponsive to the level of terrorism. Hence, during a wave of terrorism, the hotel industry faces a sharp reduction in demand from foreign tourists. As local tourists are price insensitive, relatively few Israelis are likely to alter their behavior to take advantage of any price discounting of hotel rooms. Overall, the local market does little to buffer the decline in foreign demand resulting from a wave of terrorist attacks. Given the relatively fixed number of hotel rooms at any point in time, the industry is particularly vulnerable to terrorism, since steep price and revenue reductions typically accompany any escalation in the level of violence.

Trade Effects

Nitsch and Schumacher (2004) estimated the effects of terrorism on trade openness. They speculated that the higher risks and enhanced security measures raise transaction costs and reduce the volume of international transactions. Increases in airline and port security act like a tariff by raising the cost of trading. Additionally, enhanced terrorist activities may keep goods from arriving on time or intact.

They formally estimated the effects of terrorism within each country on all of the nation's trading partners. The control variables included the distance between the two countries, dummy variables (for speaking the same language or sharing a common border), measured GDP, and population. The data set consisted of 217 countries and territories over the 1968–1979 period. They found that terrorism strongly affects the pattern of international trade. The estimated effect of terrorism is such that a doubling of the number of terrorist incidents reduces bilateral trade by 4%; hence, high-terrorism nations have a substantially reduced trade volume. The magnitude of the terrorism effect on trade is robust to a number of alternative terrorism measures.

THE EFFECTS OF TERRORISM ON FOREIGN DIRECT INVESTMENT

If terrorists target foreign firms, the risk of subsequent attacks can induce investors to move out of the now-riskier holdings of foreign assets for several reasons. First, even in the absence of a direct terrorist attack, the acquisition of the necessary resources to protect a facility from potential attacks raises operating costs. In addition to these direct costs, a firm facing terrorism risk must maintain security clearance for its employees and is subject to additional insurance charges. Second, terrorist attacks can destroy infrastructure, causing business disruptions. An attack on a railroad line may cause substantial shipping delays. Third, recruiting costs may rise because personnel from the home office may not wish to work in a terrorism-prone region. Similarly, domestic firms in high-terrorism countries may find it cheaper to shift operations to countries relatively free of terrorism.

Enders and Sandler (1996) argued that the effects of terrorism on net foreign direct investment (NFDI) in the relatively small European economies of Greece and Spain should differ from those in larger economies. Large countries, such as the United States and the United Kingdom, draw their foreign capital inflows from diversified sources and are better able to withstand attacks without a measurable diversion of inflows. Large countries also have adequate resources to thwart potential terrorist attacks and restore a feeling of security. Greece and Spain were selected as case studies because both have experienced a number of terrorist attacks directed against foreign commercial interests. In Spain, the ETA, Iraultza, and the Autonomous Anti-Capitalist Commandos (CAA) have directed attacks against foreign enterprise. An explicit aim of Iraultza was to discourage foreign investment in the Basque region. In Greece, the Revolutionary Organization 17 November and the Revolutionary Popular Struggle had the goals of attacking capitalist interests and ending the US and NATO presence in Greece.

The amount of NFDI curtailed by such attacks cannot be directly measured. Even if it were feasible to survey all potential firms to ask how their international investment plans had been altered by terrorism, such an approach would not properly measure the net effects of terrorism on NFDI. Insofar as firms perceive risks differently, a curtailment of an investment by one firm may leave an unexploited profit opportunity for another firm. The alternative is to conduct a counterfactual analysis using the transfer function methodology to estimate an equation in the form of equation (10.5). If the dependent variable, y_t, is net foreign direct investment and if x_t measures terrorism, the fitted equations should reveal the dynamic relationship between NFDI and terrorism. Once the coefficients of the equation are determined, we can calculate what would have happened to the time path of NFDI had all values of x_t been equal to zero.

Enders and Sandler (1996) estimated a transfer function for the effects of terrorism on Spain's NFDI. The form of the transfer function is similar to that of equation (10.5). One notable feature of their equation is the long lag time of eleven quarters between the advent of a terrorist incident and the response in net foreign direct investment. A typical transnational terrorist incident in Spain is estimated to cause a $23.817 million reduction in NFDI. There is a reasonable amount of memory in the system, since 59.3% of the impact remains after the first quarter.

The nature of their estimated equation is such that the effect of a one-time increase in terrorism will cause the change in NFDI to decay to zero. However, once NFDI returns to its long-run level, the cumulated values have a permanent effect on the capital stock. The relationship between NFDI and net foreign capital holdings is

$$K_t = K_{t-1} + NFDI_t - depreciation_t, \tag{10.8}$$

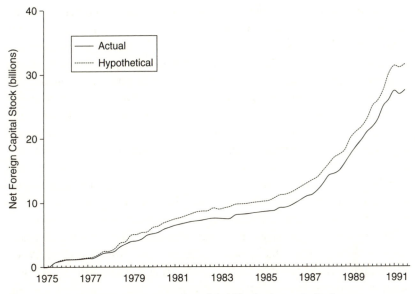

Figure 10.2. Net capital stock held by foreigners in Spain.

where K_t is total net foreign capital holdings in Spain during period t, and *depreciation$_t$* denotes the depreciation of the capital stock between periods t and $t - 1$.

Equation (10.8) indicates that the total net foreign capital holdings in Spain during period t are equal to the previous period's holdings (K_{t-1}) plus any augmentation due to net foreign direct investment less depreciation. To ascertain the total effects of terrorism in Spain, we calculated what each period's $NFDI_t$ would have been had all values of terrorism been equal to zero. We called these hypothetical values $NFDI_t^*$. Next, assuming a depreciation rate of 5%, we used equation (10.8) and the $NFDI_t^*$ sequence to construct the hypothetical capital stock had there been no terrorism. The comparison between the actual and theoretical capital stocks is shown in Figure 10.2. Our estimates show that a bout of terrorism from late 1979 through early 1981 resulted in a gap of approximately $1.8 billion. A second terrorist campaign from mid-1985 through 1987 expanded the size of the gap by nearly $3 billion, or approximately 15% of the amount of total foreign capital in Spain.

We repeated the exercise for Greece and found similar results. The major difference is that the response of NFDI to terrorism is larger and more rapid in Greece than in Spain. We were able to detect a measurable response within only a single quarter. Moreover, terrorism explains as much as 33% of the total variation in Greece's NFDI.

In an updated study, Enders, Sachsida, and Sandler (2006) analyzed the effects of terrorism on US foreign direct investment in particular countries. Clearly, US firms might want to reduce their level of investment in a country if US-directed attacks increase in that country. Similarly, US firms might want to diversify by investing abroad in response to an attack like 9/11. Let FDI_{it} denote the total holdings of US foreign direct investment in country i during period t, and let T_{it} denote the number of US-directed terrorist attacks occurring in country i during period t. Using a sample of sixty-nine countries, and controlling for international differences in factor supplies, the distance between countries, and other economic determinants of FDI, Enders, Sachsida, and Sandler found no significant effect of T_{it} on FDI_{it}. This lack of significance remained when terrorism was measured by the number of incidents with casualties and the number of incidents with deaths. However, with sixty-nine diverse countries there may be too much heterogeneity in the sample to capture the effect of terrorism on FDI. When the sample was restricted to the OECD countries, each of the three measures of terrorism was significant. On average, each US-directed incident in a country acted to reduce US FDI in that country by about $1 million. If there was a death involved, the figure increased to about $1.1 million. Nevertheless, the overall effects were quite small, amounting to 1% of US FDI; however, the effects were not uniform across countries. Given their levels of terrorism, Greece and Turkey experienced reductions in US FDI of 5.7% and 6.5%, respectively.

Of all terrorist events, Enders, Sachsida, and Sandler argued that 9/11 should have had the largest effect on US foreign direct investment decisions. Eyeballing the data in Figure 10.3 suggests that US FDI fell immediately after 9/11 and then surged. This is consistent with the notion that US firms tried to diversify the risk of another attack by expanding their international investment positions.

THE PSYCHIC COSTS OF TERRORISM AND THE LIFE SATISFACTION APPROACH

Although terrorists try to achieve their goals by promoting a general climate of fear and intimidation, it is very difficult to actually measure the psychological costs of any particular attack. It is even more difficult to measure the psychic costs of threatened attacks that may never occur. Some social scientists, such as Mueller (2004), have argued that most psychological costs of terrorism can be readily dismissed because they are nothing more than a state of mind. Yet, in a special report of the *New England Journal of*

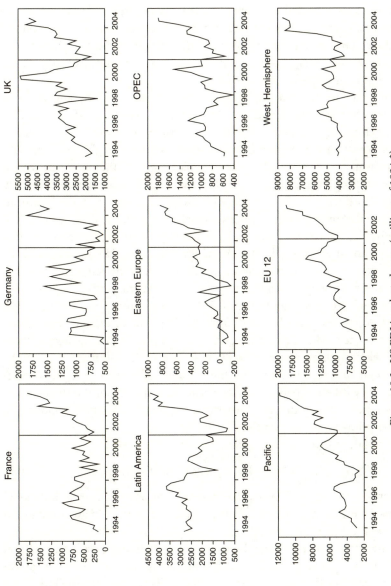

Figure 10.3. US FDI in selected areas (millions of 1994 $).

313

Medicine, Schuster and colleagues (2001) reported that even people who are not present at a traumatic event can experience mental health problems. Forty-four percent of the 560 US adults in their nationally representative survey reported substantial symptoms of stress resulting from the 9/11 attacks and/or from their children's reactions to the attacks. Symptoms included one or more of the following: feeling very upset (30%), difficulty concentrating (14%), disturbing memories (16%), trouble sleeping (11%), and feeling irritable or angry (9%).

In order to measure the psychic costs induced by ongoing terrorist campaigns, Frey, Luechinger, and Stutzer (2009) used the Life Satisfaction Approach (LSA). In a sense, the approach tries to measure people's willingness to pay for eliminating the "fear, grief and mourning" associated with terrorism. Instead of directly asking people how much they would be willing to pay to eliminate terrorism, the LSA uses an indirect method that is likely to be more accurate. For most years between 1973 and 2002, the European Barometer Survey Series asked individuals to respond to the question: "On the whole, are you very satisfied [4], fairly satisfied [3], not very satisfied [2], or not at all satisfied [1] with the life you lead?" The survey also contains economic and demographic variables such as the responder's level of income, gender, age, marital status, and employment status.

In total, the survey contained 30,244 responses from Great Britain, 7,891 from Northern Ireland, 24,185 from the Republic of Ireland, and 38,062 from France. Although each country is reasonably homogeneous, there are relatively high-terrorism regions within each country. For example, London, Northern Ireland, and the Republic of Ireland generally experience very different patterns of terrorism than the rest of the British Isles. This is desirable in that it allows the researchers to compare regions that differ primarily in their levels of terrorism.

Consider the regression equation

$$LS_{irt} = \beta_1 T_{rt} + \beta_2 \ln(m_{irt}) + \textit{other personal characteristics}_{irt}, \qquad (10.9)$$

where LS is life satisfaction; T is the level of terrorism; m is individual household income; and subscripts i, r, and t refer to individual i living in region r during time period t.

The key to understanding the methodology is to recognize that equation (10.9) can be treated like an indifference curve. In particular, it is possible to calculate the terrorism and income levels that provide the individual with a given amount of life satisfaction. For example, given the estimates in equation (10.9), suppose that T_{rt} was set to equal zero. The value of m_{irt} necessary to maintain LS_{irt} at its initial level is the financial equivalent of people's willingness to pay for the complete elimination of terrorism. The paper actually reports individuals' willingness to pay for a reduction in terrorism to the levels in the relatively tranquil parts of the nation.

When terrorism was measured in the British Isles by the number of incidents occurring in a region, the estimated value of β_1 was -7.6×10^{-5} and the t-statistic was statistically significant. Thus, the level of terrorism is associated with a reduction in life satisfaction. In Northern Ireland, the coefficient estimates for equation (10.9) indicate that people would pay an average of $7,641 to eliminate 1022.76 acts of terrorism. When equation (10.9) was estimated using French data, Frey and colleagues (2009) found that Parisians would pay an average of $2,149 to eliminate 9.58 acts of terrorism.

The LSA can be criticized because the life satisfaction variable is ordinal and may not be comparable across individuals. Clearly, a Pollyanna's "very satisfied" might be the same as a naysayer's "not at all satisfied." Moreover, the willingness-to-pay estimates seem overly large. A payment of $7,641 seems excessive for a region in which average household income is only $20,501. With roughly 672,600 households in Northern Ireland, the total payout would be over $13 billion. Similarly, is it plausible that each individual in Paris is actually willing to forfeit $2,149 in order to eliminate about 9.58 acts of terrorism? Nevertheless, Frey and colleagues (2009) argued that their estimate for Northern Ireland is reasonable given the intensity of the conflict, the reductions in civil liberties, and losses in productivity due to curfews, riots, and demonstrations.

CONCLUSIONS

The International Monetary Fund (2001b) has concluded that the costs of terrorism in terms of lost growth are small when compared to the resources spent to fight terrorism. Their report indicated that the average annual growth rate of real GDP in the industrialized nations is 2.75%. "If the impact [of terrorism] on the level of potential output were relatively sizable, say 1% of GDP, its impact on medium-term growth would be significantly smaller then current estimates of information technology in U.S. growth since the mid-1990s …" (International Monetary Fund, 2001b, p. 15). This result is consistent with the findings of Blomberg, Hess, and Orphanides (2004) and Tavares (2004). However, the indirect costs of terrorism are typically far larger than the direct costs. The indirect costs include foregone output, increased security costs, and a high risk premium. In response to a sustained level of terrorism, governments increase their homeland security expenditures. Such expenditures tend to crowd out private capital formation in such a way that the overall level of growth is reduced. Because growth effects are cumulative, slight changes in growth rates can have a substantial effect on the long-term standard of living.

There is strong evidence that these effects are proportionately larger for small economies than for large, diversified economies. Moreover, the impact of any particular terrorist incidents tends to be lowest in democratic nations. In large and diversified market economies facing a terrorist threat, price adjustments act to ease the allocation of resources away from terror-sensitive sectors into relatively secure sectors. Moreover, policymakers in large market-based economies have a menu of policy tools that can offset some of the adverse consequences of an attack such as 9/11.

Terrorists tend to target public transportation (airline and rail), with the result that industries relying on these sectors are particularly vulnerable to terrorist attacks. The tourism sector and sectors relying on international trade and FDI bear much of the losses from terrorist attacks.

In viewing all of these results, one must remember that it is very difficult to precisely measure the various costs of terrorism. Large-scale terrorist attacks generate redistributions of income that must be included in a full accounting of the overall costs of terrorism. This is especially true for the indirect costs of terrorism. The number of tourists who never arrive and the quantity of capital never formed are measures that are clearly unobservable and must be estimated using a counterfactual technique such as the transfer function methodology. The nature of the various government policy responses also needs to be considered. Had the Federal Reserve not provided additional liquidity to financial markets, the macroeconomic consequences of 9/11 might have been far greater than they actually were. Although psychological costs such as stress, anxiety, and the loss of a loved one are difficult to measure, the Life Satisfaction Approach suggests that these costs are far in excess of the direct costs of terrorist attacks.

ELEVEN

Homeland Security

The unprecedented attacks on 9/11 underscored the importance of an over-all strategy for homeland security that not only coordinates agencies' efforts to prevent terrorist attacks, but also takes decisive actions to promote recovery following an attack. The magnitude of the 9/11 incidents, with approximately 3,000 deaths and over $80 billion in property and earning losses (Kunreuther and Michel-Kerjan, 2004a, 2004b), indicates that terror-ism poses a significant risk. On 11 March 2004 (henceforth, 3/11), Madrid's commuter train bombings again emphasized the vulnerability of industrial countries to terrorist events. More recently, this ever-present risk of cat-astrophic terrorist events was underscored by the failed attempt to bomb Northwest Airlines flight 253 on approach to Detroit on 25 December 2009 and by the suicide bombings on the Moscow subway on 29 March 2010. As terrorists seek in the future to outdo the carnage of 9/11, 3/11, and other catastrophic events, they may eventually resort to the use of weapons of mass destruction (WMD) (see Chapter 12). Thus, preventive measures by the authorities must address a wide range of possible attack scenarios, including standard terrorist attacks and those involving biological and chemical agents. By the same token, plans must be in place to respond to all possible attack scenarios. The digital age and the complexity of modern-day society provide terrorists with the opportunity to cause mass disruptions in communication, energy supply lines, or transportation. Actions to safe-guard against attacks to society's transportation networks involve a trade-off between safety and the free flow of passengers. Ensuring that almost no attacks will occur may slow passenger transit – say, in subway systems – due to long delays at entry points.

In order to have effective homeland security, component agencies must act in unison not only at the same jurisdictional level but also between different jurisdictional levels. That is, the federal, state, and local agencies must cooperate. Agencies' collective action failure will lead to wasteful duplication and the inability of agents at one jurisdictional level to inform agents at another level about a pending attack or threat. The creation of the Department of Homeland Security (DHS) in 2002 was, in principle, a move to eliminate waste and foster synergy among component agencies at all jurisdictional levels in the United States. Hearings following 9/11 revealed coordination errors, especially in terms of intelligence (National Commission on Terrorist Attacks Upon the United States, 2004, or *9/11 Commission Report*). In the wake of 9/11, the US government had to take steps to provide Americans with a greater sense of security. Clearly, the ability of the 9/11 hijackers to bring weapons on board four flights demonstrated that the nation's airports were not secure. The success of the terrorists in obtaining visas and even flight training in the United States also highlighted vulnerabilities. The failure of US law enforcement and customs officials to stop the terrorists at the border, even though some were on a watchlist, also reflected the system's failure to protect Americans against terrorism prior to 9/11. On Christmas day 2009, Northwest Airlines flight 253 revealed that the "no-fly list" still presented gaps and challenges that allowed a bomb-carrying terrorist to board a flight. As a consequence, no-fly lists have been greatly expanded, and advanced imaging technology (AIT) scanners or "whole body imagers" will be increasingly deployed at US airports – 200 AIT units will be in place by the end of calendar year 2010, and a total of 878 AIT units will be in place by the end of the fiscal year 2014 (US Government Accountability Office, 2010).

Along with the war on terror, the creation of the DHS represented a bold initiative to make America safer from the threat of terrorism. The purpose of this chapter is to present and evaluate US post-9/11 efforts to curb the threat of terrorism through the creation of the DHS and other actions. Many questions are addressed, including whether the US response has been appropriate. Can US action serve as a role model for other countries confronted with transnational and domestic terrorist threats? Clearly, only rich prime-target countries can afford such a large response, as the new defensive actions alone run into the tens of billions of dollars. We are also interested in raising issues that require further analysis. For instance, what is the proper mix of defensive and proactive measures? Another concern involves the proper combination of private and public efforts and how best to finance security measures. There is also a need to explore the implications that US homeland security policies have for other countries, insofar as a more secure America may induce terrorists to seek softer targets abroad (see Chapters 5 and 9).

INITIAL REACTION TO 9/11: USA PATRIOT ACT

After the smoke had settled at the World Trade Center, the Pentagon, and in rural Pennsylvania, the Bush administration and the US Congress needed to regain the confidence of America. The first two responses were the US-led invasion of Afghanistan on 7 October 2001 and the passage of the USA PATRIOT Act, signed by President George W. Bush on 26 October 2001 (Congressional Research Service, 2002). The former was a proactive response after the Taliban failed to hand over Osama bin Laden, while the latter gave federal officials greater ability to monitor communications and prevent future terrorist acts. The USA PATRIOT Act traded off personal freedoms for collective security – a trade-off that some in the country were willing to make in light of the threat of future terrorism (see Chapter 2).

The original USA PATRIOT Act is a complicated piece of legislation that is over 340 pages long (US Congress, 2001). In Table 11.1, we indicate the act's nine major provisions in italics along with select subprovisions. The act is meant to enhance domestic security by allowing for a counterterrorism fund, a Federal Bureau of Investigation (FBI) technical support center, a National Electronic Crime Task Force Initiative, and other measures. One of the act's more controversial provisions concerns greater surveillance powers and curbs on privacy. The main subprovisions involve the power to intercept and seize a wider range of communications, including voice mail messages. A second aspect encourages collaboration among foreign and domestic law enforcement agencies – for example, the FBI and the Central Intelligence Agency (CIA). A third provision augments anti-money-laundering activities by mandating greater regulation of money transfers through actions at home and with counterparts abroad. The act also provides for augmented border protection – for example, biometric identification, a foreign-student monitoring program, machine-readable passports, and other measures. Another freedom-limiting provision increases the investigative powers of law enforcement agencies. Under this provision, the US attorney general and the US secretary of state have expanded powers to pay rewards to capture terrorists. A sixth set of provisions provides relief and compensation not only for the victims of terrorist attacks but also for safety officers injured or killed in the line of duty. Another provision increases criminal penalties against terrorists and greatly limits the statute of limitations on various terrorist acts. Penalties are also increased for those who aid terrorists. Penalties are extended to apply to acts of cyber-terrorism. The USA PATRIOT Act also allows for improved intelligence to monitor terrorists and their resources. In so doing, cooperation

Table 11.1. *Highlights of the USA PATRIOT Act (HR 3162)*

➤ *Enhanced domestic security measures against terrorism*
  - Counterterrorism fund
  - $200 million for FBI's technical support center
  - National Electronic Crime Task Force Initiative
  - Allow for antiterrorism military assistance
  - Ability to delay notice for execution of a warrant

➤ *Greater surveillance and reduced privacy protection*
  - Expanded authority to intercept wire, oral, and electronic communications for suspected terrorist or computer offenses
  - Clearance to share criminal investigative findings among foreign and domestic law enforcement agencies
  - Reduced restrictions on foreign intelligence gathering inside the United States
  - Voice mail message seizures allowed
  - Access to Foreign Intelligence Surveillance Act records for domestic law enforcement agents
  - Trade sanctions

➤ *Expanded action against money laundering*
  - Securities brokers, dealers, and financial institutions must file Suspicious Activity Reports (SARs)
  - Greater authority of the US secretary of the treasury to control activities within US financial institutions regarding foreigners' deposits
  - Greater transparency of accounts
  - Enhanced international cooperation

➤ *Augmented border protection*
  - Fingerprinting and biometric identification of some foreign visitors
  - Foreign student monitoring program
  - Machine-readable passports
  - Other improved safeguards

➤ *Increased ability to investigate terrorism*
  - Attorney general's and secretary of state's authority to pay rewards in the war on terror
  - Greater coordination among law enforcement agencies
  - Collection of DNA samples from convicted criminals and terrorists

➤ *Provision for victims of terrorism, including safety officers*

➤ *Enhanced criminal laws and penalties against terrorism*
  - Improved definitions of domestic and transnational terrorism
  - Penalties extended to those who aid, abet, or harbor terrorists
  - Reduced statute of limitations on some terrorist offenses
  - Greater penalties on terrorist offenses
  - Penalties extended to include cyber-terrorism

➤ *Improved intelligence*
  - Tracking of foreign terrorists' assets
  - Less congressional oversight on intelligence gathering
  - More cooperation internationally
  - More cooperation among federal, state, and local jurisdictions

➤ *Miscellaneous*
  - First-responder assistance
  - Deny entry to aliens who engage in money-laundering activities
  - Examine feasibility of domestic identifier system
  - Grant program to state and local agencies for domestic preparedness
  - Provide for critical infrastructure protection

Sources: US Congress (2001) and Congressional Research Service (2002).

is encouraged between international law enforcement organizations and among agencies at different jurisdictional levels within the United States. Finally, the act's miscellaneous provisions support a first-responder program at the state and local levels. Grants are mentioned as a means to bolster state and local authorities' domestic preparedness against terrorist attacks. In addition, there is a call to examine the feasibility of a citizen identification system, not unlike the one instituted in Germany during its era of left-wing terrorists in the 1970s. There is also a recognition of the need to protect critical infrastructure against terrorist attacks throughout the United States.

The USA PATRIOT Act is a noteworthy piece of legislation for at least three reasons. First, it highlights how civil liberties may be traded away following a devastating terrorist attack. The bounds of these new surveillance, investigative, and intelligence-gathering powers resulted in court challenges in subsequent years as the authorities extended their powers. In 2004, the act was declared unconstitutional by a US district court in a suit brought by the American Civil Liberties Union (ACLU) concerning a gag order that limits the ability of a recipient of a National Security Letter – a type of subpoena – from communicating with his or her attorney. The act was later reauthorized (see below) without the gag provision. Second, the USA PATRIOT Act demonstrates that taking action against terrorists involves a host of activities, including victim protection, interjurisdictional cooperation, increased criminal penalties, augmented authority, and international cooperation. Third, the PATRIOT Act is a clear forerunner of the DHS, which is reflected in the first-responder program, grants for domestic preparedness, the protection of critical infrastructure, and other activities.

Some of the act's controversial surveillance provisions were to end after 31 December 2005. These provisions concern the interception of wire, oral, and electronic communications, roving surveillance authority, voice mail seizure, computer surveillance, and gag orders. Most of the controversial provisions of the PATRIOT Act were reauthorized in two bills: the USA PATRIOT and Terrorism Prevention Reauthorization Act of 2005 and the USA PATRIOT Act Additional Reauthorizing Amendments Act of 2006. The new laws somewhat limited roving wiretaps and access to business records in order to permit greater judicial oversight and review (Electronic Privacy Information Center, 2010). In addition, the new laws broadened the definition of terrorism and increased penalties for some forms of terrorism. In the new acts, the provisions on roving surveillance and access to business records were to sunset on 31 December 2009. In March 2010, the US Congress extended these controversial powers of surveillance for another year (Electronic Privacy Information Center, 2010). Legal challenges to various provisions of the PATRIOT Acts will continue.

In the first edition of this book, we argued that, as long as transnational terrorism remains a significant security threat, surveillance provisions will be renewed despite their costs in terms of lost privacy. Thus far, this prediction has held up, notwithstanding a shift to the left in the Congress's orientation in 2008.

DEPARTMENT OF HOMELAND SECURITY

The origins of the DHS came in an executive order establishing the White House Office of Homeland Security and the Homeland Security Council on 8 October 2001, the day after the US-led invasion of Afghanistan had begun (Department of Homeland Security, 2002). The office was created to work with federal, state, and local agencies to develop an integrated national strategy to counter and prevent terrorist attacks. In the event of an attack, the office would coordinate actions to respond and to help citizens recover from the attack's consequences. The Homeland Security Council served to advise and help the president address all issues of homeland security.

In 2002, the Bush administration realized that a significant reorganization of the government was needed if a fully integrated approach to homeland security was to be achieved. Thus, President Bush called for the creation of the DHS, which would bring together twenty-two agencies in a cabinet-level department (White House, 2002, 2004). Initially, the DHS had four primary missions: to prevent terrorist events at home, to limit US vulnerability to terrorism, to minimize damage from terrorist attacks, and to recover quickly following attacks. The DHS would secure borders, the transportation sector, ports, and critical infrastructure, while mobilizing all available resources. In so doing, the DHS would coordinate agencies at all jurisdictional levels. If properly constituted, the DHS would eliminate duplication among agencies, coordinate activities among different authorities, centralize intelligence, address the WMD threat, and foster research and development efforts in counterterrorism.

Over time, the DHS's missions grew to five: preventing terrorism, securing and maintaining US borders, enforcing and administering immigration laws, safeguarding cyberspace, and promoting resilience following disasters (Department of Homeland Security, 2010). Thus, its original four missions are primarily subsumed under preventing terrorism and protecting US borders. Cyber-security may involve elements of terrorism on occasion. The DHS's expanded mission statement recognizes that it does much more than

Table 11.2. *Key Directorates, Offices, and Mission Agencies of the Department of Homeland Security*

Key Directorates and Offices: Some Important Component Parts
• Departmental Management and Operations
• Analysis and Operations   ○ Office of Intelligence and Analysis; Office of Operations Coordination and Planning
• Office of the Inspector General
• US Customs and Border Protection   ○ Office of Investigations; Office of Detention and Removal
• Transportation Security Administration (TSA)   ○ Security Operations; Transportation Sector Network Management; Law Enforcement/Federal Air Marshal Service; Security Technology; Information Technology; Intelligence and Analysis; Threat Assessment
• National Protection and Program Directorate   ○ Cyber Security and Communications; Infrastructure Protection; US-VISIT; Risk Management and Analysis
• Office of Health Affairs   ○ Office of WMD and Biodefense; Office of Medical Readiness
• Federal Emergency Management Agency (FEMA)
• US Citizenship and Immigration Services   ○ Field Operations; Refugee, Asylum, and International Operations; Fraud Detection and National Security
• Federal Law Enforcement Training Center
• Science and Technology (S&T) Directorate   ○ Borders and Maritime Security; Chemical and Biological; Human Factors/Behavioral Sciences; Infrastructure and Geophysical; Radiological and Nuclear
• Domestic Nuclear Detection Office

Three Mission Agencies
- US Coast Guard
- US Immigration and Customs Enforcement (ICE)
- US Secret Service

inhibit terrorism. For example, it guards against drug trafficking and protects against natural disasters and health crises.

In Table 11.2, the key directorates and offices of the DHS are indicated along with its three mission agencies – the US Coast Guard, US Immigration and Customs Enforcement (ICE), and the US Secret Service. In select cases, some essential subcomponents of the directorates and offices are listed.

Thus, the Transportation Security Administration (TSA), which safeguards the US transportation system, includes many subcomponents. By contrast, Analysis and Operations has two main subcomponents: the Office of Intelligence and Analysis, and the Office of Operations Coordination and Planning.

The structure of the DHS has changed dramatically since its initial formation and first few years of operation. Originally, there were four functional categories: security, enforcement, and investigations; preparedness and recovery; research, development, training, assessments, and services; and departmental management and operations. Security, enforcement, and investigations included border protection, ICE, TSA, the US Coast Guard, and the US Secret Service. As such, this early functional area absorbed about two-thirds of DHS spending. The Federal Emergency Management Agency (FEMA) and biodefense were placed in preparedness and recovery. Research, development, training, assessments, and services included an array of diverse agencies – for example, the Bureau of Citizenship and Immigration Services, and Science and Technology. A hodgepodge of component parts also characterized the initial functional area of Departmental Management and Operations. This early organizational breakdown is displayed in Table 11.A1 at the end of the chapter, along with the expenditures for fiscal years 2003–2005. The initial structure of DHS did not appear to make much sense; hence, DHS was reorganized into more compatible components and subcomponents. Henceforth, we focus on the current structure of DHS, as previously indicated in Table 11.2.

In Table 11.3, the current components of DHS are listed along with a brief explanation of their responsibilities. DHS administration is directed by Departmental Management and Operations, which provides leadership. This component also directs procurement, human capital, and finance. Analysis and Operations is the intelligence center of DHS, with just 1% of the budget. It is charged with disseminating intelligence over the component parts of DHS, while partnering with other intelligence agencies at home and abroad. In addition, Analysis and Operations forges linkages at the state and local levels. The Office of the Inspector General fosters economy and efficiency through the institution of independent audits, inspections, and investigations. Border security against terrorists, criminals, and contraband is provided by US Customs and Border Protection. It receives the largest share of the DHS budget – 20% in 2011. ICE keeps America safe and protects its interests by identifying and removing terrorists, criminals, and other illegal immigrants. It seeks to eliminate criminal and terrorist organizations that set up operations in the United States illegally. ICE includes an Office of International Affairs that works with law enforcement agents abroad to keep arms, bombs, nuclear material, and dangerous persons from US soil. The TSA has an exceedingly difficult task: keep the vast US transportation system safe without impeding the flow of people and goods. To accomplish this goal, the TSA must risk-manage. The TSA deploys technologies – for example, advanced imaging technology – to thwart terrorist threats. These technological barriers must be constantly upgraded to anticipate and counter terrorists' efforts to circumvent static barriers. Currently, the TSA employs 56,000 people and accounts for 14% of the DHS budget. The TSA is anticipated to screen 625 million airline passengers in 2010 and must account for almost 800,000 hazardous shipments daily (Department of Homeland Security, 2010). When one includes rail, mass transit, roads, pipelines, and bridges, TSA has a daunting task.

The US Coast Guard is the only branch of the armed services that is part of the DHS. In 2011, it accounts for 18% of the proposed DHS budget. The Coast Guard protects US maritime interests. Unlike the other branches of the armed services, the Coast Guard serves as a law enforcement and regulatory agency by performing drug interdiction, apprehending illegal immigrants, and protecting the US marine environment. In guarding US coastlines, the Coast Guard protects US claims to territorial waters and resources within 200 miles of the shore. The Coast Guard also saves lives in peril at sea through search-and-rescue missions. Another DHS mission agency – the US Secret Service – provides personal protection for US leadership and visiting heads of state. The Secret Service also protects against the counterfeiting of currency and the forgery of financial instruments.

A major counterterrorism activity is provided by the National Protection and Program Directorate, which offsets threats to critical US infrastructure – for example, cyber-networks and communication systems. This directorate also safeguards US infrastructure against natural disasters. Its activities include risk assessment and management, deployment of defensive measures, and direction of recovery after incidents. Like other risk-assessment components of the DHS, this directorate collaborates at various jurisdictional levels at home and abroad. The Office of Health Affairs is the main medical advisor to the DHS. Since the reorganization of the DHS, this office manages DHS biodefense and biosurveillance efforts. FEMA serves the United States in its preparation, response, and recovery from major disasters – hurricanes, floods, and earthquakes – and emergencies. The latter may include a large-scale terrorist attack.

The Federal Law Enforcement Training Center offers a consolidated approach to training law enforcement agents. Its training meets high

Table 11.3. *Department of Homeland Security: Responsibilities of Component Parts*

Component Part	Responsibilities
• *Departmental Management and Operations*	Provides leadership, guidance, and management of DHS. Includes the Office of the Secretary and Executive Management, as well as other leadership and management offices.
• *Analysis and Operations*	Gathers intelligence and interfaces with other components of DHS and lower levels of government. Also interfaces with the intelligence community. Includes the Office of Intelligence and Analysis and the Office of Operations Coordination. The latter is charged with preventing, protecting against, responding to, and recovering from terrorist attacks and natural disasters.
• *Office of the Inspector General*	Promotes DHS efficiency and effectiveness. It performs internal audits.
• *US Customs and Border Protection*	Ensures that people and cargo enter the United States legally. Keeps out illegal immigrants, terrorists, contraband, and diseased plants and animals.
• *US Immigration and Customs Enforcement (ICE)*	Removes illegal immigrants and dismantles criminal and terrorist organizations on US soil. ICE partners with police and other law enforcement agencies overseas to limit criminal and terrorist activities in the United States.
• *Transportation Security Administration (TSA)*	Safeguards the US transportation system and facilitates the flow of people and goods.
• *US Coast Guard*	Promotes safety on intercoastal waters and adjacent areas. It performs rescues at sea, interdicts drug traffickers, and fosters environmental protection. It is a branch of the armed services.
• *US Secret Service*	Protects the president, vice president, their families, and visiting heads of state. It defends the White House and some other government buildings. It also safeguards financial instruments from forgery and counterfeiting.

- *National Protection and Program Directorate*

  Safeguards the country's critical infrastructure and essential resources from man-made and natural catastrophic events. This directorate is also concerned with cyber and communication security.

- *Office of Health Affairs*

  Advises the DHS secretary and FEMA on public health issues. It addresses biological and chemical attack risks.

- *Federal Emergency Management Agency (FEMA)*

  Coordinates the government's response to and recovery from natural and man-made disasters.

- *US Citizenship and Immigration Services*

  Manages immigration and citizenship services and processing.

- *Federal Law Enforcement Training Center*

  Provides consolidated and standardized training programs to law enforcement personnel.

- *Science and Technology Directorate*

  Fosters the generation of science and knowledge for DHS. Guards the nation from chemical, biological, radiological, nuclear, cyber, and explosive attacks. Administers the University Programs and Centers for Excellence.

- *Domestic Nuclear Detection Office*

  Keeps the nation safe from criminal and terrorist attacks using nuclear or radiological material.

Source: Department of Homeland Security (2010).

standards. The Science and Technology (S&T) Directorate promotes home-land security through the acquisition of knowledge and state-of-the-art equipment for first responders and others charged with protecting the United States from terrorist and natural threats. This directorate is also concerned with thwarting chemical, biological, radiological, and nuclear terrorist attacks. In particular, S&T chooses and funds the research centers, including the first center at the University of Southern California. There are currently twelve Centers of Excellence, funded by S&T, conducting research on all aspects of terrorism. The S&T budget has increased significantly since the establishment of DHS. Finally, the Domestic Nuclear Detection Office guards the nation against illegal attempts to import radiological or nuclear material into the United States. In essence, this office coordinates federal efforts to defend against radiological and nuclear terrorism.

DHS BUDGET

Since the department's inception in 2003, the DHS budget has risen from just over $31.1 billion in 2003 to $56.3 billion in 2011. This is displayed in Figure 11.1, which is based on the adjusted total budget, excluding emer-gency funding and supplementals (Department of Homeland Security, 2004, 2006, 2008, 2010). In just nine years, the DHS budget increased by over 80%, or by almost 9% annually when averaged over the entire period. This increase far exceeds the rate of inflation. As new threats surface (for example, the underwear bomber), expensive new technologies and proce-dures are deployed, which will raise the real budget further. Even if the terrorists achieve no concessions, there is no question that they impose real costs on society as it allocates increased resources to thwart terrorism at home.

   In Table 11.4, we break down the DHS budget into spending on the pri-mary directorates, offices, and mission agencies, as described earlier. The only category added to this table is FEMA grants. These grants are given to states, cities, and rural areas to improve their first-responder capabilities in times of emergency or disaster. DHS budgets for three fiscal years – 2009, 2010, and 2011 – are shown in Table 11.4 in thousands of current-year dollars. In descending order, the largest shares of the DHS budget go to US Customs and Border Protection, US Coast Guard, TSA, FEMA, ICE, and FEMA grants. For 2011, these shares ranged from 20% to 7% of the adjusted total budget. In 2011, the largest increases in spending are associ-ated with Departmental Management and Operations, the Office of Health Affairs, the Office of the Inspector General, and TSA. The largest decrease

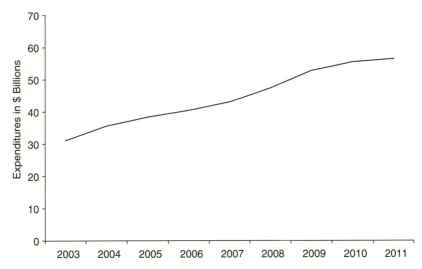

Figure 11.1. US Department of Homeland Security expenditures: 2003–2011.
Source: US Department of Homeland Security (2004, 2006, 2008, 2010).

in spending is on the Domestic Nuclear Detection Office. In total, there
is only a 2% increase in the total budget request for 2011 as compared to
2010. TSA spending will increase further as more advanced imaging technology scanners are deployed at US airports over time. In addition, there
are planned increases in the federal air marshals program in response to
Northwest Airlines flight 253. The TSA budget was $4.6 billion in 2003; it
is $8.2 billion in 2011.

FEMA grants raise some interesting public finance issues because this
program distributes money to the state and local levels in order to bolster security nationwide. Money is given out based on areas containing
high-threat urban centers, population density, and other considerations.
This redistribution scheme uses federally collected tax revenues to provide a degree of safety at all jurisdictional levels. The federal government
has a greater ability than local jurisdictions to raise tax revenues in order
to foster antiterrorism measures. Without such a redistribution scheme,
less-protected local areas will be more likely to draw the terrorist attack.
The scheme is analogous to revenue-sharing arrangements, where the federal government raises funds that are subsequently shared with state and
local governments. The formula used for such grants has been criticized as
not reflecting the expected level of terrorism and other risks. Ideally, the
grants should equalize, at the margin, the expected losses to alternative target sites by accounting for the site's *likelihood of an attack*; its *losses in case*

Table 11.4. *Department of Homeland Security Budgets:*
Fiscal Years (FY) 2009, 2010, and 2011

	FY 2009 $000	FY 2010 $000	FY 2011[a] $000	% Increase[b]
Departmental Management and Operations[c]	659,109	802,931	1,270,821	58%
Analysis and Operations	327,373	335,030	347,930	4%
Office of the Inspector General	114,513	113,874	129,806	14%
US Customs and Border Protection	11,250,652	11,449,283	11,180,018	−2%
US Immigration and Customs Enforcement	5,968,015	5,741,752	5,835,187	2%
Transportation Security Administration (TSA)	6,992,778	7,656,066	8,164,780	7%
US Coast Guard	9,624,179	10,122,963	10,078,317	0%
US Secret Service	1,640,444	1,702,644	1,811,617	6%
National Protection and Programs Directorate	1,188,263	2,432,755	2,361,715	−3%
Office of Health Affairs	157,621	139,250	212,734	53%
Federal Emergency Management Agency	5,971,159	6,194,268	6,527,406	5%
FEMA Grants[d]	4,220,858	4,165,200	4,000,590	−4%
US Citizenship and Immigration Services	2,876,348	2,859,997	2,812,357	−2%
Federal Law Enforcement Training Center	332,986	282,812	278,375	−2%
Science and Technology Directorate	932,587	1,006,471	1,018,264	1%
Domestic Nuclear Detection Office	514,191	383,037	305,820	−20%
TOTAL	52,771,076	55,388,333	56,335,737	1.71%
Less Carryovers	−61,373	−40,474	0	
Adjusted Total	52,709,703	55,347,859	56,335,737	2%
Emergency Funding/ Supplemental	3,354,503	295,503		

[a] President's requested funding.

[b] Increase over 2010.

[c] Office of the Secretary and Executive Management, the Office of the Federal Coordinator for Gulf Coast Rebuilding, the Office of the Undersecretary for Management, the Office of the Chief Financial Officer, the Office of the Chief Information Officer, and the National Special Security Events Fund.

[d] Includes the following FEMA appropriations: State and Local Programs and Emergency Management Performance Grants, and Assistance to Firefighters Grants.

Source: Department of Homeland Security (2010).

of a successful attack; and the site's *vulnerability*. This last is the probability that an attack will succeed, which can be decreased through defensive measures. The expected loss at a potential target site is a product of the attack likelihood, losses, and vulnerability. Losses can be reduced through grants that augment a location's first-responder capabilities. The worry is that alternative locations will lobby the federal government for these grants, not based on their expected losses, thereby providing terrorists with targets of opportunity. Hence, a rent-seeking collective action problem may result that favors the terrorists.[1] This is a concern for any country that must allocate defensive resources countrywide.

In Table 11.5, the DHS budget is again displayed by its main directorates, offices, and mission agencies for fiscal years 2009 and 2010. Fees for US Citizenship and Immigration Services and trust funds for FEMA grants and other purposes are indicated as a separate combined entry toward the bottom of the table. Table 11.5, however, distinguishes the expenditures going to homeland security (HS) and nonhomeland security (NHS) for each entry. As shown, large nonhomeland security components are associated with the US Coast Guard, FEMA, the US Customs and Border Protection, and the US Citizenship and Immigration Services. Most of the mandatory fees (for example, passport application fees) are not homeland security expenditures. From an economic efficiency standpoint, activities with distinct user benefits – for example, visa applications – should be financed through fees paid by the beneficiaries rather than through general tax revenues. This benefiter-pay scheme promotes efficiency by directing resources to activities where effective demand is high. Spending by Analysis and Operations, TSA, National Protection and Programs Directorate, Office of Health Affairs, and Domestic Nuclear Detection Office is classified entirely as homeland security. We used DHS budgets for fiscal years 2004 through 2010 to compute the homeland security spending shares, as follows: 64.8%, 2010; 65.9%, 2009; 61.2%, 2008; 61.6%, 2007; 66.6%, 2006; 64.7%, 2005; and 64%, 2004. This averages out to be 64.1% for the homeland security share of the DHS budget over these seven years.

The DHS is financed by the federal government through income taxes, security taxes on airline tickets, fees, and other federal taxes. Following 9/11, the state and local governments covered much of the cost associated with preventing terrorism in their jurisdictions or responding to elevated

---

[1] On the waste of competitive rent seeking, see Tollison (1982). Wasteful rent seeking occurs when agents expend resources to obtain a return that results in no net addition of output to society. The pursuit of government transfers, such as grants, may result in such waste as potential recipients expend much effort to receive a larger award.

Table 11.5. *Homeland versus Nonhomeland Security Funding Breakdown, 2009, 2010 ($ Millions)*

Gross Discretionary Funding	Fiscal Years			
	2009		2010	
	HS	Non-HS	HS	Non-HS
Departmental Management and Operations	466	176	667	235
Analysis and Operations	327	0	357	0
Office of the Inspector General	0	99	0	128
US Customs and Border Protection	8,260	1,568	8,491	1,567
US Immigration and Customs Enforcement	4,989	641	4,763	695
Transportation Security Administration	6,737	0	7,540	0
US Coast Guard	2,814	5,291	2,985	5,388
US Secret Service	1,322	91	1,390	100
National Protection and Programs Directorate	1,158	0	1,959	0
Office of Health Affairs	157	0	138	0
Federal Emergency Management Agency	4,435	2,759	3,581	3,814
US Citizenship and Immigration Services	0	152	0	364
Federal Law Enforcement Training Center	236	97	204	85
Science and Technology Directorate	800	132	826	142
Domestic Nuclear Detection Office	514	0	366	0
Total[a]	32,215	11,005	33,268	12,518
Mandatory Fees, Trust Funds	2,398	6,922	2,410	6,919
Grand Total	34,613	17,927	35,678	19,437

[a] Total may not add up due to rounding errors.
Source: Department of Homeland Security (2009).

terrorism alert levels issued by the DHS. For 2001, the National Governors Association estimated added antiterrorism expenses of $650 million, while the US Conference of Mayors estimated added counterterrorism costs of $525 million in 2001 (Bush, 2002, p. 5). Clearly, something needed to be done to give state and local governments some fiscal relief.

Some relief came within the DHS budget. The old Office of Domestic Preparedness instituted a first-responder program to support local efforts. Grants under this program initially paid for law enforcement person-nel training, wages (including overtime pay during heightened alerts), equipment, and practice exercises. Similar preparedness grants are now administered by FEMA to the states, which, in turn, distribute some of the money to local jurisdictions. In fiscal year 2010, $842 million in grants was available to build up state and local capabilities under the State Homeland Security Program (SHSP). SHSP awards are based on minimum legislated floors, risk assessments, and perceived effectiveness. This grant program, however, no longer protects against contingent expenses from terror alerts or attacks – say, to the New York subway – that put financial stress on local resources. Cities can defray some of the contingent expenses through hotel and other taxes on tourists. In the case of sporting events, ticket prices can be raised to cover terrorism-related costs associated with the events. Additional help comes from the Federal Law Enforcement Training Center, which supplies basic and advanced training in countering terrorism to state and local agents. Some of the biodefense program is set aside to assist the state and local jurisdictions. In addition, DHS Analysis and Operations provides intelligence on terrorism to state and local jurisdictions. Finally, the National Protection and Program Directorate helps state and local jurisdictions address threats to their critical infrastructure.

EVALUATION OF THE DHS

The DHS has many pluses and minuses. On the positive side, the DHS seeks to address the weakest-link problem by achieving greater security standards countrywide. This is particularly germane to the TSA's efforts to secure the nation's airports by deploying professional screeners. Prior to 9/11, airline companies hired their own screeners and faced a moral hazard problem, because airlines could pocket cost savings from security fees collected on tickets by using cheap screeners with little training (also see Hainmüller and Lemnitzer, 2003, on the failure of private airline companies to provide adequate security). The DHS utilizes the revenue-generating ability of the federal government to provide funding to lower-level jurisdictions, including small townships that, without federal assistance, are unable to prepare for biological or chemical terrorist attacks. Another favorable factor is the greater coordination that the DHS can achieve by bringing agencies performing related and complementary chores under the same department and leadership. The DHS also spearheads a crucial research and development program to investigate a wide range of issues, including identifying improved counterterrorism practices, addressing threats to US agriculture, limiting potential attacks against the nation's food supply, and understanding the root causes of terrorism. DHS has tried to recognize new exigencies and take action before the threats are realized.

Because terrorism poses a nationwide threat, action needs to be directed at the federal level, which is precisely what the DHS does. In so doing, the DHS must coordinate federal, state, and local responses, which is yet another mission of the department. Independent antiterrorism action at the state or local level will merely displace the attack to a less-protected jurisdiction. Because much of the terrorism threat within the United States is coming from abroad, the inclusion of the US Customs and Border Protection, the TSA, and the US Coast Guard is sensible.

Since the TSA assumed the responsibility for screening airline passengers and their luggage, the US Government Accountability Office (GAO) issues reports that assess the performance of federal screeners, their practices, training, and equipment. An early report indicated the need to measure screeners' performance and to provide for ongoing training (US General Accounting Office, 2003). In a subsequent report, the GAO identified technology and training constraints – for example, screeners' inability to access and complete online recurrent training programs (US Government Accountability Office, 2005). This report also indicated that the TSA's covert tests on the screening of passengers and checked baggage found that an unacceptably high number of threat objects passed undetected through screening.[2] As a consequence, improved threat image projection systems were deployed to US airports, and screeners' training was improved further. There appears to be a TSA reliance on technology – for example, explosive trace portals (ETPs) or "puffer machines" were placed in thirty-six US airports in 2006 (US Government Accountability Office, 2010). These devices are intended to detect traces of explosives on passengers that are dislodged by puffs of air. ETP deployment ensued despite disappointing operational results following tests on ETP prototypes during 2004 and 2005. As of 31 December 2009, all but 9 of the 101 deployed ETPs have been removed from the nation's airports owing to effectiveness and operational concerns (US Government Accountability Office, 2010, pp. 19–20). The remaining machines are scheduled for removal by the end of 2010. This deployment of an expensive screening technology with insufficient pre-deployment evaluation is costly. More important, such a practice may provide a false sense of security when vulnerabilities remain high.

The near-tragedy on Northwest Airlines flight 253 has again raised questions about screening technology and the efficacy of the US no-fly watchlist. Following this incident on 25 December 2009, the TSA is moving ahead with the deployment of 878 advanced imaging technology (AIT)

---

[2]   The results of these tests are classified because they could aid terrorists.

scanners. The GAO has cautioned that AIT scanners must pass rigorous in-the-field operational testing to prove their reliability in detecting explosives and weapons on passengers prior to widespread AIT deployment (US Government Accountability Office, 2009a, 2010). The GAO is particularly concerned about the ability of terrorists to escape detection by devising means of circumventing the technology – for example, hiding explosives in body cavities much as drug runners hide drugs. All technological barriers are static, thereby inviting innovative terrorists to develop countermeasures. Unfortunately, terrorists have the clear cost advantage in such technology-countermeasure contests. As mentioned earlier in the book, AIT scanners also raise privacy issues. These scanners require large floor space, which may necessitate expensive reconfiguration of screening areas at some airports.

Flight 253 also underscored that watchlists at the end of 2009 did not identify Umar Farouk Abdulmutallah, the underwear bomber, despite many warning signs. According to the GAO, watchlist practices present "potential vulnerabilities," including ones created because agencies were not screening against all records in the watchlist (US Government Accountability Office, 2010, p. 1). Earlier GAO recommendations to screen against all records had not been instituted by the National Counterterrorism Center and other US agencies responsible for pooling intelligence when developing watchlists (US Government Accountability Office, 2007). Since flight 253, watchlists have been greatly expanded, and increased interagency cooperation and communication has supposedly been implemented.

There are many other aspects of the DHS that can be improved. In its mission to bring relevant agencies within the same department, the DHS does not go far enough in terms of intelligence. There is still intelligence duplication with the FBI, the CIA, the Department of Defense (DoD), the National Security Council, and other entities collecting information on the terrorism threat. The same logic that justifies bringing twenty-two agencies within the DHS also supports including these intelligence offices *within* DHS. Currently, DHS's Analysis and Operations interfaces with these other intelligence organizations. Given its modest budget of $348 million in 2010, Analysis and Operations must depend on other US intelligence agencies for its intelligence, which underscores the importance of interagency sharing. Flight 253 is a recent example that indicates the inadequacy of this sharing. Proper intelligence is essential to all DHS missions – for example, intelligence informs the DHS about where to concentrate its research and development efforts and tells the TSA what steps should be taken to keep commercial air travel safe. Intelligence allows S&T to know what WMD threats are the most immediate. An explicit linkage between the military and the DHS is also needed. Military operations – for example, raids on al-Qaida caves in Afghanistan or its safe havens in Pakistan – can yield crucial information for homeland security. Planned military operations can create grievances that may erupt in terrorist attacks, which further justifies the proposed link.

To improve DHS operations, an augmented international viewpoint is required. By improving security for Americans and foreign visitors in the United States, DHS activities will surely divert some attacks abroad. This transference is apt to gravitate to two venues: poor countries with less capacity for homeland security and countries where the terrorists can obtain safe haven. The latter class of countries includes "failed states," where there is no stable government to maintain order. In other instances, the terrorists may operate in their own country and target foreigners. At home, terrorists can blend in easily and establish a support system (see Chapter 9; Enders and Sandler, 2006). To address these venue shifts, there must be expanded ties between the DHS and foreign authorities. This transfer of attacks puts Americans and their property at greater risk abroad. Some foreign ties exist in Analysis and Operations, ICE, TSA, the National Protection and Program Directorate, the Domestic Nuclear Detection Office, and other DHS components. However, these linkages can be strengthened because defensive measures in all targeted countries have global implications. US directives in early 2010 to some foreign governments to enhance the screening of some high-risk airline passengers traveling to the United States are useful interactions with foreign authorities to improve security without inconveniencing everyone. Immediately after flight 253, the United States wanted *all* travelers from certain countries to be subject to greater screening. A subsequent directive identified the profile of high-risk passengers who required secondary screening. DHS can promote its domestic security mission by taking an ever-increasing global viewpoint.

Terrorism Alert System

One DHS innovation merits some special evaluation. Prior to 9/11, terrorism warnings were not always shared with the public – for example, a terrorism advisory issued prior to the downing of Pan Am flight 103 on 21 December 1988 had not been made public. The failure to inform the public of a terrorism advisory can bring outrage once an incident occurs and the advisory is revealed. Apparently, the US government was aware of increased chatter on the internet about a pending terrorist attack before 9/11 but did not publicize the information. To stem future criticism, the DHS instituted a five-tier terrorism alert system: green, low threat; blue, guarded risk; yellow, elevated or significant threat; orange, high alert; and red, severe risk. For each tier, there are certain actions required by the authorities and the DHS – for example, an orange alert mandates coordinated security actions by federal, state, and local law enforcement bodies. The DHS uses the alert system, in part, to make the public more vigilant and more accepting of delays at airports, public events, and critical infrastructure.

Despite these benefits, the color-coded terrorism alert system had some shortfalls. Intelligence provides the authorities with information that the terrorists may not know that they have. In such a situation, the authorities can use this one-sided information to lay a trap for the terrorists. By making the information public, the authorities lose a strategic advantage. The original alert system also allowed the terrorists to manipulate the system. That is, the terrorists could increase their chatter or level of activity, thereby creating enhanced fear in the public and greater security expenditures by the authorities. By limiting their chatter, the terrorists could reduce DHS vigilance prior to a planned attack. The color-coded system also informed the terrorists when attacks were more difficult to execute owing to the watchfulness of the authorities. Another drawback was the proclivity of the authorities to maintain an elevated or high-alert level, because they did not want an attack to occur during a low-alert period. Not surprisingly, the alert level never fell below yellow. This practice led to public fatigue; the system lost its immediacy because vigilance was always heightened. Orange alerts were costly for state and local law enforcement agencies. The color-coded system issued nationwide alerts that did not permit action to be sufficiently tailored to venues where the potential threat was most relevant. Since 2005, DHS has partially addressed this concern by issuing some localized warnings.

On 27 January 2011, Secretary of Homeland Security Janet Napolitano announced the discontinuation of the color-coded alerts. The new system – the National Terrorism Advisory System (NTAS) – provides more detailed information about terrorist threats to first responders, airports, state and local governments, the public, and others. General countrywide alerts will typically not be issued unless warranted. The nature of the threat will be indicated along with suggested actions. Even though DHS may, at times, be providing useful information to terrorists, the fatigue factor and the proclivity to keep threat levels high are thus alleviated. Moreover, potential targets and the public will be better able to respond to threats.

OTHER ISSUES OF HOMELAND SECURITY

Homeland security here and abroad is primarily concerned with defensive measures that harden targets, foil terrorist attacks, and keep terrorists or their weapons from entering the country. Proactive responses that attack transnational terrorists or their assets directly are left to the military, the intelligence community, and other government agencies. The relative expenditure breakdown between defensive and proactive responses is difficult to ascertain. In fiscal year 2004, the US General Accounting Office (2004) offered the following breakdown among departments: DHS, $23.9 billion; DoD, $15.2 billion; Department of Justice, $2.3 billion; Department of State, $2.4 billion; Department of Health and Human Services, $3.8 billion; and other departments and agencies, $5.2 billion. In total, these antiterrorism expenditures came to $52.8 billion, which did not include spending on intelligence by the CIA, the FBI, and other agencies outside of the DHS. Of this total, proactive measures include expenditures of $15.2 billion by DoD and some of the other expenditures that went for freezing terrorist assets or bringing terrorists to justice.

US military spending on the war on terror now dwarfs DHS spending. By December 2008, the US Congress had appropriated approximately $808 billion to proactive military operations since 2001. This appropriation included $140.4 billion for fiscal year 2009 (US Government Accountability Office, 2009b). Clearly, sizable US military spending on counterterrorism also occurred during 2010–2011 in rebuilding Iraq and fighting the Taliban in Afghanistan. To our knowledge, DoD proactive spending on the war on terror is determined independently of DHS spending even though these two types of spending are related.

What Is the Proper Mix between Proactive and Defensive Measures?

In coming up with an overall homeland security strategy, the US or any terrorism-plagued government must address this issue. The proper budget for homeland security can be ascertained only if the level of proactive measures is known. If, for example, a larger offensive against the terrorists were to reduce their numbers, then less defensive homeland security would be needed. When, however, proactive responses create grievances, greater terrorism may ensue and enhanced defensive measures may be needed. Finding the proper mix poses a difficult question that requires some careful analysis. The best that we can accomplish here is to indicate some of the trade-offs that a proper study must take into account.

Proactive strategies can result in potential *long-run* savings from eliminating the current terrorist threat. This means that a multiperiod analysis is appropriate, one that accounts for the immediate proactive costs and the longer-run proactive benefits as the terrorists are reduced in number. By contrast, defensive measures provide primarily short-term benefits from current safeguards. Such measures involve a continual flow of spending because actions must be applied during *every* period in which the threat persists. In calculating defensive benefits, a researcher must net out transference externalities as attacks are shifted to less-guarded venues. As a rough rule of thumb, the *net* additional benefits per dollar of expenditure should be equated between defensive and proactive policies, if the two policies are determined simultaneously.[3] Because the unit costs of proactive and defensive responses are likely to differ, it is essential to divide the *net* additional gains from each kind of activity by its respective price. If, for example, proactive policies have a higher unit price than defensive actions, then the net marginal benefits from proactive measures must exceed those of defensive action in order to justify implementing as much proactive policy. Some combination of the two policies is required depending on their time profile of benefits, their price, and any offsetting negative consequences (for example, from transference or enhanced grievances).

Other Allocative Choices

Once an appropriate division between proactive and defensive measures is decided upon, resources must be allocated within each class based on payoffs and costs. For proactive responses, the military must account for the expected gain in terms of reduced terrorism from offensive actions. If two proactive choices are equally costly, then action favors the choice whose success is more assured and whose payoff is greater. A smaller likelihood of success can be compensated for by a larger payoff in terms of reduced terrorism.

When the DHS or its equivalent in another country is deciding allocations among alternative defensive measures, several factors must be considered: the value of the protected target, the ease of protecting the target, collateral damage, and intelligence on the terrorists' predilection for the target. A target's value is determined by the potential loss of life, the loss of property value, and its symbolic value. Collateral damage to nearby areas

---

[3] Bandyopadhyay and Sandler (2011) determined proactive and defensive spending as a two-stage sequential game, where the main active agents are two countries targeted by the same terrorist network. These authors showed that the associated market failures are complementary, so that addressing the underprovision of proactive measures serves to reduce the overspending on defensive measures.

can augment a target's value. Knowledge of the terrorists' preferences can allow the authorities to estimate how likely a target is to be hit, thereby permitting an estimate of a target's *expected value* – its likelihood-weighted losses from an attack. Keeping other things constant, defensive measures should favor high-value targets that are *likely venues and easier to protect*. The latter consideration determines how many resources must be assigned in order to achieve a given level of protection. Targets with easy-to-protect distant perimeters may require fewer defensive resources than targets that have no safety buffer. In Los Angeles, the Staples Center has no defensive perimeter, while Dodgers Stadium does. Defensive resource budgets are usually fixed, so that more protection at one place implies less at other places. Resources should be allocated among venues so that the expected *net* marginal gain is equated across targets, where these net gains account for the target's value after deducting marginal defensive costs. Given their high value, high-profile sports events and public gatherings should receive greater protection. Technological breakthroughs may result in greater effective protection as associated costs are reduced.

Private versus Public Provision of Security

Private enterprises also have a role and incentives to provide defensive measures and not rely solely on the DHS or its equivalent abroad for protection. For example, cruise ships can gain passengers and revenue if security measures appear adequate. The associated costs can, in part, be passed on in the ticket price. Adequate terrorism precautions may also save cruise ships on insurance. Cruise ships and other enterprises (for example, amusement parks and racetracks) at risk for terrorist attacks must also balance greater security costs against savings in insurance premiums. Clearly, the DHS will direct most of its protection to public venues, so private corporations will have to finance their own protection. In some cases where there are public spillovers, the DHS provides grants to assist some enterprises with terrorism protection – for example, grants are offered to oil companies.

INSURANCE AND TERRORISM

Another issue of homeland security following 9/11 has been the ability of firms to obtain terrorism insurance.[4] Without this insurance, a future terrorist incident could put firms in the impacted industry out of business.

---

[4] The information in this section draws from facts provided in Kunreuther and Michel-Kerjan (2004a, 2004b) and Wolgast (2002).

Commercial airline companies need such insurance in order to continue to provide flights to the public. Prior to 9/11, insured losses from transnational terrorist attacks had been modest: $907 million in the 24 April 1993 NatWest tower bombing in London; $725 million in the 26 February 1993 World Trade Center bombing; $671 million in the 10 April 1992 financial district bombing in London; $398 million in the 24 July 2001 aircraft bombing at the Colombo International Airport in Sri Lanka; and $259 million in the 9 February 1996 IRA South Key Docklands bombing in London (Wolgast, 2002).[5] The 9/11 attacks resulted in economic and property losses of $80 billion, of which about $40 billion was insured. These covered losses included business interruption, workers compensation, life insurance, liability payments, and property damage. With the exception of Hurricane Katrina, insured losses from the most costly natural disasters do not rival those of 9/11: $15.5 billion from Hurricane Andrew in 1992; $12.5 billion from the Northridge earthquake in 1994; $7.3 billion from Typhoon Murielle (Japan) in 1991; and $6.2 billion from Winterstorm Daria (Europe) in 1990 (Congressional Research Service, 2005; Wolgast, 2002).[6] Private insurer losses from Hurricane Katrina were estimated to be $40–60 billion (Congressional Research Service, 2005). The losses from 9/11 prompted the insurance industry to exclude terrorism coverage or to charge extremely high premiums.

Terrorism presented the insurance industry with dilemmas not characteristic of other insurance liabilities (Kunreuther and Michel-Kerjan, 2004b). The experience of 9/11 demonstrated that catastrophic losses could result from a terrorist event. For example, a radiological bomb that explodes in a major city could result in losses that would rival those of 9/11 (Gordon et al., 2005). More important, modelers have great difficulty in computing the likelihood of future terrorist events and the potential losses. This difficulty can be appreciated by reflecting on terrorism prior to 9/11, where the highest death toll from any terrorist attack had been fewer than 500 persons. The 10 April 1992 bombing of the London financial district represented the greatest pre-9/11 terrorist-induced loss, estimated at $2.9 billion.[7] Thus, historical data do little to help the insurance industry to calculate what types of risks are associated with terrorism insurance. With natural disasters, there are more data that permit actuarial calculations.

---

[5] The Oklahoma City bombing resulted in over $650 million in losses, of which $145 million was insured (Wolgast, 2002).

[6] Different sources will report different insured losses for these events. Somewhat lower figures are found in Navarro and Spencer (2001). Figures may differ because of different price deflators, exchange rates, and estimations.

[7] Only $671 million of the $2.9 billion were insured (Wolgast, 2002).

Other factors distinguish insurance risks for terrorist incidents from other contingencies. Unlike natural disasters, terrorist events can be influenced by government actions. Proactive measures can create grievances that may result in more terrorism. After the US retaliatory raid on Libya in April 1986 for its alleged involvement in the La Belle discotheque bombing, there were numerous terrorist attacks against US and UK interests worldwide (Enders and Sandler, 1993). The same experience has characterized Israeli retaliations (Brophy-Baermann and Conybeare, 1994). Another difficulty in insuring terrorist attacks is the displacement effect, where defensive actions can merely shift the attack elsewhere. This means that private or public protective measures may have no effect on the overall risk exposure of the insurance industry. In the case, say, of fire, individual actions to limit risks do not make other structures more vulnerable. Another concern in insuring terrorism is the interdependent security problem, where individual precautions may be useless unless similar steps are taken by others (Kunreuther and Heal, 2003; Kunreuther and Michel-Kerjan, 2004a, 2004b). This problem reduces individual incentives to curb risks.

If incentives to reduce risk exposure are absent, then insurance premiums may become prohibitively expensive. This was the situation in the United States after 9/11. As a temporary fix, the US government passed the Terrorism Risk Insurance Act (TRIA) on 26 November 2002. Under TRIA, the federal government paid 90% of any losses beyond the deductible from a transnational terrorist attack, while the insurance company covered the remaining 10%. In order for payment to be made, the US secretary of the treasury had to certify that the attack was transnational. TRIA allowed the insurance company to place a surcharge on all property and casualty policies in order to recoup losses. Insured buildings and firms did not have to pay any premiums for federal coverage. TRIA was in effect until 31 December 2004 and extended by the treasury secretary until the end of 2005.

On 26 December 2007, President George W. Bush signed the Terrorism Risk Insurance Program Reauthorization Act, which essentially extended TRIA through 31 December 2014. This reauthorization made a number of modifications to the original act (National Association of Insurance Commissioners, 2010). Coverage no longer depends on the terrorist attack being transnational; domestic terrorist incidents with large losses are also covered. There is a $100 billion limit on insured losses from a catastrophic terrorist event. The federal government would cover 85% of insured losses beyond deductibles; private insurers would cover 15% of these insured losses. Federal disbursements would later be recouped through policyholder surcharges. In essence, this reauthorization acknowledges the importance of a federal backstop until there are sufficient private insurers for terrorism. The reauthorization mandates further study by the comptroller general of the feasibility of affordable private insurance coverage for conventional and nonconventional terrorist attacks.

The events of 9/11 single-handedly disrupted an important aspect of the private insurance market. In so doing, terrorism created a significant market failure that required federal intervention and amelioration. Without federal action, significant portions of the transportation industry would not have had the necessary liability coverage. The insurance concerns show that the security of a market-economy nation may require actions by its government that go beyond protecting against terrorist incidents.

CONCLUDING REMARKS

In Figure 11.1, the rising cost of US defensive counterterrorism measures is evident as the DHS budget has increased in nominal terms by 9% annually. The rise in US proactive military spending has been even greater, with about $1 trillion spent on the war on terror since October 2001. These expenditures represent an ever-expanding drain on the country's resources. Other terrorism burdens, not reflected in government expenditures, involve private protection, increased insurance premiums, and lost time in security lines. Homeland security spending has increased greatly in other rich countries. One must wonder whether there is too much spending on homeland security since 9/11 and subsequent attacks. There is a clear tendency for targeted countries to overprotect their territory in the hopes of transferring attacks abroad. This collective action failure may result in too much spending (see Chapter 4).

Our evaluation of the DHS shows that, in principle, it was a move in the right direction to improve coordination among agencies involved with homeland security and to prevent duplication. However, we conclude that the DHS, by not including enough elements of the intelligence community, has not fully realized its mission. Additionally, a better liaison is needed between the military and the DHS if the latter is going to make appropriate allocations to defensive measures. The DHS needs to go further to integrate all aspects of the war on terror. This integration also requires greater interface with foreign counterparts charged with homeland security. Another concern is the TSA's reliance on technological barriers that, in some instances, can be circumvented readily by innovative terrorists. If such barriers are deployed with inadequate operational tests, then wasteful spending can result.

We have focused on the DHS because it is easy to find information about its structure, budget, and evolution. It is much more difficult to find such information about other countries' homeland security practices. Nevertheless, the issues raised here about expanding homeland security budgets apply in theory to any country that confronts terrorism at home. The need to coordinate defensive and proactive counterterrorism decisions applies universally, as does the need for strong links between intelligence agencies and homeland security. The proper allocation of defensive resources between rural and urban locations is relevant for any country's homeland security decisions.

Table 11.A1. *Total Budget Authority by Organization as of 31 January 2004 ($ Millions)*

Organization	Fiscal Years[a]		
	2003	2004	2005
Security, Enforcement, and Investigations	*21,566*	*22,606*	*24,691*
Border and Transportation Under Secretary	0	8	10
US VISIT	380	328	340
Bureau of Customs and Borders Protection	5,887	5,942	6,199
Bureau of Immigration and Customs Enforcement	3,262	3,654	4,011
Transportation Security Administration	4,648	4,405	5,297
US Coast Guard	6,196	6,935	7,471
US Secret Service	1,193	1,334	1,363
Preparedness and Recovery	*5,175*	*5,493*	*7,372*
Federal Emergency Management Agency	5,175	4,608	4,844
Biodefense	0	885	2,528
Research, Development, Training, Assessments and Services	*2,330*	*3,591*	*3,810*
Bureau of Citizenship and Immigration Services	1,422	1,653	1,711
Federal Law Enforcement Training Center	170	191	196
Information Analysis and Infrastructure Protection	185	834	864
Science and Technology	553	913	1,039
Departmental Management and Operations	*2,111*	*4,851*	*4,294*
Departmental Operations	22	211	405
Technology Investments	47	184	226
Counterterrorism Fund	10	10	20
Office of Domestic Preparedness	1,961	4,366	3,561
Inspector General	71	80	82
Total	31,182	36,541	40,167

[a] Figures for 2004 are estimates, and figures for 2005 are requests.
Source: Department of Homeland Security (2004, p. 13).

TWELVE

The Future of Terrorism

Despite the war on terror and the death of bin Laden, the one certainty is that terrorism will continue as a tactic associated with conflicts. As long as there are grievances, there will be conflict and, thus, terrorism. Terrorism will always be present owing to its cost-effectiveness and its favoring of the weak against the strong. A bomb that costs a mere few hundred dollars may cause hundreds of millions in damage – for example, the 1993 bombing of the north tower of the World Trade Center. Desperation and frustration are key motives for terrorism. Its cruelty can, at times, make it an end in itself.

Since the start of the modern era of terrorism in the late 1960s, terrorist experts have used current experiences and trends to predict the future of terrorism.[1] Predictions are based on two paradigms: (i) an induction derived from recent events, and (ii) forecasts using statistical methods.[2] Both paradigms have their shortcomings. When past experiences (attacks) are used, predictions tend to be reactive coming from an unanticipated driver – for example, the shift from leftist-based to fundamentalist transnational terrorism. Such predictions are useful until the next major unforeseen upheaval. Policy ends are better served if changing grievances, players, and tactics are recognized near their onset so that countervailing actions can be proactively engineered at the outset of change. Forecasts based on statistical techniques are less accurate as they are further projected into the future. As in the case of experienced-based predictions, a statistically fitted trend cannot foresee shocks that throw off forecasts. Trend analysis provides an "average" description that cannot identify an unusual future pattern.

---

[1] For an example, see Hoffman (1999). Examples can be found every year in the journals *Terrorism and Political Violence* and *Studies in Conflict & Terrorism*.

[2] Hoffman (1998, 1999) fall into the first category, while Enders and Sandler (1999, 2000, 2005a) fall into the second category.

The short-run nature of forecasts may be understood by considering the recent past. Starting in the early 1990s, the sharp downturn in the level of transnational terrorism (see Chapter 3, Figure 3.2) came as a surprise, as did the accompanying upturn in the *proportion* of terrorist incidents involving deaths (see Chapter 3, Figure 3.6). In this case, the influences of the end of the Cold War, the decline of leftist terrorism, and the rise of fundamentalist terrorism were unanticipated. Until the 20 March 1995 sarin gas attack on the Tokyo subway, most terrorism experts viewed the possibility of a chemical, biological, radiological, or nuclear terrorist attack as remote (Jenkins, 1975). The conventional view was that terrorists were constrained by their constituency from using such attacks because they would unleash sustained retribution by the authorities. After the sarin attack, terrorism experts began to consider potential terrorist events involving weapons of mass destruction (WMDs).[3] This concern escalated after 9/11 and the subsequent discovery of evidence in al-Qaida's hideouts in Afghanistan that the group had actively tried to acquire WMDs. The events of 9/11 and the earlier attempted implosion of the World Trade Center on 26 February 1993 had demonstrated that some groups would engage in mass-casualty terrorism. Given this realization, the possible use of WMDs had to be seriously considered along with effective countermeasures to such attacks.

This final chapter has three purposes. First, we assess the risk of terrorists acquiring and deploying WMDs. In so doing, we indicate the consequences of such attacks, their likely perpetrators and venue. Second, we evaluate the current threat of terrorism. Third, we indicate future directions for domestic and transnational terrorism. During the course of the chapter, we argue that domestic terrorism will continue to be the predominant form of terrorism, as it has been in the past. Any use of WMDs by terrorists is anticipated to be on a small scale, with a preference for chemical weapons deployed in closed places. The greatest immediate threat of mass-casualty terrorism still comes from bombs or from turning everyday objects – for example, airplanes or tanker trucks – into formidable weapons. Terrorist attacks will remain relatively low-tech and simple, because such attacks allow terrorists to stay clandestine and to operate in loose-knit networks. Moreover, these attacks are cost-effective and can still create tremendous fear in a target audience. Suicide attacks are expected to come to North America and to increase in frequency in Europe. In the first edition, we predicted suicide attacks in Europe, which the 7 July 2005 London transport bombings and

---

[3] See articles by Cameron (2004), Campbell (1997), Hoffman (1997, 1998, 1999), and Parachini (2003). This interest was bolstered by the rise in fundamentalist terrorism.

some subsequent events (for example, in Moscow) have proven to be an accurate prediction. Chemical, biological, radiological, or nuclear (CBRN) terrorist events pose a greater risk if terrorists are greatly assisted by a rogue state, particularly one with chemical or nuclear weapons.

MASS-CASUALTY TERRORIST ATTACKS

Officially, WMDs consist of any mine, bomb, or device that releases chemicals, biological organisms, or radiation in sufficient quantity to cause the loss of human life (Bunker, 2000). There is no official requirement that this loss of life be extensive – the mere application of CBRN substances is sufficient to qualify a weapon as a WMD. CBRN weapons can be small-scale, intended for discriminate targeting, or large-scale, intended for mass casualties. The use of chlorine gas by the Tamil Tigers to rout a Sri Lankan army encampment on 18 June 1990 was a small-scale attack of opportunity, whereas the dispersion of sarin by Aum Shinrikyo to murder morning commuters on 20 March 1995 was a large-scale attack with just twelve deaths (Cameron, 2004).

Nuclear terrorism can take two main forms. There can be an attack against a facility containing highly radioactive materials, such as a nuclear power plant, in the hope of causing widespread contamination (US Government Accountability Office, 2008). For example, a 9/11-type plane attack can be directed at the containment building of a nuclear power plant. Given the reinforced concrete used in these buildings, the intended goal of dispersing nuclear material may be difficult to achieve in practice in this scenario. A bomb directed at a truck transporting nuclear waste to a disposal site may be a more realistic scenario for dispersing radioactive material. A second type of attack involves exploding a nuclear device that is either stolen or built by the terrorists. The former scenario is more likely, since building a bomb would require considerable expertise and access to sufficient quantities of enriched uranium. Most experts do not see the nuclear scenarios as likely in the foreseeable future (see, for example, Ackerman, 2004; Cameron, 2004; Hoffman, 1999; Parachini, 2003). Even stealing a nuclear device presents formidable challenges given that all nations deploy significant safeguards to keep these weapons out of the hands of their enemies.

A radiological weapon usually consists of radioactive material attached to a dispersion device such as a bomb or a mine. This weapon is known as a *dirty bomb*, which is intended to have long-term economic consequences from long-lived radiation. The necessary material could be stolen from a university laboratory, a nuclear power plant, or a hospital. Terrorists may also acquire radiological material from a state sponsor. Highly radioactive daughter elements, such as plutonium, would pose the greatest threat owing to their lengthy half-lives. In some instances, this material could be spread without an explosive device. Dirty bombs are particularly worrisome because they are low-tech and can have significant consequences. Even a small device could disrupt economic and other activities if exploded in a busy harbor (for example, Long Beach, California) or along a city street (Gordon et al., 2005).

Chemical weapons fall into four general categories and are best used in confined areas where victims are exposed to greater concentrations of the poison (White, 2003). Nerve agents (for example, sarin and VX) enter a person's body through food, drink, or the skin and result in muscle spasms or the rapid discharge of bodily fluids. In some cases, these substances can cause paralysis, leading to suffocation and death. Blood agents (for example, hydrogen cyanide) are typically absorbed through breathing and result in death as they interact with bodily enzymes. Choking agents (for example, chlorine) also enter through the lungs and cause the victim's lungs to fill with fluids. Finally, blistering agents (for example, mustard gas) burn the victim's skin and cause disfigurement. Chemical weapons are the easiest of the CBRN weapons for terrorists to acquire and deploy and, thus, pose the greatest terrorism threat (Ackerman, 2004; Ivanova and Sandler, 2006, 2007). Aum Shinrikyo's action in 1995 demonstrates that proper dispersion causing widespread casualties is not always easy to achieve.

Biological agents also fall into four categories (Institute of Medicine, 2002). First, there are highly toxic poisons, such as ricin (obtained from castor beans) and botulinum toxin. These poisons lend themselves to assassinations or small-scale poisonings. Second, there are viruses – smallpox, viral hemorrhagic fevers, and virulent influenzas – that can kill thousands or more if a population is exposed. Such viruses can be spread from person to person. A vaccine can protect a population if administered in time, but the vaccine carries its own risks, and the authorities must know of the exposure in sufficient time. The Department of Homeland Security is stockpiling smallpox vaccine under its biodefense program (see Chapter 11). Third, there are bacteria such as anthrax, which is difficult to "weaponize" so that the bacteria can be inhaled in sufficient quantities by the victims. The optimum aerosol particle size is one to five microns, which is sufficiently small to remain airborne for hours and sufficiently light to be readily dispersed through air-exchange systems in buildings and other closed spaces. The anthrax letters in 2001 contained particles in this size range. Moreover, the spore concentration was 10^{12} per gram, sufficient to infect most people who entered the contaminated buildings (Institute of Medicine, 2002, p. 72). If the infection is caught in time, there are effective antibiotics that can protect infected persons – the key is to know of the exposure. Fourth, there are plagues, including the black plague and tularemia. Sufficiently fine aerosols can be used to disperse all of the biological agents. Efforts by Aum Shinrikyo, al-Qaida, and others to acquire such agents show that terrorists have an interest in engaging in biological terrorist attacks. This then necessitates large expenditures on biodefense even if the probability of an attack is small.

As demonstrated by 9/11, mass-casualty terrorist attacks do not require a WMD. Fully fueled airplanes used as bombs, the destruction of chemical plants, large-scale car bombings, fuel trucks used as bombs, and large-scale explosions in a confined space (for example, a tunnel or subway station) can all result in high death tolls. Just the release of deadly chemicals from a plant can kill thousands. Recent statistical analysis of transnational terrorism reveals a greater reliance on deadly car bombings since 9/11 (see Chapter 9). To outdo the carnage of 9/11, terrorists would have to resort to a CBRN attack or an attack on a high-rise building. In the latter case, an attack on a low floor is apt to cause large-scale casualties by limiting the number who can escape. As they escalate attacks in order to gain greater media attention, a time may come when terrorists will stage a large-scale CBRN incident. The likelihood of this eventuality is investigated in the next few sections.

For ready reference, Table 12.1 indicates the five types of mass-casualty terrorist events along with their subclasses.

PAST MASS-CASUALTY ATTACKS

To put terrorist carnage in perspective, Table 12.2 lists some of the major mass-casualty terrorist attacks, starting with the 22 July 1946 bombing by Zionist terrorists of the British military headquarters at the King David Hotel, Jerusalem. This bombing greatly contributed to the British decision that its occupation was leading to larger costs than the benefits derived. This incident was the role model for the massive bombings of the 1980s and beyond. The 1980 Bologna railway station bombing by right-wing terrorists was one of the largest European bombings in terms of casualties until the late 1990s and the Chechen bombings in Moscow. The Madrid commuter train bombings of 11 March 2004 were the deadliest nonaerial European terrorist attack so far. Throughout the modern era of terrorism, public transport – rail, bus, and plane – has been a favorite venue for major attacks.

Table 12.1. *Potential Mass-Casualty Terrorist Attacks*

- *Nuclear terrorism*
  - Attack against a nuclear facility
  - Exploding a nuclear bomb

- *Radiological terrorism*
  - Radiological device (for example, dirty bomb)
  - Spreading radioactive contaminants without a bomb

- *Chemical attacks*
  - Nerve agents (for example, sarin, VX)
  - Blood agents (for example, hydrogen cyanide)
  - Choking agents (for example, chlorine)
  - Blistering agents (for example, mustard gas)

- *Biological attacks*
  - Poison (for example, ricin, botulinum toxin)
  - Viruses (for example, smallpox, viral hemorrhagic fevers, virulent flu)
  - Bacteria (for example, anthrax, brucellosis)
  - Plagues (for example, black plague, tularemia)

- *Conventional attacks with mass casualties*
  - Airplanes used as bombs
  - Blowing up a chemical plant
  - Large-scale car bombing
  - Fuel trucks used as bombs
  - Large-scale explosions in a confined space

Sources: Institute of Medicine (2002), White (2003), and authors' research.

A landmark suicide truck bombing was the October 1983 bombing of the US Marines' barracks that killed 241 people and caused the United States to withdraw its peacekeepers from Lebanon. The Tamil Tigers adopted this form of attack in their domestic terrorist campaign for independence.

A number of features of Table 12.2 are noteworthy. First, no mass-casualty incident had killed more than 500 persons until the hijackings on 9/11. Second, most major events involved either blowing up a plane in midair or a car or truck bomb. The bombings in Bombay on 12 March 1993 and the bombings and armed attacks in Mumbai (the old Bombay) on 26 November 2008 are two important exceptions. Third, some of these events were simultaneous attacks. Fourth, suicide attacks have been associated with a number of the deadliest attacks since 1983. Fifth, compared to the carnage of past mass-casualty incidents, the successful use of a WMD could result in

Table 12.2. *Select Mass-Casualty Terrorist Attacks*

Date	Event	Perpetrator	Death Toll
22 July 1946	Bombing of local British military headquarters at King David Hotel, Jerusalem.	Irgun Zvai Leumi	91
2 Aug. 1980	Bombing of Bologna railway station.	Armed Revolutionary Nuclei	84
23 Oct. 1983	Suicide truck bombing of US Marines' barracks in Beirut.	Hezbollah	241
23 June 1985	Downing of Air-India Boeing 747 en route from Montreal to London.	Sikh extremists	329
15 March 1987	Car bombing of the main bus terminal in Colombo, Sri Lanka.	Tamil Tigers	105
21 Dec. 1988	Downing of Pan Am flight 103 en route from London to New York.	Libyan intelligence agent	270
19 Sept. 1989	Downing of Union des Transports (UTA) flight 772 en route from Brazzaville to Paris.	Libyan intelligence agents	171
12 March 1993	Thirteen bombings in Bombay.	Pakistani agents	317
19 April 1995	Truck bombing of the Alfred P. Murrah Federal Building in Oklahoma.	Timothy McVeigh	168
7 Aug. 1998	Simultaneous bombings of US embassies in Nairobi, Kenya, and Dar es Salaam, Tanzania.	al-Qaida	301
13 Sept. 1998	Car bombing of an eight-story Moscow apartment building. Bombs on 8 and 9 September in Dagestan and Moscow also killed 64 and 94, respectively.	Chechen rebels	118
11 Sept. 2001	Four suicide hijackings that crashed into the World Trade Center towers, the Pentagon, and a field in rural Pennsylvania.	al-Qaida	2,871[a]
23 October 2002	Barricade hostage seizure of Moscow Theater.	Chechen rebels	178

(continued)

Table 12.2 *(continued)*

Date	Event	Perpetrator	Death Toll
11 March 2004	Bombing of commuter trains and stations during morning rush hour in Madrid.	al-Qaida	191
1 Sept. 2004	Barricade hostage seizure of schoolchildren and parents in Beslan.	Chechen rebels	385
7 July 2005	London subway and bus bombings by four suicide terrorists.	Homegrown terrorists with al-Qaida sympathies	56
26 Nov. 2008	Mumbai bombings and armed attacks on the Oberoi Hotel, the Taj Mahal Palace Hotel, the central train station, a children's hospital, Leopold Café, and other locations.	Lashkar-e-Taiba	175

[a] Updated death toll as of 26 April 2010 at National Obituary Archive–Honor Roll (2010), http://www.arrangeonline.com/notablePersons/honorroll.asp.
Sources: Quillen (2002a, 2002b), Mickolus et al. (2009).

casualties that dwarf those of past events. For example, Aum Shinrikyo's 1995 subway attack could have resulted in casualty figures in excess of those of 9/11 had the sarin been purer and had it been dispersed more effectively (Cameron, 2004). Clearly, terrorist attacks involving WMDs could surpass a casualty threshold that no previous incident has approached.

COSTS OR CONSEQUENCES OF CBRN TERRORISM

The consequences of a CBRN terrorist attack could be devastating, exceeding those of 9/11. In recent years, there have been many studies that have attempted to quantify the potential monetary and human losses that could arise from various CBRN attack scenarios. The exact calculations are dependent on many parameters: the type of attack, the size of the attack, and environmental conditions. Consider an anthrax aerosol attack on a city. The ensuing consequences depend on the purity and concentration of the anthrax agent, the number of people exposed, the venue of the exposure (for example, a confined space or outdoors), the efficiency of the dispersal, and the effectiveness of the post-exposure response (Kaufman, Meltzer, and Schmid, 1997). For a sarin attack, many of these same parameters play a role,

Table 12.3. *Select Consequence Scenarios for CBRN Attacks*

Scenario	Consequences	Source
• 1,000 kilograms of *sarin gas* disperse in a large city	$34 billion 6,000 deaths	US GAO (2008)[a]
• 10 kilograms of *anthrax* slurry in a large city	$254 billion 80,000 deaths	US GAO (2008)[a]
• aerosol spray of *anthrax* spores with 100,000 people exposed	$26.2 billion 38,875 deaths	Kaufman, Meltzer, and Schmid (1997)
• aerosol spray of *Brucella melitensis* with 100,000 people exposed	$0.477 billion 413 deaths	Kaufman, Meltzer, and Schmid (1997)
• aerosol spray of *Francisella tularensis* with 100,000 people exposed	$5.4 billion 6,188 deaths	Kaufman, Meltzer, and Schmid (1997)
• *dirty bomb* with 15,000 curies of caesium-137	$43 billion A few deaths	US GAO (2008)[a]
• *dirty bomb* in the twin ports of Los Angeles and Long Beach, CA – 120-day shutdown with bridge damage	$34 billion 212,165 jobs	Gordon et al. (2005)
• *nuclear bomb* of one kiloton in a large city	$205 billion 1.3 million deaths	US GAO (2005)

[a] US Government Accountability Office (2008), which reports scenario research by Risk Management Solutions, Inc.

as was vividly illustrated in the 1995 Tokyo subway attack, where lives were spared because the sarin had been diluted and the dispersal method had been inadequate. The damage from a dirty bomb hinges on the dispersal method, the amount of radioactive material, and its placement. Gordon et al. (2005) investigated various dirty bomb scenarios in which two bombs are placed in the twin ports of Los Angeles and Long Beach, which handle half of US seaborne international trade. In their worst case scenario, in which the Vincent Thomas Bridge linking the two ports is damaged, losses run to $34 billion and cost the local economy 212,165 jobs. If, alternatively, a small nuclear bomb is detonated in a city, then the main determinants of its damage and carnage hinge on the bomb's kilotonnage and the population size and density at the target (US Government Accountability Office, 2005).

In Table 12.3, a few select scenarios are indicated, along with their estimated consequences and the source study. Both deaths and monetary losses can vary greatly. There are also scenarios, not shown, involving nuclear bombs with damage running into the trillions of dollars and millions of lives lost (US Government Accountability Office, 2008).

These scenarios raise some essential issues. An important question is how to prepare for such attacks in order to mitigate the damage. For biological attacks, Abt (2005) indicated that biodetectors are crucial in order to identify an attack at its onset. Once an attack is detected, exposed victims must be tracked and then treated with vaccines and prophylactics. This requires advance deployment of vaccines and other inhibitors. A proper response program and treatment facilities must be in place. Finally, the population must be sufficiently educated to assist in the response procedure in the event of an attack. Mathematical models have been developed to compare different response strategies for their cost-effectiveness.[4]

Another question concerns how much should be spent to prepare for low-probability CBRN scenarios with potentially devastating consequences. Preparation may require huge defensive expenditures that can stress a nation's budget. Risk management techniques allow nations to allocate scarce defensive resources among various CBRN contingencies based on target vulnerability, attack likelihood, and potential losses. That is, the same considerations that determine the allocation of defensive measures for conventional terrorist attacks apply, in principle, to protecting against alternative CBRN attacks. The difference is that many CBRN scenarios may have such a miniscule probability of occurring that no protection is best for many contingencies despite dire consequences. Nations are wise to seek inexpensive mitigation programs that can greatly limit consequences in the event of an incident. Prevention programs that, say, safeguard nuclear material typically have huge benefit-cost ratios.

Potential CBRN losses also raise an insurance question that is yet to be resolved. Private insurers exclude CBRN terrorist attacks from their coverage. Moreover, the Terrorism Risk Insurance Act (TRIA) does not currently cover such attacks (US Government Accountability Office, 2008). The extension of TRIA to CBRN terrorist attacks is currently under consideration. This extension is likely because the federal government will have to

---

[4] In a fascinating paper, Kaplan, Craft, and Wein (2002) compared two vaccination programs – trace vaccination (TV) and mass vaccination (MV) – based on a multi-equation dynamic model. TV is meant "to isolate symptomatic cases, trace and vaccinate their contacts, quarantine febrile contacts, but vaccinate more broadly if the outbreak cannot be contained by these measures." (p. 10935) As its name implies, MV involves inoculating everyone in the urban region once exposure is detected. These authors showed that MV results in far fewer deaths and more rapid eradication. TV gives rise to missing contacts who can spread the disease. In a subsequent paper, Wein, Craft, and Kaplan (2003) used queuing equations to identify an optimal distribution strategy for antibiotics in the event of an anthrax attack. These innovative papers demonstrate that mathematical modeling can inform policymakers on the most effective response to biological terrorist attacks.

help victims of a CBRN attack recover losses in the absence of any insurance. An extension of TRIA to cover CBRN attacks would not only give the government a way of sharing some of the losses with private insurers, but would also provide for premiums to defray possible future payouts.

ASSESSING THE LIKELIHOOD OF CBRN ATTACKS

This assessment requires recognition of those factors that either inhibit or promote CBRN attacks. Inhibitors are many and so far represent a formidable barrier. Most groups are inhibited from CBRN attacks by a need to maintain constituency support and funding, which might end with the indiscriminate use of a WMD. This is particularly true of separatist, ethnonationalist, and leftist terrorists, but is not true of fundamentalists and some nontraditional extremists – for example, Aum Shinrikyo (Gurr, 2004; Post, 2004). There is also the retribution worry – a WMD attack might result in an all-out effort by the authorities to destroy the group, not unlike what happened to al-Qaida in the aftermath of 9/11. The latter experience, however, shows that complete eradication is not so easy.

Technical considerations also hamper the use of WMDs. First, there is a weaponization hurdle that must be overcome. For example, the implosion required to set off a nuclear bomb is a formidable technical requirement. Second, the requisite ingredients must be acquired, which is a relevant consideration for some, but not all, WMDs. Third, efforts to acquire these materials put members in jeopardy from sting and counterterrorist operations. Fourth, there are handling risks to members from chemical, biological, and radiological agents that must be managed.

As they adopted loosely connected organizational structures in order to minimize infiltration risk, some terrorist groups compromised their ability to acquire CBRN weapons (Merrari, 1999). This follows because reduced centralization limits the resources and personnel that can be coordinated in order to make the necessary technological breakthroughs. Aum Shinrikyo stayed centralized and, hence, sustained an organization-wide setback when their headquarters were raided in 1995. By contrast, al-Qaida's decentralized structure protected it during the post-9/11 attacks, but at the price of not being able to develop CBRN weapons.

A final impediment is the cost-effectiveness of conventional attacks. As long as conventional incidents can create sufficient anxiety at a lower cost than nonconventional incidents, terrorists will not find the latter attractive. The recent cost-effectiveness of suicide attacks make them a likely alternative to WMD in the near term. A suicide attack on a US shopping mall

356 The Political Economy of Terrorism

Table 12.4. *Inhibiting and Promoting Factors Regarding Terrorists' Use of WMDs*

- *Inhibiting factors*
  - ➢ Losing constituency support and fund raising
  - ➢ Absorbing retribution/reaction from target
  - ➢ Acquiring required ingredients
  - ➢ Managing handling risk to members
  - ➢ Surmounting weaponization hurdle
  - ➢ Succumbing to counterterrorist efforts (including sting operations)
  - ➢ Loose organizational structure and the need for clandestine operations
  - ➢ Cost-effectiveness of conventional attacks

- *Promoting factors*
  - ➢ Possessing fundamentalist beliefs that demonize a target population
  - ➢ Possessing millenarian, apocalyptic, or messianic vision
  - ➢ Having deep-seated grievance that requires destruction of one's enemy
  - ➢ Reacting to excessive proactive measures
  - ➢ Supporting efforts by a rogue or failed state

would attract much media attention. Moreover, suicide attacks are easily managed using the current loosely tied terrorist structures.

Other factors are believed to promote terrorist WMD attacks. The rise of fundamentalist terrorists, who demonize a target population, increases the likelihood of such attacks, as does the presence of terrorists possessing millenarian, apocalyptic, or messianic visions (Post, 2004). These groups are not trying to win over a constituency and view the act as an end in itself; thus, they are not constrained in the carnage that they cause. Their deep-seated grievances require the destruction of the "enemy." Heavy-handed proactive measures by targeted governments may heighten grievances and encourage the acquisition of more formidable weapons (Rosendorff and Sandler, 2004). Such proactive responses may also enhance recruitment, thereby attracting members with the capabilities needed to produce WMDs. Another facilitator is support by rogue or failed states. This may be particularly true for chemical weapons, because twenty-six nations currently possess chemical weapons, and others seek them (White, 2003, p. 251).

Table 12.4 lists the inhibiting and promoting factor regarding terrorists' use of WMDs. Most terrorist experts see *small-scale* chemical and radiological attacks as likely in the near term. Large-scale CBRN attacks and/ or nuclear bombs are not likely given the overwhelming influence of the numerous impediments. Loose terrorist structures, the cost-effectiveness of conventional attacks, and the weaponization hurdle are the main inhibitors that should continue to limit the possibility of large-scale WMD terrorism in the foreseeable future, despite the presence of some extremists willing to cross the WMD threshold.

CBRN ATTACKS: PAST RECORD

A good way to gauge the likelihood of WMD terrorism is to examine a past record of such attacks. Table 12.5 displays some past incidents involving chemical, biological, and radiological agents. This list includes only some of the important events. For a more complete list, consult Ackerman (2004) and the Center for Nonproliferation Studies, Monterey Institute of International Studies. The Monterey WMD Terrorism Database contains over 1,200 incidents; about a third of these are hoaxes (Ackerman, 2004). This database is intended to be as inclusive as possible and, hence, includes some events that do not fit the definition of terrorism – for example, criminal incidents with no political motive.

As indicated in Table 12.5, Aum Shinrikyo launched a sarin attack near the judicial building in Matsumoto, Japan, in June 1994, well in advance of the 20 March 1995 sarin attack on the Tokyo subway. Aum Shinrikyo tried a hydrogen cyanide attack at a Tokyo train station on 5 May 1995, but the device was deactivated before anyone was injured. The chemical attack on the Sri Lankan army outpost by the Tamil Tigers was very limited and put their own members at risk when the chlorine gas drifted back over their members. No subsequent chemical attacks were tried by the Tamil Tigers.

There have been three noteworthy biological incidents, two involving religious cults and one by an unknown perpetrator. This latter incident concerns the anthrax letters. Given its temporal proximity to 9/11, the anthrax incident created more anxiety than its consequences warranted, with just five dead and seventeen people sickened. The most notable thing about this incident is the weapon-grade anthrax used in the attack, leading authorities to suspect someone involved with the government's biological weapons program. If these anthrax spores had been placed surreptitiously into one of the targeted buildings' ventilation systems, the number of deaths could have been quite large. This incident indicates the possibility of such attacks. Moreover, it highlights the fact that the weaponization hurdle may be circumvented by taking materials from a government's weapons program or a research laboratory. This theft risk also involves chemical, radiological, and nuclear attacks.

Table 12.5. *Past Incidents of Chemical, Biological, and Radiological Terrorism*

- *Chemical attacks*
  - ➤ April 1984: Christian Patriots stockpiled thirty gallons of cyanide to poison reservoirs in Chicago and Washington, DC.
  - ➤ 18 June 1990: Tamil Tigers used chlorine gas to rout a Sri Lankan army encampment, injuring sixty.
  - ➤ 28 March 1992: Kurdistan Workers' Party (PKK) put cyanide in three water tanks at a Turkish air force base outside Istanbul. There were no injuries.
  - ➤ 26 February 1993: Sodium cyanide canister was placed near the fertilizer bomb at the World Trade Center. The heat of the bomb destroyed the chemical.
  - ➤ 27 June 1994: Aum Shinrikyo members released sarin gas near the judicial building in Matsumoto, Japan. Eight people died and 150 were injured.
  - ➤ 15 March 1995: Attaché case with vents and fans found at Tokyo subway station. Planned attack attributed to Aum Shinrikyo.
  - ➤ 20 March 1995: Aum's sarin attack on Tokyo's subway station during morning rush hour. Twelve died and over 1,000 were sickened.
  - ➤ 5 May 1995: Hydrogen cyanide device set to go off in a men's room in Shinjuku station by Aum members. Device deactivated in time.
- *Biological attacks*
  - ➤ October 1984: Followers of Bhagwan Shree Rajneesh poisoned twelve salad bars with salmonella in The Dalles, Oregon, in hopes of winning a local election. 751 people were sickened.
  - ➤ April 1990: Aum members dispersed botulinum toxin near the Japanese Diet. There were no injuries.
  - ➤ 11 September 2001 and 9 October 2001: The mailing of anthrax letters to US elected officials and the news media. Five people were killed and seventeen were sickened.
- *Radiological attacks*
  - ➤ November 1995: Chechen rebels bury caesium-137 in Moscow's Izmailovsky Park. Authorities were warned. No injuries were reported.
  - ➤ 1998: Chechen rebels attached radioactive materials to a mine near a railway line in Argun, Chechnya. No injuries were reported.

Sources: Ackerman (2004), Cameron (2004), Campbell (1997), especially for Aum Shinrikyo incidents, Hoffman (1998), Institute of Medicine (2002), Merrari (1999), and Parachini (2003).

In Table 12.5, the two noteworthy radiological incidents both involved Chechen rebels and resulted in no casualties. The second incident is of interest because it indicates that terrorists once tried to set off a crude dirty bomb.

Ivanova and Sandler (2006) used the Monterey WMD Terrorism Database to investigate the association of regime characteristics and the

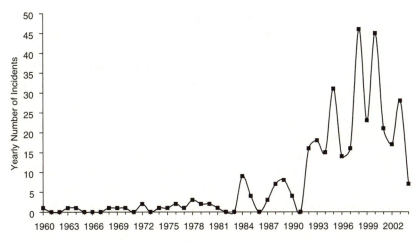

Figure 12.1. CBRN terrorist incidents: 1960–2004. *Source:* Ivanova and Sandler (2006).

likelihood of CBRN terrorist incidents. These authors first culled the data of criminal and doubtful incidents. The latter incidents involve threats and hoaxes, where there was no clear evidence that the alleged perpetrators had acquired a CBRN agent. Figure 12.1 displays the number of CBRN terrorist incidents for 1960–2004. Clearly, there were very few CBRN incidents before 1988; hence, Ivanova and Sandler (2006) concentrated their statistical analysis on the period 1988–2004. Their sample had the following breakdown: chemical incidents, 65.5%; biological incidents, 13.3%; radiological incidents, 8.2%; nuclear incidents, 2.5%; combination incidents, 2.2%; and unknown incidents, 8.2%. With the use of an odds-ratio test (see Chapter 2), these authors found that democratic regimes, rather than autocracies, were the more likely venue for CBRN incidents. The corresponding odds ratio is 4.64, which is highly significant. Also, past venue countries had a strong rule of law. Thus, these authors concluded that failed states may be where some terrorist groups form or take refuge, but that these states had not been the venue of choice for CBRN terrorist incidents. Contrary to conventional wisdom, Ivanova and Sandler found that religious fundamentalist and nationalist/separatist groups were no more likely than others to engage in CBRN terrorist attacks.

In a follow-up study, Ivanova and Sandler (2007) ascertained what factors – regime characteristics and perpetrator types – determined the likelihood of CBRN terrorist incidents. They showed that religious cults and terrorist groups with a transnational orientation posed the largest CBRN threat to society. Moreover, democratic and corrupt regimes are the likely venues for CBRN attacks. They also found that once a country had experienced a CBRN incident, the country was much more likely to experience future incidents. These findings support allocating some resources to guarding against and preparing for CBRN terrorism. In the United States, democratic values are strong, and some small-scale CBRN terrorist incidents have occurred. Nevertheless, one must remember that conventional terrorist incidents have killed, on average, twice as many persons per incident as CBRN incidents – that is, just over one person versus 0.5 persons (Ivanova and Sandler, 2007). Thus, CBRN risks must be kept in perspective when the government allocates defensive resources for these incidents.

The past record supports the expert's assessment that a chemical attack is the most likely and that a nuclear attack is highly unlikely. Radiological and biological attacks have intermediate probabilities. With the exception of the Tokyo subway attack, the past record does not include CBRN use that would have resulted in thousands of casualties, the result one tends to associate with WMDs. The most likely future scenario is the continued reliance by terrorists on an occasional large-scale conventional attack like those of 9/11 and 3/11. Nevertheless, some resources will need to be allocated to biodefense and to preparing for chemical and/or radiological terrorist attacks.

SHAPE OF TERRORISM TO COME

We now come to the most difficult task – that of predicting the future of terrorism. We take a conservative approach and base our predictions on our knowledge of terrorism since 1968 and the body of past empirical work. Our intention is to come up with predictions that are likely to hold; our intention is not to be provocative.

Domestic terrorism will continue to overshadow transnational terrorism in terms of the number of incidents. With so many civil conflicts raging around the globe, this is a safe prediction. Moreover, domestic terrorist incidents typically outnumber transnational incidents by more than eight to one. Both domestic and transnational terrorism will remain cyclical in nature, so that a downturn should not necessarily be projected into the future. Terrorists will continue to respond to countermeasures by shifting tactics, venues, and targets in order to exploit opportunities. They will also be inventive in developing innovations to circumvent countermeasures; this is particularly true in terms of technological barriers, such as full body scanners. Thus, authorities should not place too much faith in new technologies. Successful innovations on the part of terrorists will rapidly be disseminated worldwide.

As long as religious-based terrorism remains the dominant influence in transnational terrorist attacks, these attacks will remain more deadly *per incident* than during the 1970s and 1980s. Suicide terrorist incidents will increase in prevalence in Europe and will occur in the United States. On average, suicide attacks are twelve to thirteen times more deadly per incident than a typical transnational incident and have caused some targeted governments to make major concessions (Pape, 2003, 2005). Suicide missions are logistically simple and relatively inexpensive, making them attractive to some terrorist groups. Geographically, the region of concentration for transnational terrorist attacks will be the Middle East, followed by Asia and Eurasia. Most transnational terrorist incidents against US and European interests will occur in one of these three regions. Because of the augmentation in homeland security in both the United States and Europe, the venue for transnational terrorism will remain the poorer countries, those less able to protect against such attacks, where terrorists can blend in with the indigenous populations. The regional shift to the Middle East, Asia, and Eurasia began with the rise of fundamentalist terrorism in the 1980s (Enders and Sandler, 2006). On rare occasions, terrorists will resort to a large-scale conventional attack; only a couple of terrorist spectaculars are anticipated each year. Any use of WMDs will probably involve chemical weapons on a local scale.

Terrorists will increasingly rely on the internet as a way to link far-flung networks and to coordinate attacks. The internet has greatly facilitated the ability of terrorist groups to expand their territorial reach and to become less vulnerable by keeping links loose. For some groups, individual cells are quite autonomous. In Iraq, the late Abu Masab al-Zarqawi used the internet to post videos of beheadings and hostages pleading for their lives as a means to heighten anxiety and public pressure in order to induce governments and firms to withdraw their personnel. In many ways, the internet is serving the same purpose as city walls in medieval times, when severed heads were displayed to warn off one's enemies. Many terrorists groups have web sites where they post political statements, list grievances, claim responsibility for past attacks, and recruit new members. The internet also allows for the possibility of cyber-terrorism, where a politically motivated attack is directed at disrupting some organization's computers, servers, and web postings. Cyber-terrorism can also take the form of viruses and worms when disseminated for a political purpose. To date, most terrorist groups have used the internet to facilitate their operations rather than to disrupt the operations of a target organization.

Future terrorist attacks are likely to be directed at economic targets. For example, diseases can be introduced into American cattle herds as a way to create significant losses. Research Centers of Excellence have been established by the Department of Homeland Security (DHS) at Texas A & M University, with links to other universities, to protect against terrorists-induced animal diseases, and at the University of Minnesota to limit terrorist attacks on the US food supply. The first DHS Research Center of Excellence at the University of Southern California assesses the risks to critical infrastructure (for example, ports, communication networks, energy grids, and transportation links) from terrorist attacks. This center is also developing policy recommendations for protecting this infrastructure through hardening and redundancy (for example, "parallel" electricity transmission lines).

CONCLUDING REMARKS

As stated at the outset, terrorism is here to stay. Terrorism levels the playing field between the weak and the strong and, as such, provides the weak with a cost-effective means to engage in conflict. We do not see the nature of terrorism showing much change in the near term. Although expenditures on counters to WMDs will increase annually, we do not view a large-scale WMD attack as being very likely in the foreseeable future. The bomb will remain the terrorists' favorite mode of attack. Nevertheless, terrorists will exploit modern technology and adapt innovations to their purposes, as they have done with the internet. Such innovations mean that counterterrorism measures will become ever more costly. This increased expense is bolstered by an increase in the variety of potential attacks.

References

Abadie, Alberto (2006), "Poverty, Political Freedom and the Roots of Terrorism," *American Economic Review*, 96(2), 50–6.

Abadie, Alberto and Javier Gardeazabal (2003), "The Economic Cost of Conflict: A Case Study of the Basque Country," *American Economic Review*, 93(1), 113–32.

(2008), "Terrorism and the World Economy," *European Economic Review*, 52(1), 1–27.

Abt, Clark C. (2005), "Current and Improved Biodefense Cost-Benefit Assessment," in Harry W. Richardson, Peter Gordon, and James E. Moore II (eds.), *The Economic Impact of Terrorist Attacks* (Cheltenham, UK: Edward Elgar), 119–32.

Ackerman, Gary (2004), "WMD Terrorism Research: Where to from Here?," unpublished manuscript, Center for Nonproliferation Studies, Monterey Institute of International Studies, Monterey, CA.

Alexander, Yonah and Dennis Pluchinsky (1992), *Europe's Red Terrorists: The Fighting Communist Organizations* (London: Frank Cass).

Anderton, Charles H. and John R. Carter (2005), "On Rational Choice Theory and the Study of Terrorism," *Defence and Peace Economics*, 16(4), 275–82.

Arce, Daniel G. and Todd Sandler (2005), "Counterterrorism: A Game-Theoretic Analysis," *Journal of Conflict Resolution*, 49(2), 183–200.

(2007), "Terrorist Signalling and the Value of Intelligence," *British Journal of Political Science*, 37(4), 573–86.

(2009), "Fitting In: Group Effects and the Evolution of Fundamentalism," *Journal of Policy Modeling*, 31(5), 739–57.

(2010), "Terrorist Spectaculars: Backlash Attacks and the Focus of Intelligence," *Journal of Conflict Resolution*, 54(2), 354–73.

Arquilla, John and David Ronfeldt (eds.) (2001), *Networks and Netwars* (Santa Monica, CA: RAND).

Asal, Victor and R. Karl Rethemeyer (2008), "The Nature of the Beast: Terrorist Organizational Characteristics and Organizational Lethality," *Journal of Politics*, 70(2), 437–49.

Atkinson, Scott E., Todd Sandler, and John Tschirhart (1987), "Terrorism in a Bargaining Framework," *Journal of Law and Economics*, 30(1), 1–21.

Azam, Jean-Paul (2005), "Suicide-Bombing as Inter-Generational Investment," *Public Choice*, 122(1–2), 177–98.

Azam, Jean-Paul and Véronique Thelen (2010), "Foreign Aid versus Military Intervention in the War on Terror," *Journal of Conflict Resolution*, 54(2), 237–61.

Baccara, Mariagiovanna and Heski Bar-Isaac (2009), "Interrogation Methods and Terror Networks," in Nasrullah Memon, Jonathan D. Farley, David L. Hicks, and Torben Rosenorn (eds.), *Mathematical Methods in Counterterrorism* (New York: Springer), 271–90.

Bai, Jushan and Pierre Perron (1998), "Estimating and Testing Linear Models with Multiple Structural Changes," *Econometrica*, 66(1), 47–78.

   (2003), "Computation and Analysis of Multiple Structural Change Models," *Journal of Applied Econometrics*, 18(1), 1–22.

Bandyopadhyay, Subhayu and Todd Sandler (2011), "The Interplay between Preemptive and Defensive Counterterrorism Measures: A Two-Stage Game," *Economica*, 78(3), 546–564.

Bandyopadhyay, Subhayu, Todd Sandler, and Javed Younas (2011), "Foreign Aid as Counterterrorism Policy," *Oxford Economic Papers*, 63(3), 423–47.

Bapat, Navin A. (2006), "State Bargaining with Transnational Terrorist Groups," *International Studies Quarterly*, 50(1), 213–29.

Barros, Carlos P. and Luis Gil-Alana (2006), "The Timing of ETA Terrorist Attacks," *Journal of Policy Modeling*, 28(3), 335–46.

Basile, Mark (2004), "Going to the Source: Why Al Qaida's Financial Network Is Likely to Withstand the Current War on Terrorist Financing," *Studies in Conflict & Terrorism*, 27(3), 169–85.

Becker, Gary S. and Kevin M. Murphy (2001), "Prosperity Will Rise Out of the Ashes." *Wall Street Journal* (Eastern ed.), 29 October 2001, A.22.

Berman, Eli and David D. Laitin (2005), "Hard Targets: Theory and Evidence on Suicide Attacks," unpublished manuscript, University of California at San Diego, San Diego, CA.

Berrebi, Claude and Darius Lakdawalla (2007), "How Does Terrorism Risk Vary Across Space and Time? An Analysis Based on Israeli Experience," *Defence and Peace Economics*, 18(2), 113–31.

Bier, Vicki, Santiago Oliveros, and Larry Samuelson (2007), "Choosing What to Protect: Strategic Defensive Allocation against an Unknown Attacker," *Journal of Public Economic Theory*, 9(4), 563–87.

Blomberg, S. Brock (2009), "Perspective Paper 9.1," in Bjorn Lomborg (ed.), *Global Crises, Global Solutions*, 2nd ed. (Cambridge: Cambridge University Press), 563–76.

Blomberg, S. Brock, Rozlyn C. Engel, and Reid Sawyer (2010), "On the Duration and Sustainability of Transnational Terrorist Organizations," *Journal of Conflict Resolution*, 54(2), 303–30.

Blomberg, S. Brock, Gregory D. Hess, and Athanasios Orphanides (2004), "The Macroeconomic Consequences of Terrorism," *Journal of Monetary Economics*, 51(5), 1007–32.

Blomberg, S. Brock, Gregory D. Hess, and Akila Weerapana (2004), "Economic Conditions and Terrorism," *European Journal of Political Economy*, 20(2), 463–78.

Bloom, Mia (2005), *Dying to Kill: The Allure of Suicide Terror* (New York: Columbia University Press).

Brachman, Jarret, Brian Fishman, and Joseph Felter (2008), "The Power of Truth: Questions for Ayman al-Zawahiri," Combating Terrorism Center, US Military Academy, West Point, NY, [http://ctc.usma.edu], accessed 10 October 2008.

Brandt, Patrick T. and Todd Sandler (2009), "Hostage Taking: Understanding Terrorism Event Dynamics," *Journal of Policy Modeling*, 31(5), 758–78.

(2010), "What Do Transnational Terrorists Target? Has It Changed? Are We Safer?," *Journal of Conflict Resolution*, 54(2), 214–36.

(2011), "Dynamics of Complementarity in Transnational Terrorist Targeting Decisions, 1968–2008," unpublished manuscript, University of Texas at Dallas, Richardson, TX.

Brophy-Baermann, Bryan and John A. C. Conybeare (1994), "Retaliating against Terrorism: Rational Expectations and the Optimality of Rules versus Discretion," *American Journal of Political Science*, 38(1), 196–210.

Browne, Julie and Eric S. Dickson (2010), "We Don't Talk to Terrorists: On the Rhetoric and Practice of Secret Negotiations," *Journal of Conflict Resolution*, 54(3), 379–407.

Bruce, Neil (2001), *Public Finance and the American Economy*, 2nd ed. (Boston: Addison Wesley).

Bueno de Mesquita, Ethan (2005a), "Conciliation, Commitment and Counterterrorism: A Formal Model," *International Organization*, 59(1), 145–76.

(2005b), "The Quality of Terror," *American Journal of Political Science*, 49(3), 515–30.

(2007), "Politics and the Suboptimal Provision of Counterterror," *International Organization*, 61(1), 9–36.

(2008), "Terrorist Factions," *Quarterly Journal of Political Science*, 3(4), 399–418.

Bueno de Mesquita, Ethan and Eric S. Dickson (2007), "The Propaganda of the Deed: Terrorism, Counterterrorism, and Mobilization," *American Journal of Political Science*, 51(2), 364–81.

Bunker, Robert (2000), "Weapons of Mass Disruption and Terrorism," *Terrorism and Political Violence*, 12(1), 37–46.

Bureau of Economic Analysis (2001), "Business Situation," *Survey of Current Business*, 81(11), [http://www.bea.doc.gov/bea/ARTICLES/2001/11november/1101bsa.pdf], accessed 10 January 2005.

Bureau of Labor Statistics (2003), "Extended Mass Layoffs and the 9/11 Attacks," *Monthly Labor Review: The Editor's Desk*, [http://www.bls.gov/opub/ted/2003/sept/wk2/art03.htm], accessed 10 January 2005.

Busea, Mikel, Aurelia Valiño, Joost Heijs, Thomas Baumert, and Javier Gonzalez Gomez (2007), "The Economic Cost of March 11: Measuring Direct Economic Cost of the Terrorist Attack on March 11, 2004 in Madrid," *Terrorism and Political Violence*, 19(4), 489–509.

Bush, George W. (2002), *Securing the Homeland: Strengthening the Nation* (Washington, DC: White House).

Cameron, Gavin (2004), "Weapons of Mass Destruction Terrorism Research: Past and Future," in Andrew Silke (ed.), *Research on Terrorism: Trends, Achievements and Failures* (London: Frank Cass), 72–90.

Campbell, James K. (1997), "Excerpts from Research Study 'Weapons of Mass Destruction and Terrorism: Proliferation by Non-State Actors,'" *Terrorism and Political Violence*, 9(2), 24–50.

Caplan, Bryan (2006), "Terrorism: The Relevance of the Rational Choice Model," *Public Choice*, 128(1–2), 91–107.

Carceles-Poveda, Eva and Yair Tauman (2011), "A Strategic Analysis of the War against Transnational Terrorism," *Games and Economic Behavior*, 71(1), 49–65.

CBS News (2010), "Times Square Car Bomb – How Much Did it Cost?," [www.cbsnews.com/8301-31727_162-20004452-10391695.html], accessed 20 September 2010.

Chen, Andrew H. and Thomas F. Siems (2004), "The Effects of Terrorism on Global Capital Markets," *European Journal of Political Economy*, 20(2), 249–66.

Combs, Cindy C. (2003), *Terrorism in the Twenty-First Century*, 3rd ed. (Upper Saddle River, NJ: Prentice-Hall).

Congressional Budget Office (2004), *The Budget and Economic Outlook: An Update*, [http://www.cbo.gov/ftpdocs/57xx/doc5773/08-24-BudgetUpdate.pdf], accessed 12 January 2005.

Congressional Research Service (2002), "The USA Patriot Act: A Sketch," CRS Report No. RS21203, Library of Congress, Washington, DC, [http://www.fas.org/irp/RS21203.pdf], accessed 11 July 2004.

(2005), "Hurricane Katrina: Insurance Losses and National Capacities for Financing Disaster Risk," CRS Report No. RL33086, Library of Congress, Washington, DC, [http://www.au.af.mil/au/awc/awcgate/crs/rl33086.pdf], accessed 19 April 2010.

Cornes, Richard and Todd Sandler (1996), *The Theory of Externalities, Public Goods, and Club Goods*, 2nd ed. (Cambridge: Cambridge University Press).

Crenshaw, Martha (1981), "The Causes of Terrorism," *Comparative Politics*, 13(4), 379–99.

Cross, John G. (1969), *The Economics of Bargaining* (New York: Basic Books).

(1977), "Negotiations as a Learning Process," *Journal of Conflict Resolution*, 21(4), 581–606.

Das, Satya (2008), "Some Mechanisms of Terror Cycles," *Journal of Economic Behavior and Organization*, 67(3–4), 644–56.

Davis, Darren W. and Brian D. Silver (2004), "Civil Liberties vs. Security: Public Opinion in the Context of the Terrorist Attacks on America," *American Journal of Political Science*, 48(1), 38–46.

Department of Homeland Security (DHS) (2002), "DHS Organization," [http://www.dhs.gov/dhspublic/display?theme=59&content=312&print=true], accessed 25 August 2003.

(2003), "Budget in Brief," [http://www.dhs.gov/xlibrary/assets/FY_2004_BUDGET_IN_BRIEF.pdf], accessed 19 April 2010.

(2004), "Budget in Brief, Fiscal Year 2005," [http://www.dhs.gov/xlibrary/assets/FY_2005_BIB_4.pdf], accessed 19 April 2010.

(2006), "Budget in Brief, Fiscal Year 2007," [http://www.dhs.gov/xlibrary/assets/Budget_BIB-FY2007.pdf], accessed 19 April 2010.

(2008), "Budget in Brief, Fiscal Year 2009," [http://www.dhs.gov/xlibrary/assets/budget_bib-fy2009.pdf], accessed 19 April 2010.

(2009), "Budget-in-Brief, Fiscal Year 2010," [http:/www.dhs.gov/xlibrary/assets/budget_bib_fy2010.pdf], accessed 19 April 2010.

(2010), "Budget in Brief, Fiscal Year 2011," [http://www.dhs.gov/xlibrary/assets/budget_bib_fy2011.pdf], accessed 19 April 2010.

Department of Justice (2004), website on victim compensation, [http://www.usdoj.gov/final_report.pdf], accessed 14 March 2005.

Dershowitz, Alan (2002), *Why Terrorism Works: Understanding the Threat, Responding to the Challenge* (New Haven, CT: Yale University Press).

Dixit, Avinash and Susan Skeath (2004), *Games of Strategy*, 2nd ed. (New York: W.W. Norton & Co.).

Doyle, Michael W. (1997), *Ways of War and Peace* (New York: W. W. Norton & Co.)

Drakos, Konstantinos (2004), "Terrorism-Induced Structural Shifts in Financial Risk: Airline Stocks in the Aftermath of the September 11th Terror Attacks," *European Journal of Political Economy*, 20(2), 436–46.

Drakos, Konstantinos and Andreas Gofas (2006), "In Search of the Average Transnational Terrorist Attack Venue," *Defence and Peace Economics*, 17(2), 73–93.

Drakos, Konstantinos and Ali M. Kutan (2003), "Regional Effects of Terrorism on Tourism in Three Mediterranean Countries," *Journal of Conflict Resolution*, 47(5), 621–41.

Durch, William J. (1993), "Paying the Tab: Financial Crisis," in William J. Durch (ed.), *The Evolution of UN Peacekeeping: Case Studies and Comparative Analysis* (New York: St. Martin's Press), 39–55.

Eckstein, Zvi and Daniel Tsiddon (2004), "Macroeconomic Consequences of Terror: Theory and the Case of Israel," *Journal of Monetary Economics*, 51(5), 971–1002.

The Economist (2003), "Al-Qaeda Operations Are Rather Cheap," *The Economist*, 369(8344), 45.

(2004), "Terror's New Depths," *The Economist*, 373(8392), 23–5.

Eldor, Rafi and Rafi Melnick (2004), "Financial Markets and Terrorism," *European Journal of Political Economy*, 20(2), 367–86.

Electronic Privacy Information Center (2010), "PATRIOT Act Extension?," [http://epic.org/privacy/terrorism/usapatriot/extension/], accessed 17 April 2010.

Enders, Walter (2010), *Applied Econometric Time Series*, 3rd ed. (Hoboken, NJ: John Wiley & Sons).

Enders, Walter and Paan Jindapon (2010), "Network Externalities and the Structure of Terror Networks," *Journal of Conflict Resolution*, 54(2), 262–80.

Enders, Walter, Adolfo Sachida, and Todd Sandler (2006), "The Impact of Transnational Terrorism on U.S. Foreign Direct Investment," *Political Research Quarterly*, 59(4), 517–31.

Enders, Walter and Todd Sandler (1991), "Causality between Transnational Terrorism and Tourism: The Case of Spain," *Terrorism*, 14(1), 49–58.

(1993), "The Effectiveness of Anti-Terrorism Policies: A Vector-Autoregression-Intervention Analysis," *American Political Science Review*, 87(4), 829–44.

(1995), "Terrorism: Theory and Applications," in Keith Hartley and Todd Sandler (eds.), *Handbook of Defense Economics, Vol. I* (Amsterdam: North-Holland), 213–49.

(1996), "Terrorism and Foreign Direct Investment in Spain and Greece," *Kyklos*, 49(3), 331–52.

(1999), "Transnational Terrorism in the Post-Cold War Era," *International Studies Quarterly*, 43(2), 145–67.

(2000), "Is Transnational Terrorism Becoming More Threatening? A Time-Series Investigation," *Journal of Conflict Resolution*, 44(3), 307–32.

(2005a), "After 9/11: Is It All Different Now?," *Journal of Conflict Resolution*, 49(2), 259–77.

(2005b), "Transnational Terrorism 1968–2000: Thresholds, Persistence, and Forecasts," *Southern Economic Journal*, 71(3), 467–82.

(2006), "Distribution of Transnational Terrorism among Countries by Income Classes and Geography after 9/11," *International Studies Quarterly*, 50(2), 367–93.

Enders, Walter, Todd Sandler, and Jon Cauley (1990a), "UN Conventions, Technology, and Retaliation in the Fight against Terrorism: An Econometric Evaluation," *Terrorism and Political Violence*, 2(1), 83–105.

(1990b), "Assessing the Impact of Terrorist-Thwarting Policies: An Intervention Time Series Approach," *Defence Economics*, 2(1), 1–18.

Enders, Walter, Todd Sandler, and Khusrav Gaibulloev (2011), "Domestic versus Transnational Terrorism: Data, Decomposition, and Dynamics," *Journal of Peace Research*, 48(3), 319–37.

Enders, Walter, Todd Sandler, and Gerald F. Parise (1992), "An Econometric Analysis of the Impact of Terrorism on Tourism," *Kyklos*, 45(4), 531–54.

Enders, Walter and Xuejuan Su (2007), "Rational Terrorists and Optimal Network Structure," *Journal of Conflict Resolution*, 51(1), 33–57.

Engene, Jan O. (2007), "Five Decades of Terrorism in Europe: The TWEED dataset," *Journal of Peace Research*, 44(1), 109–21.

Eubank, William L. and Leonard B. Weinberg (1994), "Does Democracy Encourage Terrorism?," *Terrorism and Political Violence*, 6(4), 417–35.

(2001), "Terrorism and Democracy: Perpetrators and Victims," *Terrorism and Political Violence*, 13(1), 155–64.

Eyerman, Joe (1998), "Terrorism and Democratic States: Soft Targets or Accessible Systems?," *International Interactions*, 24(2), 151–70.

Faria, João R. (2003), "Terror Cycles," *Studies in Nonlinear Dynamics and Econometrics*, 7(1), 1–11.

Faria, João R. and Daniel G. Arce (2005), "Terror Support and Recruitment," *Defence and Peace Economics*, 16(4), 263–73.

Farley, Jonathan D. (2003), "Breaking Al Qaeda: A Mathematical Analysis of Counterterrorism Operations," *Studies in Conflict & Terrorism*, 26(6), 399–411.

Farrow, Scott (2007), "The Economics of Homeland Security Expenditures: Foundational Expected Cost-Effectiveness Approaches," *Contemporary Economic Policy*, 25(1), 14–26.

Feichtinger, G., R. F. Hartl, P. M. Kort, and A. J. Novak (2001), "Terrorism Control in the Tourism Industry," *Journal of Optimization Theory and Applications*, 108(2), 283–96.

Feinstein, Jonathan S. and Edward H. Kaplan (2010), "Analysis of a Strategic Terror Organization," *Journal of Conflict Resolution*, 54(2), 281–302.

Fleck, Robert K. and Christopher Kilby (2010), "Changing Aid Regimes? US Foreign Aid from the Cold War to the War on Terror," *Journal of Development Economics*, 91(1), 185–97.

Fleischer, Aliza and Steven Buccola (2002), "War, Terror, and the Tourism Market in Israel," *Applied Economics*, 34(11), 1335–43.

Frey, Bruno S. (2004), *Dealing with Terrorism – Stick or Carrot?* (Cheltenham, UK: Edward Elgar).

Frey, Bruno S. and Simon Luechinger (2003), "How to Fight Terrorism: Alternatives to Deterrence," *Defence and Peace Economics*, 14(4), 237–49.

Frey, Bruno S., Simon Luechinger, and Alois Stutzer (2009), "The Life Satisfaction Approach to Valuing Public Goods: The Case of Terrorism," *Public Choice* 138(3–4), 317–45.

Gaibulloev, Khusrav and Todd Sandler (2008), "Growth Consequences of Terrorism in Western Europe," *Kyklos*, 61(3), 411–24.

(2009a), "Hostage Taking: Determinants of Terrorist Logistical and Negotiation Success," *Journal of Peace Research*, 46(6), 739–56.

(2009b), "The Impact of Terrorism and Conflicts on Growth in Asia," *Economics & Politics*, 21(3), 359–83.

(2011), "The Adverse Effect of Transnational and Domestic Terrorism on Growth in Africa," *Journal of Peace Research*, 48(3), 355–71.

Gallagher, Robert P. (2003), "The Psychological Impact of 9–11 on College Students and Suggestions for How Counseling Centers Can Prepare for War and/or Future Terroristic Attacks," *Commission for Counseling and Psychological Services Newsletter*, [http://www.acpa.nche.edu/comms/comm07/feature3-03.htm], accessed 18 February 2005.

Gartenstein-Ross, Daveed (2010), "Death by 1000 Cuts," *Foreign Policy*, online edition [http://www.foreignpolicy.com/articles/2010/11/23/death_by_a_thousand_cuts], accessed 4 January 2011.

Gerges, Fawaz A. and Christopher Isham (2003), "Sign of Weakness? Do Overseas Terror Strikes Suggest Al Qaeda Inability to Hit US?," *ABC News*, November 22.

Gordon, Peter, James E. Moore II, Harry W. Richardson, and Qisheng Pan (2005), "The Economic Impact of a Terrorist Attack on the Twin Ports of Los Angeles–Long Beach," in Harry W. Richardson, Peter Gordon, and James E. Moore II (eds.), *The Economic Impacts of Terrorist Attacks* (Cheltenham, UK: Edward Elgar), 262–86.

Graham, Sarah (2001), "9–11: The Psychological Aftermath," *Scientific American*, [http://www.sciam.com/article.cfm?articleID=00092E93-AAAB-1C75-9B81809E-C588EF21], accessed 18 February 2005.

Guardian (2007), "Mass Murderers Jailed for 40 Years as Judge Delivers Verdicts on Spain's 9/11," [http://www.guardian.co.uk/world/2007/nov/01/spain.international], accessed 10 September 2010.

Gurr, Ted Robert (2004), "Which Minorities Might Use Weapons of Mass Destruction?," unpublished manuscript, Minorities at Risk Project, University of Maryland, College Park.

Gutfraind, Alexander (2009), "Understanding Terrorist Organizations with a Dynamic Model," *Studies in Conflict & Terrorism*, 32(1), 45–55.

Hainmüller, Jens and Jan Martin Lemnitzer (2003), "Why Do Europeans Fly Safer? The Politics of Airport Security in Europe and the US," *Terrorism and Political Violence*, 15(4), 1–36.

Heal, Geoffrey and Howard Kunreuther (2003), "You Only Die Once: Managing Discrete Interdependent Risks," unpublished manuscript, Columbia University, New York, NY.

(2005), "IDS Models of Airline Security," *Journal of Conflict Resolution*, 49(2), 201–17.

Hirshleifer, Jack (1983), "From the Weakest-Link to Best-Shot: The Voluntary Provision of Public Goods," *Public Choice*, 41(3), 371–86.

Hoffman, Bruce (1997), "The Confluence of International and Domestic Trends in Terrorism," *Terrorism and Political Violence,* 9(1), 1–15.

(1998), *Inside Terrorism* (New York: Columbia University Press).

(1999), "Terrorism Trends and Prospects," in Ian O. Lesser, Bruce Hoffman, John Arquilla, David Ronfeldt, and Michele Zanini (eds.), *Countering the New Terrorism* (Santa Monica, CA: RAND), 7–38.

(2003), "The Logic of Suicide Terrorism," *The Atlantic Monthly,* 291(5), 40–7.

(2006), *Inside Terrorism,* revised and expanded edition (New York: Columbia University Press).

Horgan, John (2005), *The Psychology of Terrorism* (New York: Routledge).

Im, Eric I., Jon Cauley, and Todd Sandler (1987), "Cycles and Substitutions in Terrorist Activities: A Spectral Approach," *Kyklos,* 40(2), 238–55.

Institute of Medicine (2002), *Biological Threats and Terrorism: Assessing the Science and Response Capabilities* (Washington, DC: National Academy Press).

International Monetary Fund (IMF) (2001a), *Intensified Fund Involvement in Anti-Money Laundering Work and Combating the Financing of Terrorism* (Washington, DC: IMF).

(2001b), "How Has September 11 Influenced the Global Economy?," *World Economic Outlook,* 18 December 2001, 14–33.

(2009), "The IMF and the Fight against Money Laundering and the Financing of Terrorism," [http:/www.imf.org/external/np/exr/facts/aml.htm], accessed 14 March 2010.

Intriligator, Michael D. (2010), "The Economics of Terrorism," *Economic Inquiry,* 48(1), 1–13.

Islam, Muhammad Q. and Wassim N. Shahin (1989), "Economic Methodology Applied to Political Hostage-Taking in Light of the Iran-Contra Affair," *Southern Economic Journal,* 55(4), 1019–24.

Ito, Harumi and Darin Lee (2005), "Assessing the Impact of the September 11 Terrorist Attacks on U.S. Airline Demand," *Journal of Economics and Business,* 57(1), 79–95.

Ivanova, Kate and Todd Sandler (2006), "CBRN Incidents: Political Regimes, Perpetrators, and Targets," *Terrorism and Political Violence,* 18(3), 423–48.

(2007), "CBRN Attack Perpetrators: An Empirical Study," *Foreign Policy Analysis,* 3(4), 273–94.

Jacobson, Daniel and Edward H. Kaplan (2007), "Suicide Bombings and Targeted Killings in (Counter-) Terror Games," *Journal of Conflict Resolution,* 51(5), 772–92.

Jain, Sanjay and Sarun Mukand (2004), "The Economics of High-Visibility Terrorism," *European Journal of Political Economy,* 20(2), 479–94.

Jenkins, Brian (1975), "Will Terrorists Go Nuclear?," Report No. P-5541, RAND Corp., Santa Monica, CA.

Jindapon, Paan and William S. Neilson (2009), "The Impact of Societal Risk Attitudes on Terrorism and Counterterrorism," *Economics & Politics,* 21(3), 433–51.

Kaplan, Edward H., David L. Craft, and Lawrence M. Wein (2002), "Emergency Response to a Smallpox Attack: The Case for Mass Vaccination," *Proceedings of the National Academy of Sciences,* 99(16), 10935–40.

Kaufman, Arnold F., Martin I. Meltzer, and George P. Schmid (1997), "The Economic Impact of a Bioterrorist Attack: Are Prevention and Postattack Intervention Programs Justifiable?," *Emerging Infectious Diseases,* 3(2), 83–94.

Krueger, Alan B. and David Laitin (2008), "Kto Kogo? A Cross-Country Study of the Origins and Targets of Terrorism," in Philip Keefer and Norman Loayza (eds.), *Terrorism, Economic Development, and Political Openness* (New York: Cambridge University Press), 148–73.

Krueger, Alan B. and Jitka Maleckova (2003), "Education, Poverty, and Terrorism: Is There a Causal Connection?," *Journal of Economic Perspectives,* 17(4), 119–44.

Kunreuther, Howard and Geoffrey Heal (2003), "Interdependent Security," *Journal of Risk and Uncertainty,* 26(2–3), 231–49.

Kunreuther, Howard and Erwann Michel-Kerjan (2004a), "Policy Watch: Challenge for Terrorism Risk Insurance in the United States," *Journal of Economic Perspectives,* 18(4), 201–14.

(2004b), "Dealing with Extreme Events: New Challenges for Terrorist Risk Coverage," unpublished manuscript, Wharton School, University of Pennsylvania, Philadelphia.

Kunreuther, Howard, Erwann Michel-Kerjan, and Beverly Porter (2003), "Assessing, Managing and Financing Extreme Events: Dealing with Terrorism," Working Paper 10179, National Bureau of Economic Research, Cambridge, MA.

Landes, William M. (1978), "An Economic Study of US Aircraft Hijackings, 1961–1976," *Journal of Law and Economics,* 21(1), 1–31.

Lapan, Harvey E. and Todd Sandler (1988), "To Bargain or Not to Bargain: That Is the Question," *American Economic Review,* 78(2), 16–20.

(1993), "Terrorism and Signalling," *European Journal of Political Economy,* 9(3), 383–97.

Laqueur, Walter (ed.) (1976), *The Israel-Arab Reader: A Documentary History of the Middle East Conflict* (New York: Bantam).

(1978), *The Terrorism Reader: A Historical Anthology* (New York: New American Library).

Lee, Beom S., Walter Enders, and Todd Sandler (2009), "9/11: What Did We Know and When Did We Know It?," *Defence and Peace Economics,* 20(2), 79–93.

Lee, Dwight R. (1988), "Free Riding and Paid Riding in the Fight against Terrorism," *American Economic Review,* 78(2), 22–6.

Lee, Dwight R. and Todd Sandler (1989), "On the Optimal Retaliation against Terrorists: The Paid-Rider Option," *Public Choice,* 62(2), 141–52.

Levitt, Matthew (2003), "Stemming the Flow of Terrorist Financing: Practical and Conceptual Challenges," *Fletcher Forum of World Affairs,* 27(1), 59–70.

Lexis Nexis (2004), "Academic Search Engine," [http://web.lexis-nexis.com/universe], accessed throughout September and October 2004.

Li, Quan (2005), "Does Democracy Promote Transnational Terrorist Incidents?," *Journal of Conflict Resolution,* 49(2), 278–97.

Li, Quan and Drew Schaub (2004), "Economic Globalization and Transnational Terrorism," *Journal of Conflict Resolution,* 48(2), 230–58.

Lichbach, Mark I. (1987), "Deterrence or Escalation? The Puzzle of Aggregate Studies of Repression and Dissent," *Journal of Conflict Resolution,* 31(2), 266–97.

Lindelauf, Roy, Peter Borm, and Herbert Hamers (2009), "On Heterogeneous, Covert Networks," in Nasrullah Memon, Jonathan L. Farley, David L. Hicks, and Torben Rosenorn (eds.), *Mathematical Methods in Counterterrorism* (New York: Springer), 215–28.

London Chamber of Commerce and Industry (2005), *The Economic Effects of Terrorism on London – Experiences of Firms in London's Business Community* (London: Press and Public Affairs, London Chamber of Commerce and Industry).

McGough, Lauren (2009), "Mathematically Modeling Terrorist Cells: Examining the Strength of Small Sizes," in Nasrullah Memon, Jonathan L. Farley, David L. Hicks, and Torben Rosenorn (eds.), *Mathematical Methods in Counterterrorism* (New York: Springer), 55–67.

Memon, Nasrullah, Jonathan D. Farley, David L. Hicks, and Torben Rosenorn (eds.) (2009), *Mathematical Methods in Counterterrorism* (Wien: Springer-Verlag).

Merrari, Ariel (1999), "Terrorism as a Strategy of Struggle: Past and Future," *Terrorism and Political Violence*, 11(4), 52–65.

Metcalfe, Robert, Nattavudh Powdthavee, and Paul Dolan (2011), "Destruction and Distress: Using a Quasi-Experiment to Show the Effects of the September 11 Attacks on Subjective Well-Being in the United Kingdom," *Economic Journal*, 121(1), F81–F103.

Mickolus, Edward F. (1980), *Transnational Terrorism: A Chronology of Events 1968–1979* (Westport, CT: Greenwood Press).

    (1982), *International Terrorism: Attributes of Terrorist Events, 1968–1977* (ITERATE 2), Inter-University Consortium for Political and Social Research, Ann Arbor, MI.

    (2008), *Terrorism, 2005–2007: A Chronology* (Westport, CT: Praeger Security International).

Mickolus, Edward F., Todd Sandler, and Jean M. Murdock (1989), *International Terrorism in the 1980s: A Chronology of Events*, 2 vols. (Ames: Iowa State University).

Mickolus, Edward F., Todd Sandler, Jean M. Murdock, and Peter Flemming (2009), *International Terrorism: Attributes of Terrorist Events, 1968–2008* (ITERATE) (Dunn Loring, VA: Vinyard Software).

Mickolus, Edward F. and Susan L. Simmons (1997), *Terrorism, 1992–1995: A Chronology of Events and a Selectively Annotated Bibliography* (Westport, CT: Greenwood Press).

Mills, Susan R. (1990), "The Financing of UN Peacekeeping Operations: The Need for a Sound Financial Basis," in Indar Jit Rikhye and Kjell Skjelsback (eds.), *The United Nations and Peacekeeping: Results, Limitations and Prospects: The Lessons of 40 Years of Experience* (Houndmills, UK: Macmillan), 91–110.

Moghadam, Assaf (2006), "Suicide Terrorism, Occupation, and the Globalization of Martyrdom: A Critique of Dying to Win," *Studies in Conflict & Terrorism*, 29(8), 707–27.

Mueller, John (2004), "A False Sense of Insecurity?," *Regulation*, 27(3), 42–6.

Nash, John F. (1950), "The Bargaining Problem," *Econometrica*, 18(2), 155–62.

Nasr, Kameel (1997), *Arab and Israeli Terrorism: The Causes and Effects of Political Violence, 1936–1993* (Jefferson, NC: McFarland and Co.).

National Association of Insurance Commissioners (2010), "Terrorism Risk Insurance Act (TRIA)," [http://www.naic.org/topics/topic_tria.htm], accessed 19 April 2010.

National Commission on Terrorist Attacks Upon the United States (2004), *The 9/11 Commission Report* (New York: W.W. Norton & Company).

National Consortium for the Study of Terrorism and Responses to Terrorism (START) (2009a), *Global Terrorism Database*, CD-ROM (College Park, MD: University of Maryland).

(2009b), *Global Terrorism Database: GTD Variables and Inclusion Criteria*, Version 3.0, [http://www.start.umd.edu/gtd/downloads/codebook.pdf], accessed 15 April 2010.

National Obituary Archive–Honor Roll (2010), "Death Toll from 9/11," [http//:www.arrangeonline.com/notablePersons/honorroll.asp], accessed 29 April 2010.

Navarro, Peter and Aron Spencer (2001), "September 11, 2001: Assessing the Costs of Terrorism," *Milken Institute Review*, Fourth Quarter 2001, 16–31.

Nelson, Paul S. and John L. Scott (1992), "Terrorism and the Media: An Empirical Analysis," *Defence Economics,* 3(4), 329–39.

Nitsch, Volker and Dieter Schumacher (2004), "Terrorism and International Trade: An Empirical Investigation," *European Journal of Political Economy*, 20(2), 423–33.

Office of Management and Budget (2010), *Budget of the U.S. Government* (Washington, DC: U.S. Government Printing Office).

Organization of Economic Cooperation and Development (OECD) (2003), "Financial Action Task Force on Money Laundering," [http://www1.oecd.org/fatf], accessed 16 September 2003.

Overgaard, Per B. (1994), "Terrorist Attacks as a Signal of Resources," *Journal of Conflict Resolution,* 38(3), 452–78.

Pape, Robert A. (2003), "The Strategic Logic of Suicide Terrorism," *American Political Science Review*, 97(3), 343–61.

(2005), *Dying to Win: The Strategic Logic of Suicide Terrorism* (New York: Random House).

Parachini, John (2003), "Putting WMD Terrorism into Perspective," *The Washington Quarterly*, 26(4), 37–50.

Pearl, Marc A. (1987), "Terrorism – Historical Perspective on U.S. Congressional Action," *Terrorism*, 10(2), 139–43.

Pedahzur, Ami (2005), *Suicide Terrorism* (Malden, MA: Polity Press).

Piazza, James A. (2008), "Incubators of Terror: Do Failed and Failing States Promote Transnational Terrorism?," *International Studies Quarterly*, 52(3), 469–88.

Pizan, Abraham and Aliza Fleischer (2002), "Severity versus Frequency of Acts of Terrorism: Which Has a Larger Impact on Tourism Demand?," *Journal of Travel Research*, 40(3), 337–9.

Post, Jerrold M. (2004), "Differentiating the Threat of Chemical/Biological Terrorism: Motivations and Constraints," unpublished manuscript, George Washington University, Washington, DC.

Post, Jerrold M., Keven G. Ruby, and Eric D. Shaw (2000), "From Car Bombs to Logic Bombs: The Growing Threat from Information Terrorism," *Terrorism and Political Violence,* 12(2), 97–122.

(2002), "The Radical Group in Context 1: An Integrated Framework for the Analysis of Group Risk for Terrorism," *Studies in Conflict & Terrorism*, 25(2), 73–100.

Powell, Robert (2007), "Defending against Terrorist Attacks with Limited Resources," *American Political Science Review*, 101(3), 527–41.

Prieto, Daniel B. (2005), "Mass Transit Security after the London Bombings." Testimony presented to the Commonwealth of Massachusetts Joint Committee on Public Safety and Homeland Security, 4 August 2005.

Quillen, Chris (2002a), "A Historical Analysis of Mass Casualty Bombers," *Studies in Conflict & Terrorism*, 25(5), 279–92.

(2002b), "Mass Casualty Bombings Chronology," *Studies in Conflict & Terrorism*, 25(2), 293–302.

Rapoport, David C. (1984), "Fear and Trembling: Terrorism in Three Religious Traditions," *American Political Science Review*, 78(3), 658–77.

(2004), "Modern Terror: The Four Waves," in Audrey K. Cronin and James M. Ludes (eds.), *Attacking Terrorism: Elements of a Grand Strategy* (Washington, DC: Georgetown University Press), 46–73.

Rohner, Dominic and Bruno S. Frey (2007), "Blood and Ink! The Common-Interest Game between Terrorists and the Media," *Public Choice*, 133(1–2), 129–45.

Rosendorff, B. Peter and Todd Sandler (2004), "Too Much of a Good Thing? The Proactive Response Dilemma," *Journal of Conflict Resolution*, 48(5), 657–71.

(2010), "Suicide Terrorism and the Backlash Effect," *Defence and Peace Economics*, 21(5–6), 443–57.

Ross, Jeffrey Ian (1993), "Structural Causes of Oppositional Political Terrorism: Towards a Causal Model," *Journal of Peace Research*, 30(3), 317–29.

Sageman, Marc (2004), *Understanding Terror Networks* (Philadelphia: University of Pennsylvania Press).

Sandler, Todd (1992), *Collective Action: Theory and Applications* (Ann Arbor: University of Michigan Press).

(1995), "On the Relationship between Democracy and Terrorism," *Terrorism and Political Violence*, 7(4), 1–9.

(1997), *Global Challenges: An Approach to Environmental, Political, and Economic Problems* (Cambridge: Cambridge University Press).

(2003), "Collective Action and Transnational Terrorism," *World Economy*, 26(6), 779–802.

(2004), *Global Collective Action* (Cambridge: Cambridge University Press).

(2005), "Collective versus Unilateral Responses to Terrorism," *Public Choice*, 124(1–2), 75–93.

(2009), "The Past and Future of Terrorism Research," *Revista de Economia Aplicada*, 50(1), 5–25.

(2010), "Terrorism Shocks: Domestic versus Transnational Responses," *Studies in Conflict & Terrorism*, 33(10), 893–910.

Sandler, Todd and Daniel G. Arce (2003), "Terrorism & Game Theory," *Simulation & Gaming*, 34(3), 319–37.

Sandler, Todd, Daniel G. Arce, and Walter Enders (2009), "Transnational Terrorism," in Bjørn Lomborg (ed.), *Global Crises, Global Solutions*, 2nd ed. (Cambridge: Cambridge University Press), 516–62.

(2011), "An Evaluation of INTERPOL's Cooperative-Based Counterterrorism Linkage," *Journal of Law and Economics*, 54(1), 79–110.

Sandler, Todd and Walter Enders (2004), "An Economic Perspective on Transnational Terrorism," *European Journal of Political Economy*, 20(2), 301–16.

(2005), "Transnational Terrorism: An Economic Analysis," in Harry W. Richardson, Peter Gordon, and James E. Moore II (eds.), *The Economic Impact of Terrorist Attacks* (Cheltenham, UK: Edward Elgar), 11–34.

Sandler, Todd and Harvey E. Lapan (1988), "The Calculus of Dissent: An Analysis of Terrorists' Choice of Targets," *Synthese*, 76(2), 245–61.

Sandler, Todd and Keith Sargent (1995), "Management of Transnational Commons: Coordination, Publicness, and Treaty Formation," *Land Economics*, 71(2), 145–62.

Sandler, Todd and John Scott (1987), "Terrorist Success in Hostage-Taking Incidents: An Empirical Study," *Journal of Conflict Resolution*, 31(1), 35–53.

Sandler, Todd and Kevin Siqueira (2006), "Global Terrorism: Deterrence versus Preemption," *Canadian Journal of Economics*, 50(4), 1370–87.

Sandler, Todd, John Tschirhart, and Jon Cauley (1983), "A Theoretical Analysis of Transnational Terrorism," *American Political Science Review*, 77(1), 36–54.

Savun, Burcu and Brian J. Phillips (2009), "Democracy, Foreign Policy, and Terrorism," *Journal of Conflict Resolution*, 53(6), 878–904.

Scheuer, Michael (2006), *Through Our Enemies' Eyes*, revised ed. (Washington, DC: Potomac Books).

Schmid, Alex P. (1992), "Terrorism and Democracy," *Terrorism and Political Violence*, 4(4), 14–25.

Schulze, Richard H. and Andreas Vogt (2003), "It's War! Fighting Post-11 September Global Terrorism through a Doctrine of Preemption," *Terrorism and Political Violence*, 15(1), 1–30.

Schuster, Mark, Bradley Stein, Lisa Jaycox, Rebecca Collins, Grant Marshall, Marc Elliott, Anne Zhou, Davis Kanouse, Janina Morrison, and Sandra Berry (2001), "A National Survey of Stress Reactions after the September 11, 2001 Terrorist Attacks," *New England Journal of Medicine*, 345(20), 1507–12.

Seale, Patrick (1992), *Abu Nidal: Gun for Hire* (New York: Random House).

Selten, Reinhard (1988), "A Simple Game Model of Kidnappings," in Reinhard Selten (ed.), *Models of Strategic Rationality* (Boston: Kluwer Academic), 77–93.

Shahin, Wassim N. and Muhammad Q. Islam (1992), "Combating Political Hostage-Taking: An Alternative Approach," *Defence Economics*, 3(4), 321–7.

Shapiro, Jacob N. (2007), "Terrorist Organizations' Vulnerabilities and Inefficiencies," in Jeanne K. Giraldo and Harold A. Trinkunas (eds.), *Terrorism Financing and State Responses: A Comparative Perspective* (Stanford, CA: Stanford University Press), 56–71, 308–313.

Shapiro, Jacob N. and David A. Siegel (2007), "Underfunding in Terrorist Organizations," *International Studies Quarterly*, 51(2), 405–29.

Shapiro, Robert (2004), "Al-Qaida and the GDP: How Much Would Terrorism Damage the U.S. Economy? Less Than You'd Expect," *Slate*, [http://slate.msn.com/id/2079298/], accessed 28 October 2004.

Sieff, Martin (2006), "More Delays on MANPADs," [http://www.spacewar.com/reports/More_Delays_On_MANPADs_999.html], accessed on 14 March 2010.

Silke, Andrew (2001), "When Sums Go Bad: Mathematical Models and Hostage Situations," *Terrorism and Political Violence*, 13(2), 49–66.

Siqueira, Kevin (2005), "Political and Militant Wings within Dissident Movements and Organizations," *Journal of Conflict Resolution*, 49(2), 218–36.

Siqueira, Kevin and Todd Sandler (2006), "Terrorists versus the Government: Strategic Interaction, Support, and Sponsorship," *Journal of Conflict Resolution*, 50(6), 878–98.

(2007), "Terrorist Backlash, Terrorism Mitigation, and Policy Delegation," *Journal of Public Economics*, 91(9), 1800–15.

(2010), "Terrorist Networks, Support, and Delegation," *Public Choice*, 142(1–2), 237–53.

Sloboda, Brian W. (2003), "Assessing the Effects of Terrorism on Tourism by the Use of Time Series Methods," *Tourism Economics*, 9(2), 179–90.

Tanzi, Vincent (1972), "A Note on Exclusion, Pure Public Goods and Pareto Optimality," *Public Finance*, 27(1), 75–8.

Tavares, Jose (2004), "The Open Society Assesses Its Enemies: Shocks, Disasters and Terrorist Attacks," *Journal of Monetary Economics*, 51(5), 1039–70.

Technical Support Working Group (2003), "Infrastructure Protection," [http://www.tswg.gov/tswg/ip/ip_ma.htm], accessed 12 April 2004.

Tollison, Robert D. (1982), "Rent-seeking: A Survey," *Kyklos*, 35(4), 575–602.

United Nations (2002a), "Report of the Policy Working Group on the United Nations and Terrorism," A/57/273-S/2002/875, United Nations, New York.

(2002b), "Measures to Eliminate International Terrorism," A/57/273, S/2002/875, United Nations, New York.

(2003), "United Nations: Treaty Collection: Conventions on Terrorism," [http://untreaty.un.org/English/Terrorism.asp], accessed 28 August 2003.

(2009), "Status of International Legal Instruments Related to the Prevention and Suppression of International Terrorism," [http://www.un.org/ga/sixth/64/Terrorism_Table_64th.pdf], accessed 14 March 2010.

(2010), "United Nations: Treaty Collection: Conventions on Terrorism," [http://treaties.un.org/Pages/DB.aspx?path=DB/studies/page2_en.xm/&menu=MTDSG], accessed 24 March 2010.

United Nations Security Council (2001), "Resolution 1373 (2001)," S/Res/1373 (2001), United Nations, New York.

United States Congress (2001), "HR 3162, US Patriot Act," *Congressional Record* 146, S10969, 24 October, US Congress, Washington, DC, [http://www.epic.org/privacy/terrorism/hr3162.html], accessed 11 July 2004.

United States Department of State (various years), *Patterns of Global Terrorism* (Washington, DC: US Department of State).

(2002), "Yemen: The Economic Cost of Terrorism," [http://www.state.gov/s/ct/rls/fs/2002/15028.htm], accessed 12 December 2004.

United States General Accounting Office (2003), "Airport Passenger Screening: Preliminary Observations on Progress Made and Challenges Remaining," GAO-03-1173, US General Accounting Office, Washington, DC.

(2004), "Combating Terrorism: Evaluation of Selected Characteristics in National Strategies Related to Terrorism," GAO-04-408T, US General Accounting Office, Washington, DC.

United States Government Accountability Office (2005), "Aviation Security: Screener Training and Performance Measurement Strengthened, but More Work Remains," GAO-05-457, US Government Accountability Office, Washington, DC.

(2007), "Terrorist Watchlist Screening Opportunities Exist to Enhance Management Oversight, Reduce Vulnerabilities in Agency Screening Processes, and Expand Use of the List," GAO-08-110, US Government Accountability Office, Washington, DC.

(2008), "Terrorism Insurance: Status of Coverage Availability for Attacks Involving Nuclear, Biological, Chemical, or Radiological Weapons," GAO-09-39, US Government Accountability Office, Washington, DC.

(2009a), "Aviation Security: DHS and TSA Have Researched, Developed, and Begun Deploying Passenger Checkpoint Screening Technologies, but Continue to Face Challenges," GAO-10-128, US Government Accountability Office, Washington, DC.

(2009b), "Global War on Terrorism: Reported Obligations for the Department of Defense," GAO-09-449R, US Government Accountability Office, Washington, DC.

(2010), "Homeland Security: Better Use of Terrorist Watchlist Information and Improvements in Deployment of Passenger Screening Checkpoint Technologies Could Further Strengthen Security," GAO-10-401T, US Government Accountability Office, Washington, DC.

USA Today (2004), "Second Uzbek Explosion Rips Bomb-Making Factory," [http://www.usatoday.com/news/world/2004-03-29-uzbek-blast_x.htm?POE=NEWI], accessed 12 April 2004.

Vicary, Simon (1990), "Transfers and the Weakest-Link: An Extension of Hirshleifer's Analysis," *Journal of Public Economics,* 43(3), 375–94.

Vicary, Simon and Todd Sandler (2002), "Weakest-Link Public Goods: Giving In-Kind or Transferring Money," *European Economic Review,* 46(8), 1501–20.

Victoroff, Jeff (2005), "The Mind of the Terrorist: A Review and Critique of Psychological Approaches," *Journal of Conflict Resolution,* 49(1), 3–42.

Viscusi, W. Kip and Richard J. Zeckhauser (2003), "Sacrificing Civil Liberties to Reduce Terrorism Risks," *Journal of Risk and Uncertainty,* 26(2–3), 99–120.

Wein, Lawrence M., David L. Craft, and Edward H. Kaplan (2003), "Emergency Response to an Anthrax Attack," *Proceedings of the National Academy of Sciences,* 100(7), 4346–51.

Weinberg, Leonard B. and William L. Eubank (1998), "Terrorism and Democracy: What Recent Events Disclose," *Terrorism and Political Violence,* 10(1), 108–18.

White, Jonathan R. (2003), *Terrorism: 2002 Update*, 4th ed. (Belmont, CA: Wadsworth/Thomson Learning).

White House (2002), "Press Release," [http://www.whitehouse.gov/news/releases/2002/06/print/20020618-5.html], accessed 25 August 2003.

(2003), "Progress Report on the Global War on Terrorism," [http://www.state.gov/s/ct/rls/rpt/24087.htm], accessed 5 February 2004.

(2004), "Department of Homeland Security," [http://www.whitehouse.gov/omb/budget/fy2005/pdf/budget/homeland.pdf], accessed 15 June 2004.

(2008), "Fact Sheet: President Bush Has Kept America Safe, President Bush Fundamentally Reshaped Our Strategy to Protect the American People," [http://georgewbush-whitehouse.archives.gov/news/resleases/2008/12/20081217-5.html], accessed 12 December 2010.

Wilkinson, Paul (1986), *Terrorism and the Liberal State*, revised ed. (London: Macmillan).

(1997), "The Media and Terrorism: A Reassessment," *Terrorism and Political Violence,* 9(2), 51–64.

(2001), *Terrorism versus Democracy: The Liberal State Response* (London: Frank Cass).

Wilson, Margaret A. (2000), "Toward a Model of Terrorist Behavior in Hostage-Taking Incidents," *Journal of Conflict Resolution,* 44(4), 403–24.

Wintrobe, Ronald (2002), "Can Suicide Bombers be Rational?," unpublished manuscript, Department of Economics, University of Western Ontario, London, Ontario.

(2006), "Extremism, Suicide Terror, and Authoritarianism," *Public Choice*, 128(1), 169–95.

Wolgast, Michael (2002), "Global Terrorism and the Insurance Industry: New Challenges and Policy Responses," presented at DIW workshop, The Economic Consequences of Global Terrorism, Berlin, 14–15 June 2002.

Wolinsky, Frederick D., Kathleen W. Wyrwich, Kurt Kroenke, Ajit Babu, and William Tierney (2003), "9–11, Personal Stress, Mental Health, and Sense of Control among Older Adults," *The Journals of Gerontology*, 58B(3), 5146–5150.

Woo, Gordon (2009), "Intelligence Constraints on Terrorist Network Plots," in Nasrullah Memon, Jonathan L. Farley, David L. Hicks, and Torben Rosenorn (eds.), *Mathematical Methods in Counterterrorism* (New York: Springer), 205–14.

World Bank (various years), *World Development Report* (New York: Oxford University Press).

Zhuang, Jun and Vicki M. Bier (2007), "Balancing Terrorism and Natural Disasters – Defensive Strategy with Endogenous Attacker Effort," *Operations Research*, 55(5), 976–91.

Author Index

Subject Index